NO FEAR

NO FEAR

The Canterbury Tales
The Scarlet Letter

NO FEAR

SHAKESPEARE

As You Like It
The Comedy of Errors
Hamlet
Henry IV, Parts One and Two
Henry V
Julius Caesar
King Lear
Macbeth
The Merchant of Venice
A Midsummer Night's Dream
Much Ado About Nothing
Othello
Richard III
Romeo and Juliet
Sonnets
The Taming of the Shrew
The Tempest
Twelfth Night

THE
SCARLET LETTER

Cover Illustration by Michael Wertz
Book layout by Christina Renzi

SPARKNOTES is a registered trademark of SparkNotes LLC.

Spark Publishing
A Division of Barnes & Noble
120 Fifth Avenue
New York, NY 10011
www.sparknotes.com

ISBN: 978-1-4114-2697-9

Library of Congress Cataloging-in-Publication Data

Hawthorne, Nathaniel, 1804–1864.
  The scarlet letter / [Nathaniel Hawthorne].
      p. cm. — (No fear literature)
  A modern English translation of The scarlet letter. SparkNotes contributers: James Bickford, Andrew Sylvester, Emma Chastain, and John Crowther.
  ISBN 978-1-4114-2697-9 (pbk.)
1. Boston (Mass.) —History—Colonial period, ca. 1600–1775—Fiction. 2. Triangles (Interpersonal relations)—Fiction. 3. Illegitimate children—Fiction. 4. Married women—Fiction. 5. Puritans—Fiction. 6. Adultery—Fiction. 7. Revenge—Fiction. 8. Clergy—Fiction. I. Title.
  PS1868.A2S73 2009
  813'.3—dc22

                    2009005105

Please submit changes or report errors to www.sparknotes.com/errors.

Printed and bound in the United States

10 9 8 7 6 5

FEAR NOT.

Have you ever tried to read *The Scarlet Letter* but realized midway through the second sentence that you were already lost? *No Fear: The Scarlet Letter* will change all that. You won't have to worry about losing the thread anymore. Whenever Hawthorne's sentences become too convoluted to follow, or when you can't even figure out what he's talking about, simply look across at the right-hand page and we'll set you back on track. Soon you'll be reading Hawthorne's own words fearlessly—and actually enjoying it.

No Fear: The Scarlet Letter puts Hawthorne's language side by side with a facing-page modern English translation—the kind of English people actually speak today. When Hawthorne's prose makes your head spin, our translation will help you sort out what's happening, who's saying what, and why.

Contents

Characters

HESTER PRYNNE—The book's protagonist and the wearer of the scarlet letter that gives the book its title. The letter is a patch of fabric elaborately embroidered by Hester with an *A*, identifying Hester as an "adulterer." As a young woman, Hester married an elderly scholar who sent her ahead to America, where he planned to meet her after finishing up some business. While waiting for her husband, who had still not arrived after two years, she has an affair with the Puritan minister Arthur Dimmesdale. The affair led to the birth of their child, Pearl, and to her public shaming at the opening of the novel. For her immoral behavior, Hester is banished to the outskirts of town. She is largely friendless, but through her kindness and talent as a seamstress she becomes a respected, if alienated, member of society.

PEARL—Hester's illegitimate daughter. Pearl is a young girl with a moody, mischievous spirit and the ability to perceive things others do not. She quickly discerns the truth about her mother and Dimmesdale, though neither will confirm her suspicions. The townspeople say that she barely seems human and spread rumors that her unknown father is actually the Devil. Pearl has grown up with her mother outside of the town, and she often terrorizes the town's children, who view her as a curiosity. She is wise beyond her years, frequently engaging in ironic play having to do with her mother's scarlet letter.

ROGER CHILLINGWORTH—Hester's husband. "Roger Chillingworth" is actually a pseudonym used by Hester's husband to disguise his identity from the townspeople. He is an old scholar (he is much older than Hester) who had sent Hester to America while he settled his affairs in Europe. He arrives in Boston belatedly after being shipwrecked and captured by Native Americans. Upon his arrival in town, he finds Hester and her illegitimate child being publicly displayed for the crime of adultery. He lusts for revenge, and thus decides to stay in Boston despite his wife's betrayal and disgrace. He uses his knowledge to disguise himself as a doctor, intent on discovering and tormenting Hester's anonymous lover.

REVEREND ARTHUR DIMMESDALE—Hester's anonymous lover. As a young theologian, Dimmesdale studied at some of England's greatest universities before immigrating to America, specifically Boston, to work as a minister. In a moment of weakness, he becomes Hester's lover and the father of her child, though he will not acknowledge this fact publicly. Dimmesdale's commitments to his congregation are in constant conflict with his feelings of sinfulness and need to confess. The adulation he receives from them only serves to exacerbate his sense of guilt and self-loathing. Dimmesdale torments himself physically and psychologically for his sins, and his health deteriorates through the course of the novel, even as his prestige as a minister continues to increase.

GOVERNOR BELLINGHAM—A wealthy, elderly gentleman who spends much of his time consulting with the other town leaders. Bellingham tends to adhere strictly to the rules, but he is easily swayed by Dimmesdale's eloquence. He remains blind to the misbehaviors taking place in his own house: His sister, Mistress Hibbins, is a witch.

MISTRESS HIBBINS—A widow and sister of Governor Bellingham. She is commonly known to be a witch who ventures into the forest at night to ride with the "Black Man."

REVEREND MR. JOHN WILSON—Boston's elder clergyman. Reverend Wilson is a scholarly yet grandfatherly figure. Like Governor Bellingham, Wilson follows the community's rules strictly but can be swayed by Dimmesdale's eloquence. Unlike Dimmesdale, his junior colleague, Wilson preaches hellfire and damnation and advocates harsh punishment of sinners.

NARRATOR—Former surveyor of the Salem Custom House some 200 years after the events described in the novel take place. The unnamed narrator discovers an old manuscript in the building's attic that tells the story of Hester Prynne. When he loses his job, he decides to write a fictional treatment of the narrative.

NO FEAR

THE
SCARLET LETTER

The Custom House: Introductory to The Scarlet Letter

It is a little remarkable, that—though disinclined to talk over-much of myself and my affairs at the fireside, and to my personal friends—an autobiographical impulse should twice in my life have taken possession of me, in addressing the public. The first time was three or four years since, when I favored the reader—inexcusably, and for no earthly reason, that either the indulgent reader or the intrusive author could imagine—with a description of my way of life in the deep quietude of an Old Manse. And now—because, beyond my deserts, I was happy enough to find a listener or two on the former occasion—I again seize the public by the button, and talk of my three years' experience in a Custom-House. The example of the famous "P. P., Clerk of this Parish," was never more faithfully followed. The truth seems to be, however, that, when he casts his leaves forth upon the wind, the author addresses, not the many who will fling aside his volume, or never take it up, but the few who will understand him, better than most of his schoolmates and lifemates. Some authors, indeed, do far more than this, and indulge themselves in such confidential depths of revelation as could fittingly be addressed, only and exclusively, to the one heart and mind of perfect sympathy; as if the printed book, thrown at large on the wide world, were certain to find out the divided segment of the writer's own nature, and complete his circle of existence by bringing him into communion with it. It is scarcely decorous, however, to speak all, even where we speak impersonally. But—as thoughts are frozen and utterance benumbed, unless the speaker stand in some true relation with his audience—it may be pardonable to imagine that a friend, a kind and apprehensive, though not the closest friend, is listening to our talk; and then, a native reserve being thawed by this genial consciousness, we may prate of the circumstances that lie around us, and even of ourself, but still keep the inmost Me behind its veil. To this extent and within these limits, an author, methinks, may be autobiographical, without violating either the reader's rights or his own.

It will be seen, likewise, that this Custom-House sketch has a certain propriety, of a kind always recognized in literature, as explaining how a large portion of the following pages came into my possession, and as offering proofs of the authenticity of a narrative therein contained. This, in fact—a desire to put myself in my true position as

The Custom House: A Prologue to *The Scarlet Letter*

I'm not inclined to talk much about myself and my business, even to friends, so it's a little odd that I've twice had the impulse to write an autobiography. The first time was three or four years ago, when I published (for no good reason) a story about my way of life in the deep calm of the Old Manse. Because a few people read that story (and even those few readers were more than the story deserved), I'm buttonholing the public again, this time to talk about my three years' experience in a Custom House. No writer has ever followed the example of "P.P., Clerk of this Parish" more faithfully. It seems that when an author sends his book into the world, he's addressing not the people who will set it aside, or never start it in the first place, but the few who will understand him even better than his friends and family do. Some authors go way beyond this, and let themselves write intimate stuff that's really only appropriate for a true soulmate—as if throwing the printed book to the world could bring them into contact with that person. It's not appropriate to spill your guts, even when you're writing impersonally. Still, since thoughts are frozen and voices silent unless the writer has some true relationship with his audience, I might be forgiven for imagining that a friend—a kind, insightful, though not especially close friend—is reading as I write. My natural reserve will be thawed by the friend's warmth, and we'll be able to chat about events, and even about ourselves—but I'll keep my innermost self private. In this way, I think an author can write about his life without crossing the line with the reader or with himself.

P. Clerk of this : Satire of long- d and pointless noirs, written by Alexander Pope.

This sketch of the Custom House takes the polite step, as is common in literature, of explaining how the story that follows came into my possession, and offering proof that the story is real. I'm only writing this sketch and addressing the public personally because I want to say that I am not the author of *The Scarlet Letter*, but merely

editor, or very little more, of the most prolix among the tales that make up my volume,—this, and no other, is my true reason for assuming a personal relation with the public. In accomplishing the main purpose, it has appeared allowable, by a few extra touches, to give a faint representation of a mode of life not heretofore described, together with some of the characters that move in it, among whom the author happened to make one.

In my native town of Salem, at the head of what, half a century ago, in the days of old King Derby; was a bustling wharf,—but which is now burdened with decayed wooden warehouses, and exhibits few or no symptoms of commercial life; except, perhaps, a bark or brig, half-way down its melancholy length, discharging hides; or, nearer at hand, a Nova Scotia schooner, pitching out her cargo of firewood,—at the head, I say, of this dilapidated wharf, which the tide often overflows, and along which, at the base and in the rear of the row of buildings, the track of many languid years is seen in a border of unthrifty grass,—here, with a view from its front windows adown this not very enlivening prospect, and thence across the harbour, stands a spacious edifice of brick. From the loftiest point of its roof, during precisely three and a half hours of each forenoon, floats or droops, in breeze or calm, the banner of the republic; but with the thirteen stripes turned vertically, instead of horizontally, and thus indicating that a civil, and not a military post of Uncle Sam's government, is here established. Its front is ornamented with a portico of half a dozen wooden pillars, supporting a balcony, beneath which a flight of wide granite steps descends towards the street. Over the entrance hovers an enormous specimen of the American eagle, with outspread wings, a shield before her breast, and, if I recollect aright, a bunch of intermingled thunderbolts and barbed arrows in each claw. With the customary infirmity of temper that characterizes this unhappy fowl, she appears, by the fierceness of her beak and eye and the general truculency of her attitude, to threaten mischief to the inoffensive community; and especially to warn all citizens, careful of their safety, against intruding on the premises which she overshadows with her wings. Nevertheless, vixenly as she looks, many people are seeking, at this very moment, to shelter themselves under the wing of the federal eagle; imagining, I presume, that her bosom has all the softness and snugness of an

NO FEAR

its editor, or a little more than its editor. While explaining how *The Scarlet Letter* came into my hands, I've also added a few details about a previously undescribed way of life and the characters who live it—one of whom happens to be me.

In my native Salem, there is a wharf that was bustling fifty years ago but is now decaying and almost empty, aside from a few trading ships unloading their cargo. The tide often overflows the wharf, and overgrown grass tells the story of many slow years. At the end of this dilapidated wharf, overlooking the bleak view, is a big brick building. For three and a half hours each morning, from the roof of the building, a U.S. flag floats or droops, depending on the weather. The flag's stripes are turned vertically to show that the building has a civil purpose, not a military one. In the front of the building, six wooden pillars support a balcony, and a flight of wide stone steps descends to the street. Over the entrance hovers a huge American eagle, with spread wings, a shield over her chest, and, if I'm remembering right, a bunch of thunderbolts and barbed arrows in each claw. With the customary bad temper of this unhappy species, the eagle looks like she's threatening the inoffensive community with her fierce beak and eye, and her overall bad attitude. She looks like she's warning people who care about their safety not to set foot in the building. Despite her scary appearance, many people are, at this very moment, trying to shelter themselves under the wing of the federal government. I guess they imagine she's as soft and cozy as a down pillow. But the bird is vicious in even her best moods, and sooner or later (usually sooner), she flings off the shelter-seekers with her claw, beak, or arrows.

eider-down pillow. But she has no great tenderness, even in her best of moods, and, sooner or later,—oftener soon than late,—is apt to fling off her nestlings with a scratch of her claw, a dab of her beak, or a rankling wound from her barbed arrows.

The pavement round about the above-described edifice—which we may as well name at once as the Custom-House of the port—has grass enough growing in its chinks to show that it has not, of late days, been worn by any multitudinous resort of business. In some months of the year, however, there often chances a forenoon when affairs move onward with a livelier tread. Such occasions might remind the elderly citizen of that period, before the last war with England, when Salem was a port by itself; not scorned, as she is now, by her own merchants and ship-owners, who permit her wharves to crumble to ruin, while their ventures go to swell, needlessly and imperceptibly, the mighty flood of commerce at New York or Boston. On some such morning, when three or four vessels happen to have arrived at once,—usually from Africa or South America,—or to be on the verge of their departure thitherward, there is a sound of frequent feet, passing briskly up and down the granite steps. Here, before his own wife has greeted him, you may greet the sea-flushed ship-master, just in port, with his vessel's papers under his arm in a tarnished tin box. Here, too, comes his owner, cheerful or sombre, gracious or in the sulks, accordingly as his scheme of the now accomplished voyage has been realized in merchandise that will readily be turned to gold, or has buried him under a bulk of incommodities, such as nobody will care to rid him of. Here, likewise,—the germ of the wrinkle-browed, grizzly-bearded, careworn merchant,—we have the smart young clerk, who gets the taste of traffic as a wolf-cub does of blood, and already sends adventures in his master's ships, when he had better be sailing mimic boats upon a mill-pond. Another figure in the scene is the outward-bound sailor, in quest of a protection; or the recently arrived one, pale and feeble, seeking a passport to the hospital. Nor must we forget the captains of the rusty little schooners that bring firewood from the British provinces; a rough-looking set of tarpaulins, without the alertness of the Yankee aspect, but contributing an item of no slight importance to our decaying trade.

Cluster all these individuals together, as they sometimes were, with other miscellaneous ones to diversify the group, and, for the

NO FEAR

The streets around this building—which I might as well say now is the Custom House of the port—have grass growing in their cracks, which shows how slow business has been. Some months, though, we'll happen to have a busier morning. Such occasions might remind older citizens of the time before the War of 1812, when Salem was a thriving port—not scorned, as it is now, by its own merchants and ship owners, who let Salem crumble while they send their business to Boston and New York, who don't need or notice it. On one of those rare busy mornings, when three or four boats were coming or going to Africa or South America, you can hear many people walking briskly up and down the granite steps of the Custom House. Before he's seen his own wife, the sea-flushed ship's captain comes here, newly arrived to port, holding his ship's papers in a tarnished tin box under one arm. The ship's owner is here, too. He's cheerful, somber, gracious, or sulking, depending on whether his new merchandise will sell or will be impossible to get rid of. And here is a fresh young clerk, the seed of the wrinkled, grizzled, tired merchant he'll become. He gets a taste for traffic like a wolf-cub gets a taste for blood. He's already sending out merchandise of his own in his master's ships, at an age when he should be sailing toy ships on a pond. Another figure on the scene is the outward-bound sailor, seeking proof of American citizenship. Or the recently arrived sailor, pale and feeble, requesting papers to visit the hospital. And we can't forget the captains of the rusty little schooners hauling firewood: they're a rough-looking bunch of tarps, but important to our decaying trade.

Group all of these people together, as they sometimes were, and throw in a few random others, and it makes the Custom House into

time being, it made the Custom-House a stirring scene. More frequently, however, on ascending the steps, you would discern—in the entry, if it were summer time, or in their appropriate rooms, if wintry or inclement weather—a row of venerable figures, sitting in old-fashioned chairs, which were tipped on their hind legs back against the wall. Oftentimes they were asleep, but occasionally might be heard talking together, in voices between speech and a snore, and with that lack of energy that distinguishes the occupants of alms-houses, and all other human beings who depend for subsistence on charity, on monopolized labor, or any thing else but their own independent exertions. These old gentlemen—seated, like Matthew, at the receipt of custom, but not very liable to be summoned thence, like him, for apostolic errands—were Custom-House officers.

Furthermore, on the left hand as you enter the front door, is a certain room or office, about fifteen feet square, and of a lofty height; with two of its arched windows commanding a view of the aforesaid dilapidated wharf, and the third looking across a narrow lane, and along a portion of Derby Street. All three give glimpses of the shops of grocers, block-makers, slop-sellers, and ship-chandlers; around the doors of which are generally to be seen, laughing and gossiping, clusters of old salts, and such other wharf-rats as haunt the Wapping of a seaport. The room itself is cobwebbed, and dingy with old paint; its floor is strewn with gray sand, in a fashion that has elsewhere fallen into long disuse; and it is easy to conclude, from the general slovenliness of the place, that this is a sanctuary into which womankind, with her tools of magic, the broom and mop, has very infrequent access. In the way of furniture, there is a stove with a voluminous funnel; an old pine desk, with a three-legged stool beside it; two or three wooden-bottom chairs, exceedingly decrepit and infirm; and,—not to forget the library,—on some shelves, a score or two of volumes of the Acts of Congress, and a bulky Digest of the Revenue Laws. A tin pipe ascends through the ceiling, and forms a medium of vocal communication with other parts of the edifice. And here, some six months ago,—pacing from corner to corner, or lounging on the long-legged stool, with his elbow on the desk, and his eyes wandering up and down the columns of the morning newspaper,—you might have recognized, honored reader, the same individual who welcomed you into

quite a scene. More often, however, as you climbed the staircase you would notice venerable men sitting in old-fashioned chairs, which were tipped on their hind legs back against the wall. In the summer these men were in the entry; in wintry or bad weather, in their offices. They were often asleep, but sometimes you could hear them talking together in a half-snore, with that lack of energy characteristic of beggars, or people who live on charity, or anything other than their own work. These old men sat like the apostle Matthew when he collected taxes, though they were far less likely to be called off on a holy mission. They were Custom House officers.

On the left-hand side as you walk in the front door is an office, fifteen feet square and very tall. Two of its arched windows overlook the run-down wharf, and the third looks out on a narrow lane and part of Derby Street. All three windows give glimpses of shops: grocers, block-makers, slop-sellers, and ship-chandlers. Old sailors and other wharf-rats can be seen laughing and gossiping outside these stores. The room itself is cobwebbed and dingy with old paint; its floor is covered in gray sand, in a fashion that's out of style everywhere else. It's easy to tell that women, with their magic brooms and mops, haven't had much access to the room. The furniture includes a stove with a large funnel, an old pine desk with a three-legged stool beside it, two or three beat-up wooden chairs, and a few dozen volumes of the Acts of Congress. A tin pipe rises through the ceiling, allowing communication with other parts of the building. Six months ago, you might have found me here, pacing from corner to corner or lounging on the long-legged stool with my elbow on the desk, skimming the morning paper—the same person who welcomed you into his cheery study, where the sunshine glimmers pleasantly through the willow branches on the western side of the Old Manse. But no more. The political tides washed me out of office, and a worthier man enjoys my old dignity and salary.

his cheery little study, where the sunshine glimmered so pleasantly through the willow branches, on the western side of the Old Manse. But now, should you go thither to seek him, you would inquire in vain for the Loco-foco Surveyor. The besom of reform has swept him out of office; and a worthier successor wears his dignity and pockets his emoluments.

This old town of Salem—my native place, though I have dwelt much away from it, both in boyhood and maturer years—possesses, or did possess, a hold on my affections, the force of which I have never realized during my seasons of actual residence here. Indeed, so far as its physical aspect is concerned, with its flat, unvaried surface, covered chiefly with wooden houses, few or none of which pretend to architectural beauty,—its irregularity, which is neither picturesque nor quaint, but only tame,—its long and lazy street, lounging wea-risomely through the whole extent of the peninsula, with Gallows Hill and New Guinea at one end, and a view of the alms-house at the other,—such being the features of my native town, it would be quite as reasonable to form a sentimental attachment to a disarranged checkerboard. And yet, though invariably happiest elsewhere, there is within me a feeling for old Salem, which, in lack of a better phrase, I must be content to call affection. The sentiment is probably assign-able to the deep and aged roots which my family has struck into the soil. It is now nearly two centuries and a quarter since the original Briton, the earliest emigrant of my name, made his appearance in the wild and forest-bordered settlement, which has since become a city. And here his descendants have been born and died, and have min-gled their earthy substance with the soil; until no small portion of it must necessarily be akin to the mortal frame wherewith, for a little while, I walk the streets. In part, therefore, the attachment which I speak of is the mere sensuous sympathy of dust for dust. Few of my countrymen can know what it is; nor, as frequent transplantation is perhaps better for the stock, need they consider it desirable to know.

But the sentiment has likewise its moral quality. The figure of that first ancestor, invested by family tradition with a dim and dusky grandeur, was present to my boyish imagination, as far back as I can remember. It still haunts me, and induces a sort of home-feeling with the past, which I scarcely claim in reference to the present phase of the town. I seem to have a stronger claim to a residence here

NO FEAR

Salem is my hometown, though I've moved away many times. It has—or had, at any rate—a hold on my heart, the strength of which I never recognized when I was living here. The town is flat, covered in unattractive wooden houses. It's odd. Its long, lazy street has Gallows Hill and New Guinea at one end and the poorhouse at the other. Liking this town makes as much sense as being fond of a checkerboard with pieces scattered on it. Yet though I'm always happier in other places, I have a certain affection for Old Salem. I probably feel this way because my family has deep roots here. It was more than 200 years ago that my first ancestor arrived in the wild, forest-bordered settlement that is now Salem. His descendents have been born, died, and were buried in Salem's soil, which must resemble my own body. Part of my affection for Salem is this connection between their bones and my own. Moving as often as they do, few Americans know such a bond—and since frequent movement is better for the family line, it's okay that they don't know.

There's a moral aspect to this connection, as well. For as long as I can remember, I have known about my first Salem ancestor, that dim and grand figure. The idea of him still haunts me and makes me feel as though my home is Old Salem, not the run-down port town Salem is today. I feel bound to the town today because of this serious, bearded, sable-cloaked man who, with his Bible and his sword, once

on account of this grave, bearded, sable-cloaked, and steeple-crowned progenitor,—who came so early, with his Bible and his sword, and trode the unworn street with such a stately port, and made so large a figure, as a man of war and peace,—a stronger claim than for myself, whose name is seldom heard and my face hardly known. He was a soldier, legislator, judge; he was a ruler in the Church; he had all the Puritanic traits, both good and evil. He was likewise a bitter persecutor; as witness the Quakers, who have remembered him in their histories, and relate an incident of his hard severity towards a woman of their sect, which will last longer, it is to be feared, than any record of his better deeds, although these were many. His son, too, inherited the persecuting spirit, and made himself so conspicuous in the martyrdom of the witches, that their blood may fairly be said to have left a stain upon him. So deep a stain, indeed, that his old dry bones, in the Charter Street burial-ground, must still retain it, if they have not crumbled utterly to dust! I know not whether these ancestors of mine bethought themselves to repent, and ask pardon of Heaven for their cruelties; or whether they are now groaning under the heavy consequences of them, in another state of being. At all events, I, the present writer, as their representative, hereby take shame upon myself for their sakes, and pray that any curse incurred by them—as I have heard, and as the dreary and unprosperous condition of the race, for many a long year back, would argue to exist—may be now and henceforth removed.

Doubtless, however, either of these stern and black-browed Puritans would have thought it quite a sufficient retribution for his sins, that, after so long a lapse of years, the old trunk of the family tree, with so much venerable moss upon it, should have borne, as its topmost bough, an idler like myself. No aim, that I have ever cherished, would they recognize as laudable; no success of mine—if my life, beyond its domestic scope, had ever been brightened by success—would they deem otherwise than worthless, if not positively disgraceful. "What is he?" murmurs one gray shadow of my forefathers to the other. "A writer of story-books! What kind of a business in life,—what mode of glorifying God, or being serviceable to mankind in his day and generation,—may that be? Why, the degenerate fellow might as well have been a fiddler!" Such are the compliments bandied between my great-grandsires and myself, across the gulf of time! And yet, let them scorn

walked the new streets of Salem with a stately air. He was a large figure, a man of war and peace. By comparison, I'm almost anonymous. He was a soldier, a legislator, and a judge. He was a powerful minister, with both the good and the evil traits of the Puritans. He persecuted many people. The Quakers remember him for that, particularly for his severe judgment of one woman, which may last longer than the record of his many good deeds. His son inherited the same fondness for persecution: He convicted so many witches that you could say their blood is on his hands. The stain is so deep that it must still be on his dry old bones, if they haven't crumbled to dust yet. I don't know whether these ancestors of mine repented for their cruelties or whether they are now groaning in Hell. As their representative, I take their shame on myself and pray that any curse on their dreary descendents will be removed.

I'm sure that either of these stern Puritans would consider an idle descendent like me punishment enough for his sins. They would not have approved of any of my goals. All of my success—if I've even had any worldly success—would seem worthless to them, or even disgraceful. "What is he?" I hear one gray shadow of an ancestor murmur to another. "A story writer! What kind of business is that? Does it glorify God, or serve mankind? He might as well have been a fiddle-player!" Such are the compliments my ancestors give me across time. Yet although they scorn me, I have strong traits of theirs.

me as they will, strong traits of their nature have intertwined themselves with mine.

Planted deep, in the town's earliest infancy and childhood, by these two earnest and energetic men, the race has ever since subsisted here; always, too, in respectability; never, so far as I have known, disgraced by a single unworthy member; but seldom or never, on the other hand, after the first two generations, performing any memorable deed, or so much as putting forward a claim to public notice. Gradually, they have sunk almost out of sight; as old houses, here and there about the streets, get covered half-way to the eaves by the accumulation of new soil. From father to son, for above a hundred years, they followed the sea; a gray-headed shipmaster, in each generation, retiring from the quarter-deck to the homestead, while a boy of fourteen took the hereditary place before the mast, confronting the salt spray and the gale, which had blustered against his sire and grandsire. The boy, also, in due time, passed from the forecastle to the cabin, spent a tempestuous manhood, and returned from his world-wanderings, to grow old, and die, and mingle his dust with the natal earth. This long connection of a family with one spot, as its place of birth and burial, creates a kindred between the human being and the locality, quite independent of any charm in the scenery or moral circumstances that surround him. It is not love, but instinct. The new inhabitant—who came himself from a foreign land, or whose father or grandfather came—has little claim to be called a Salemite; he has no conception of the oyster-like tenacity with which an old settler, over whom his third century is creeping, clings to the spot where his successive generations have been imbedded. It is no matter that the place is joyless for him; that he is weary of the old wooden houses, the mud and dust, the dead level of site and sentiment, the chill east wind, and the chillest of social atmospheres;—all these, and whatever faults besides he may see or imagine, are nothing to the purpose. The spell survives, and just as powerfully as if the natal spot were an earthly paradise. So has it been in my case. I felt it almost as a destiny to make Salem my home; so that the mould of features and cast of character which had all along been familiar here—ever, as one representative of the race lay down in his grave, another assuming, as it were, his sentry-march along the Main Street—might still in my little day be seen and recognized in the old

NO FEAR

Deeply planted by these two men so many years ago, the family tree has grown here ever since. We have always been respectable, never disgraced—but never memorable, either, after the first two generations. Our family sank gradually out of sight, like an old house slowly buried under new soil. For more than a hundred years our men went to sea. A gray-haired shipmaster would retire, and a fourteen-year-old boy in our family would take his place at the mast, facing down the same salt spray and storms his ancestors had. That boy eventually advanced and then came home to grow old, die, and be buried in the place of his birth. This long connection between Salem and our family has created a strong bond, which has nothing to do with the scenery or the surroundings. It is not love but instinct. A newcomer whose family has been here a mere generation or three cannot call himself a Salemite. He has no concept of the tenacity with which someone like me clings, to the place where his ancestors have lived. It doesn't matter that the town brings me no joy, that I am tired of the old wooden houses, the mud and the dust, the flat land and flatter emotions of Salem, its cold wind and colder social atmosphere. The place has cast a spell on me that's as powerful as if Salem were an earthly paradise. It almost felt like I was destined to make Salem my home, to continue my family's long presence here. But this connection has become unhealthy, and must be broken. Human beings can't grow in the same worn-out soil year after year, any more than a potato can. My children have been born elsewhere and, if I have anything to say about it, will settle elsewhere.

town. Nevertheless, this very sentiment is an evidence that the connection, which has become an unhealthy one, should at last be severed. Human nature will not flourish, any more than a potato, if it be planted and replanted, for too long a series of generations, in the same worn-out soil. My children have had other birthplaces, and, so far as their fortunes may be within my control, shall strike their roots into unaccustomed earth.

On emerging from the Old Manse, it was chiefly this strange, indolent, unjoyous attachment for my native town, that brought me to fill a place in Uncle Sam's brick edifice, when I might as well, or better, have gone somewhere else. My doom was on me. It was not the first time, nor the second, that I had gone away,—as it seemed, permanently,—but yet returned, like the bad half-penny; or as if Salem were for me the inevitable centre of the universe. So, one fine morning, I ascended the flight of granite steps, with the President's commission in my pocket, and was introduced to the corps of gentlemen who were to aid me in my weighty responsibility, as chief executive officer of the Custom-House.

I doubt greatly—or rather, I do not doubt at all—whether any public functionary of the United States, either in the civil or military line, has ever had such a patriarchal body of veterans under his orders as myself. The whereabouts of the Oldest Inhabitant was at once settled, when I looked at them. For upwards of twenty years before this epoch, the independent position of the Collector had kept the Salem Custom-House out of the whirlpool of political vicissitude, which makes the tenure of office generally so fragile. A soldier,—New England's most distinguished soldier,—he stood firmly on the pedestal of his gallant services; and, himself secure in the wise liberality of the successive administrations through which he had held office, he had been the safety of his subordinates in many an hour of danger and heart-quake. General Miller was radically conservative; a man over whose kindly nature habit had no slight influence; attaching himself strongly to familiar faces, and with difficulty moved to change, even when change might have brought unquestionable improvement. Thus, on taking charge of my department, I found few but aged men. They were ancient sea-captains, for the most part, who, after being tost on every sea, and standing up sturdily against life's tempestuous blast, had finally drifted into

NO FEAR

This strange, lazy, joyless attachment to Salem brought me here to work at the Custom House when I might have gone somewhere else. It was my doom. I had moved away a few times before—permanently, it seemed. But every time I came back like a bad penny, as if Salem were the center of the universe for me. So one fine morning I climbed the stone steps, with a commission from the president in my pocket. I was introduced to the group of gentlemen who were to help me with my grave responsibilities as chief executive officer of the Custom House.

I'm sure no public servant of the United States has ever had a more experienced group of veterans under his direction. For almost twenty years before I took the job, the custom-collector was an independent position, which protected the Custom House from shifts in the political winds. New England's most distinguished soldier, General Miller, had authority from his service experience. No politician would ever fire him, and he protected his employees. General Miller was radically conservative. He was a man of habit, strongly attached to familiar faces and reluctant to change, even when change would have improved things. So when I took over my department, I found only a few old men. They were old sailors, mostly. Having faced stormy seas and stood sturdily in the face of the strong winds of life, they had finally drifted into this quiet corner of the world. With little to worry them here, except for the passing terror of presidential elections, they each acquired a new lease on life. Though they were as susceptible to old age and sickness as other men, they must have had some charm to keep death away. I heard a few of them were sick or confined to their beds and didn't dream of making an appearance at work for most of the year. But after their sluggish winter, they would creep out

this quiet nook; where, with little to disturb them, except the periodical terrors of a Presidential election, they one and all acquired a new lease of existence. Though by no means less liable than their fellow-men to age and infirmity, they had evidently some talisman or other that kept death at bay. Two or three of their number, as I was assured, being gouty and rheumatic, or perhaps bed-ridden, never dreamed of making their appearance at the Custom-House, during a large part of the year; but, after a torpid winter, would creep out into the warm sunshine of May or June, go lazily about what they termed duty, and, at their own leisure and convenience, betake themselves to bed again. I must plead guilty to the charge of abbreviating the official breath of more than one of these venerable servants of the republic. They were allowed, on my representation, to rest from their arduous labors, and soon afterwards—as if their sole principle of life had been zeal for their country's service; as I verily believe it was—withdrew to a better world. It is a pious consolation to me, that, through my interference, a sufficient space was allowed them for repentance of evil and corrupt practices, into which, as a matter of course, every Custom-House officer must be supposed to fall. Neither the front nor the back entrance of the Custom-House opens on the road to Paradise.

The greater part of my officers were Whigs. It was well for their venerable brotherhood, that the new Surveyor was not a politician, and, though a faithful Democrat in principle, neither received nor held his office with any reference to political services. Had it been otherwise,—had an active politician been put into this influential post, to assume the easy task of making head against a Whig Collector, whose infirmities withheld him from the personal administration of his office,—hardly a man of the old corps would have drawn the breath of official life, within a month after the exterminating angel had come up the Custom-House steps. According to the received code in such matters, it would have been nothing short of duty, in a politician, to bring every one of those white heads under the axe of the guillotine. It was plain enough to discern, that the old fellows dreaded some such discourtesy at my hands. It pained, and at the same time amused me, to behold the terrors that attended my advent; to see a furrowed cheek, weather-beaten by half a century of storm, turn ashy pale at the glance of so harmless an individual

into the warm sunshine of May or June. They would lazily do their duties (as they called them) and, when they felt like it, go back to bed again. I have to plead guilty to shortening the service of several of these valuable public servants. I let them stop doing their official duties, and as if their only aim in life had been to serve their country, they soon went to a better place. I am consoled by the thought that I gave these men the time and space to repent their sins and corruption, which every Custom House officer falls prey to. Neither the front nor the back door of the Custom House opens onto the road to paradise.

Whigs: One of
major political
ties in the mid-
3th century. The
crats were the
er major party.

Most of my officers were Whigs. It was lucky for them that I was no politician. Though a faithful Democrat in principle, my appointment to the job wasn't political. If I had been a partisan Democrat, placed in this job to do the easy task of seizing power from an elderly Whig customs-collector whose illness kept him from fulfilling his duties, I would have fired almost every officer in my first month on the job. I would have been the Angel of Death himself. Indeed, the unspoken rules of politics would have made it my duty to give those white-haired guys the axe. It was easy to see the old fellows were nervous around me. I found it both funny and painful to see the terror with which they greeted my arrival. Old men, weather beaten by fifty years at sea, would turn pale when I glanced at them. Little harmless me! When they spoke to me, their voices trembled—the same voices that used to bellow commands. They knew, the clever old men, that by the established political rules (and, in some cases, by their own inability to work) they should have been replaced by younger, healthier

as myself; to detect, as one or another addressed me, the tremor of a voice, which, in long-past days, had been wont to bellow through a speaking-trumpet, hoarsely enough to frighten Boreas himself to silence. They knew, these excellent old persons, that, by all established rule,—and, as regarded some of them, weighed by their own lack of efficiency for business,—they ought to have given place to younger men, more orthodox in politics, and altogether fitter than themselves to serve our common Uncle. I knew it too, but could never quite find in my heart to act upon the knowledge. Much and deservedly to my own discredit, therefore, and considerably to the detriment of my official conscience, they continued, during my incumbency, to creep about the wharves, and loiter up and down the Custom-House steps. They spent a good deal of time, also, asleep in their accustomed corners, with their chairs tilted back against the wall; awaking, however, once or twice in a forenoon, to bore one another with the several thousandth repetition of old sea-stories, and mouldy jokes, that had grown to be pass-words and countersigns among them.

The discovery was soon made, I imagine, that the new Surveyor had no great harm in him. So with lightsome hearts, and the happy consciousness of being usefully employed,—in their own behalf, at least, if not for our beloved country,—these good old gentlemen went through the various formalities of office. Sagaciously, under their spectacles, did they peep into the holds of vessels! Mighty was their fuss about little matters, and marvellous, sometimes, the obtuseness that allowed greater ones to slip between their fingers! Whenever such a mischance occurred,—when a wagon-load of valuable merchandise had been smuggled ashore, at noonday, perhaps, and directly beneath their unsuspicious noses,—nothing could exceed the vigilance and alacrity with which they proceeded to lock, and double-lock, and secure with tape and sealing-wax, all the avenues of the delinquent vessel. Instead of a reprimand for their previous negligence, the case seemed rather to require an eulogium on their praiseworthy caution, after the mischief had happened; a grateful recognition of the promptitude of their zeal, the moment that there was no longer any remedy!

Unless people are more than commonly disagreeable, it is my foolish habit to contract a kindness for them. The better part of my

men who voted Democratic. I knew it, too, but I could never bring myself to do anything about it. To my well-deserved shame, and with a guilty official conscience, I let the old men hang out on the wharves and loiter on the Custom House steps. They spent a lot of time asleep in their usual corners, chairs tilted back against the walls. They'd wake up once or twice every morning to bore each other with the several thousandth repetition of old sea stories and moldy jokes, which had turned into passwords for them.

They must have quickly realized I was harmless. So with light hearts and the happy knowledge that they were usefully employed (the jobs were useful to *them*, even if they weren't much use to the country) these good old men went through the motions. Looking wisely under their spectacles, they peeped into the holds of mighty ships. They made a big fuss about little things and showed an amazing ability to let serious matters slip through their fingers. Whenever something bad happened—for example, when an entire wagonload of valuable goods was smuggled ashore at noon, right underneath their unsuspicious noses—nothing could outdo their fast and useless reaction. They'd lock and double-lock and tape up and wax over every opening of the ship. Instead of scolding them for their negligence, it seemed I was supposed to praise them for springing into action the moment there was nothing left to do.

It's a foolish habit of mine to be nice to anyone who isn't extremely irritating. If a man has strong points, I focus on those.

companion's character, if it have a better part, is that which usually comes uppermost in my regard, and forms the type whereby I recognize the man. As most of these old Custom-House officers had good traits, and as my position in reference to them, being paternal and protective, was favorable to the growth of friendly sentiments, I soon grew to like them all. It was pleasant, in the summer forenoons,—when the fervent heat, that almost liquefied the rest of the human family, merely communicated a genial warmth to their half-torpid systems,—it was pleasant to hear them chatting in the back entry, a row of them all tipped against the wall, as usual; while the frozen witticisms of past generations were thawed out, and came bubbling with laughter from their lips. Externally, the jollity of aged men has much in common with the mirth of children; the intellect, any more than a deep sense of humor, has little to do with the matter; it is, with both, a gleam that plays upon the surface, and imparts a sunny and cheery aspect alike to the green branch, and gray, mouldering trunk. In one case, however, it is real sunshine; in the other, it more resembles the phosphorescent glow of decaying wood.

It would be sad injustice, the reader must understand, to represent all my excellent old friends as in their dotage. In the first place, my coadjutors were not invariably old; there were men among them in their strength and prime, of marked ability and energy, and altogether superior to the sluggish and dependent mode of life on which their evil stars had cast them. Then, moreover, the white locks of age were sometimes found to be the thatch of an intellectual tenement in good repair. But, as respects the majority of my corps of veterans, there will be no wrong done, if I characterize them generally as a set of wearisome old souls, who had gathered nothing worth preservation from their varied experience of life. They seemed to have flung away all the golden grain of practical wisdom, which they had enjoyed so many opportunities of harvesting, and most carefully to have stored their memories with the husks. They spoke with far more interest and unction of their morning's breakfast, or yesterday's, to-day's, or to-morrow's dinner, than of the shipwreck of forty or fifty years ago, and all the world's wonders which they had witnessed with their youthful eyes.

The father of the Custom-House—the patriarch, not only of this little squad of officials, but, I am bold to say, of the respectable body

NO FEAR

Since most of these old Custom House officials had good traits, and since my paternal, protective position created a friendly environment, I grew to like them all. On summer mornings, when heat that would liquefy younger people only warmed these old ones, it was nice to hear them all chatting in the back entry, chairs tipped against the wall, as usual. They would thaw out and tell the frozen old jokes of past generations. On the outside, the jolliness of old men is like the happiness of children. There is nothing deep or intellectual about it. Both the elderly and the young light up with laughter on their surface, whether that surface is a green branch or a gray, moldy trunk. But for the young that light is real sunshine; for the aged, it's the glow of decaying wood.

It would be unfair, you must understand, to suggest that all of my officers were senile. For starters, they weren't all old. Some were in their prime, skillful and energetic, and much better than the sluggish jobs they'd been cursed with. And sometimes white hair covered a brain that worked well. But most of them were wearying old souls who had gained little of value from their wide experience. In terms of wisdom, they'd thrown out the baby and kept the bathwater. They spoke with far more interest about today's breakfast, or yesterday's, today's, or tomorrow's dinner than about the shipwrecks and wonders their youthful eyes had seen.

The father figure of the Custom House (indeed, of Custom Houses throughout the United States) was a certain permanent Inspector.

of tide-waiters all over the United States—was a certain permanent Inspector. He might truly be termed a legitimate son of the revenue system, dyed in the wool, or rather, born in the purple; since his sire, a Revolutionary colonel, and formerly collector of the port, had created an office for him, and appointed him to fill it, at a period of the early ages which few living men can now remember. This Inspector, when I first knew him, was a man of fourscore years, or thereabouts, and certainly one of the most wonderful specimens of winter-green that you would be likely to discover in a lifetime's search. With his florid cheek, his compact figure, smartly arrayed in a bright-buttoned blue coat, his brisk and vigorous step, and his hale and hearty aspect, altogether, he seemed—not young, indeed—but a kind of new contrivance of Mother Nature in the shape of man, whom age and infirmity had no business to touch. His voice and laugh, which perpetually reëchoed through the Custom-House, had nothing of the tremulous quaver and cackle of an old man's utterance; they came strutting out of his lungs, like the crow of a cock, or the blast of a clarion. Looking at him merely as an animal,—and there was very little else to look at,—he was a most satisfactory object, from the thorough healthfulness and wholesomeness of his system, and his capacity, at that extreme age, to enjoy all, or nearly all, the delights which he had ever aimed at, or conceived of. The careless security of his life in the Custom-House, on a regular income, and with but slight and infrequent apprehensions of removal, had no doubt contributed to make time pass lightly over him. The original and more potent causes, however, lay in the rare perfection of his animal nature, the moderate proportion of intellect, and the very trifling admixture of moral and spiritual ingredients; these latter qualities, indeed, being in barely enough measure to keep the old gentleman from walking on all-fours. He possessed no power of thought, no depth of feeling, no troublesome sensibilities; nothing, in short, but a few commonplace instincts, which, aided by the cheerful temper that grew inevitably out of his physical well-being, did duty very respectably, and to general acceptance, in lieu of a heart. He had been the husband of three wives, all long since dead; the father of twenty children, most of whom, at every age of childhood or maturity, had likewise returned to dust. Here, one would suppose, might have been sorrow enough to imbue the sunniest disposition, through and through, with a

NO FEAR

You could say he was dyed in the wool, or maybe born in royal purple. In the early days of the country, this man's father, a colonel in the Revolutionary War and former custom-collector in Salem, created an office for his son. When I first met this Inspector, he was eighty years old, and one of the most vital specimens you could ever hope to meet. With his rosy cheeks, compact body, blue coat with bright buttons, quick step, and hearty appearance, he looked—not young, exactly—but like some new creation of Mother Nature's: a man-like creature whom age and illness couldn't touch. His voice and laugh, which always echoed in the Custom House, didn't quaver like an old man's; they strutted like the crow of a rooster or the blast of a trumpet. He was a remarkable animal: healthy, wholesome, and still capable of enjoying nearly all of life's pleasures. His carefree job security and regular paycheck, marred only by slight and passing fears of being fired, had made time kind to him. The original cause of his wonderful state, though, was in his animal nature, his modest intellect, and the smallness of his moral and spiritual awareness. Indeed, he had barely enough mind and soul to keep him from walking on all fours. He had no power of thought, no deep feelings, no real emotion. Really, instead of a heart, he had nothing but a few common instincts and the cheerfulness that comes from good health. He had married three women, all long dead, and fathered twenty children, many of whom were dead too. You'd think so much death would darken even the sunniest temperament. But not so with our old Inspector. One brief sigh took care of all his sad memories. The next minute he was as ready to play as any boy, far readier even than his assistant, who at nineteen years was by far the older and more serious man.

sable tinge. Not so with our old Inspector! One brief sigh sufficed to carry off the entire burden of these dismal reminiscences. The next moment, he was as ready for sport as any unbreeched infant; far readier than the Collector's junior clerk, who, at nineteen years, was much the elder and graver man of the two.

I used to watch and study this patriarchal personage with, I think, livelier curiosity than any other form of humanity there presented to my notice. He was, in truth, a rare phenomenon; so perfect in one point of view; so shallow, so delusive, so impalpable, such an absolute nonentity, in every other. My conclusion was that he had no soul, no heart, no mind; nothing, as I have already said, but instincts; and yet, withal, so cunningly had the few materials of his character been put together, that there was no painful perception of deficiency, but, on my part, an entire contentment with what I found in him. It might be difficult—and it was so—to conceive how he should exist hereafter, so earthy and sensuous did he seem; but surely his existence here, admitting that it was to terminate with his last breath, had been not unkindly given; with no higher moral responsibilities than the beasts of the field, but with a larger scope of enjoyment than theirs, and with all their blessed immunity from the dreariness and duskiness of age.

One point, in which he had vastly the advantage over his four-footed brethren, was his ability to recollect the good dinners which it had made no small portion of the happiness of his life to eat. His gourmandism was a highly agreeable trait; and to hear him talk of roast-meat was as appetizing as a pickle or an oyster. As he possessed no higher attribute, and neither sacrificed nor vitiated any spiritual endowment by devoting all his energies and ingenuities to subserve the delight and profit of his maw, it always pleased and satisfied me to hear him expatiate on fish, poultry, and butcher's meat, and the most eligible methods of preparing them for the table. His reminiscences of good cheer, however ancient the date of the actual banquet, seemed to bring the savor of pig or turkey under one's very nostrils. There were flavors on his palate, that had lingered there not less than sixty or seventy years, and were still apparently as fresh as that of the mutton-chop which he had just devoured for his breakfast. I have heard him smack his lips over dinners, every guest at which, except himself, had long been food for worms. It

NO FEAR

I used to watch and study this father figure with greater curiosity than any other specimen of humanity I met. He was a rare phenomenon: so perfect in some ways, so shallow and deluded and blank in others. I concluded that he had no soul at all, no heart, no mind, nothing but instincts. Yet the few bits of his character had been assembled so cleverly that there were no obvious gaps. Indeed, I found him entirely satisfactory. It was hard to imagine him in the afterlife, since he was so earthly, but even if his life were to end with his final breath, it was not unkindly granted. The man had no more moral responsibilities than animals do, but he enjoyed profounder pleasures, and he had their immunity from the dreariness of old age.

One great advantage the Inspector had over animals was his ability to remember good dinners, which had given his life so much happiness. His love of food was a wonderful trait: To hear him talk of roast meat made me as hungry as eating an appetizer. Since he had no higher sensibilities, he didn't sacrifice any spirituality by devoting all his energy to pleasing his mouth. Because I didn't have to worry about his nonexistent soul, I always enjoyed listening to him talk about fish, poultry, and meat and how best to cook them. When he described a feast, no matter how long ago he had enjoyed it, it was like the smell of the pig or turkey was right under your nose. He could taste flavors that hit his palate sixty or seventy years ago as clearly as the meat he'd just devoured for breakfast. I have heard him smack his lips remembering dinner parties, every guest at which (besides him) has been worm food for years. It was amazing to see how the ghosts of long-ago meals were always rising up before him—not in anger or blame, but as if they were grateful for the appreciation. It was as if the ghosts wanted to recreate old pleasures.

was marvellous to observe how the ghosts of bygone meals were continually rising up before him; not in anger or retribution, but as if grateful for his former appreciation, and seeking to reduplicate an endless series of enjoyment, at once shadowy and sensual. A tenderloin of beef, a hind-quarter of veal, a spare-rib of pork, a particular chicken, or a remarkably praiseworthy turkey, which had perhaps adorned his board in the days of the elder Adams, would be remembered; while all the subsequent experience of our race, and all the events that brightened or darkened his individual career, had gone over him with as little permanent effect as the passing breeze. The chief tragic event of the old man's life, so far as I could judge, was his mishap with a certain goose, which lived and died some twenty or forty years ago; a goose of most promising figure, but which, at table, proved so inveterately tough that the carving-knife would make no impression on its carcass; and it could only be divided with an axe and handsaw.

But it is time to quit this sketch; on which, however, I should be glad to dwell at considerably more length, because, of all men whom I have ever known, this individual was fittest to be a Custom-House officer. Most persons, owing to causes which I may not have space to hint at, suffer moral detriment from this peculiar mode of life. The old Inspector was incapable of it, and, were he to continue in office to the end of time, would be just as good as he was then, and sit down to dinner with just as good an appetite.

There is one likeness, without which my gallery of Custom-House portraits would be strangely incomplete; but which my comparatively few opportunities for observation enable me to sketch only in the merest outline. It is that of the Collector, our gallant old General, who, after his brilliant military service, subsequently to which he had ruled over a wild Western territory, had come hither, twenty years before, to spend the decline of his varied and honorable life.

The brave soldier had already numbered, nearly or quite, his threescore years and ten, and was pursuing the remainder of his earthly march, burdened with infirmities which even the martial music of his own spirit-stirring recollections could do little towards lightening. The step was palsied now, that had been foremost in the

The piece of beef, veal, pork, chicken, or turkey he might have eaten when John Adams was president are all remembered to this day. Not so all the history he's seen, nor the successes and failures of his career. Those have affected him as little as a passing breeze. As far as I can tell, the most tragic event of the old man's life was a mishap with a certain goose, which lived and died twenty or forty years ago. The bird looked quite delicious but turned out to be so tough that the carving knife couldn't cut it, and it had to be tackled with an axe and a saw.

But it is time to abandon this sketch of the Inspector, though I would be glad to dwell on it a lot longer, since of all the men I have known, he was the best suited to being a Custom House officer. Most people, for reasons I may not have the space to explain, are morally weakened by this job. But the old Inspector was incapable of being corrupted, since there was nothing in him to corrupt. Had he remained at the Custom House until the end of time, he would emerge just as good as when he went in, and sit down to dinner with just as good an appetite.

There's one portrait my Custom House gallery would be incomplete without. I haven't had many opportunities to observe the subject, though, so I can only sketch a little outline. The portrait is of the Collector, gallant old General Miller. After brilliant military service, after which he ruled a Western territory, the General came to Salem twenty years ago to live out his last decades.

The brave soldier was nearly seventy years old when I met him, and was burdened with illnesses even his stirring military recollections could not lessen. His once-commanding step had grown weak. He needed a servant's assistance and the iron railing just to slowly, painfully climb the Custom House stairs and reach his chair beside

charge. It was only with the assistance of a servant, and by leaning his hand heavily on the iron balustrade, that he could slowly
and painfully ascend the Custom-House steps, and, with a toilsome
progress across the floor, attain his customary chair beside the fireplace. There he used to sit, gazing with a somewhat dim serenity of
aspect at the figures that came and went; amid the rustle of papers,
the administering of oaths, the discussion of business, and the casual
talk of the office; all which sounds and circumstances seemed but
indistinctly to impress his senses, and hardly to make their way into
his inner sphere of contemplation. His countenance, in this repose,
was mild and kindly. If his notice was sought, an expression of courtesy and interest gleamed out upon his features; proving that there
was light within him, and that it was only the outward medium of
the intellectual lamp that obstructed the rays in their passage. The
closer you penetrated to the substance of his mind, the sounder it
appeared. When no longer called upon to speak, or listen, either of
which operations cost him an evident effort, his face would briefly
subside into its former not uncheerful quietude. It was not painful to behold this look; for, though dim, it had not the imbecility
of decaying age. The framework of his nature, originally strong and
massive, was not yet crumbled into ruin.

To observe and define his character, however, under such disad-
vantages, was as difficult a task as to trace out and build up anew,
in imagination, an old fortress, like Ticonderoga, from a view of its
gray and broken ruins. Here and there, perchance, the walls may
remain almost complete; but elsewhere may be only a shapeless
mound, cumbrous with its very strength, and overgrown, through
long years of peace and neglect, with grass and alien weeds.

Nevertheless, looking at the old warrior with affection,—for,
slight as was the communication between us, my feeling towards
him, like that of all bipeds and quadrupeds who knew him, might
not improperly be termed so,— I could discern the main points
of his portrait. It was marked with the noble and heroic qualities
which showed it to be not by a mere accident, but of good right,
that he had won a distinguished name. His spirit could never, I conceive, have been characterized by an uneasy activity; it must, at any
period of his life, have required an impulse to set him in motion;
but, once stirred up, with obstacles to overcome, and an adequate

the fireplace. He would sit there, gazing with a dim calm at the people who came and went. The rustle of paper, the oaths, and the chit-chat of the office didn't make an impression on him. His face was mild and kind. If someone spoke to him, his face would light up with courtesy and attention: His mind remained sharp though his senses had dulled. The more you learned of his mind, the sounder it appeared. When he wasn't speaking or listening—and it took some physical effort for him to do either—his face would return to its former calmness. He wasn't hard to look at: Though he had dimmed, he wasn't losing his mind. And his physical frame, once so strong and massive, was not yet entirely ruined.

In that condition, however, observing and defining his character was as difficult as trying to plan and rebuild a fortress by looking at its gray and broken ruins. A wall might stand here and there, but elsewhere only a shapeless mound remained, overgrown with grass and weeds after long years of peace and neglect.

I looked at the old warrior with affection. We hadn't talked much, but like all the men and animals who knew him, it's fair to say I felt affectionate about him. And through these kind eyes, I could see the main points of his portrait. His noble and heroic qualities showed that his reputation was well deserved. I can't imagine that he was ever restless. It must have taken a certain impulse to set him in motion. Once he was stirred up, though, and had obstacles to overcome and a worthy goal, it wasn't in the man to quit or fail. Heat had once defined him, and wasn't extinct yet. That heat was never the kind that flashes and flickers; rather, it was a deep red glow, like iron

object to be attained, it was not in the man to give out or fail. The heat that had formerly pervaded his nature, and which was not yet extinct, was never of the kind that flashes and flickers in a blaze, but, rather, a deep, red glow, as of iron in a furnace. Weight, solidity, firmness; this was the expression of his repose, even in such decay as had crept untimely over him, at the period of which I speak. But I could imagine, even then, that, under some excitement which should go deeply into his consciousness,—roused by a trumpet-peal, loud enough to awaken all of his energies that were not dead, but only slumbering,—he was yet capable of flinging off his infirmities like a sick man's gown, dropping the staff of age to seize a battle-sword, and starting up once more a warrior. And, in so intense a moment, his demeanour would have still been calm. Such an exhibition, however, was but to be pictured in fancy; not to be anticipated, nor desired. What I saw in him—as evidently as the indestructible ramparts of Old Ticonderoga, already cited as the most appropriate simile—were the features of stubborn and ponderous endurance, which might well have amounted to obstinacy in his earlier days; of integrity, that, like most of his other endowments, lay in a somewhat heavy mass, and was just as unmalleable and unmanageable as a ton of iron ore; and of benevolence, which, fiercely, as he led the bayonets on at Chippewa or Fort Erie, I take to be of quite as genuine a stamp as what actuates any or all the polemical philanthropists of the age. He had slain men with his own hand, for aught I know;—certainly, they had fallen, like blades of grass at the sweep of the scythe, before the charge to which his spirit imparted its triumphant energy;—but, be that as it might, there was never in his heart so much cruelty as would have brushed the down off a butterfly's wing. I have not known the man, to whose innate kindliness I would more confidently make an appeal.

Many characteristics—and those, too, which contribute not the least forcibly to impart resemblance in a sketch—must have vanished, or been obscured, before I met the General. All merely graceful attributes are usually the most evanescent; nor does Nature adorn the human ruin with blossoms of new beauty, that have their roots and proper nutriment only in the chinks and crevices of decay, as she sows wall-flowers over the ruined fortress of Ticonderoga. Still, even in respect of grace and beauty, there were points well worth

in a furnace. Old as he was when I met him, the man still exuded weight, solidity, and firmness. I could imagine that even at his age he could throw off his infirmities like a hospital gown and become a warrior once more, if the moment called for it. And even then he would have kept his calm demeanor. Such a moment, however, was only to be imagined, not expected or even desired. What I saw in the General—who was like a wall that remains standing in a ruin—was endurance, which might well have been stubborn hard-headedness in his younger days; integrity, which was so heavy it was as immovable as a ton of iron; and benevolence, which, though he'd led bayonet charges, was as genuine as an philanthropist's. He may have killed men with his own hands for all I know, and he certainly killed them with his troops, but there wasn't enough cruelty in his heart to brush the down off a butterfly's wing. I have not met a kinder man.

Yet many of the General's character traits must have faded or vanished entirely before I met him. Our most graceful attributes are often the most fleeting, and nature doesn't decorate decaying men with wildflowers like the ones that bloom on ruined fortresses. Even so, the General had some grace and beauty worth noting. A ray of humor would come from him now and then, and glimmer pleasantly on our faces. His fondness for the sight and smell of flowers revealed an elegance rarely seen in young men. An old soldier might

noting. A ray of humor, now and then, would make its way through the veil of dim obstruction, and glimmer pleasantly upon our faces. A trait of native elegance, seldom seen in the masculine character after childhood or early youth, was shown in the General's fondness for the sight and fragrance of flowers. An old soldier might be supposed to prize only the bloody laurel on his brow; but here was one, who seemed to have a young girl's appreciation of the floral tribe.

There, beside the fireplace, the brave old General used to sit; the Surveyor—though seldom, when it could be avoided, taking upon himself the difficult task of engaging him in conversation—was fond of standing at a distance, and watching his quiet and almost slumberous countenance. He seemed away from us, although we saw him but a few yards off; remote, though we passed close beside his chair; unattainable, though we might have stretched forth our hands and touched his own. It might be, that he lived a more real life within his thoughts, than amid the unappropriate environment of the Collector's office. The evolutions of the parade; the tumult of the battle; the flourish of old, heroic music, heard thirty years before;—such scenes and sounds, perhaps, were all alive before his intellectual sense. Meanwhile, the merchants and ship-masters, the spruce clerks, and uncouth sailors, entered and departed; the bustle of this commercial and Custom-House life kept up its little murmur round about him; and neither with the men nor their affairs did the General appear to sustain the most distant relation. He was as much out of place as an old sword—now rusty, but which had flashed once in the battle's front, and showed still a bright gleam along its blade—would have been, among the inkstands, paper-folders, and mahogany rulers, on the Deputy Collector's desk.

There was one thing that much aided me in renewing and re-creating the stalwart soldier of the Niagara frontier,—the man of true and simple energy. It was the recollection of those memorable words of his,—"I'll try, Sir!"—spoken on the very verge of a desperate and heroic enterprise, and breathing the soul and spirit of New England hardihood, comprehending all perils, and encountering all. If, in our country, valor were rewarded by heraldic honor, this phrase—which it seems so easy to speak, but which only he, with such a task of danger and glory before him, has ever spoken—would be the best and fittest of all mottoes for the General's shield of arms.

be expected to think only of the glories he won in battle, but here was one who loved flowers as much as any young girl.

There, beside the fireplace, the brave old General used to sit, while the Surveyor would stand at a distance, without starting a conversation, watching his quiet, sleepy face. The General seemed far away, even though he was just a few yards off. We could have reached out and touched him, but still he seemed unattainable. Maybe his own thoughts were more real to him than the Custom House. Perhaps military parades, battles, and heroic music were still alive to him. Meanwhile, the merchants and ship masters, the young aides and foul-mouthed sailors, came and went. The Custom House bustled around the General, and he barely seemed to notice. He was as out of place as a rusty old sword, which had once flashed in battle and still gleamed slightly, would have been among the papers, file folders, and rulers on the Deputy Collector's desk.

There was one thing that helped me re-create this brave soldier, and that was remembering his words, "I'll try, sir." The General spoke them as he set out to battle in the War of 1812. Those words summed up New England hardiness, acknowledged danger, and faced everything. If our country honored bravery with a coat of arms, that phrase would be the General's motto. The words seem easy to speak, but only he has ever spoken them while facing such danger and glory.

It contributes greatly towards a man's moral and intellectual health, to be brought into habits of companionship with individuals unlike himself, who care little for his pursuits, and whose sphere and abilities he must go out of himself to appreciate. The accidents of my life have often afforded me this advantage, but never with more fulness and variety than during my continuance in office. There was one man, especially, the observation of whose character gave me a new idea of talent. His gifts were emphatically those of a man of business; prompt, acute, clear-minded; with an eye that saw through all perplexities, and a faculty of arrangement that made them vanish, as by the waving of an enchanter's wand. Bred up from boyhood in the Custom-House, it was his proper field of activity; and the many intricacies of business, so harassing to the interloper, presented themselves before him with the regularity of a perfectly comprehended system. In my contemplation, he stood as the ideal of his class. He was, indeed, the Custom-House in himself; or, at all events, the main-spring that kept its variously revolving wheels in motion; for, in an institution like this, where its officers are appointed to subserve their own profit and convenience, and seldom with a leading reference to their fitness for the duty to be performed, they must perforce seek elsewhere the dexterity which is not in them. Thus, by an inevitable necessity, as a magnet attracts steel-filings, so did our man of business draw to himself the difficulties which everybody met with. With an easy condescension, and kind forbearance towards our stupidity,—which, to his order of mind, must have seemed little short of crime,—would he forthwith, by the merest touch of his finger, make the incomprehensible as clear as daylight. The merchants valued him not less than we, his esoteric friends. His integrity was perfect; it was a law of nature with him, rather than a choice or a principle; nor can it be otherwise than the main condition of an intellect so remarkably clear and accurate as his, to be honest and regular in the administration of affairs. A stain on his conscience, as to any thing that came within the range of his vocation, would trouble such a man very much in the same way, though to a far greater degree, than an error in the balance of an account, or an ink-blot on the fair page of a book of record. Here, in a word,—and it is a rare instance in my life,—I had met with a person thoroughly adapted to the situation which he held.

NO FEAR

It's good for a man's soul and mind to hang out with people unlike himself. When someone doesn't care about your hobbies and interests, you must stretch yourself to appreciate theirs. I've met many different people in my life, but never more so than during my time in the Custom House. There was one man in particular who broadened my idea of what talent could be. He had the gifts of a businessman. He was prompt, perceptive, and clear headed, with an eye that saw through complexity and a mind that made it vanish as if he'd waved a wand. Having spent his life since boyhood in the Custom House, he knew every aspect of its business. The details that might mystify a stranger, he understood perfectly. To my mind, he was the best of his type. He was the Custom House itself. At the very least, he was what kept its wheels in motion. At a place like this, where officers are hired because the job helps them, and because they're good at the job, the men must look to someone for the skills they lack themselves. Like a magnet attracts filings, this man of business attracted everyone else's difficulties. Though we must have seemed criminally stupid to him, he solved our problems with kind patience and lighthearted condescension. At a little touch of his finger, he made the incomprehensible as clear as daylight. The merchants valued him just as much as we did. He was a man of perfect integrity, as his clear intellect almost required. A blemish on his professional conscience would trouble him even more than the many small errors he corrected in the office. This was a man perfectly adapted to his situation—a rare thing in life.

Such were some of the people with whom I now found myself connected. I took it in good part at the hands of Providence, that I was thrown into a position so little akin to my past habits; and set myself seriously to gather from it whatever profit was to be had. After my fellowship of toil and impractical schemes, with the dreamy brethren of Brook Farm; after living for three years within the subtle influence of an intellect like Emerson's; after those wild, free days on the Assabeth, indulging fantastic speculations beside our fire of fallen boughs, with Ellery Channing; after talking with Thoreau about pine-trees and Indian relics, in his hermitage at Walden; after growing fastidious by sympathy with the classic refinement of Hillard's culture; after becoming imbued with poetic sentiment at Longfellow's hearth-stone;—it was time, at length, that I should exercise other faculties of my nature, and nourish myself with food for which I had hitherto had little appetite. Even the old Inspector was desirable, as a change of diet, to a man who had known Alcott. I looked upon it as an evidence, in some measure, of a system naturally well balanced, and lacking no essential part of a thorough organization, that, with such associates to remember, I could mingle at once with men of altogether different qualities, and never murmur at the change.

Literature, its exertions and objects, were now of little moment in my regard. I cared not, at this period, for books; they were apart from me. Nature,—except it were human nature,—the nature that is developed in earth and sky, was, in one sense, hidden from me; and all the imaginative delight, wherewith it had been spiritualized, passed away out of my mind. A gift, a faculty, if it had not departed, was suspended and inanimate within me. There would have been something sad, unutterably dreary, in all this, had I not been conscious that it lay at my own option to recall whatever was valuable in the past. It might be true, indeed, that this was a life which could not, with impunity, be lived too long; else, it might make me permanently other than I had been, without transforming me into any shape which it would be worth my while to take. But I never considered it as other than a transitory life. There was always a prophetic instinct, a low whisper in my ear, that, within no long period, and whenever a new change of custom should be essential to my good, a change would come.

NO FEAR

These were the people I worked with. I figured it was a stroke of luck to have a job so different from anything I had done before, and I decided to learn as much as I could from the people and the place.

After dreaming up impractical schemes at Brook Farm, after living for three years under the subtle intellect of Emerson, after the days of wild wondering on the Assabeth with Ellery Channing, after talking with Thoreau about pine trees and Indian relics at his place in Walden, after growing more discerning with the refined Hillard, after getting poetic before Longfellow's fire—after all of this, it was time for me to use other aspects of my mind and nourish myself with work I had not previously desired. Even the old Inspector was a welcome change for a man who had known Alcott. I took my ability to mix with men so different from those I had known as evidence of my own well-balanced nature.

Brook Farm: ̶a̶n community ̶o̶utside Boston.

Assabeth: River outside Boston.

The ambitions and the toils of literature mattered little to me then. I did not care for books at that time. Nature—not human nature, but the nature of earth and sky—was hidden from me, and the imagination with which I had observed it passed from my mind. If this gift did not leave me altogether, at least it became frozen and useless. There would have been something unspeakably sad about this loss if I hadn't realized that I could recall the best parts of my past whenever I wished. If I had lived that way for too long, it could have changed me forever—and for the worse. But I never thought of my time at the Custom House as more than a passing phase. There was always a voice in the back of my head telling me that when I needed a change, change would come.

Meanwhile, there I was, a Surveyor of the Revenue, and, so far as I have been able to understand, as good a Surveyor as need be. A man of thought, fancy, and sensibility, (had he ten times the Surveyor's proportion of those qualities,) may, at any time, be a man of affairs, if he will only choose to give himself the trouble. My fellow-officers, and the merchants and sea-captains with whom my official duties brought me into any manner of connection, viewed me in no other light, and probably knew me in no other character. None of them, I presume, had ever read a page of my inditing, or would have cared a fig the more for me, if they had read them all; nor would it have mended the matter, in the least, had those same unprofitable pages been written with a pen like that of Burns or of Chaucer, each of whom was a Custom-House officer in his day, as well as I. It is a good lesson—though it may often be a hard one—for a man who has dreamed of literary fame, and of making for himself a rank among the world's dignitaries by such means, to step aside out of the narrow circle in which his claims are recognized, and to find how utterly devoid of significance, beyond that circle, is all that he achieves, and all he aims at. I know not that I especially needed the lesson, either in the way of warning or rebuke; but, at any rate, I learned it thoroughly; nor, it gives me pleasure to reflect, did the truth, as it came home to my perception, ever cost me a pang, or require to be thrown off in a sigh. In the way of literary talk, it is true, the Naval Officer—an excellent fellow, who came into office with me, and went out only a little later—would often engage me in a discussion about one or the other of his favorite topics, Napoleon or Shakspeare. The Collector's junior clerk, too,—a young gentleman who, it was whispered, occasionally covered a sheet of Uncle Sam's letter-paper with what, (at the distance of a few yards,) looked very much like poetry,—used now and then to speak to me of books, as matters with which I might possibly be conversant. This was my all of lettered intercourse; and it was quite sufficient for my necessities.

No longer seeking nor caring that my name should be blazoned abroad on title-pages, I smiled to think that it had now another kind of vogue. The Custom-House marker imprinted it, with a stencil and black paint, on pepper-bags, and baskets of anatto, and cigar-boxes, and bales of all kinds of dutiable merchandise, in testimony that these commodities had paid the impost, and

Surveyor: Chief administrator of the Custom House.

In the meantime, there I was: a Surveyor of the Revenue, and a good one at that. A man of intelligence, imagination, and taste can become a man of business if he chooses. My fellow officers and the others who dealt with me thought me no different from anyone else in the Custom House. None of them had read a page of my writing, nor would have thought more of me had they read every last one. It wouldn't have mattered if my poor pages had been written by Burns or Chaucer—both Custom House officers in their day. It's good, if hard, for a writer who dreams of literary fame to realize that outside his own little circle, he's completely insignificant and unknown. I don't think I really needed that lesson, but I learned it well. I'm proud to say that it didn't even hurt. In the way of literary talk, it's true that the Naval Officer (a very good man who worked with me) would often talk to me about Napoleon or Shakespeare. And the Collector's young assistant was rumored to write poetry at work. We'd talk about books now and then, as though I might know something about them. This was the sum of my literary conversation, and it was quite sufficient for my needs.

No longer hoping to see my name printed on the title page of a book, I smiled to think that it had a new kind of popularity. The Custom House printed it, with a stencil and black paint, on bags of pepper and other spices, on cigar boxes and bales of all sorts. My name declared that these goods had paid their taxes and been inspected by the office. By such a strange means, my name was

gone regularly through the office. Borne on such queer vehicle of fame, a knowledge of my existence, so far as a name conveys it, was carried where it had never been before, and, I hope, will never go again.

But the past was not dead. Once in a great while, the thoughts, that had seemed so vital and so active, yet had been put to rest so quietly, revived again. One of the most remarkable occasions, when the habit of by-gone days awoke in me, was that which brings it within the law of literary propriety to offer the public the sketch which I am now writing.

In the second story of the Custom-House, there is a large room, in which the brick-work and naked rafters have never been covered with panelling and plaster. The edifice—originally projected on a scale adapted to the old commercial enterprise of the port, and with an idea of subsequent prosperity destined never to be realized— contains far more space than its occupants know what to do with. This airy hall, therefore, over the Collector's apartments, remains unfinished to this day, and, in spite of the aged cobwebs that festoon its dusky beams, appears still to await the labor of the carpenter and mason. At one end of the room, in a recess, were a number of barrels, piled one upon another, containing bundles of official documents. Large quantities of similar rubbish lay lumbering the floor. It was sorrowful to think how many days, and weeks, and months, and years of toil, had been wasted on these musty papers, which were now only an encumbrance on earth, and were hidden away in this forgotten corner, never more to be glanced at by human eyes. But, then, what reams of other manuscripts—filled, not with the dulness of official formalities, but with the thought of inventive brains and the rich effusion of deep hearts—had gone equally to oblivion; and that, moreover, without serving a purpose in their day, as these heaped up papers had, and—saddest of all—without purchasing for their writers the comfortable livelihood which the clerks of the Custom-House had gained by these worthless scratchings of the pen! Yet not altogether worthless, perhaps, as materials of local history. Here, no doubt, statistics of the former commerce of Salem might be discovered, and memorials of her princely merchants,— old King Derby,—old Billy Gray,—old Simon Forrester,—and many another magnate in his day; whose powdered head, however, was

spread to places where it had never been before and where I hope it will never go again.

But the past was not yet dead. Once in a long while, my thoughts from years gone by were revived again. It was one of those occasions, when my writerly habits reappeared, that justifies the publication of this sketch.

In the second story of the Custom House there is a large room, in which the brickwork and naked rafters have never been covered with paneling and plaster. The building, which was built for boom times, and with the expectation that business would only grow, contains far more space than its occupants can use. So this room over the apartment of the Collector has never been finished. Although there are cobwebs festooning the beams, it looks like it's still waiting for attention from the carpenter and the plasterer. At one end of the room, in an alcove, were a number of barrels piled on each other, filled with bundles of official documents. A lot of other trash was on the floor. It was sad to think how many days, and weeks, and months, and years of work had been wasted on those musty papers, which were now just a burden, hidden away in this corner, where no one would ever see them again. But then again, so many manuscripts filled with the thoughts of clever minds and the feelings of deep hearts have met the same fate as these official documents and without earning their writers the comfortable living Custom House officials had made with their worthless scribblings. And maybe the official documents weren't even worthless. If nothing else, they preserved valuable local history: commerce statistics from the old days of Salem, memories of the merchants who did business then, whose heirs wasted the fortunes they had accumulated. There was family history in those papers too: records of the plain beginnings of Salem's "aristocracy" in the days long before the Revolution.

scarcely in the tomb, before his mountain-pile of wealth began to dwindle. The founders of the greater part of the families which now compose the aristocracy of Salem might here be traced, from the petty and obscure beginnings of their traffic, at periods generally much posterior to the Revolution, upward to what their children look upon as long-established rank.

Prior to the Revolution, there is a dearth of records; the earlier documents and archives of the Custom-House having, probably, been carried off to Halifax, when all the King's officials accompanied the British army in its flight from Boston. It has often been a matter of regret with me; for, going back, perhaps, to the days of the Protectorate, those papers must have contained many references to forgotten or remembered men, and to antique customs, which would have affected me with the same pleasure as when I used to pick up Indian arrow-heads in the field near the Old Manse.

But, one idle and rainy day, it was my fortune to make a discovery of some little interest. Poking and burrowing into the heaped-up rubbish in the corner; unfolding one and another document, and reading the names of vessels that had long ago foundered at sea or rotted at the wharves and those of merchants, never heard of now on 'Change, nor very readily decipherable on their mossy tombstones; glancing at such matters with the saddened, weary, half-reluctant interest which we bestow on the corpse of dead activity,—and exerting my fancy, sluggish with little use, to raise up from these dry bones an image of the old town's brighter aspect, when India was a new region, and only Salem knew the way thither,—I chanced to lay my hand on a small package, carefully done up in a piece of ancient yellow parchment. This envelope had the air of an official record of some period long past, when clerks engrossed their stiff and formal chirography on more substantial materials than at present. There was something about it that quickened an instinctive curiosity, and made me undo the faded red tape, that tied up the package, with the sense that a treasure would here be brought to light. Unbending the rigid folds of the parchment cover, I found it to be a commission, under the hand and seal of Governor Shirley, in favor of one Jonathan Pue, as Surveyor of his Majesty's Customs for the port of Salem, in the Province of Massachusetts Bay. I remembered to have read (probably in Felt's Annals) notice of the

NO FEAR

Few records survive from before the Revolution. Those older documents were probably carried off by the British army when it retreated from Boston to Halifax. I have often regretted that. Those papers, some going back as far as the English Revolution, more than a hundred years before our own, must have contained references to forgotten men and obscure customs that would have given me the same pleasure I used to get from picking up Indian arrowheads in the field by my house.

But one lazy, rainy day I made a discovery of some interest. I was poking around in the piles of rubbish and unfolding one document after another, reading the names of ships that had rotted or sunk long ago and the names of merchants gone to their graves. I glanced at those papers with the saddened, weary interest with which we study dry history. I used my rusty imagination to call up old Salem in happier days, when India was newly discovered and only Salem ships could sail there. I happened to place my hand on a small package, carefully wrapped in a piece of ancient yellow parchment. The envelope seemed like an official record of a period long past, when everyone used better paper. Something about the package made me curious. I untied the faded red tape with the sense that a treasure was about to come to light. Raising the rigid fold of the parchment cover, I found it to be a commission signed by Governor Shirley, naming Jonathan Pine as Surveyor of His Majesty's Customs for the Port of Salem, in the Province of Massachusetts Bay. I remembered reading in some old book a notice of the death of Mr. Surveyor Pine, about eighty years ago. I'd recently seen in the newspaper that his remains had been dug up when they renovated St. Peter's Church. Nothing remained but his skeleton, some bits of fabric, and a majestic wig, which, unlike the head on which it rested, was very well preserved. Examining the papers that were wrapped in this commission, I found more traces of Mr. Pine's brain and its workings than even his grave now contained.

decease of Mr. Surveyor Pue, about fourscore years ago; and likewise, in a newspaper of recent times, an account of the digging up of his remains in the little grave-yard of St. Peter's Church, during the renewal of that edifice. Nothing, if I rightly call to mind, was left of my respected predecessor, save an imperfect skeleton, and some fragments of apparel, and a wig of majestic frizzle; which, unlike the head that it once adorned, was in very satisfactory preservation. But, on examining the papers which the parchment commission served to envelop, I found more traces of Mr. Pue's mental part, and the internal operations of his head, than the frizzled wig had contained of the venerable skull itself.

They were documents, in short, not official, but of a private nature, or, at least, written in his private capacity, and apparently with his own hand. I could account for their being included in the heap of Custom-House lumber only by the fact, that Mr. Pue's death had happened suddenly; and that these papers, which he probably kept in his official desk, had never come to the knowledge of his heirs, or were supposed to relate to the business of the revenue. On the transfer of the archives to Halifax, this package, proving to be of no public concern, was left behind, and had remained ever since unopened.

The ancient Surveyor—being little molested, I suppose, at that early day, with business pertaining to his office—seems to have devoted some of his many leisure hours to researches as a local antiquarian, and other inquisitions of a similar nature. These supplied material for petty activity to a mind that would otherwise have been eaten up with rust. A portion of his facts, by the by, did me good service in the preparation of the article entitled "Main Street," included in the present volume. The remainder may perhaps be applied to purposes equally valuable, hereafter; or not impossibly may be worked up, so far as they go, into a regular history of Salem, should my veneration for the natal soil ever impel me to so pious a task. Meanwhile, they shall be at the command of any gentleman, inclined, and competent, to take the unprofitable labor off my hands. As a final disposition, I contemplate depositing them with the Essex Historical Society.

But the object that most drew my attention, in the mysterious package, was a certain affair of fine red cloth, much worn and faded. There were traces about it of gold embroidery, which, however, was

NO FEAR

These were not official documents. They were his private thoughts, written in his own hand. Maybe they were among all this junk because Mr. Pine's death had happened suddenly, and these papers, which he probably kept in his official desk, had not been discovered by his heirs or else were thought to be Custom House papers. When the British carried everything off to Halifax, this package, being of no public concern, was left behind. It had not been opened since.

I guess there wasn't much business in those days, and old Mr. Pine must have filled the hours by researching local history. The research kept his mind from rusting. I used some of his research for a story entitled "Main Street," included here. The rest I may use for other purposes, or perhaps as the basis for a history of Salem, if my fondness for my birthplace ever makes me so inclined. In the meantime, it will be available to anyone with the desire and the ability to take on that task. I imagine I'll leave the papers to the Essex Historical Society in the end. But what most drew my attention to the mysterious package was a piece of fine red cloth, now worn and faded. There were hints of gold embroidery on it, but almost none of the glitter was left. It had been made with wonderfully skilled needlework: Women who would know say the stitches are evidence of a forgotten art. When I examined this rag of scarlet cloth (for time and moths had reduced it to that state), it took the shape of a letter.

It was the capital letter *A*. Each side was exactly three and a quarter inches long. It was clearly meant as a piece of decorative clothing, but how it was worn and what honor it signified was a riddle I had

greatly frayed and defaced; so that none, or very little, of the glitter was left. It had been wrought, as was easy to perceive, with wonderful skill of needlework; and the stitch (as I am assured by ladies conversant with such mysteries) gives evidence of a now forgotten art, not to be recovered even by the process of picking out the threads. This rag of scarlet cloth,—for time, and wear, and a sacrilegious moth, had reduced it to little other than a rag,—on careful examination, assumed the shape of a letter. It was the capital letter A. By an accurate measurement, each limb proved to be precisely three inches and a quarter in length. It had been intended, there could be no doubt, as an ornamental article of dress; but how it was to be worn, or what rank, honor, and dignity, in by-past times, were signified by it, was a riddle which (so evanescent are the fashions of the world in these particulars) I saw little hope of solving. And yet it strangely interested me. My eyes fastened themselves upon the old scarlet letter, and would not be turned aside. Certainly, there was some deep meaning in it, most worthy of interpretation, and which, as it were, streamed forth from the mystic symbol, subtly communicating itself to my sensibilities, but evading the analysis of my mind.

While thus perplexed,—and cogitating, among other hypotheses, whether the letter might not have been one of those decorations which the white men used to contrive, in order to take the eyes of Indians,—I happened to place it on my breast. It seemed to me,—the reader may smile, but must not doubt my word,—it seemed to me, then, that I experienced a sensation not altogether physical, yet almost so, as of burning heat; and as if the letter were not of red cloth, but red-hot iron. I shuddered, and involuntarily let it fall upon the floor.

In the absorbing contemplation of the scarlet letter, I had hitherto neglected to examine a small roll of dingy paper, around which it had been twisted. This I now opened, and had the satisfaction to find, recorded by the old Surveyor's pen, a reasonably complete explanation of the whole affair. There were several foolscap sheets, containing many particulars respecting the life and conversation of one Hester Prynne, who appeared to have been rather a noteworthy personage in the view of our ancestors. She had flourished during a period between the early days of Massachusetts and the close of the

little hope of solving, since fashions chance so quickly. And yet it interested me. My eyes locked onto the old scarlet letter and could not turn away. Surely there was some deep meaning in it, worthy of interpretation. I was sure that meaning streamed from the mystic symbol, speaking to my senses but escaping my mind.

Perplexed, and thinking that the letter might have been a decoration that white men used to distract the Indians, I placed the scarlet letter on my breast. I seemed to feel—you may smile, but do not doubt my word—I seemed to feel a burning heat, as though the letter were made of red-hot iron and not red cloth. I shuddered and involuntarily let it fall to the floor.

Absorbed in the scarlet letter, I hadn't noticed a small roll of dingy paper. The letter had been twisted around it. I opened the roll. To my satisfaction, I found that it was an almost complete explanation of the whole affair, written with the old Surveyor's pen. There were several sheets with many details about the life and sayings of a Hester Prynne. She seemed to have been a notable person who lived in the mid to late 1600s. Old men and women who were alive in the time of Mr. Surveyor Pine told him that they remembered Hester Prynne from their youth. They recalled her as very old, but in good

seventeenth century. Aged persons, alive in the time of Mr. Surveyor Pue, and from whose oral testimony he had made up his narrative, remembered her, in their youth, as a very old, but not decrepit woman, of a stately and solemn aspect. It had been her habit, from an almost immemorial date, to go about the country as a kind of voluntary nurse, and doing whatever miscellaneous good she might; taking upon herself, likewise, to give advice in all matters, especially those of the heart; by which means, as a person of such propensities inevitably must, she gained from many people the reverence due to an angel, but, I should imagine, was looked upon by others as an intruder and a nuisance. Prying farther into the manuscript, I found the record of other doings and sufferings of this singular woman, for most of which the reader is referred to the story entitled "The Scarlet Letter"; and it should be borne carefully in mind, that the main facts of that story are authorized and authenticated by the document of Mr. Surveyor Pue. The original papers, together with the scarlet letter itself,—a most curious relic,—are still in my possession, and shall be freely exhibited to whomsoever, induced by the great interest of the narrative, may desire a sight of them. I must not be understood as affirming, that, in the dressing up of the tale, and imagining the motives and modes of passion that influenced the characters who figure in it, I have invariably confined myself within the limits of the old Surveyor's half a dozen sheets of foolscap. On the contrary, I have allowed myself, as to such points, nearly or altogether as much license as if the facts had been entirely of my own invention. What I contend for is the authenticity of the outline.

This incident recalled my mind, in some degree, to its old track. There seemed to be here the groundwork of a tale. It impressed me as if the ancient Surveyor, in his garb of a hundred years gone by, and wearing his immortal wig,—which was buried with him, but did not perish in the grave,—had met me in the deserted chamber of the Custom-House. In his port was the dignity of one who had borne his Majesty's commission, and who was therefore illuminated by a ray of the splendor that shone so dazzlingly about the throne. How unlike, alas! The hang-dog look of a republican official, who, as the servant of the people, feels himself less than the least, and below the lowest, of his masters. With his own ghostly hand, the obscurely seen, but majestic, figure had imparted to me

health, with a stately and serious appearance. For as long as almost anyone could remember, she had gone around the countryside as a sort of volunteer nurse. She did whatever good she could and gave advice freely, especially in matters of the heart. Some looked on her as an angel, but I'm sure others considered her a busybody and a nuisance. Reading this manuscript further, I found a record of other deeds and sorrows of this exceptional woman. You can read about them in the story *The Scarlet Letter*. Bear in mind that the main facts of the story are attested to by the document of Mr. Surveyor Pine. I still have the original papers, along with the scarlet letter itself. I would be glad to show them to anyone who would like to see. You must not think that in dressing up the tale, and imagining the motives and the passions of the people in it, I have limited myself to what is written on those six sheets. On the contrary, I have allowed myself as much imaginative license as if I had made up the whole thing. But the outline of the story is true.

When I found the letter, my mind turned to writing once again. There seemed to be a story here. The tale made a strong impression on me, as though the old Surveyor himself had appeared before me in his outdated clothing and immortal wig. He carried himself with the dignity of someone who had received a royal commission and with it a touch of the royal splendor. The public servants in a democracy are different: They feel themselves to be lower than the least of their many masters. With his own ghostly hand, the Surveyor had given me the scarlet letter and the rolled-up manuscript. With his own ghostly voice, he had told me that he was my official ancestor, and I must bring his work before the public. "Do this," said the ghost of Mr. Surveyor Pine, nodding his head with that memorable

the scarlet symbol, and the little roll of explanatory manuscript. With his own ghostly voice, he had exhorted me, on the sacred consideration of my filial duty and reverence towards him,—who might reasonably regard himself as my official ancestor,—to bring his mouldy and moth-eaten lucubrations before the public. "Do this," said the ghost of Mr. Surveyor Pue, emphatically nodding the head that looked so imposing within its memorable wig, "do this, and the profit shall be all your own! You will shortly need it; for it is not in your days as it was in mine, when a man's office was a life-lease, and oftentimes an heirloom. But, I charge you, in this matter of old Mistress Prynne, give to your predecessor's memory the credit which will be rightfully its due!" And I said to the ghost of Mr. Surveyor Pue,—"I will!"

On Hester Prynne's story, therefore, I bestowed much thought. It was the subject of my meditations for many an hour, while pacing to and fro across my room, or traversing, with a hundredfold repetition, the long extent from the front-door of the Custom-House to the side-entrance, and back again. Great were the weariness and annoyance of the old Inspector and the Weighers and Gaugers, whose slumbers were disturbed by the unmercifully lengthened tramp of my passing and returning footsteps. Remembering their own former habits, they used to say that the Surveyor was walking the quarter-deck. They probably fancied that my sole object— and, indeed, the sole object for which a sane man could ever put himself into voluntary motion—was, to get an appetite for dinner. And to say the truth, an appetite, sharpened by the east-wind that generally blew along the passage, was the only valuable result of so much indefatigable exercise. So little adapted is the atmosphere of a Custom-House to the delicate harvest of fancy and sensibility, that, had I remained there through ten Presidencies yet to come, I doubt whether the tale of "The Scarlet Letter" would ever have been brought before the public eye. My imagination was a tarnished mirror. It would not reflect, or only with miserable dimness, the figures with which I did my best to people it. The characters of the narrative would not be warmed and rendered malleable, by any heat that I could kindle at my intellectual forge. They would take neither the glow of passion nor the tenderness of sentiment, but retained all the rigidity of dead corpses, and stared me in the face with a fixed

wig upon it, "do this, and the profit will be yours. You will need it soon: The Surveyor's job is less secure than it was in my day. But give me the credit I deserve when you tell the story of old Mistress Prynne." And I said to the ghost, "I will."

So I thought a lot about Hester Prynne's story. I thought about it for many hours, pacing back and forth across my room or walking along the porch of the Custom House. I greatly irritated the old Inspector and the officers, waking them as I passed again and again. Like the old sailors they were, they used to say that I was walking the quarterdeck. They probably thought I was working up an appetite for dinner. Why else would a man put himself in motion? And truth be told, an appetite was often all I got for my efforts. The Custom House is so ill-suited to the cultivation of imagination that I doubt I could ever have written *The Scarlet Letter* if I had stayed there. My mind was a tarnished mirror. It would not reflect a clear image of the characters I was trying to create. My intellect could not generate enough heat to warm and soften them. The emerging characters had no glow of passion or tenderness of feeling. As stiff as corpses, they stared me in the face with a ghastly grin of contempt and defiance. "What do you want with us?" their expression seemed to say. "You have traded your writer's gifts for a little bit of public money. Go, then, and earn your paycheck." The nearly lifeless characters I was creating mocked me for my incompetence, often with good reason.

and ghastly grin of contemptuous defiance. "What have you to do with us?" that expression seemed to say. "The little power you might once have possessed over the tribe of unrealities is gone! You have bartered it for a pittance of the public gold. Go, then, and earn your wages!" In short, the almost torpid creatures of my own fancy twitted me with imbecility, and not without fair occasion.

It was not merely during the three hours and a half which Uncle Sam claimed as his share of my daily life, that this wretched numbness held possession of me. It went with me on my sea-shore walks and rambles into the country, whenever—which was seldom and reluctantly—I bestirred myself to seek that invigorating charm of Nature, which used to give me such freshness and activity of thought, the moment that I stepped across the threshold of the Old Manse. The same torpor, as regarded the capacity for intellectual effort, accompanied me home, and weighed upon me in the chamber which I most absurdly termed my study. Nor did it quit me, when, late at night, I sat in the deserted parlour, lighted only by the glimmering coal-fire and the moon, striving to picture forth imaginary scenes, which, the next day, might flow out on the brightening page in many-hued description.

If the imaginative faculty refused to act at such an hour, it might well be deemed a hopeless case. Moonlight, in a familiar room, falling so white upon the carpet, and showing all its figures so distinctly,—making every object so minutely visible, yet so unlike a morning or noontide visibility,—is a medium the most suitable for a romance-writer to get acquainted with his illusive guests. There is the little domestic scenery of the well-known apartment; the chairs, with each its separate individuality; the centre-table, sustaining a work-basket, a volume or two, and an extinguished lamp; the sofa; the book-case; the picture on the wall;—all these details, so completely seen, are so spiritualized by the unusual light, that they seem to lose their actual substance, and become things of intellect. Nothing is too small or too trifling to undergo this change, and acquire dignity thereby. A child's shoe; the doll, seated in her little wicker carriage; the hobby-horse;—whatever, in a word, has been used or played with, during the day, is now invested with a quality of strangeness and remoteness, though still almost as vividly present as by daylight. Thus, therefore, the floor of our familiar room

NO FEAR

But it wasn't only for the three and a half hours that I worked every day that this horrible numbness took over. It went with me on my seashore walks and country rambles, whenever I reluctantly headed out to seek inspiration outdoors. It used to be that Nature sparked my thoughts the instant I stepped out of the Old Manse. The same dull feeling came home with me every night and weighed on me in what I called, absurdly, my study. It was there late at night when I sat in the deserted parlor, illuminated by moonlight and coal fire, struggling to think of scenes to write the next day.

If my imagination refused to act at that hour, it was probably hopeless. Moonlight, in a familiar room, falling whitely on a carpet, both revealing and transforming everything, is the perfect spur for the imagination of a novelist. The objects in my living room, from the chairs to the pictures, are so changed by the moonlight that they seem to lose their substance and become creations of the mind. Nothing is too small or insignificant to be changed in this way. A child's shoe or doll or rocking horse, whatever had been used that day, is given a quality of strangeness and remoteness, though it's still almost as visible as it is in daylight. The floor of the familiar room becomes a neutral territory, somewhere between the real world and fairyland. The actual and the imaginary can meet, and each imparts its nature to the other. Ghosts might enter here without scaring us, since they seem so appropriate in this place. We wouldn't be surprised to look around and see the form of a beloved person, now dead, sitting quietly in a streak of magic moonshine, looking as if it had never left the fireside.

has become a neutral territory, somewhere between the real world and fairy-land, where the Actual and the Imaginary may meet, and each imbue itself with the nature of the other. Ghosts might enter here, without affrighting us. It would be too much in keeping with the scene to excite surprise, were we to look about us and discover a form, beloved, but gone hence, now sitting quietly in a streak of this magic moonshine, with an aspect that would make us doubt whether it had returned from afar, or had never once stirred from our fireside.

The somewhat dim coal-fire has an essential influence in producing the effect which I would describe. It throws its unobtrusive tinge throughout the room, with a faint ruddiness upon the walls and ceiling, and a reflected gleam from the polish of the furniture. This warmer light mingles itself with the cold spirituality of the moonbeams, and communicates, as it were, a heart and sensibilities of human tenderness to the forms which fancy summons up. It converts them from snow-images into men and women. Glancing at the looking-glass, we behold—deep within its haunted verge—the smouldering glow of the half-extinguished anthracite, the white moonbeams on the floor, and a repetition of all the gleam and shadow of the picture, with one remove farther from the actual, and nearer to the imaginative. Then, at such an hour, and with this scene before him, if a man, sitting all alone, cannot dream strange things, and make them look like truth, he need never try to write romances.

But, for myself, during the whole of my Custom-House experience, moonlight and sunshine, and the glow of fire-light, were just alike in my regard; and neither of them was of one whit more avail than the twinkle of a tallow-candle. An entire class of susceptibilities, and a gift connected with them,—of no great richness or value, but the best I had,—was gone from me.

It is my belief, however, that, had I attempted a different order of composition, my faculties would not have been found so pointless and inefficacious. I might, for instance, have contented myself with writing out the narratives of a veteran ship-master, one of the Inspectors, whom I should be most ungrateful not to mention; since scarcely a day passed that he did not stir me to laughter and admiration by his marvellous gifts as a story-teller. Could I have preserved the picturesque force of his style, and the humorous col-

NO FEAR

The dim coal fire contributes to the effect, as well. It throws its light around the room, giving a faint, orange-red tinge to the walls and ceiling and an extra gleam to the furniture. This warmer light mixes itself with the cold spirituality of the moonbeams. It gives a heart and human tenderness to whatever one imagines. It changes those creations from black-and-white pictures into men and women. Glancing at the mirror, we can see within its haunted depths the glow of the dying coal fire and the white moonbeams on the floor. In that mirror, all the gleam and shadow is taken one step farther from the real and made one step closer to the imaginative. If, with all of this inspiration, a man still cannot dream strange things and make them look like truth, he should never try to write fantastic stories.

But during all of my time at the Custom House, moonlight, sunshine, and the glow of a fire all seemed the same to me. None of them did a thing more for me than the light of a common candle. My writing gift might not have been very rich or valuable, but it was the best I had, and it was gone.

Yet I think if I had tried to write in a different way, I would not have been so frustrated. I could have written the stories one of the Inspectors told. An old ship captain, he made me laugh with his marvelous tales almost every day. If I could have preserved his forceful style and humorous descriptions, the result would have been something new in literature. Or I could have found a more serious undertaking. It was foolish, with the reality of this daily life pressing on me, to try to fling myself back into another age or to create

oring which nature taught him how to throw over his descriptions, the result, I honestly believe, would have been something new in literature. Or I might readily have found a more serious task. It was a folly, with the materiality of this daily life pressing so intrusively upon me, to attempt to fling myself back into another age; or to insist on creating the semblance of a world out of airy matter, when, at every moment, the impalpable beauty of my soap-bubble was broken by the rude contact of some actual circumstance. The wiser effort would have been, to diffuse thought and imagination through the opaque substance of to-day, and thus to make it a bright transparency; to spiritualize the burden that began to weigh so heavily; to seek, resolutely, the true and indestructible value that lay hidden in the petty and wearisome incidents, and ordinary characters, with which I was now conversant. The fault was mine. The page of life that was spread out before me seemed dull and commonplace, only because I had not fathomed its deeper import. A better book than I shall ever write was there; leaf after leaf presenting itself to me, just as it was written out by the reality of the flitting hour, and vanishing as fast as written, only because my brain wanted the insight and my hand the cunning to transcribe it. At some future day, it may be, I shall remember a few scattered fragments and broken paragraphs, and write them down, and find the letters turn to gold upon the page.

These perceptions have come too late. At the instant, I was only conscious that what would have been a pleasure once was now a hopeless toil. There was no occasion to make much moan about this state of affairs. I had ceased to be a writer of tolerably poor tales and essays, and had become a tolerably good Surveyor of the Customs. That was all. But, nevertheless, it is any thing but agreeable to be haunted by a suspicion that one's intellect is dwindling away; or exhaling, without your consciousness, like ether out of a phial; so that, at every glance, you find a smaller and less volatile residuum. Of the fact, there could be no doubt; and, examining myself and others, I was led to conclusions in reference to the effect of public office on the character, not very favorable to the mode of life in question. In some other form, perhaps, I may hereafter develop these effects. Suffice it here to say, that a Custom-House officer, of long continuance, can hardly be a very praiseworthy or respectable

an imaginary world out of thin air. Every soap bubble of imagination was popped when I came back into contact with the real world. It would have been wiser to work from and transform the world around me in writing. I could have found the true value in the trivial happenings and ordinary men that made up my daily life. The fault was mine. My life seemed dull because I hadn't understood its deeper meaning. There was a better book in the reality of that experience than I will ever write. It showed itself to me page after page, vanishing as fast as it was written because my brain lacked the insight and my hand lacked the skill to copy it down. Maybe some day I will recall bits and pieces of my life in that place and write about it. I suspect my writing would turn to gold on the page.

But it was too late for those thoughts. At that moment, I was only aware that what would once have been a pleasure had become hopeless drudgework. There was no point in complaining. I had stopped being a writer of fairly mediocre tales and essays. Now I was a fairly good Surveyor of the Customs. That was all. But it still isn't pleasant to be haunted by the sense that, without realizing it, your mind is dwindling away with every breath. Looking at myself and the men around me, I decided that public office was bad for the imagination. I may write about that another time. Here, it is enough to say that for many reasons a Custom House officer of long service is rarely a praiseworthy or respectable person. He holds his job subject to political whim, and he does not produce a thing.

personage, for many reasons; one of them, the tenure by which he holds his situation, and another, the very nature of his business, which—though, I trust, an honest one—is of such a sort that he does not share in the united effort of mankind.

An effect—which I believe to be observable, more or less, in every individual who has occupied the position—is, that, while he leans on the mighty arm of the Republic, his own proper strength departs from him. He loses, in an extent proportioned to the weakness or force of his original nature, the capability of self-support. If he possess an unusual share of native energy, or the enervating magic of place do not operate too long upon him, his forfeited powers may be redeemable. The ejected officer—fortunate in the unkindly shove that sends him forth betimes, to struggle amid a struggling world— may return to himself, and become all that he has ever been. But this seldom happens. He usually keeps his ground just long enough for his own ruin, and is then thrust out, with sinews all unstrung, to totter along the difficult footpath of life as he best may. Conscious of his own infirmity,—that his tempered steel and elasticity are lost,— he for ever afterwards looks wistfully about him in quest of support external to himself. His pervading and continual hope—a hallucination, which, in the face of all discouragement, and making light of impossibilities, haunts him while he lives, and, I fancy, like the convulsive throes of the cholera, torments him for a brief space after death—is, that, finally, and in no long time, by some happy coincidence of circumstances, he shall be restored to office. This faith, more than any thing else, steals the pith and availability out of whatever enterprise he may dream of undertaking. Why should he toil and moil, and be at so much trouble to pick himself up out of the mud, when, in a little while hence, the strong arm of his Uncle will raise and support him? Why should he work for his living here, or go to dig gold in California, when he is so soon to be made happy, at monthly intervals, with a little pile of glittering coin out of his Uncle's pocket? It is sadly curious to observe how slight a taste of office suffices to infect a poor fellow with this singular disease. Uncle Sam's gold—meaning no disrespect to the worthy old gentleman—has, in this respect, a quality of enchantment like that of the Devil's wages. Whoever touches it should look well to himself, or he may find the bargain to go hard against him, involving, if not

NO FEAR

Almost everyone who takes the job is weakened by it. While he leans on the mighty arm of the federal government, he loses his own strength. He becomes less able to support himself. If he is unusually energetic, or does not hold the job for long, then he may recover his powers. The officer lucky enough to be fired may become himself once again. But this rarely happens. A man usually keeps the job just long enough for it to ruin him. Then he is shoved into the world in his weakened state to struggle along the difficult path of life. Aware of his own weakness, knowing that his strength and flexibility are gone forever, he looks around for something else to support him. His constant hope is that somehow or another he will be restored to his former post. This hallucination haunts him while he lives and, I imagine, even for a brief time after his death. It sucks away his enthusiasm for any other undertaking. Why should he struggle and strive when he knows that, before too long, Uncle Sam will raise him up again? Why work for a living, or go dig gold in California, when a government salary will soon make him happy again? It is truly sad to see how little time in the Custom House it takes to infect a man with this peculiar disease. I don't mean to disrespect worthy old Uncle Sam, but his gold is cursed like the Devil's. Whoever touches it should beware. If the gold doesn't cost his soul, it may still take his strength, courage, dependability, truthfulness, self-reliance, and all the best parts of his character.

his soul, yet many of its better attributes; its sturdy force, its courage and constancy, its truth, its self-reliance, and all that gives the emphasis to manly character.

Here was a fine prospect in the distance! Not that the Surveyor brought the lesson home to himself, or admitted that he could be so utterly undone, either by continuance in office, or ejectment. Yet my reflections were not the most comfortable. I began to grow melancholy and restless; continually prying into my mind, to discover which of its poor properties were gone, and what degree of detriment had already accrued to the remainder. I endeavoured to calculate how much longer I could stay in the Custom-House, and yet go forth a man. To confess the truth, it was my greatest apprehension,—as it would never be a measure of policy to turn out so quiet an individual as myself, and it being hardly in the nature of a public officer to resign,—it was my chief trouble, therefore, that I was likely to grow gray and decrepit in the Surveyorship, and become much such another animal as the old Inspector. Might it not, in the tedious lapse of official life that lay before me, finally be with me as it was with this venerable friend,—to make the dinner-hour the nucleus of the day, and to spend the rest of it, as an old dog spends it, asleep in the sunshine or the shade? A dreary look-forward this, for a man who felt it to be the best definition of happiness to live throughout the whole range of his faculties and sensibilities! But, all this while, I was giving myself very unnecessary alarm. Providence had meditated better things for me than I could possibly imagine for myself.

A remarkable event of the third year of my Surveyorship—to adopt the tone of "P. P."—was the election of General Taylor to the Presidency. It is essential, in order to form a complete estimate of the advantages of official life, to view the incumbent at the in-coming of a hostile administration. His position is then one of the most singularly irksome, and, in every contingency, disagreeable, that a wretched mortal can possibly occupy; with seldom an alternative of good, on either hand, although what presents itself to him as the worst event may very probably be the best. But it is a strange experience, to a man of pride and sensibility, to know that his interests are within the control of individuals who neither love nor understand him, and by whom, since one or the other must needs hap-

NO FEAR

This was a great thing to look forward to. Not that I applied this example to myself or admitted that I might end up like that whether I kept my job or lost it. Still, my mind was ill at ease. I became depressed and restless, constantly examining my mind to see what abilities I had lost already. I tried to calculate how much longer I could stay in the Custom House and still remain a man. To tell the truth, it was my greatest fear that I would grow old there and become an animal like the old Inspector. No one would fire a quiet person like me, and quitting wasn't what someone in my position did. Could I turn out like the venerable old man? Would dinner be the high point of my day, and would I spend the rest as a dog does, sleeping in the sun or in the shade? It was a dismal prospect for a man who was happiest when all his senses and his faculties were engaged. But I was worrying needlessly, as it turned out. Fortune had conceived of better things for me than I could have imagined for myself.

In the third year of my Surveyorship, General Taylor was elected president. To fully understand the life of an official, one must imagine him at the moment the other party comes to power. His position is then as unpleasant as one can imagine, with no good alternatives—although what seems the worst outcome may turn out to be the best. It is a strange experience for a man of pride and feeling to know that his interests are in the control of strangers who don't like or understand him. Under those circumstances, he would rather be injured than assisted by them. How strange for someone who has taken no part in the election to realize he is an object of the blood thirst of the victors! Few traits of human nature are uglier than the tendency to grow cruel when you have power. If the mem-

pen, he would rather be injured than obliged. Strange, too, for one who has kept his calmness throughout the contest, to observe the bloodthirstiness that is developed in the hour of triumph, and to be conscious that he is himself among its objects! There are few uglier traits of human nature than this tendency—which I now witnessed in men no worse than their neighbours—to grow cruel, merely because they possessed the power of inflicting harm. If the guillotine, as applied to office-holders, were a literal fact, instead of one of the most apt of metaphors, it is my sincere belief, that the active members of the victorious party were sufficiently excited to have chopped off all our heads, and have thanked Heaven for the opportunity! It appears to me—who have been a calm and curious observer, as well in victory as defeat—that this fierce and bitter spirit of malice and revenge has never distinguished the many triumphs of my own party as it now did that of the Whigs. The Democrats take the offices, as a general rule, because they need them, and because the practice of many years has made it the law of political warfare, which, unless a different system be proclaimed, it were weakness and cowardice to murmur at. But the long habit of victory has made them generous. They know how to spare, when they see occasion; and when they strike, the axe may be sharp, indeed, but its edge is seldom poisoned with ill-will; nor is it their custom ignominiously to kick the head which they have just struck off.

In short, unpleasant as was my predicament, at best, I saw much reason to congratulate myself that I was on the losing side, rather than the triumphant one. If, heretofore, I had been none of the warmest of partisans, I began now, at this season of peril and adversity, to be pretty acutely sensible with which party my predilections lay; nor was it without something like regret and shame, that, according to a reasonable calculation of chances, I saw my own prospect of retaining office to be better than those of my Democratic brethren. But who can see an inch into futurity, beyond his nose? My own head was the first that fell!

The moment when a man's head drops off is seldom or never, I am inclined to think, precisely the most agreeable of his life. Nevertheless, like the greater part of our misfortunes, even so serious a contingency brings its remedy and consolation with it, if the sufferer will but make the best, rather than the worst, of the acci-

bers of the victorious party had had an actual guillotine rather than a metaphorical one, I do believe they would have beheaded us and thanked God for the chance to do so. It seems to me that my party has never taken as malicious a revenge as the victorious Whigs. The Democrats take the jobs because they need them and because that's just the way it's done—and because to propose a change is considered a sign of weakness. But their many victories have made them generous. They know how to spare a man when there is reason to do so. When they strike, their axe is sharp, but they don't kick the decapitated head for good measure.

Though my situation wasn't pleasant, I saw good reason to congratulate myself for being on the election's losing side. Though I hadn't taken sides in the election, I began to take sides after it. I was pretty sure where my affections lay, and I was sorry and a little embarrassed that my fellow Democratic colleagues might lose their jobs while I kept mine. But who can see even a moment into the future? My head was the first to go.

The moment when a man's head is chopped off is almost never the happiest of his life. But like any misfortune it has some benefits, if one will only make the best of things. In my case, the consolations were already apparent. Indeed, I had thought of them long before. I had been weary of the Custom House and vaguely thinking of

dent which has befallen him. In my particular case, the consolatory topics were close at hand, and, indeed, had suggested themselves to my meditations a considerable time before it was requisite to use them. In view of my previous weariness of office, and vague thoughts of resignation, my fortune somewhat resembled that of a person who should entertain an idea of committing suicide, and, altogether beyond his hopes, meet with the good hap to be murdered. In the Custom-House, as before in the Old Manse, I had spent three years; a term long enough to rest a weary brain; long enough to break off old intellectual habits, and make room for new ones; long enough, and too long, to have lived in an unnatural state, doing what was really of no advantage nor delight to any human being, and withholding myself from toil that would, at least, have stilled an unquiet impulse in me. Then, moreover, as regarded his unceremonious ejectment, the late Surveyor was not altogether ill-pleased to be recognized by the Whigs as an enemy; since his inactivity in political affairs,—his tendency to roam, at will, in that broad and quiet field where all mankind may meet rather than confine himself to those narrow paths where brethren of the same household must diverge from one another,—had sometimes made it questionable with his brother Democrats whether he was a friend. Now, after he had won the crown of martyrdom, (though with no longer a head to wear it on,) the point might be looked upon as settled. Finally, little heroic as he was, it seemed more decorous to be overthrown in the downfall of the party with which he had been content to stand, than to remain a forlorn survivor, when so many worthier men were falling; and, at last, after subsisting for four years on the mercy of a hostile administration, to be compelled then to define his position anew, and claim the yet more humiliating mercy of a friendly one.

Meanwhile, the press had taken up my affair, and kept me, for a week or two, careering through the public prints, in decapitated state, like Irving's Headless Horseman; ghastly and grim, and longing to be buried, as a politically dead man ought. So much for my figurative self. The real human being, all this time, with his head safely on his shoulders, had brought himself to the comfortable conclusion, that every thing was for the best; and, making an investment in ink, paper, and steel-pens, had opened his long-disused

resigning from it, so my fate was like that of a suicidal man who has the good luck to be murdered. I had spent three years in the Custom House, long enough to rest a weary brain, to break off old habits of mind and make room for new ones. I had spent long enough—too long, really—doing a job unfit for man and keeping myself away from real work. And I was glad to be called an enemy by the Whigs, since my tendency to go my own way led many Democrats to question my loyalty. Now that I was a martyr for their cause, there was no longer any doubt. And though I didn't imagine myself a hero, it did seem better to fall along with the party and many worthier men than to remain a lone survivor, changing sides after each election.

Meanwhile, the press took up my cause. They kept me in the news for a week or two like Washington Irving's Headless Horseman, longing to be buried in the political graveyard. So much for my metaphorical self. The actual man, head still firmly on his shoulders, had concluded that this was all for the best. I bought ink, paper, and pens; opened my long-unused writing desk; and was again a literary man.

writing-desk, and was again a literary man.

Now it was, that the lucubrations of my ancient predecessor, Mr. Surveyor Pue, came into play. Rusty through long idleness, some little space was requisite before my intellectual machinery could be brought to work upon the tale, with an effect in any degree satisfactory. Even yet, though my thoughts were ultimately much absorbed in the task, it wears, to my eye, a stern and sombre aspect; too much ungladdened by genial sunshine; too little relieved by the tender and familiar influences which soften almost every scene of nature and real life, and, undoubtedly, should soften every picture of them. This uncaptivating effect is perhaps due to the period of hardly accomplished revolution, and still seething turmoil, in which the story shaped itself. It is no indication, however, of a lack of cheerfulness in the writer's mind; for he was happier, while straying through the gloom of these sunless fantasies, than at any time since he had quitted the Old Manse. Some of the briefer articles, which contribute to make up the volume, have likewise been written since my involuntary withdrawal from the toils and honors of public life, and the remainder are gleaned from annuals and magazines, of such antique date that they have gone round the circle, and come back to novelty again. Keeping up the metaphor of the political guillotine, the whole may be considered as the Posthumous Papers of a Decapitated Surveyor; and the sketch which I am now bringing to a close, if too autobiographical for a modest person to publish in his lifetime, will readily be excused in a gentleman who writes from beyond the grave. Peace be with all the world! My blessing on my friends! My forgiveness to my enemies! For I am in the realm of quiet!

The life of the Custom-House lies like a dream behind me. The old Inspector,—who, by the by, I regret to say, was overthrown and killed by a horse, some time ago; else he would certainly have lived for ever,—he, and all those other venerable personages who sat with him at the receipt of custom, are but shadows in my view; white-headed and wrinkled images, which my fancy used to sport with, and has now flung aside for ever. The merchants,—Pingree, Phillips, Shepard, Upton, Kimball, Bertram, Hunt,—these, and many other names, which had such a classic familiarity for my ear six months ago,—these men of traffic, who seemed to occupy so important a

NO FEAR

It was then that the records of my ancient predecessor, Mr. Surveyor Pine, came into play. Rusty as I was, it was a while before I could do much of anything with the tale. Even now, though I put a lot into it, the story seems to have a stern and serious aspect. It shows too little of the sunshine that brightens real life and should brighten every image of it. This effect may be partly due to the period in which the story is set, which was one of recent revolution and still-seething turmoil. But it does not stem from any unhappiness in my mind. Indeed, I was happier wandering in the gloom of these sunless fantasies than I have been since leaving the Old Manse. Some of the shorter stories, which are included in this volume, have similarly been written since my withdrawal from public life. The rest were published in magazines so long ago that they have come full circle are now as good as new. To keep up the metaphor of the political guillotine, the volume may be thought of as the *Posthumous Papers of a Decapitated Surveyor*. This sketch, which may be too autobiographical for a modest person to publish in his lifetime, will be excused if written by a political dead man. Peace to all, my blessings to my friends, and forgiveness to my enemies, for I have passed from the political world.

The life of the Custom House is like a dream to me now. I'm sorry to say that the old Inspector was thrown from his horse and killed. He would have lived forever otherwise. Now he and the other officers are like shadows to me: white-headed and wrinkled images that my imagination once played with but never will again. The many merchants who were so familiar and seemed so important only six months ago—how soon they have faded from my memory! I struggle to recall them now. And soon Salem itself will loom over me through the haze of memory, as though it were an overgrown village in cloud-land and not part of the real world. Salem is no longer a

position in the world,—how little time has it required to disconnect me from them all, not merely in act, but recollection! It is with an effort that I recall the figures and appellations of these few. Soon, likewise, my old native town will loom upon me through the haze of memory, a mist brooding over and around it; as if it were no portion of the real earth but an overgrown village in cloud-land, with only imaginary inhabitants to people its wooden houses, and walk its homely lanes, and the unpicturesque prolixity of its main street. Henceforth, it ceases to be a reality of my life. I am a citizen of somewhere else. My good townspeople will not much regret me; for—though it has been as dear an object as any, in my literary efforts, to be of some importance in their eyes, and to win myself a pleasant memory in this abode and burial-place of so many of my forefathers—there has never been, for me, the genial atmosphere which a literary man requires, in order to ripen the best harvest of his mind. I shall do better amongst other faces; and these familiar ones, it need hardly be said, will do just as well without me.

It may be, however,—O, transporting and triumphant thought!—that the great-grandchildren of the present race may sometimes think kindly of the scribbler of bygone days, when the antiquary of days to come, among the sites memorable in the town's history, shall point out the locality of The Town-Pump!

reality of my life. I live elsewhere now. The townspeople won't miss me much. Though I have tried to win their esteem with my writing, the town never gave me a pleasant atmosphere required by a literary man. I will do better with other faces around me—and the familiar ones, I hardly need to say, will do just fine without me.

Perhaps—oh, what an amazing thought—their great-grandchildren will think kindly thoughts about me in days to come, when the local historians point out where the town pump once stood.

Chapter 1: The Prison Door

Athrong of bearded men, in sad-colored garments and gray, steeple-crowned hats, intermixed with women, some wearing hoods, and others bareheaded, was assembled in front of a wooden edifice, the door of which was heavily timbered with oak, and studded with iron spikes.

The founders of a new colony, whatever Utopia of human virtue and happiness they might originally project, have invariably recognized it among their earliest practical necessities to allot a portion of the virgin soil as a cemetery, and another portion as the site of a prison. In accordance with this rule, it may safely be assumed that the forefathers of Boston had built the first prison-house, somewhere in the vicinity of Cornhill, almost as seasonably as they marked out the first burial-ground, on Isaac Johnson's lot, and round about his grave, which subsequently became the nucleus of all the congregated sepulchres in the old church-yard of King's Chapel. Certain it is, that, some fifteen or twenty years after the settlement of the town, the wooden jail was already marked with weather-stains and other indications of age, which gave a yet darker aspect to its beetle-browed and gloomy front. The rust on the ponderous iron-work of its oaken door looked more antique than any thing else in the new world. Like all that pertains to crime, it seemed never to have known a youthful era. Before this ugly edifice, and between it and the wheel-track of the street, was a grass-plot, much overgrown with burdock, pig-weed, apple-peru, and such unsightly vegetation, which evidently found something congenial in the soil that had so early borne the black flower of civilized society, a prison. But, on one side of the portal, and rooted almost at the threshold, was a wild rose-bush, covered, in this month of June, with its delicate gems, which might be imagined to offer their fragrance and fragile beauty to the prisoner as he went in, and to the condemned criminal as he came forth to his doom, in token that the deep heart of Nature could pity and be kind to him.

This rose-bush, by a strange chance, has been kept alive in history; but whether it had merely survived out of the stern old wilderness, so long after the fall of the gigantic pines and oaks that

Chapter 1: The Prison Door

A crowd of dreary-looking men and women stood outside of a heavy oak door studded with iron spikes.

The founders of a new colony, regardless of the utopia they may hope for, always build two things first: a cemetery and a prison. So it is safe to assume that the founders of Boston built their first prison somewhere in the vicinity of Cornhill just as they marked the first burial ground on Isaac Johnson's land. It took only fifteen or twenty years for the wooden jail to take on water stains and other signs of age, which darkened its already gloomy appearance. The rust on the door's iron spikes looked older than anything else in the New World. Like all things touched by crime, it seemed that the prison had never been young or new. In front of the prison there was a grassy area overgrown with weeds, which must have found something welcoming in the soil that had supported the black flowers of society. But on one side of the ugly prison door there was a wild rose bush, which was covered with delicate buds on this June day. It was as if Nature had taken pity and offered some beauty to the criminals walking in to serve their terms or heading out to face their executions.

Johnson: One
of Boston's earliest
settlers, whose land
eventually became
the site of a cemetery and church.

This rose bush, by an odd chance, is still alive today. Some say that its wild heartiness has preserved it, even after the giant pines and oaks that once overshadowed it have fallen. Others claim that it

originally overshadowed it,—or whether, as there is fair authority for believing, it had sprung up under the footsteps of the sainted Ann Hutchinson, as she entered the prison-door,—we shall not take upon us to determine. Finding it so directly on the threshold of our narrative, which is now about to issue from that inauspicious portal, we could hardly do otherwise than pluck one of its flowers and present it to the reader. It may serve, let us hope, to symbolize some sweet moral blossom, that may be found along the track, or relieve the darkening close of a tale of human frailty and sorrow.

e Hutchinson:
st and pioneer
rganized Puri-
ligious groups
and preached
them without
ing authorized
do so by any
urch authority.
was tried and
communicated
ampioning the
and dignity of
women.

sprang up under the footsteps of the sainted Anne Hutchinson as she entered the prison. But it isn't my place to decide. Finding the bush directly on the threshold of my story, I can only pluck one of its flowers and present it to the reader. I hope the flower may serve as a symbol of some sweet moral lesson to be found here or offer relief from this dark tale of human frailty and sorrow.

Chapter 2: The Marketplace

The grass-plot before the jail, in Prison Lane, on a certain summer morning, not less than two centuries ago, was occupied by a pretty large number of the inhabitants of Boston; all with their eyes intently fastened on the iron-clamped oaken door. Amongst any other population, or at a later period in the history of New England, the grim rigidity that petrified the bearded physiognomies of these good people would have augured some awful business in hand. It could have betokened nothing short of the anticipated execution of some noted culprit, on whom the sentence of a legal tribunal had but confirmed the verdict of public sentiment. But, in that early severity of the Puritan character, an inference of this kind could not so indubitably be drawn. It might be that a sluggish bond-servant, or an undutiful child, whom his parents had given over to the civil authority, was to be corrected at the whipping-post. It might be, that an Antinomian, a Quaker, or other heterodox religionist, was to be scourged out of the town, or an idle and vagrant Indian, whom the white man's fire-water had made riotous about the streets, was to be driven with stripes into the shadow of the forest. It might be, too, that a witch, like old Mistress Hibbins, the bitter-tempered widow of the magistrate, was to die upon the gallows. In either case, there was very much the same solemnity of demeanour on the part of the spectators; as befitted a people amongst whom religion and law were almost identical, and in whose character both were so thoroughly interfused, that the mildest and the severest acts of public discipline were alike made venerable and awful. Meagre, indeed, and cold, was the sympathy that a transgressor might look for, from such bystanders at the scaffold. On the other hand, a penalty which, in our days, would infer a degree of mocking infamy and ridicule, might then be invested with almost as stern a dignity as the punishment of death itself.

It was a circumstance to be noted, on the summer morning when our story begins its course, that the women, of whom there were several in the crowd, appeared to take a peculiar interest in whatever penal infliction might be expected to ensue. The age had not so much refinement, that any sense of impropriety restrained the wearers of petticoat and farthingale from stepping forth into the public ways, and wedging their not unsubstantial persons, if occasion were, into

Chapter 2: The Marketplace

One summer morning in the early seventeenth century, a large number of Boston residents were gathered in front of the prison, staring at its oak door. In another place or time, the grim faces of these good people would have suggested a terrible event, such as the impending execution of a criminal so notorious that the court's verdict merely confirms what the community already knows. But given the harsh Puritan character, one could not be so sure about the cause for this scene. Perhaps a lazy servant or rebellious child was about to be publicly whipped. Maybe a religious heretic was to be beaten out of town or an Indian, drunk on the settlers' whiskey, was to be lashed back into the woods. It could be that a witch like old Mistress Hibbins, the foul-tempered widow of the local judge, was to be hanged. Whatever their reason for being there, the crowd gathered on that morning was quite solemn. This cold demeanor suited a community in which religion and law so intermixed in the hearts of the people that mild punishments were just as terrifying as the serious ones. A criminal could expect little sympathy on his execution day. Back then, even a light penalty—the sort that might be laughed off today—was handed out as sternly as a death sentence.

It should be noted that on the summer morning when our story begins, the women in the crowd seemed especially interested in the forthcoming punishment. This was not a refined age. No sense of impropriety kept these women from elbowing their way to the front, even at a hanging. In their morals as in their bodies, these women were coarser than women these days. Today, six or seven generations removed from those ancestors, women are smaller and more

the throng nearest to the scaffold at an execution. Morally, as well as materially, there was a coarser fibre in those wives and maidens of old English birth and breeding, than in their fair descendants, separated from them by a series of six or seven generations; for, throughout that chain of ancestry, every successive mother has transmitted to her child a fainter bloom, a more delicate and briefer beauty, and a slighter physical frame, if not a character of less force and solidity, than her own. The women, who were now standing about the prison-door, stood within less than half a century of the period when the man-like Elizabeth had been the not altogether unsuitable representative of the sex. They were her countrywomen; and the beef and ale of their native land, with a moral diet not a whit more refined, entered largely into their composition. The bright morning sun, therefore, shone on broad shoulders and well-developed busts, and on round and ruddy cheeks, that had ripened in the far-off island, and had hardly yet grown paler or thinner in the atmosphere of New England. There was, moreover, a boldness and rotundity of speech among these matrons, as most of them seemed to be, that would startle us at the present day, whether in respect to its purport or its volume of tone.

"Goodwives," said a hard-featured dame of fifty, "I'll tell ye a piece of my mind. It would be greatly for the public behoof, if we women, being of mature age and church-members in good repute, should have the handling of such malefactresses as this Hester Prynne. What think ye, gossips? If the hussy stood up for judgment before us five, that are now here in a knot together, would she come off with such a sentence as the worshipful magistrates have awarded? Marry, I trow not!"

"People say," said another, "that the Reverend Master Dimmesdale, her godly pastor, takes it very grievously to heart that such a scandal should have come upon his congregation."

"The magistrates are God-fearing gentlemen, but merciful overmuch,—that is a truth," added a third autumnal matron. "At the very least, they should have put the brand of a hot iron on Hester Prynne's forehead. Madam Hester would have winced at that, I warrant me. But she,—the naughty baggage,—little will she care what they put upon the bodice of her gown! Why, look you, she may cover it with a brooch, or such like heathenish adornment, and so walk the streets as brave as ever!"

delicate in frame and character. But the women standing in front of that prison door were less than fifty years from the time when manly Queen Elizabeth was the model for femininity. Being the queen's countrywomen, these women were raised on the same English beef and ale, which combined with an equally coarse moral diet to make them who they were. So the bright sun shone that morning on a group of broad shoulders, large busts, and round, rosy cheeks that were raised on English stock and not yet made pale or thin by the New England air. The bold and frank speech of these women would also startle us today, both in its meaning and its volume.

en Elizabeth:
achelor queen
presided over
golden age in
English history.

"Ladies," said one hard-faced woman of fifty, "I'll give you a piece of my mind. It would serve the public good if mature, church-going women like us were allowed to deal with hussies like Hester Prynne. What do you say, ladies? If the five of us passed judgment on this slut, would she have gotten off as lightly as she has before the magistrates? I don't think so."

"People say," said another woman, "that the Reverend Master Dimmesdale, her pastor, is very grieved that a scandal like this has occurred in his congregation."

"The magistrates may be God-fearing, but they are too merciful—and that's the truth!" added a middle-aged woman. "At the very least, they should have branded Hester Prynne's forehead with a hot iron. She would have winced then, for sure. But—the dirty whore—what will she care about something pinned to her dress? She could cover it with a brooch or some other sinful jewelry and walk the streets as proud as ever."

"Ah, but," interposed, more softly, a young wife, holding a child by the hand, "let her cover the mark as she will, the pang of it will be always in her heart."

"What do we talk of marks and brands, whether on the bodice of her gown, or the flesh of her forehead?" cried another female, the ugliest as well as the most pitiless of these self-constituted judges. "This woman has brought shame upon us all, and ought to die. Is there not law for it? Truly there is, both in the Scripture and the stat-ute-book. Then let the magistrates, who have made it of no effect, thank themselves if their own wives and daughters go astray!"

"Mercy on us, goodwife," exclaimed a man in the crowd, "is there no virtue in woman, save what springs from a wholesome fear of the gallows? That is the hardest word yet! Hush, now, gossips; for the lock is turning in the prison-door, and here comes Mistress Prynne herself."

The door of the jail being flung open from within, there appeared, in the first place, like a black shadow emerging into the sunshine, the grim and grisly presence of the town-beadle, with a sword by his side and his staff of office in his hand. This personage prefig-ured and represented in his aspect the whole dismal severity of the Puritanic code of law, which it was his business to administer in its final and closest application to the offender. Stretching forth the official staff in his left hand, he laid his right upon the shoulder of a young woman, whom he thus drew forward; until, on the thresh-old of the prison-door, she repelled him, by an action marked with natural dignity and force of character, and stepped into the open air, as if by her own of free-will. She bore in her arms a child, a baby of some three months old, who winked and turned aside its little face from the too vivid light of day; because its existence, heretofore, had brought it acquainted only with the gray twilight of a dungeon, or other darksome apartment of the prison.

When the young woman—the mother of this child—stood fully revealed before the crowd, it seemed to be her first impulse to clasp the infant closely to her bosom; not so much by an impulse of moth-erly affection, as that she might thereby conceal a certain token, which was wrought or fastened into her dress. In a moment, how-ever, wisely judging that one token of her shame would but poorly

NO FEAR

"Well," interrupted a young wife, holding her child by the hand, "she can cover the mark however she likes, but it will still weigh on her heart."

"Why talk about marks and brands, whether they're on her gown or the skin of her forehead?" shouted another woman, the most ugly and merciless of this self-righteous and judgmental group. "This woman has brought shame to all of us, and she ought to die. Isn't there a law that says so? There truly is, in both the Bible and the statutes. The magistrates will have only themselves to thank when, having disregarded these laws, they find that their wives and daughters are sleeping around."

"Have mercy, ma'am," shouted a man in the crowd. "Are women only virtuous when they fear punishment? That's the worst thing I've heard today! Quiet now, you gossips. The prison door is opening. Here comes Mistress Prynne herself."

beadle: Minor official designated to keep order ing certain town proceedings.

The prison door was flung open. The town beadle appeared first, looking like a black shadow emerging into the sunlight. He was a grim figure, with a sword by his side and the staff of office in his hand. The beadle represented the laws of the Puritans, and it was his job to deliver the punishments they required. Holding the official staff in front of him with his left hand, he laid his right on the shoulder of a young woman. He led her forward until, on the threshold of the prison door, she freed herself. With dignity and force, she stepped into the fresh air as though it were her free choice to do so. She carried a child in her arms—a three-month-old baby that squinted and turned its face away from the bright sun. Until that moment, it had only known the dim, gray light of the prison.

When the young woman (the child's mother) stood in plain view of the crowd, her first instinct was to clasp her baby tightly to her chest. She seemed to do so not out of motherly affection but rather to hide something attached to her dress. Realizing, however, that one shameful thing would not hide another, she took her baby on her arm. With a burning blush, but a proud smile and eyes that

serve to hide another, she took the baby on her arm, and, with a burning blush, and yet a haughty smile, and a glance that would not be abashed, looked around at her townspeople and neighbours. On the breast of her gown, in fine red cloth, surrounded with an elaborate embroidery and fantastic flourishes of gold thread, appeared the letter A. It was so artistically done, and with so much fertility and gorgeous luxuriance of fancy, that it had all the effect of a last and fitting decoration to the apparel which she wore; and which was of a splendor in accordance with the taste of the age, but greatly beyond what was allowed by the sumptuary regulations of the colony.

The young woman was tall, with a figure of perfect elegance, on a large scale. She had dark and abundant hair, so glossy that it threw off the sunshine with a gleam, and a face which, besides being beautiful from regularity of feature and richness of complexion, had the impressiveness belonging to a marked brow and deep black eyes. She was lady-like, too, after the manner of the feminine gentility of those days; characterized by a certain state and dignity, rather than by the delicate, evanescent, and indescribable grace, which is now recognized as its indication. And never had Hester Prynne appeared more lady-like, in the antique interpretation of the term, than as she issued from the prison. Those who had before known her, and had expected to behold her dimmed and obscured by a disastrous cloud, were astonished, and even startled, to perceive how her beauty shone out, and made a halo of the misfortune and ignominy in which she was enveloped. It may be true, that, to a sensitive observer, there was something exquisitely painful in it. Her attire, which, indeed, she had wrought for the occasion, in prison, and had modelled much after her own fancy, seemed to express the attitude of her spirit, the desperate recklessness of her mood, by its wild and picturesque peculiarity. But the point which drew all eyes, and, as it were, transfigured the wearer,—so that both men and women, who had been familiarly acquainted with Hester Prynne, were now impressed as if they beheld her for the first time,—was that Scarlet Letter, so fantastically embroidered and illuminated upon her bosom. It had the effect of a spell, taking her out of the ordinary relations with humanity, and inclosing her in a sphere by herself.

"She hath good skill at her needle, that's certain," remarked one of the female spectators; "but did ever a woman, before this brazen

NO FEAR

smptuary laws: laws restricting le's consumptions of luxury ts, particularly clothing.

refused to be embarrassed, she looked around at her neighbors. On the front of her dress, in fine red cloth embellished with gold thread, was the letter *A*. The piece was so artistically done that it seemed like the perfect final touch for her outfit—an outfit that was as rich as the tastes of the age but far fancier than anything permitted by the sumptuary laws of the colony.

The young woman was tall and elegant. Her thick, dark hair gleamed in the sunlight. Her beautiful face, with well-formed features and perfect complexion, was impressive in a way that young faces rarely are. She held herself in a stately and dignified manner, like upper-class ladies of that time, not delicate like women are today. And Hester Prynne had never appeared more ladylike than when she stepped out from that prison. Those who knew her and expected to see her diminished by her circumstance were startled to find that her beauty radiated like a halo to obscure the clouds of misfortune that surrounded her. Even so, the sensitive observer might have detected something exquisitely painful in the scene. Her outfit, which she had fashioned for the occasion while in her cell, was extravagant in a way that seemed to reflect her reckless mood. But all eyes were drawn to the embroidered scarlet letter, which so transformed its wearer that people who had known Hester Prynne felt they were seeing her for the first time. The letter had the effect of a spell, removing her from ordinary humanity and placing her in a world by herself.

"She's certainly good with a needle," commented one female observer, "but did a woman ever parade her skill in the way this hussy, contrive such a way of showing it! Why, gossips, what is it but to laugh in the faces of our godly magistrates, and make a pride out of what they, worthy gentlemen, meant for a punishment?"

"It were well," muttered the most iron-visaged of the old dames, "if we stripped Madam Hester's rich gown off her dainty shoulders; and as for the red letter, which she hath stitched so curiously, I'll bestow a rag of mine own rheumatic flannel, to make a fitter one!"

"O, peace, neighbours, peace!" whispered their youngest companion. "Do not let her hear you! Not a stitch in that embroidered letter, but she has felt it in her heart."

The grim beadle now made a gesture with his staff.

"Make way, good people, make way, in the King's name," cried he. "Open a passage; and, I promise ye, Mistress Prynne shall be set where man, woman, and child may have a fair sight of her brave apparel, from this time till an hour past meridian. A blessing on the righteous Colony of the Massachusetts, where iniquity is dragged out into the sunshine! Come along, Madam Hester, and show your scarlet letter in the market-place!"

A lane was forthwith opened through the crowd of spectators. Preceded by the beadle, and attended by an irregular procession of stern-browed men and unkindly-visaged women, Hester Prynne set forth towards the place appointed for her punishment. A crowd of eager and curious schoolboys, understanding little of the matter in hand, except that it gave them a half-holiday, ran before her progress, turning their heads continually to stare into her face, and at the winking baby in her arms, and at the ignominious letter on her breast. It was no great distance, in those days, from the prison-door to the market-place. Measured by the prisoner's experience, however, it might be reckoned a journey of some length; for, haughty as her demeanour was, she perchance underwent an agony from every footstep of those that thronged to see her, as if her heart had been flung into the street for them all to spurn and trample upon. In our nature, however, there is a provision, alike marvellous and merciful, that the sufferer should never know the intensity of what he endures by its present torture, but chiefly by the pang that rankles after it. With almost a serene deportment, therefore, Hester Prynne passed through this portion of her ordeal, and came to a sort of scaffold, at the western extremity of

harlot has today? Girls, she is laughing in the faces of our godly magistrates and proudly flaunting the symbol they intended as a punishment!"

"It would be well-deserved," muttered a hard-faced old woman, "if we tore Madame Hester's rich gown off her precious shoulders. As for the red letter which she has so skillfully made, I'll give her a scrap of my own crimson flannel to make a better one!"

"Oh quiet, ladies, quiet!" whispered their youngest companion. "Don't let her hear you! Every stitch in that letter took a toll on her heart."

The grim beadle made a gesture with his staff.

"Make way, good people! Make way, in the King's name!" he cried. "Make a path, and I promise you that Mistress Prynne will be placed where man, woman, and child will have a good view of her fine garments from now until one o'clock. God bless the righteous colony of Massachusetts, where misdeeds are dragged out into the sunshine! Come along, Madame Hester, and show your scarlet letter in the marketplace!"

A path immediately opened in the crowd of spectators. With the beadle in front, and a procession of foul-faced men and women behind, Hester Prynne walked toward the spot chosen for her punishment. An eager group of curious schoolboys ran ahead. Although they understood little of what was going on except that school had closed early that day, they kept turning around to stare at Hester, the baby in her arms and the shameful letter on her breast. In those days, the prison door sat close to the marketplace. For the prisoner, though, it was a long walk. As confident as she may have seemed, Hester would have felt every step of every person in the crowd as though they had landed on her heart. But human nature blesses us with a strange and merciful quirk: In our moments of suffering, we don't realize how much we hurt. It's only afterward that we feel the worst pain. So with almost serene composure, Hester Prynne endured this portion of her ordeal. She came to a crude scaffold at the western end of the marketplace. The scaffold stood below the eaves of Boston's oldest church and seemed to be a permanent feature of the place.

the market-place. It stood nearly beneath the eaves of Boston's earliest church, and appeared to be a fixture there.

In fact, this scaffold constituted a portion of a penal machine, which now, for two or three generations past, has been merely historical and traditionary among us, but was held, in the old time, to be as effectual an agent in the promotion of good citizenship, as ever was the guillotine among the terrorists of France. It was, in short, the platform of the pillory; and above it rose the framework of that instrument of discipline, so fashioned as to confine the human head in its tight grasp, and thus hold it up to the public gaze. The very idea of ignominy was embodied and made manifest in this contrivance of wood and iron. There can be no outrage, methinks, against our common nature—whatever be the delinquencies of the individual,—no outrage more flagrant than to forbid the culprit to hide his face for shame; as it was the essence of this punishment to do. In Hester Prynne's instance, however, as not unfrequently in other cases, her sentence bore, that she should stand a certain time upon the platform, but without undergoing that gripe about the neck and confinement of the head, the proneness to which was the most devilish characteristic of this ugly engine. Knowing well her part, she ascended a flight of wooden steps, and was thus displayed to the surrounding multitude, at about the height of a man's shoulders above the street.

Had there been a Papist among the crowd of Puritans, he might have seen in this beautiful woman, so picturesque in her attire and mien, and with the infant at her bosom, an object to remind him of the image of Divine Maternity, which so many illustrious painters have vied with one another to represent; something which should remind him, indeed, but only by contrast, of that sacred image of sinless motherhood, whose infant was to redeem the world. Here, there was the taint of deepest sin in the most sacred quality of human life, working such effect, that the world was only the darker for this woman's beauty, and the more lost for the infant that she had borne.

The scene was not without a mixture of awe, such as must always invest the spectacle of guilt and shame in a fellow-creature, before society shall have grown corrupt enough to smile, instead of shuddering, at it. The witnesses of Hester Prynne's disgrace had not yet passed beyond their simplicity. They were stern enough to look

NO FEAR

Scaffolds may seem like little more than historical curiosities now, but they once formed an integral part of a penal system that was thought to promote good citizenship as effectively as the guillotines of the French Revolution. The scaffold was the site of public humiliation. On it stood the pillory, a device that held the human head steady, exhibiting it to the public gaze. The very idea of shame was embodied in this frame of wood and iron. No matter how bad the offense, there is nothing more severe, I think, than to forbid someone to hide his face in shame. This punishment did precisely that. In Hester Prynne's case, as sometimes happens, her sentence required her to stand for a certain time on the platform, but without having her head held still—the worst part of the punishment. Knowing her role, she climbed the wooden steps and stood on display above the crowd.

If a Catholic had been present in that crowd of Puritans, the sight of this beautiful woman with an infant at her breast might have reminded him of the Virgin Mary. But Hester Prynne would have stood in great contrast to that sinless mother whose infant was sent to redeem the world. Here, sin created a stain on the most sacred quality of human life. This beautiful woman and her child made the world a darker place.

The scene was somewhat awful, as spectacles of guilt and shame always are, until that time when society becomes so corrupt that it laughs when it should be shuddering. The witnesses of Hester Prynne's disgrace were still simple, innocent folk. They were stern enough to have watched her execution—had she been sentenced to

upon her death, had that been the sentence, without a murmur at its severity, but had none of the heartlessness of another social state, which would find only a theme for jest in an exhibition like the present. Even had there been a disposition to turn the matter into ridicule, it must have been repressed and overpowered by the solemn presence of men no less dignified than the Governor, and several of his counsellors, a judge, a general, and the ministers of the town; all of whom sat or stood in a balcony of the meeting-house, looking down upon the platform. When such personages could constitute a part of the spectacle, without risking the majesty or reverence of rank and office, it was safely to be inferred that the infliction of a legal sentence would have an earnest and effectual meaning. Accordingly, the crowd was sombre and grave. The unhappy culprit sustained herself as best a woman might, under the heavy weight of a thousand unrelenting eyes, all fastened upon her, and concentred at her bosom. It was almost intolerable to be borne. Of an impulsive and passionate nature, she had fortified herself to encounter the stings and venomous stabs of public contumely, wreaking itself in every variety of insult; but there was a quality so much more terrible in the solemn mood of the popular mind, that she longed rather to behold all those rigid countenances contorted with scornful merriment, and herself the object. Had a roar of laughter burst from the multitude,—each man, each woman, each little shrill-voiced child, contributing their individual parts,—Hester Prynne might have repaid them all with a bitter and disdainful smile. But, under the leaden infliction which it was her doom to endure, she felt, at moments, as if she must needs shriek out with the full power of her lungs, and cast herself from the scaffold down upon the ground, or else go mad at once.

Yet there were intervals when the whole scene, in which she was the most conspicuous object, seemed to vanish from her eyes, or, at least, glimmered indistinctly before them, like a mass of imperfectly shaped and spectral images. Her mind, and especially her memory, was preternaturally active, and kept bringing up other scenes than this roughly hewn street of a little town, on the edge of the Western wilderness; other faces than were lowering upon her from beneath the brims of those steeple-crowned hats. Reminiscences, the most trifling and immaterial, passages of infancy and school-days, sports,

die—without uttering a word about the cruelty of it. But they were not so heartless as to joke about the matter. And even if they had wanted to laugh, the presence of the governor and his advisers, a judge, a general, and the town's ministers standing in the church balcony would have kept them quiet. When important men like these could participate in this kind of event without risking their reputations, it signified that these sentences were a serious matter. The crowd was fittingly solemn, and the unhappy criminal handled herself as best a woman could with a thousand merciless eyes fixated on her bosom. The situation was nearly intolerable. Impulsive and passionate by nature, Hester Prynne had prepared herself for the stings and stabs of public scorn, which might come in any variety of insult. But the gloomy, serious mood of the crowd was much worse. She wished that everyone would laugh and shout at her instead. If they had only laughed, Hester Prynne could return a bitter, disdainful smile. But under the heavy weight of their solemnity, she felt at times that she would either cry out with all her might and hurl herself off of the platform or else go mad.

But at other times the entire scene, in which she played the largest part, seemed to vanish before her eyes or flicker like a ghostly vision. Hester Prynne's mind and memory were hyperactive. She kept recalling scenes far removed from this small town on the edge of the wilderness and faces other than those glowering at her now. The silliest and slightest memories came back to her: moments from her infancy, childhood, and the early days of her adulthood all came flooding through, mixed up with more serious and more recent memories. Each memory was as vivid as the next, as if they were all

childish quarrels, and the little domestic traits of her maiden years, came swarming back upon her, intermingled with recollections of whatever was gravest in her subsequent life; one picture precisely as vivid as another; as if all were of similar importance, or all alike a play. Possibly, it was an instinctive device of her spirit, to relieve itself, by the exhibition of these phantasmagoric forms, from the cruel weight and hardness of the reality.

Be that as it might, the scaffold of the pillory was a point of view that revealed to Hester Prynne the entire track along which she had been treading, since her happy infancy. Standing on that miserable eminence, she saw again her native village, in Old England, and her paternal home; a decayed house of gray stone, with a poverty-stricken aspect, but retaining a half-obliterated shield of arms over the portal, in token of antique gentility. She saw her father's face, with its bald brow, and reverend white beard, that flowed over the old-fashioned Elizabethan ruff; her mother's, too, with the look of heedful and anxious love which it always wore in her remembrance, and which, even since her death, had so often laid the impediment of a gentle remonstrance in her daughter's pathway. She saw her own face, glowing with girlish beauty, and illuminating all the interior of the dusky mirror in which she had been wont to gaze at it. There she beheld another countenance, of a man well stricken in years, a pale, thin, scholar-like visage, with eyes dim and bleared by the lamp-light that had served them to pore over many ponderous books. Yet those same bleared optics had strange, penetrating power, when it was their owner's purpose to read the human soul. This figure of the study and the cloister, as Hester Prynne's womanly fancy failed not to recall, was slightly deformed, with the left shoulder a trifle higher than the right. Next rose before her, in memory's picture-gallery, the intricate and narrow thoroughfares, the tall, gray houses, the huge cathedrals, and the public edifices, ancient in date and quaint in architecture, of a Continental city; where a new life had awaited her, still in connection with the misshapen scholar; a new life, but feeding itself on time-worn materials, like a tuft of green moss on a crumbling wall. Lastly, in lieu of these shifting scenes, came back the rude market-place of the Puritan settlement, with all the townspeople assembled and levelling their stern regards at Hester Prynne,—yes,

equally important or all equally unreal, like scenes in a play. Maybe her spirit was instinctively relieving itself from the cruelness of reality by showing her these fantasies.

Be that as it may, the scaffold now revealed the path of Hester Prynne's life. Standing on that unhappy stage, she saw her hometown in England and the home in which she grew up. That crumbling house of gray stone looked poor, but the half-visible coat of arms that hung over the doorway indicated a former nobility. She saw her father's face, with its bold forehead and venerable white beard flowing over an Elizabethan ruff. She saw her mother's face too, with its look of anxious and earnest love, which had served as a gentle guide to Hester even after her mother's death. Hester also saw her own face glowing with girlish beauty, lighting up the mirror into which she had often gazed. But she saw another face in that mirror: the pale, thin face of a man whose years had worn on him, the weary face and bleary eyes of a scholar who had read many books. Yet those same bleary eyes had a strange, penetrating power that could see into a human soul. Hester Prynne couldn't help but remember this monkish figure, slightly deformed with his left shoulder a touch higher than his right. The next image that came to her mind was of a continental city, with intricate, narrow streets; tall gray houses; huge cathedrals; and ancient public buildings. A new life had awaited her there, still connected to the misshapen scholar—a new life, but one that fed off of the past, like a tuft of moss on a crumbling wall. Finally, in place of these shifting scenes, came the image of the primitive marketplace of the Puritan settlement, where all the townspeople had gathered to point their stern gazes at Hester Prynne. She stood on the platform of the pillory, an infant on her arm and the letter A—surrounded in scarlet and wonderfully embroidered with gold thread—upon her bosom!

iff collar worn both men and en in the 16th 7th centuries.

at herself,—who stood on the scaffold of the pillory, an infant on her arm, and the letter A, in scarlet, fantastically embroidered with gold thread, upon her bosom!

Could it be true? She clutched the child so fiercely to her breast, that it sent forth a cry; she turned her eyes downward at the scarlet letter, and even touched it with her finger, to assure herself that the infant and the shame were real. Yes!—these were her realities,—all else had vanished!

NO FEAR

Could this really be happening? She clutched the child to her breast so fiercely that it began to cry. She looked down at the scarlet letter and even touched it with her finger to be sure that the infant and the shame were both real. They were real, and everything else had vanished!

Chapter 3: The Recognition

From this intense consciousness of being the object of severe and universal observation, the wearer of the scarlet letter was at length relieved by discerning, on the outskirts of the crowd, a figure which irresistibly took possession of her thoughts. An Indian, in his native garb, was standing there; but the red men were not so infrequent visitors of the English settlements, that one of them would have attracted any notice from Hester Prynne, at such a time; much less would he have excluded all other objects and ideas from her mind. By the Indian's side, and evidently sustaining a companionship with him, stood a white man, clad in a strange disarray of civilized and savage costume.

He was small in stature, with a furrowed visage, which, as yet, could hardly be termed aged. There was a remarkable intelligence in his features, as of a person who had so cultivated his mental part that it could not fail to mould the physical to itself, and become manifest by unmistakable tokens. Although, by a seemingly careless arrangement of his heterogeneous garb, he had endeavoured to conceal or abate the peculiarity, it was sufficiently evident to Hester Prynne, that one of this man's shoulders rose higher than the other. Again, at the first instant of perceiving that thin visage, and the slight deformity of the figure, she pressed her infant to her bosom, with so convulsive a force that the poor babe uttered another cry of pain. But the mother did not seem to hear it.

At his arrival in the market-place, and some time before she saw him, the stranger had bent his eyes on Hester Prynne. It was carelessly, at first, like a man chiefly accustomed to look inward, and to whom external matters are of little value and import, unless they bear relation to something within his mind. Very soon, however, his look became keen and penetrative. A writhing horror twisted itself across his features, like a snake gliding swiftly over them, and making one little pause, with all its wreathed intervolutions in open sight. His face darkened with some powerful emotion, which, nevertheless, he so instantaneously controlled by an effort of his will, that, save at a single moment, its expression might have passed for calmness. After a brief space, the convulsion grew almost imperceptible, and finally subsided into the depths of his nature. When he

Chapter 3: The Recognition

Hester's intense awareness of the public's attention was finally relieved by the shocking sight of a figure at the far edge of the crowd. An Indian in his native dress was standing there. Indians were not such uncommon visitors in the English settlements that Hester Prynne would have noticed one at such a time, much less been captivated by his presence. But next to the Indian, seeming like his friend, stood a white man, dressed in a strange mixture of English and Indian garments.

He was a short man with a face that was wrinkled but not that old. His features indicated great intelligence, as though he had so cultivated his mind that it began to shape his body. It was clear to Hester Prynne that one of the man's shoulders rose higher than the other, though the man had tried to conceal the fact with a seemingly careless arrangement of his strange clothing. Upon first seeing that thin face and slightly deformed figure, Hester pressed her infant to her breast so hard that the poor child cried out. But Hester did not seem to hear it.

When the stranger first arrived in the marketplace—long before Hester Prynne saw him—he had fixed his eyes on her. His initial glance was careless, like that of a man accustomed to his own thoughts, who only values the outside world for its relation to his own mind. But soon his gaze became sharp and penetrating. Horror slithered over his features like a fast-moving snake, pausing only for a moment to show its many coils. His face darkened with a powerful emotion which, nonetheless, he instantly controlled with his will. Except for that single moment of emotion, his expression seemed perfectly calm. After a little while, his convulsion became almost imperceptible, until it entirely faded into the depths of his being. When he found the eyes of Hester Prynne fixed on his, and saw that she seemed to recognize him, he slowly and calmly raised his finger and laid it on his lips.

found the eyes of Hester Prynne fastened on his own, and saw that she appeared to recognize him, he slowly and calmly raised his finger, made a gesture with it in the air, and laid it on his lips.

Then, touching the shoulder of a townsman who stood next to him, he addressed him in a formal and courteous manner.

"I pray you, good Sir," said he, "who is this woman?—and wherefore is she here set up to public shame?"

"You must needs be a stranger in this region, friend," answered the townsman, looking curiously at the questioner and his savage companion; "else you would surely have heard of Mistress Hester Prynne, and her evil doings. She hath raised a great scandal, I promise you, in godly Master Dimmesdale's church."

"You say truly," replied the other. "I am a stranger, and have been a wanderer, sorely against my will. I have met with grievous mishaps by sea and land, and have been long held in bonds among the heathen-folk, to the southward; and am now brought hither by this Indian, to be redeemed out of my captivity. Will it please you, therefore, to tell me of Hester Prynne's,—have I her name rightly?—of this woman's offences, and what has brought her to yonder scaffold?"

"Truly, friend, and methinks it must gladden your heart, after your troubles and sojourn in the wilderness," said the townsman, "to find yourself, at length, in a land where iniquity is searched out, and punished in the sight of rulers and people; as here in our godly New England. Yonder woman, Sir, you must know, was the wife of a certain learned man, English by birth, but who had long dwelt in Amsterdam, whence, some good time agone, he was minded to cross over and cast in his lot with us of the Massachusetts. To this purpose, he sent his wife before him, remaining himself to look after some necessary affairs. Marry, good Sir, in some two years, or less, that the woman has been a dweller here in Boston, no tidings have come of this learned gentleman, Master Prynne; and his young wife, look you, being left to her own misguidance—"

"Ah!—aha!—I conceive you," said the stranger, with a bitter smile. "So learned a man as you speak of should have learned this too in his books. And who, by your favor, Sir, may be the father of yonder babe—it is some three or four months old, I should judge—which Mistress Prynne is holding in her arms?"

Then he touched the shoulder of a nearby townsman and asked in a formal and courteous tone:

"My dear sir, may I ask who is this woman? And why is she being held up for public shame?"

"You must be a stranger, my friend," the townsman replied, looking curiously at the questioner and his Indian companion, "or you certainly would have heard about the evil deeds of Mistress Hester Prynne. She has caused a great scandal, I assure you, in Master Dimmesdale's church."

"You speak the truth," replied the other. "I am a stranger. I have been wandering, against my will, for a long time. I have suffered terrible bad luck at sea and on land. I have been held prisoner by the Indians to the south, and have been brought here by this Indian to be ransomed from captivity. So could I ask you to tell me of Hester Prynne's—if I have her name right—of this woman's crimes and why she is standing on this platform?"

"Certainly, friend. It must make you glad, after your wanderings in the wilderness," said the townsman, "to finally find yourself somewhere that wickedness is rooted out and punished, as it is here in our godly New England. That woman, sir, was the wife of a learned man. He was English by birth but had lived for a long time in Amsterdam. Some years ago, he decided to cross the ocean and join us in Massachusetts. He sent his wife ahead of him and stayed behind to tend to some business. Well, sir, in the two short years— maybe less—that the woman lived here in Boston, having heard nothing from this wise gentleman, Master Prynne . . . his young wife, you see, was left to mislead herself."

"Ah! Aha! I understand you," said the stranger with a bitter smile. "A man as wise as you say he was should have learned of that danger in his books. And who, beg your pardon, sir, is the father of the young child—some three of four months old, it seems—that Mistress Prynne is holding in her arms?"

"Of a truth friend, that matter remaineth a riddle; and the Daniel who shall expound it is yet a-wanting," answered the townsman. "Madam Hester absolutely refuseth to speak, and the magistrates have laid their heads together in vain. Peradventure the guilty one stands looking on at this sad spectacle, unknown of man, and forgetting that God sees him."

"The learned man," observed the stranger, with another smile, "should come himself to look into the mystery."

"It behooves him well, if he be still in life," responded the townsman. "Now, good Sir, our Massachusetts magistracy, bethinking themselves that this woman is youthful and fair, and doubtless was strongly tempted to her fall;—and that, moreover, as is most likely, her husband may be at the bottom of the sea;—they have not been bold to put in force the extremity of our righteous law against her. The penalty thereof is death. But, in their great mercy and tenderness of heart, they have doomed Mistress Prynne to stand only a space of three hours on the platform of the pillory, and then and thereafter, for the remainder of her natural life, to wear a mark of shame upon her bosom."

"A wise sentence!" remarked the stranger, gravely bowing his head. "Thus she will be a living sermon against sin, until the ignominious letter be engraved upon her tombstone. It irks me, nevertheless, that the partner of her iniquity should not, at least, stand on the scaffold by her side. But he will be known!—he will be known!—he will be known!"

He bowed courteously to the communicative townsman, and, whispering a few words to his Indian attendant, they both made their way through the crowd.

While this passed, Hester Prynne had been standing on her pedestal, still with a fixed gaze towards the stranger; so fixed a gaze, that, at moments of intense absorption, all other objects in the visible world seemed to vanish, leaving only him and her. Such an interview, perhaps, would have been more terrible than even to meet him as she now did, with the hot, midday sun burning down upon her face, and lighting up its shame; with the scarlet token of infamy on her breast; with the sin-born infant in her arms; with a whole people, drawn forth as to a festival, staring at the features that should have been seen only in the quiet gleam of the fireside, in the

aniel: Biblical het who inter- d dreams and ns in the court ng Nebuchad- nezzar.

"To tell the truth, friend, that's still a puzzle, and the Daniel who can solve it has not been found," answered the townsman. "Madame Hester absolutely refuses to speak, and the magistrates have put their heads together in vain. Perhaps the guilty man stands here in the crowd, observing this sad spectacle, and forgetting that God sees him when no one else does."

"That wise scholar," observed the stranger with another smile, "should come here to look into the mystery."

"It would serve him well, if he is still alive," responded the townsman. "Now, good sir, our Massachusetts magistrates realize that this woman is young and pretty and was surely tempted to her sin. What's more, her husband probably died at sea. So they have not punished her with death, as they very well might have. In their great mercy, they have sentenced her to stand for a mere three hours on the platform of the pillory and then to wear a mark of shame on her bosom for the rest of her life."

"A wise sentence," the stranger said, solemnly bowing his head. "She will be like a living sermon against sin, until the shameful letter is engraved on her tombstone. Yet it bothers me that her partner in wickedness does not stand beside her on the platform. But he will be known. He will be known! He will be known!"

He bowed politely to the informative townsman and whispered a few words to his Indian companion. Then they made their way through the crowd.

While this was going on, Hester Prynne stood on her platform, eyes still fixed upon the stranger. She stared so intently that sometimes the rest of the world seemed to vanish, leaving only the two of them. Perhaps such a private interview would have been even more terrible than the encounter they were having now: the noonday sun burning her face and illuminating its shame; the scarlet letter on her breast; the child, conceived in sin, resting in her arms; the crowd, assembled as though for a festival, staring at her features, which would have otherwise only been visible in the intimacy of the fireside, in the quiet of her home, or beneath a veil at church. As terrible

happy shadow of a home, or beneath a matronly veil, at church. Dreadful as it was, she was conscious of a shelter in the presence of these thousand witnesses. It was better to stand thus, with so many betwixt him and her, than to greet him, face to face, they two alone. She fled for refuge, as it were, to the public exposure, and dreaded the moment when its protection should be withdrawn from her. Involved in these thoughts, she scarcely heard a voice behind her, until it had repeated her name more than once, in a loud and solemn tone, audible to the whole multitude.

"Hearken unto me, Hester Prynne!" said the voice.

It has already been noticed, that directly over the platform on which Hester Prynne stood was a kind of balcony, or open gallery, appended to the meeting-house. It was the place whence proclamations were wont to be made, amidst an assemblage of the magistracy, with all the ceremonial that attended such public observances in those days. Here, to witness the scene which we are describing, sat Governor Bellingham himself, with four sergeants about his chair, bearing halberds, as a guard of honor. He wore a dark feather in his hat, a border of embroidery on his cloak, and a black velvet tunic beneath; a gentleman advanced in years, and with a hard experience written in his wrinkles. He was not ill fitted to be the head and representative of a community, which owed its origin and progress, and its present state of development, not to the impulses of youth, but to the stern and tempered energies of manhood, and the sombre sagacity of age; accomplishing so much, precisely because it imagined and hoped so little. The other eminent characters, by whom the chief ruler was surrounded, were distinguished by a dignity of mien, belonging to a period when the forms of authority were felt to possess the sacredness of divine institutions. They were, doubtless, good men, just, and sage. But, out of the whole human family, it would not have been easy to select the same number of wise and virtuous persons, who should be less capable of sitting in judgment on an erring woman's heart, and disentangling its mesh of good and evil, than the sages of rigid aspect towards whom Hester Prynne now turned her face. She seemed conscious, indeed, that whatever sympathy she might expect lay in the larger and warmer heart of the multitude; for, as she lifted her eyes towards the balcony, the unhappy woman grew pale and trembled.

as it was, she felt that these thousand witnesses were sheltering her. It was better to stand before all of them than to meet this stranger alone and face-to-face. She took refuge in her public exposure and dreaded the moment when its protection would be taken from her. Absorbed in these thoughts, she barely heard the voice behind her until it had repeated her name more than once, in a loud and serious tone that the whole crowd could hear.

"Hear me, Hester Prynne!" said the voice.

As mentioned earlier, attached to the meeting house was a sort of balcony that hung directly over the platform on which Hester Prynne stood. Proclamations were often made to the assembled magistrates from this balcony, with all the ceremony that was common in those days. Here, to witness the scene, sat Governor Bellingham himself, with four sergeants beside him as a guard of honor. Bellingham wore a dark feather in his hat, an embroidered border on his cloak, and a black velvet shirt underneath. He was an older gentleman, with the wrinkles of hard-won experience. He was well suited to lead a community founded not with the impulses of youth but rather on the controlled energies of manhood and the sober wisdom of age. This was a community that had accomplished so much because it imagined and hoped for so little. The prominent men who surrounded the governor were distinguished by the dignity with which they carried themselves. Their attitude was fitting for a time when worldly authority was considered as holy as religious office. These were certainly good men, fair and wise. But it would have been hard to find wise and fair men who were less qualified to sit in judgment on the heart of a fallen woman, and distinguish the good from the evil there. It was to these men that Hester now turned her face. She seemed to know that any sympathy she might hope for would have to come from the crowd rather than these men. As she lifted her eyes toward the balcony, the unhappy woman grew pale and trembled.

The voice which had called her attention was that of the reverend and famous John Wilson, the eldest clergyman of Boston, a great scholar, like most of his contemporaries in the profession, and withal a man of kind and genial spirit. This last attribute, however, had been less carefully developed than his intellectual gifts, and was, in truth, rather a matter of shame than self-congratulation with him. There he stood, with a border of grizzled locks beneath his skull-cap; while his gray eyes, accustomed to the shaded light of his study, were winking, like those of Hester's infant, in the unadulterated sunshine. He looked like the darkly engraved portraits which we see prefixed to old volumes of sermons; and had no more right than one of those portraits would have, to step forth, as he now did, and meddle with a question of human guilt, passion, and anguish.

"Hester Prynne," said the clergyman, "I have striven with my young brother here, under whose preaching of the word you have been privileged to sit,"—here Mr. Wilson laid his hand on the shoulder of a pale young man beside him,—"I have sought, I say, to persuade this godly youth, that he should deal with you, here in the face of Heaven, and before these wise and upright rulers, and in hearing of all the people, as touching the vileness and blackness of your sin. Knowing your natural temper better than I, he could the better judge what arguments to use, whether of tenderness or terror, such as might prevail over your hardness and obstinacy; insomuch that you should no longer hide the name of him who tempted you to this grievous fall. But he opposes to me, (with a young man's over-softness, albeit wise beyond his years,) that it were wronging the very nature of woman to force her to lay open her heart's secrets in such broad daylight, and in presence of so great a multitude. Truly, as I sought to convince him, the shame lay in the commission of the sin, and not in the showing of it forth. What say you to it, once again, brother Dimmesdale? Must it be thou or I that shall deal with this poor sinner's soul?"

There was a murmur among the dignified and reverend occupants of the balcony; and Governor Bellingham gave expression to its purport, speaking in an authoritative voice, although tempered with respect towards the youthful clergyman whom he addressed.

"Good Master Dimmesdale," said he, "the responsibility of this woman's soul lies greatly with you. It behooves you, therefore, to exhort her to repentance, and to confession, as a proof and consequence thereof."

NO FEAR

The voice that had called her name belonged to John Wilson, the oldest minister in Boston. He was a great scholar, like most ministers of his day, and a warm, kind man. But he had not cultivated his warmth as carefully as his mind: Indeed, he was more ashamed of that quality than proud of it. He stood there in the broad daylight with his white curls poking out underneath his skullcap. His gray eyes, accustomed to the dim light of his study, squinted like those of Hester's baby. He looked like one of the engraved portraits in an old book of sermons. And he had no more right than one of those portraits to step into and judge, as he did now, the world of human guilt, passion, and pain.

"Hester Prynne," said the clergyman, "I have been arguing with my young brother here, whose preaching of the Gospel you have been privileged to hear." Mr. Wilson laid his hand on the shoulder of a pale young man beside him. "I have tried, I say, to persuade this godly young man to confront you with the wickedness of your sin here in front of God, these rulers, and all the people. Knowing you better than I do, he could better judge what arguments to use against your stubborn refusal to reveal the man who tempted you into this state. But this young man refuses. He says, with a wise but too-soft heart, that it would be a wrong against your feminine nature to force you to reveal the secrets of your heart in the broad daylight and before this crowd. I have tried to convince him that the shame lays in your sin, not in your confession. So what do you say, brother Dimmesdale? Will it be you or me who deals with this poor sinner's soul?"

There was a murmur among the dignitaries on the balcony. In a respectful but authoritative voice, Governor Bellingham spoke aloud what everyone else had whispered:

"Good Master Dimmesdale," he said, "you are responsible for this woman's soul. You ought, therefore, to encourage her to repent and to confess as proof of her repentance."

The directness of this appeal drew the eyes of the whole crowd upon the Reverend Mr. Dimmesdale; a young clergyman, who had come from one of the great English universities, bringing all the learning of the age into our wild forest-land. His eloquence and religious fervor had already given the earnest of high eminence in his profession. He was a person of very striking aspect, with a white, lofty, and impending brow, large, brown, melancholy eyes, and a mouth which, unless when he forcibly compressed it, was apt to be tremulous, expressing both nervous sensibility and a vast power of self-restraint. Notwithstanding his high native gifts and scholar-like attainments, there was an air about this young minister,—an apprehensive, a startled, a half-frightened look,—as of a being who felt himself quite astray and at a loss in the pathway of human existence, and could only be at ease in some seclusion of his own. Therefore, so far as his duties would permit, he trode in the shadowy by-paths, and thus kept himself simple and child-like; coming forth, when occasion was, with a freshness, and fragrance, and dewy purity of thought, which, as many people said, affected them like the speech of an angel.

Such was the young man whom the Reverend Mr. Wilson and the Governor had introduced so openly to the public notice, bidding him speak, in the hearing of all men, to that mystery of a woman's soul, so sacred even in its pollution. The trying nature of his position drove the blood from his cheek, and made his lips tremulous.

"Speak to the woman, my brother," said Mr. Wilson. "It is of moment to her soul, and therefore, as the worshipful Governor says, momentous to thine own, in whose charge hers is. Exhort her to confess the truth!"

The Reverend Mr. Dimmesdale bent his head, in silent prayer, as it seemed, and then came forward.

"Hester Prynne," said he, leaning over the balcony, and looking down steadfastly into her eyes, "thou hearest what this good man says, and seest the accountability under which I labor. If thou feelest it to be for thy soul's peace, and that thy earthly punishment will thereby be made more effectual to salvation, I charge thee to speak out the name of thy fellow-sinner and fellow-sufferer! Be not silent

The directness of the governor's appeal focused all eyes in the crowd on the Reverend Mr. Dimmesdale. He was a young minister who had graduated from one of the great English universities and brought his learning to this undeveloped land. His eloquence and religious passion had already earned him great respect. He was a striking man, with a high, white forehead and sad brown eyes. His lips often trembled if he didn't press them together—a sign of both his nervous temperament and enormous self-restraint. Though he possessed impressive natural gifts and significant scholarly achievements, this young minister also had a startled, half-frightened look about him. It was as though he felt lost on the pathway of life and comfortable only in solitude. As often as he could, he wandered alone. In this way, he kept himself simple and childlike. When he did come forth to speak, his freshness and purity of thought led many people to compare him to an angel.

llingham: Former vernor of Massasetts who caused a minor scandal after marrying a man betrothed to his friend.

This was the young man whom the Reverend Mr. Wilson and Governor Bellingham had introduced so publicly and encouraged to address, in front of everyone, the mystery of a woman's soul, which was sacred even in sin. The difficult position in which he was placed drained the blood from his face and set his lips trembling.

"Speak to the woman, my brother," said Mr. Wilson. "It is essential to her soul and, therefore, as the honorable Governor says, essential to yours as well, since you are responsible for hers. Tell her to confess the truth!"

The Reverend Mr. Dimmesdale bowed his head in what appeared to be silent prayer and then stepped forward.

"Hester Prynne," he said, leaning over the balcony and looking into her eyes with a steady gaze, "you hear what this good man says and see the authority that compels me to speak. If you feel that speaking will comfort your soul and make your present punishment effective for your eternal salvation, then I charge you to speak out the name of your fellow sinner and fellow sufferer! Do

from any mistaken pity and tenderness for him; for, believe me, Hester, though he were to step down from a high place, and stand there beside thee, on thy pedestal of shame, yet better were it so, than to hide a guilty heart through life. What can thy silence do for him, except it tempt him,—yea, compel him, as it were—to add hypocrisy to sin? Heaven hath granted thee an open ignominy, that thereby thou mayest work out an open triumph over the evil within thee, and the sorrow without. Take heed how thou deniest to him— who, perchance, hath not the courage to grasp it for himself—the bitter, but wholesome, cup that is now presented to thy lips!"

The young pastor's voice was tremulously sweet, rich, deep, and broken. The feeling that it so evidently manifested, rather than the direct purport of the words, caused it to vibrate within all hearts, and brought the listeners into one accord of sympathy. Even the poor baby, at Hester's bosom, was affected by the same influence; for it directed its hitherto vacant gaze towards Mr. Dimmesdale, and held up its little arms, with a half-pleased, half-plaintive murmur. So powerful seemed the minister's appeal, that the people could not believe but that Hester Prynne would speak out the guilty name; or else that the guilty one himself, in whatever high or lowly place he stood, would be drawn forth by an inward and inevitable necessity, and compelled to ascend the scaffold.

Hester shook her head.

"Woman, transgress not beyond the limits of Heaven's mercy!" cried the Reverend Mr. Wilson, more harshly than before. "That little babe hath been gifted with a voice, to second and confirm the counsel which thou hast heard. Speak out the name! That, and thy repentance, may avail to take the scarlet letter off thy breast."

"Never!" replied Hester Prynne, looking, not at Mr. Wilson, but into the deep and troubled eyes of the younger clergyman. "It is too deeply branded. Ye cannot take it off. And would that I might endure his agony, as well as mine!"

"Speak, woman!" said another voice, coldly and sternly, proceeding from the crowd about the scaffold. "Speak; and give your child a father!"

"I will not speak!" answered Hester, turning pale as death, but responding to this voice, which she too surely recognized. "And my child must seek a heavenly Father; she shall never know an earthly one!"

NO FEAR

not be silent out of tenderness or pity for him. Believe me, Hester, even if he stepped down from a place of power to stand beside you on that platform, it would be better for him to do so than to hide a guilty heart for the rest of his life. What can your silence do for him, except tempt him—almost force him—to add hypocrisy to his sins? Heaven has granted you a public shame so that you can enjoy a public triumph over the evil within you. Beware of denying him the bitter but nourishing cup from which you now drink! He may not have the courage to grasp that cup himself."

The young pastor's voice trembled sweetly, deep and broken. The feeling that it so clearly expressed, more than any words it spoke, brought sympathy from the hearts of the audience. Even the baby at Hester's bosom was affected, for it began to gaze at Mr. Dimmesdale. It held up its arms and made a half-pleased, half-pleading sound. The minister's appeal was so powerful that all who heard felt sure that either Hester Prynne would be moved to speak the guilty man's name, or the guilty one himself—however powerful or lowly—would be compelled to join her on the platform.

Hester shook her head.

"Woman, do not test the limits of Heaven's mercy!" cried the Reverend Mr. Wilson, more harshly than before. "Your little baby, being granted a voice, agrees with the advice that you have heard. Reveal the name! That act, and your repentance, may be enough to remove the scarlet letter from you breast."

"Never," replied Hester Prynne, looking not at Mr. Wilson but into the deep and troubled eyes of the younger minister. "The scar is too deep. You cannot remove it. And if I could, I would endure his agony as well as my own!"

"Speak, woman!" said another voice, cold and stern, from the crowd. "Speak, and give your child a father!"

"I will not speak!" answered Hester, turning pale as death, but responding to this voice, which she recognized all too well. "My child must seek a heavenly father; she will never have an earthly one!"

"She will not speak!" murmured Mr. Dimmesdale, who, leaning over the balcony, with his hand upon his heart, had awaited the result of his appeal. He now drew back, with a long respiration. "Wondrous strength and generosity of a woman's heart! She will not speak!"

Discerning the impracticable state of the poor culprit's mind, the elder clergyman, who had carefully prepared himself for the occasion, addressed to the multitude a discourse on sin, in all its branches, but with continual reference to the ignominious letter. So forcibly did he dwell upon this symbol, for the hour or more during which his periods were rolling over the people's heads, that it assumed new terrors in their imagination, and seemed to derive its scarlet hue from the flames of the infernal pit. Hester Prynne, meanwhile, kept her place upon the pedestal of shame, with glazed eyes, and an air of weary indifference. She had borne, that morning, all that nature could endure; and as her temperament was not of the order that escapes from too intense suffering by a swoon, her spirit could only shelter itself beneath a stony crust of insensibility, while the faculties of animal life remained entire. In this state, the voice of the preacher thundered remorselessly, but unavailingly, upon her ears. The infant, during the latter portion of her ordeal, pierced the air with its wailings and screams; she strove to hush it, mechanically, but seemed scarcely to sympathize with its trouble. With the same hard demeanour, she was led back to prison, and vanished from the public gaze within its iron-clamped portal. It was whispered, by those who peered after her, that the scarlet letter threw a lurid gleam along the dark passage-way of the interior.

"She will not speak!" murmured Mr. Dimmesdale, who had been leaning over the balcony with his hand over his heart as he had waited to see how Hester would respond. Now he drew back with a deep breath. "The strength and generosity of a woman's heart! She will not speak!"

Mr. Wilson had prepared for this occasion. Realizing that Hester would not be moved, he gave the crowd a sermon on the many kinds of sin, though he always referred to the shameful letter. He emphasized this symbol with such force during his hour-long speech that it took on new terrors in the minds of the people. The letter seemed as red as hellfire. Meanwhile, Hester Prynne remained on the shameful platform, her eyes glazed over with weary indifference. She had endured all that she could that morning. Since she was not the type to faint, her soul could only shelter itself with the appearance of a hardened exterior. But Hester heard and saw everything. In this state, the voice of the preacher thundered into her ears without remorse, but also without effect. Toward the end of the sermon, the infant pierced the air with its cries. Hester tried to quiet it almost mechanically, but she seemed to barely sympathize with its pain. With the same frozen features, she was led back to prison and disappeared from public sight behind the iron-studded door. Those who watched her go in whispered that the scarlet letter cast a red glow along the dark prison passageway.

Chapter 4: The Interview

After her return to the prison, Hester Prynne was found to be in a state of nervous excitement that demanded constant watchfulness, lest she should perpetrate violence on herself, or do some half-frenzied mischief to the poor babe. As night approached, it proving impossible to quell her insubordination by rebuke or threats of punishment, Master Brackett, the jailer, thought fit to introduce a physician. He described him as a man of skill in all Christian modes of physical science, and likewise familiar with whatever the savage people could teach, in respect to medicinal herbs and roots that grew in the forest. To say the truth, there was much need of professional assistance, not merely for Hester herself, but still more urgently for the child; who, drawing its sustenance from the maternal bosom, seemed to have drank in with it all the turmoil, the anguish, and despair, which pervaded the mother's system. It now writhed in convulsions of pain, and was a forcible type, in its little frame, of the moral agony which Hester Prynne had borne throughout the day.

Closely following the jailer into the dismal apartment, appeared that individual, of singular aspect, whose presence in the crowd had been of such deep interest to the wearer of the scarlet letter. He was lodged in the prison, not as suspected of any offence, but as the most convenient and suitable mode of disposing of him, until the magistrates should have conferred with the Indian sagamores respecting his ransom. His name was announced as Roger Chillingworth. The jailer, after ushering him into the room, remained a moment, marvelling at the comparative quiet that followed his entrance; for Hester Prynne had immediately become as still as death, although the child continued to moan.

"Prithee, friend, leave me alone with my patient," said the practitioner. "Trust me, good jailer, you shall briefly have peace in your house; and, I promise you, Mistress Prynne shall hereafter be more amenable to just authority than you may have found her heretofore."

"Nay, if your worship can accomplish that," answered Master Brackett, "I shall own you for a man of skill indeed! Verily, the woman hath been like a possessed one; and there lacks little, that I should take in hand to drive Satan out of her with stripes."

Chapter 4: The Interview

Hester Prynne was extremely agitated upon returning to the prison. She was kept under constant watch for fear that in her emotional state she might injure herself or her child. But, despite scolding and threats of punishment, she couldn't be calmed. As night approached, Master Brackett, the jailer, called a doctor—a man trained in both Western medicine and the roots and herbs of the Indians. In truth, the doctor was desperately needed, but more for the baby than for Hester. It seemed as though the child had absorbed Hester's emotions—her pain and despair—when she drank in her milk. The baby writhed in pain, a living symbol of the moral agony Hester Prynne had suffered.

The jailer entered the prison cell. Following closely behind him was the oddly dressed stranger from the crowd, who had been of such interest to Hester. He was staying in the prison, not because he was suspected of any crime, but only until the magistrates and the Indian chiefs could agree on the price of his ransom. His name was announced as Roger Chillingworth. After leading the man into the cell, the jailer marveled at how quiet the prison had become. Though the baby was still crying, Hester Prynne was as still as death.

"Please, friend, leave me alone with my patient," said the stranger. "Trust me, my good jailer—there will be peace here shortly. And I promise you that Mistress Prynne will be more obedient from now on."

"Well, sir, if you can accomplish that," replied Master Brackett, "I will tell everyone of your medical skill! The woman's been acting like she's possessed, and I'm about ready to whip the Devil out of her."

The stranger had entered the room with the characteristic quietude of the profession to which he announced himself as belonging. Nor did his demeanour change, when the withdrawal of the prison-keeper left him face to face with the woman, whose absorbed notice of him, in the crowd, had intimated so close a relation between himself and her. His first care was given to the child; whose cries, indeed, as she lay writhing on the trundle-bed, made it of peremptory necessity to postpone all other business to the task of soothing her. He examined the infant carefully, and then proceeded to unclasp a leathern case, which he took from beneath his dress. It appeared to contain certain medical preparations, one of which he mingled with a cup of water.

"My old studies in alchemy," observed he, "and my sojourn, for above a year past, among a people well versed in the kindly properties of simples, have made a better physician of me than many that claim the medical degree. Here, woman! The child is yours,—she is none of mine,—neither will she recognize my voice or aspect as a father's. Administer this draught, therefore, with thine own hand."

Hester repelled the offered medicine, at the same time gazing with strongly marked apprehension into his face.

"Wouldst thou avenge thyself on the innocent babe?" whispered she.

"Foolish woman!" responded the physician, half-coldly, half-soothingly. "What should ail me to harm this misbegotten and miserable babe? The medicine is potent for good; and were it my child,—yea, mine own, as well as thine!—I could do no better for it."

As she still hesitated, being, in fact, in no reasonable state of mind, he took the infant in his arms, and himself administered the draught. It soon proved its efficacy, and redeemed the leech's pledge. The moans of the little patient subsided; its convulsive tossings gradually ceased; and in a few moments, as is the custom of young children after relief from pain, it sank into a profound and dewy slumber. The physician, as he had a fair right to be termed, next bestowed his attention on the mother. With calm and intent scrutiny, he felt her pulse, looked into her eyes,—a gaze that made her heart shrink and shudder, because so familiar, and yet so strange and cold,—and, finally, satisfied with his investigation, proceeded

NO FEAR

The stranger had entered the room with the characteristic stillness of the doctor he claimed to be. His expression did not change
when the jailer left him alone with the woman whose earlier preoc-
cupation with him suggested a close connection. The child cried out
for attention, so the stranger first turned to the task of soothing her.
He examined her carefully before taking a leather case from underneath his clothes. The case seemed to contain various medicines,
one of which he mixed into a cup of water.

"My studies in alchemy," he said, "and my travels for more than a
year among the Indians, who know the medical properties of many
plants, have made me a better doctor than many who went to school
for it. Here, woman—the child is yours, not mine. She won't recognize my voice or my face. Give her this potion yourself."

Hester, staring with fear into his face, refused to take the
medicine.

"Would you take your revenge on this innocent child?" she
whispered.

"You foolish woman!" the doctor responded, half coldly and
half soothingly. "Why would I want to hurt this miserable, ill-con-
ceived child? This medicine will do her much good. Were it my own
child—my own, and yours as well—I could do no better for it."

Hester was still worked up from the day's events. When she hesitated again, he took the infant in his arms and administered the
medicine himself. It worked quickly, proving the doctor's good
word. The baby's moans subsided, it stopped writhing, and before
long it was fast asleep. The doctor—as he had a right to be called—
then turned his attention to the mother. With a calm intensity, he
felt her pulse and looked into her eyes. His gaze made her shrink
away: It was so familiar, yet so cold and distant. Finally, satisfied
with his investigation, he mixed another potion.

to mingle another draught.

"I know not Lethe nor Nepenthe," remarked he; "but I have learned many new secrets in the wilderness, and here is one of them,—a recipe that an Indian taught me, in requital of some lessons of my own, that were as old as Paracelsus. Drink it! It may be less soothing than a sinless conscience. That I cannot give thee. But it will calm the swell and heaving of thy passion, like oil thrown on the waves of a tempestuous sea."

He presented the cup to Hester, who received it with a slow, earnest look into his face; not precisely a look of fear, yet full of doubt and questioning, as to what his purposes might be. She looked also at her slumbering child.

"I have thought of death," said she,—"have wished for it,—would even have prayed for it, were it fit that such as I should pray for any thing. Yet, if death be in this cup, I bid thee think again, ere thou beholdest me quaff it. See! It is even now at my lips."

"Drink, then," replied he, still with the same cold composure. "Dost thou know me so little, Hester Prynne? Are my purposes wont to be so shallow? Even if I imagine a scheme of vengeance, what could I do better for my object than to let thee live,—than to give thee medicines against all harm and peril of life,—so that this burning shame may still blaze upon thy bosom?"—As he spoke, he laid his long forefinger on the scarlet letter, which forthwith seemed to scorch into Hester's breast, as if it had been red-hot. He noticed her involuntary gesture, and smiled.—"Live, therefore, and bear about thy doom with thee, in the eyes of men and women,—in the eyes of him whom thou didst call thy husband,—in the eyes of yonder child! And, that thou mayest live, take off this draught."

Without further expostulation or delay, Hester Prynne drained the cup, and, at the motion of the man of skill, seated herself on the bed where the child was sleeping; while he drew the only chair which the room afforded, and took his own seat beside her. She could not but tremble at these preparations; for she felt that—having now done all that humanity, or principle, or, if so it were, a refined cruelty, impelled him to do, for the relief of physical suffering—he was next to treat with her as the man whom she had most deeply and irreparably injured.

NO FEAR

Lethe: River in Greek mythology, whose waters bring forgetfulness.

Nepenthe: Drug, perhaps made of opium, that eases sorrow.

Paraclesus: Swiss physician and philosopher.

"I don't know about Lethe or Nepenthe," he said, "but I have learned many new secrets in the woods. This is one of them. An Indian taught me the recipe, in return for teaching him some medicines that were as old as Paraclesus. Drink it! It may be less soothing than a sinless conscience, but I can't give you that. But it will calm the storm of your passion, like oil thrown on the waves of a stormy sea."

He gave the cup to Hester. As she took it, she gave his face a slow and serious look. She wasn't exactly afraid, but she was full of doubt and confusion. She looked over to her sleeping child.

"I have thought about death," she said, "wished for it. I would even have prayed for it if I were worthy to pray. Yet if this cup is full of death, think twice before you watch me drink it. Look—the cup is at my lips!"

"So drink it," he replied with the same cold expression. "Do you know me so poorly, Hester Prynne? Are my aims that petty? Even if I had dreamed up a scheme for revenge, how I could I do better than to let you live, to give you every good medicine I know, so that this burning shame could remain on your bosom?" As he spoke, he placed his long forefinger on the scarlet letter, which seemed to burn Hester's breast as though it had been red hot. He saw her flinch with pain, and he smiled. "Live, and carry your punishment with you: In the eyes of men and women, in the eyes of the man you called your husband, and in the eyes of that child! Drink this potion and live."

Hester Prynne quickly drank the cup. At the doctor's beckoning she sat on the bed, where the child was sleeping. He took the only chair in the room and pulled it beside her. She trembled as he did so. Hester felt that—being done with his obligations to humanity, or principle, or perhaps only a refined cruelty—he was now going to treat her as a deeply wounded husband would.

"Hester," said he, "I ask not wherefore, nor how, thou hast fallen into the pit, or say rather, thou hast ascended to the pedestal of infamy, on which I found thee. The reason is not far to seek. It was my folly, and thy weakness. I,—a man of thought,—the book-worm of great libraries,—a man already in decay, having given my best years to feed the hungry dream of knowledge,—what had I to do with youth and beauty like thine own! Misshapen from my birth-hour, how could I delude myself with the idea that intellectual gifts might veil physical deformity in a young girl's fantasy! Men call me wise. If sages were ever wise in their own behoof, I might have fore-seen all this. I might have known that, as I came out of the vast and dismal forest, and entered this settlement of Christian men, the very first object to meet my eyes would be thyself, Hester Prynne, standing up, a statue of ignominy, before the people. Nay, from the moment when we came down the old church-steps together, a mar-ried pair, I might have beheld the bale-fire of that scarlet letter blaz-ing at the end of our path!"

"Thou knowest," said Hester,—for, depressed as she was, she could not endure this last quiet stab at the token of her shame,—"thou know-est that I was frank with thee. I felt no love, nor feigned any."

"True!" replied he. "It was my folly! I have said it. But, up to that epoch of my life, I had lived in vain. The world had been so cheer-less! My heart was a habitation large enough for many guests, but lonely and chill, and without a household fire. I longed to kindle one! It seemed not so wild a dream,—old as I was, and sombre as I was, and misshapen as I was,—that the simple bliss, which is scat-tered far and wide, for all mankind to gather up, might yet be mine. And so, Hester, I drew thee into my heart, into its innermost cham-ber, and sought to warm thee by the warmth which thy presence made there!"

"I have greatly wronged thee," murmured Hester.

"We have wronged each other," answered he. "Mine was the first wrong, when I betrayed thy budding youth into a false and unnatu-ral relation with my decay. Therefore, as a man who has not thought and philosophized in vain, I seek no vengeance, plot no evil against thee. Between thee and me, the scale hangs fairly balanced. But, Hester, the man lives who has wronged us both! Who is he?"

NO FEAR

"Hester," he said, "I don't ask why or how you have fallen into this pit—no!—ascended this pedestal of infamy on which I have found you. The reason is obvious. It was my foolishness and your weakness. I am a learned man; I have devoured many libraries. I gave my best years to the pursuit of knowledge, and now I am falling apart. What business did I have with youth and beauty such as yours? I was born defective—how could I fool myself into thinking that my intellectual gifts might convince a young girl to overlook my physical deformity? People say that I am wise. If that wisdom had extended to my own life, I might have foreseen all of this. I might have known that, as I came out of the dark forest and into this Christian settlement, I would lay my eyes upon you, Hester Prynne, standing up like a statue of shame before the people. Yes, from the moment of our marriage, I might have glimpsed the scarlet letter burning at the end of our road!"

"You know," said Hester, who even as depressed as she was could not take that last little insult, "you know that I was honest with you. I felt no love for you and did not pretend to feel any."

"True," he replied. "It was my foolishness! But I had lived in vain until the moment we met. The world had been so gloomy! My heart was a house large enough for many guests, but lonely and cold, with no home fire burning. I longed to light one! It didn't seem like a crazy dream—even as old and serious and ill-formed as I was—that simple human joy could be mine too. And so, Hester, I drew you into my heart, into its innermost room, and tried to warm you with the warmth that you gave me."

"I have greatly wronged you," mumbled Hester.

"We have wronged each other," he answered. "My wrong was the first: I tricked your youth and beauty into an unnatural marriage with my decrepitude. I haven't read all that philosophy for nothing: I learned enough to seek no revenge and plot no evil against you. You and I are even. But, Hester, there is a man who has wronged us both! Who is he?"

"Ask me not!" replied Hester Prynne, looking firmly into his face. "That thou shalt never know!"

"Never, sayest thou?" rejoined he, with a smile of dark and self-relying intelligence. "Never know him! Believe me, Hester, there are few things,—whether in the outward world, or, to a certain depth, in the invisible sphere of thought,—few things hidden from the man, who devotes himself earnestly and unreservedly to the solution of a mystery. Thou mayest cover up thy secret from the prying multitude. Thou mayest conceal it, too, from the ministers and magistrates, even as thou didst this day, when they sought to wrench the name out of thy heart, and give thee a partner on thy pedestal. But, as for me, I come to the inquest with other senses than they possess. I shall seek this man, as I have sought truth in books; as I have sought gold in alchemy. There is a sympathy that will make me conscious of him. I shall see him tremble. I shall feel myself shudder, suddenly and unawares. Sooner or later, he must needs be mine!"

The eyes of the wrinkled scholar glowed so intensely upon her, that Hester Prynne clasped her hands over her heart, dreading lest he should read the secret there at once.

"Thou wilt not reveal his name? Not the less he is mine," resumed he, with a look of confidence, as if destiny were at one with him, "He bears no letter of infamy wrought into his garment, as thou dost; but I shall read it on his heart. Yet fear not for him! Think not that I shall interfere with Heaven's own method of retribution, or, to my own loss, betray him to the gripe of human law. Neither do thou imagine that I shall contrive aught against his life, no, nor against his fame; if, as I judge, he be a man of fair repute. Let him live! Let him hide himself in outward honor, if he may! Not the less he shall be mine!"

"Thy acts are like mercy," said Hester, bewildered and appalled. "But thy words interpret thee as a terror!"

"One thing, thou that wast my wife, I would enjoin upon thee," continued the scholar. "Thou hast kept the secret of thy paramour. Keep, likewise, mine! There are none in this land that know me. Breathe not, to any human soul, that thou didst ever call me husband! Here, on this wild outskirt of the earth, I shall pitch my tent; for, elsewhere a wanderer, and isolated from human interests, I find here a woman, a man, a child, amongst whom and myself there exist the closest ligaments. No matter whether of love or hate; no

NO FEAR

"Do not ask!" replied Hester Prynne, looking him firmly in the face. "You will never know!"

"Never, you say?" he retorted, with a dark and knowing smile. "Never know him! Believe me, Hester, few things remain hidden from a man who devotes himself to solving their mystery. You can keep your secret from the prying masses. You can conceal it from the ministers and magistrates, as you did today when they tried to wrench the name from your heart. But I come to this investigation with skills they lack. I will seek this man as I have sought truth in books, as I have sought gold in alchemy. We share a connection that will reveal this man to me. When he trembles, I will feel it. Sooner or later, he will be mine."

The eyes of the wrinkled scholar glowed so intensely that Hester Prynne put her hand over her heart to keep him from reading the secret hidden there.

"You won't reveal his name? He is still mine," he continued, with a look of confidence, as though destiny were on his side. "He wears no letter of shame on his clothes, as you do, but I will read the shame in his heart. But do not fear for him! Don't think that I will interfere with Heaven's own revenge or give him up to the magistrates. I will not plot to injure him or ruin his reputation. Let him live! Let him hide himself in worldly honor, if he can! He will still be mine!"

"Your actions seem like mercy," said Hester, confused and pale, "but your words are terrifying!"

"One thing, woman who was my wife, I would demand from you," continued the scholar. "You have kept your lover's secret. Keep mine, too! No one knows me here. Don't tell a soul that you ever called me husband! I will pitch my tent here, at the edge of civilization. I have been a wanderer, cut off from mankind, but here there is a woman, a man, and a child to whom I am closely bound. Whether it's through love or hate, right or wrong. You and yours, Hester Prynne, belong to me. My home is where you are and where he is. But do not betray me!"

matter whether of right or wrong! Thou and thine, Hester Prynne, belong to me. My home is where thou art, and where he is. But betray me not!"

"Wherefore dost thou desire it?" inquired Hester, shrinking, she hardly knew why, from this secret bond. "Why not announce thyself openly, and cast me off at once?"

"It may be," he replied, "because I will not encounter the dishonor that besmirches the husband of a faithless woman. It may be for other reasons. Enough, it is my purpose to live and die unknown. Let, therefore, thy husband be to the world as one already dead, and of whom no tidings shall ever come. Recognize me not, by word, by sign, by look! Breathe not the secret, above all, to the man thou wottest of. Shouldst thou fail me in this, beware! His fame, his position, his life, will be in my hands. Beware!"

"I will keep thy secret, as I have his," said Hester.

"Swear it!" rejoined he.

And she took the oath.

"And now, Mistress Prynne," said old Roger Chillingworth, as he was hereafter to be named, "I leave thee alone; alone with thy infant, and the scarlet letter! How is it, Hester? Doth thy sentence bind thee to wear the token in thy sleep? Art thou not afraid of nightmares and hideous dreams?"

"Why dost thou smile so at me?" inquired Hester, troubled at the expression of his eyes. "Art thou like the Black Man that haunts the forest round about us? Hast thou enticed me into a bond that will prove the ruin of my soul?"

"Not thy soul," he answered, with another smile. "No, not thine!"

"Why do you want this?" asked Hester, shrinking from this secret bond, though she hardly knew why. "Why not reveal yourself to everyone and denounce me openly?"

"Perhaps," he replied, "because I want to avoid the dishonor that comes to the husband of a cheating woman. Or perhaps I have other reasons. It should be enough for you that I wish to live and die unknown. So tell the world that your husband is already dead, and never to be heard from again. Give no hint that you recognize me! Most of all, do not tell your man about me! If you fail me in this, beware! His reputation, his career, and his life will be in my hands. Beware!"

"I will keep your secret, as I have kept his," said Hester.

"Swear to it!" he replied.

And she swore the oath.

"And now, Mistress Prynne," said old Roger Chillingworth, as he would be known from then on, "I leave you alone with your infant and your scarlet letter! What about it, Hester? Does your sentence require you to wear it while you sleep? Aren't you afraid of nightmares?"

"Why do you smile at me like that?" asked Hester, troubled by the look in his eyes. "Are you like the Black Man that haunts the forest? Have you lured me into a promise that will cost me my soul?"

Black Man: The Devil.

"Not your soul," he answered, with another smile. "Oh, no, not yours."

Chapter 5: Hester at Her Needle

Hester Prynne's term of confinement was now at an end. Her prison-door was thrown open, and she came forth into the sunshine, which, falling on all alike, seemed, to her sick and morbid heart, as if meant for no other purpose than to reveal the scarlet letter on her breast. Perhaps there was a more real torture in her first unattended footsteps from the threshold of the prison, than even in the procession and spectacle that have been described, where she was made the common infamy, at which all mankind was summoned to point its finger. Then, she was supported by an unnatural tension of the nerves, and by all the combative energy of her character, which enabled her to convert the scene into a kind of lurid triumph. It was, moreover, a separate and insulated event, to occur but once in her lifetime, and to meet which, therefore, reckless of economy, she might call up the vital strength that would have sufficed for many quiet years. The very law that condemned her—a giant of stern features, but with vigor to support, as well as to annihilate, in his iron arm—had held her up, through the terrible ordeal of her ignominy. But now, with this unattended walk from her prison-door, began the daily custom, and she must either sustain and carry it forward by the ordinary resources of her nature, or sink beneath it. She could no longer borrow from the future, to help her through the present grief. To-morrow would bring its own trial with it; so would the next day, and so would the next; each its own trial, and yet the very same that was now so unutterably grievous to be borne. The days of the far-off future would toil onward, still with the same burden for her to take up, and bear along with her, but never to fling down; for the accumulating days, and added years, would pile up their misery upon the heap of shame. Throughout them all, giving up her individuality, she would become the general symbol at which the preacher and moralist might point, and in which they might vivify and embody their images of woman's frailty and sinful passion. Thus the young and pure would be taught to look at her, with the scarlet letter flaming on her breast,—at her, the child of honorable parents,—at her, the mother of a babe, that would hereafter be a woman,—at her, who had once been innocent,—as the figure, the body, the reality of sin. And over her grave, the infamy that she must carry thither would be her only monument.

Chapter 5: Hester at Her Needle

Hester Prynne's prison sentence was over. The prison door was thrown open, and she walked out into the sunshine. Although the light fell equally on everyone, to Hester it seemed designed to show off the scarlet letter on her breast. Those first steps out of the prison may have been a greater torture than the elaborate public humiliation described before, when the entire town gathered to point its finger at her. At least then, her concentration and fierce combativeness allowed her to transform the scene into a sort of grotesque victory. And that was just a one-time event—the kind that happens only once in a lifetime—so she could expend several years' worth of energy to endure it. The law that condemned her was like an iron-fisted giant, and it had the strength to either support or destroy her. It had held her up throughout that terrible ordeal. But now, with this lonely walk from the prison door, her new reality began. This would be her everyday life, and she could use only everyday resources to endure it, or else she would be crushed by it. Tomorrow would bring its own struggle, and the next day, and the day after that—every day its own struggle, just like the one that was so unbearable today. The days in the distant future would arrive with the same burden for her to bear and to never put down. The accumulating days and years would pile up their misery upon the heap of shame. Through them all, she would be a symbol for the preacher and the moralist to point at: the symbol of feminine frailty and lust. The young and pure would be taught to look at Hester and the scarlet letter burning on her breast. She was the child of good parents, the mother of a baby that would grow to womanhood; she had once been innocent herself. But now she would become the embodiment of sin, and her infamy would be the only monument over her grave.

It may seem marvellous, that, with the world before her,—kept by no restrictive clause of her condemnation within the limits of the Puritan settlement, so remote and so obscure,—free to return to her birthplace, or to any other European land, and there hide her character and identity under a new exterior, as completely as if emerging into another state of being,—and having also the passes of the dark, inscrutable forest open to her, where the wildness of her nature might assimilate itself with a people whose customs and life were alien from the law that had condemned her,—it may seem marvellous, that this woman should still call that place her home, where, and where only, she must needs be the type of shame. But there is a fatality, a feeling so irresistible and inevitable that it has the force of doom, which almost invariably compels human beings to linger around and haunt, ghost-like, the spot where some great and marked event has given the color to their lifetime; and still the more irresistibly, the darker the tinge that saddens it. Her sin, her igno-miny, were the roots which she had struck into the soil. It was as if a new birth, with stronger assimilations than the first, had converted the forest-land, still so uncongenial to every other pilgrim and wan-derer, into Hester Prynne's wild and dreary, but life-long home. All other scenes of earth—even that village of rural England, where happy infancy and stainless maidenhood seemed yet to be in her mother's keeping, like garments put off long ago—were foreign to her, in comparison. The chain that bound her here was of iron links, and galling to her inmost soul, but never could be broken.

It might be, too,—doubtless it was so, although she hid the secret from herself, and grew pale whenever it struggled out of her heart, like a serpent from its hole,—it might be that another feeling kept her within the scene and pathway that had been so fatal. There dwelt, there trode the feet of one with whom she deemed herself connected in a union, that, unrecognized on earth, would bring them together before the bar of final judgment, and make that their marriage-altar, for a joint futurity of endless retribution. Over and over again, the tempter of souls had thrust this idea upon Hester's contemplation, and laughed at the passionate and desperate joy with which she seized, and then strove to cast it from her. She barely looked the idea in the face, and hastened to bar it in its dungeon. What she compelled herself to believe,—what, finally, she reasoned

NO FEAR

It may seem unbelievable that, with the whole world open to her, this woman would remain in the one and only place where she would face this shame. The conditions of her sentence didn't force her to stay in that remote and obscure Puritan settlement. She was free to return to her birthplace—or anywhere else in Europe—where she could hide under a new identify, as though she had become a new person. Or she could have simply fled to the forest, where her wild nature would be a good fit among Indians unfamiliar with the laws that had condemned her. But an irresistible fatalism exists that forces people to haunt the place where some dramatic event shaped their lives. And the sadder the event, the greater the bond. Hester's sin and shame rooted her in that soil. It was as if the birth of her child had turned the harsh wilderness of New England into her life-long home. Every other place on Earth—even the English village where she had been a happy child and a sinless young woman—was now foreign to her. The chain that bound her to this place was made of iron, and though it troubled her soul, it could not be broken.

Perhaps there was also another feeling that kept her in this place that was so tragic for her. This had to be true, though she hid the secret from herself and grew pale whenever it slithered, like a snake, out of her heart. A man lived there who she felt was joined with her in a union that, though unrecognized on earth, would bring them together on their last day. The place of final judgment would be their marriage altar, binding them in eternity. Over and over, the Devil had suggested this idea to Hester and then laughed at the desperate, passionate joy with which she grasped at it, then tried to cast it off. She barely acknowledged the thought before quickly locking it away. What she forced herself to believe—the reason why she chose to stay in New England—was based half in truth and half in self-delusion. This place, she told herself, had been the scene of her

upon, as her motive for continuing a resident of New England,—was half a truth, and half a self-delusion. Here, she said to herself, had been the scene of her guilt, and here should be the scene of her earthly punishment; and so, perchance, the torture of her daily shame would at length purge her soul, and work out another purity than that which she had lost; more saint-like, because the result of martyrdom.

Hester Prynne, therefore, did not flee. On the outskirts of the town, within the verge of the peninsula, but not in close vicinity to any other habitation, there was a small thatched cottage. It had been built by an earlier settler, and abandoned, because the soil about it was too sterile for cultivation, while its comparative remoteness put it out of the sphere of that social activity which already marked the habits of the emigrants. It stood on the shore, looking across a basin of the sea at the forest-covered hills, towards the west. A clump of scrubby trees, such as alone grew on the peninsula, did not so much conceal the cottage from view, as seem to denote that here was some object which would fain have been, or at least ought to be, concealed. In this little, lonesome dwelling, with some slender means that she possessed, and by the license of the magistrates, who still kept an inquisitorial watch over her, Hester established herself, with her infant child. A mystic shadow of suspicion immediately attached itself to the spot. Children, too young to comprehend wherefore this woman should be shut out from the sphere of human charities, would creep nigh enough to behold her plying her needle at the cottage-window, or standing in the door-way, or laboring in her little garden, or coming forth along the pathway that led townward; and, discerning the scarlet letter on her breast, would scamper off, with a strange, contagious fear.

Lonely as was Hester's situation, and without a friend on earth who dared to show himself, she, however, incurred no risk of want. She possessed an art that sufficed, even in a land that afforded comparatively little scope for its exercise, to supply food for her thriving infant and herself. It was the art—then, as now, almost the only one within a woman's grasp—of needle-work. She bore on her breast, in the curiously embroidered letter, a specimen of her delicate and imaginative skill, of which the dames of a court might gladly have availed themselves, to add the richer and more spiritual adornment

guilt, so it should be the scene of her punishment. Maybe the torture of her daily shame would finally cleanse her soul and make her pure again. This purity would be different than the one she had lost: more saint-like because she had been martyred.

So Hester Prynne did not leave. On the outskirts of town, far from other houses, sat a small cottage. It had been built by an earlier settler but was abandoned because the surrounding soil was too sterile for planting and it was too remote. It stood on the shore, looking across the water at the forest-covered hills to the west. A clump of scrubby trees did not so much conceal the cottage as suggest that it was meant to be hidden. The magistrates granted Hester a license—though they kept close watch on her—and so she took what money she had and settled with her infant child in this lonesome little home. A shadow of mystery and suspicion immediately descended on the cottage. Children would creep close enough to watch Hester sewing, or standing in the doorway, or working in her little garden, or walking along the path to town. Though they were too young to understand why this woman had been shunned, they would run off with a strange fear when they saw the scarlet letter on her breast.

Though Hester was lonely, without a friend on Earth who dared visit her, she was never in danger of going hungry. She possessed a skill that allowed her to feed her growing baby and herself, though there was less demand in New England for her work than there might have been in her homeland. Her profession was—and still is—almost the only art available to women: needlework. The intricately embroidered letter that Hester wore on her breast was an example of her delicate and imaginative skill. Ladies at court would have gladly added such a testament of human creativity to their

of human ingenuity to their fabrics of silk and gold. Here, indeed, in the sable simplicity that generally characterized the Puritanic modes of dress, there might be an infrequent call for the finer productions of her handiwork. Yet the taste of the age, demanding whatever was elaborate in compositions of this kind, did not fail to extend its influence over our stern progenitors, who had cast behind them so many fashions which it might seem harder to dispense with. Public ceremonies, such as ordinations, the installation of magistrates, and all that could give majesty to the forms in which a new government manifested itself to the people, were, as a matter of policy, marked by a stately and well-conducted ceremonial, and a sombre, but yet a studied magnificence. Deep ruffs, painfully wrought bands, and gorgeously embroidered gloves, were all deemed necessary to the official state of men assuming the reins of power; and were readily allowed to individuals dignified by rank or wealth, even while sumptuary laws forbade these and similar extravagances to the plebeian order. In the array of funerals, too,—whether for the apparel of the dead body, or to typify, by manifold emblematic devices of sable cloth and snowy lawn, the sorrow of the survivors,—there was a frequent and characteristic demand for such labor as Hester Prynne could supply. Baby-linen—for babies then wore robes of state—afforded still another possibility of toil and emolument.

By degrees, nor very slowly, her handiwork became what would now be termed the fashion. Whether from commiseration for a woman of so miserable a destiny; or from the morbid curiosity that gives a fictitious value even to common or worthless things; or by whatever other intangible circumstance was then, as now, sufficient to bestow, on some persons, what others might seek in vain; or because Hester really filled a gap which must otherwise have remained vacant; it is certain that she had ready and fairly requited employment for as many hours as she saw fit to occupy with her needle. Vanity, it may be, chose to mortify itself, by putting on, for ceremonials of pomp and state, the garments that had been wrought by her sinful hands. Her needle-work was seen on the ruff of the Governor; military men wore it on their scarfs, and the minister on his band; it decked the baby's little cap; it was shut up, to be mildewed and moulder away, in the coffins of the dead. But it is not recorded that, in a single instance, her skill was called in aid to

gold and silver garments. The drab simplicity that often character-ized Puritan clothing might have reduced the demand for such fine handiwork, but even here the taste of the age produced a desire for elaborate decoration on some occasions. Our Puritan ancestors, who had done away with more essential luxuries, had trouble resisting. Public ceremonies, such as the ordination of ministers or the instal-lation of magistrates, were customarily characterized by a serious yet deliberate magnificence. Ruffled collars, delicately made armbands, and gorgeously embroidered gloves were viewed as necessary acces-sories when men assumed positions of power. These luxuries were permitted to those with status or wealth, even though strict laws kept such extravagances from lesser folk. At funerals, too, there was great demand for work of Hester Prynne's sort. The dead body had to be dressed, and the sorrow of the mourners had to be demon-strated through emblems of black cloth and white embroidery. Baby clothes—since babies were dressed like royalty back then—offered another opportunity for Hester to ply her trade.

By degrees, Hester's handiwork quickly became fashionable. Perhaps people felt sorry for her, or enjoyed the morbid curiosity that her work inspired. Or perhaps they patronized her for some other reason entirely. Perhaps Hester really did fill a need in the marketplace. Maybe the vain chose to degrade themselves by wear-ing garments made by sinful hands on those occasions when they enjoyed the greatest recognition. Whatever the reason, she had well-paying work for as many hours as she cared to labor. Hester's nee-dlework was seen on the collar of the Governor; military men wore it on their sashes; the minister on his armband. It decorated babies' caps and was buried with the dead. But there is no record of Hester ever making a white veil to cover the pure blushes of a bride. This exception indicated the relentless condemnation society reserved for her sin.

embroider the white veil which was to cover the pure blushes of a bride. The exception indicated the ever relentless vigor with which society frowned upon her sin.

Hester sought not to acquire any thing beyond a subsistence, of the plainest and most ascetic description, for herself, and a simple abundance for her child. Her own dress was of the coarsest materials and the most sombre hue; with only that one ornament,—the scarlet letter,—which it was her doom to wear. The child's attire, on the other hand, was distinguished by a fanciful, or, we might rather say, a fantastic ingenuity, which served, indeed, to heighten the airy charm that early began to develop itself in the little girl, but which appeared to have also a deeper meaning. We may speak further of it hereafter. Except for that small expenditure in the decoration of her infant, Hester bestowed all her superfluous means in charity, on wretches less miserable than herself, and who not unfrequently insulted the hand that fed them. Much of the time, which she might readily have applied to the better efforts of her art, she employed in making coarse garments for the poor. It is probable that there was an idea of penance in this mode of occupation, and that she offered up a real sacrifice of enjoyment, in devoting so many hours to such rude handiwork. She had in her nature a rich, voluptuous, Oriental characteristic,—a taste for the gorgeously beautiful, which, save in the exquisite productions of her needle, found nothing else, in all the possibilities of her life, to exercise itself upon. Women derive a pleasure, incomprehensible to the other sex, from the delicate toil of the needle. To Hester Prynne it might have been a mode of expressing, and therefore soothing, the passion of her life. Like all other joys, she rejected it as sin. This morbid meddling of conscience with an immaterial matter betokened, it is to be feared, no genuine and stedfast penitence, but something doubtful, something that might be deeply wrong, beneath.

In this manner, Hester Prynne came to have a part to perform in the world. With her native energy of character, and rare capacity, it could not entirely cast her off, although it had set a mark upon her, more intolerable to a woman's heart than that which branded the brow of Cain. In all her intercourse with society, however, there was nothing that made her feel as if she belonged to it. Every gesture, every word, and even the silence of those with whom she came in

NO FEAR

Hester never sought to earn anything beyond subsistence for herself and a simple abundance for her child. Her own clothing was made of rough materials in somber colors, with only the one decoration—the scarlet letter—which she was doomed to wear. The child's clothing, on the other hand, was distinguished by a fantastic ingenuity. Her whimsical dress heightened the lively charm the young girl developed early on, but it appeared to have a deeper meaning too. I'll tell you more about that later. Aside from the small expense used to dress her child, Hester gave all of her disposable income to charity. She gave to wretches who were happier than she was and who often insulted the hand that fed them. She spent a great deal of time making crude garments for the poor, though she could have easily spent it practicing and perfecting her art. It's likely that Hester viewed this dull, unfulfilling of work as a sort of penance, sacrificing hours that could otherwise be spent in enjoyment. She had a taste for the rich and elaborate, the gorgeously beautiful, which she could only satisfy in her exquisite needlework. Women derive a pleasure, unimaginable to men, from the delicate work of their needles. To Hester Prynne it might have been a way of expressing, and therefore of calming, the passions of her life. But like all other joys, she rejected it as sin. Rather than demonstrating true repentance, this cheerless blending of morality with insignificant matters, I'm afraid, exposed something deeply wrong with her conscience.

**: In the Bible, first murderer, d by God as a ning to others.

⟶

Through her work, Hester Prynne found her role in the world. With her energy and abilities, the world could not entirely cast her away, even though it had set a mark upon her more awful for a woman than the mark of Cain. In all her interactions with society, Hester never felt as though she belonged. Every gesture, every word, and even the silence of those she met reminded her that she was banished, as removed from the com-

contact, implied, and often expressed, that she was banished, and as much alone as if she inhabited another sphere, or communicated with the common nature by other organs and senses than the rest of human kind. She stood apart from mortal interests, yet close beside them, like a ghost that revisits the familiar fireside, and can no longer make itself seen or felt; no more smile with the household joy, nor mourn with the kindred sorrow; or, should it succeed in manifesting its forbidden sympathy, awakening only terror and horrible repugnance. These emotions, in fact, and its bitterest scorn besides, seemed to be the sole portion that she retained in the universal heart. It was not an age of delicacy; and her position, although she understood it well, and was in little danger of forgetting it, was often brought before her vivid self-perception, like a new anguish, by the rudest touch upon the tenderest spot. The poor, as we have already said, whom she sought out to be the objects of her bounty, often reviled the hand that was stretched forth to succor them. Dames of elevated rank, likewise, whose doors she entered in the way of her occupation, were accustomed to distil drops of bitterness into her heart; sometimes through that alchemy of quiet malice, by which women can concoct a subtile poison from ordinary trifles; and sometimes, also, by a coarser expression, that fell upon the sufferer's defenceless breast like a rough blow upon an ulcerated wound. Hester had schooled herself long and well; she never responded to these attacks, save by a flush of crimson that rose irrepressibly over her pale cheek, and again subsided into the depths of her bosom. She was patient,—a martyr, indeed,—but she forbore to pray for her enemies; lest, in spite of her forgiving aspirations, the words of the blessing should stubbornly twist themselves into a curse.

Continually, and in a thousand other ways, did she feel the innumerable throbs of anguish that had been so cunningly contrived for her by the undying, the ever-active sentence of the Puritan tribunal. Clergymen paused in the street to address words of exhortation, that brought a crowd, with its mingled grin and frown, around the poor, sinful woman. If she entered a church, trusting to share the Sabbath smile of the Universal Father, it was often her mishap to find herself the text of the discourse. She grew to have a dread of children; for they had imbibed from their parents a vague idea of something horrible in this dreary woman, gliding silently through

munity as if she lived on another planet. She was like a ghost that haunts a familiar fireside, unable to make itself seen or felt, unable to smile at the joys of everyday life nor mourn its sorrow. And when the ghost manages to display its forbidden feelings, it only produces terror and repugnance in others. This horror, along with bitter scorn, seemed to be the only feeling the world had left for her. This was not a gentle era. Though Hester never forgot her position in society, she often felt its pain anew. As I said, the poor she tried to help often rejected the hand she extended to help them. The well-to-do ladies, whose houses she entered in the course of her work, had the habit of slyly insulting her, concocting insults out of slight matters in the way that women can. Other times, they would attack her more directly, their harsh words hitting her defenseless breast like a rough blow upon an open wound. But Hester had trained herself well. She never responded to these attacks, except that her cheeks would slowly turn red before the blush faded into the depths of her heart. She was patient—a true martyr. Yet she kept herself from praying for her enemies for fear that, despite her best intentions, her words of forgiveness might twist themselves into a curse.

Over and over, in a thousand different ways, Hester felt the innumerable throbs of pain that had been so cleverly devised for her by the all-encompassing sentence of the Puritan authorities. Ministers stopped in the streets to give speeches that drew a crowd of half-smiling and half-frowning people around the poor, sinful woman. If she entered a church to enjoy the holy day of rest, she often found herself the subject of the sermon. She grew to dread children, since they had learned from their parents that there was something vaguely horrible about this woman who walked silently through town with only her daughter by her side. After allowing her to pass,

the town, with never any companion but one only child. Therefore, first allowing her to pass, they pursued her at a distance with shrill cries, and the utterance of a word that had no distinct purport to their own minds, but was none the less terrible to her, as proceeding from lips that babbled it unconsciously. It seemed to argue so wide a diffusion of her shame, that all nature knew of it; it could have caused her no deeper pang, had the leaves of the trees whispered the dark story among themselves,—had the summer breeze murmured about it,—had the wintry blast shrieked it aloud! Another peculiar torture was felt in the gaze of a new eye. When strangers looked curiously at the scarlet letter,—and none ever failed to do so,—they branded it afresh into Hester's soul; so that, oftentimes, she could scarcely refrain, yet always did refrain, from covering the symbol with her hand. But then, again, an accustomed eye had likewise its own anguish to inflict. Its cool stare of familiarity was intolerable. From first to last, in short, Hester Prynne had always this dreadful agony in feeling a human eye upon the token; the spot never grew callous; it seemed, on the contrary, to grow more sensitive with daily torture.

But sometimes, once in many days, or perchance in many months, she felt an eye—a human eye—upon the ignominious brand, that seemed to give a momentary relief, as if half of her agony were shared. The next instant, back it all rushed again, with still a deeper throb of pain; for, in that brief interval, she had sinned anew. Had Hester sinned alone?

Her imagination was somewhat affected, and, had she been of a softer moral and intellectual fibre, would have been still more so, by the strange and solitary anguish of her life. Walking to and fro, with those lonely footsteps, in the little world with which she was outwardly connected, it now and then appeared to Hester,—if altogether fancy, it was nevertheless too potent to be resisted,—she felt or fancied, then, that the scarlet letter had endowed her with a new sense. She shuddered to believe, yet could not help believing, that it gave her a sympathetic knowledge of the hidden sin in other hearts. She was terror-stricken by the revelations that were thus made. What were they? Could they be other than the insidious whispers of the bad angel, who would fain have persuaded the struggling woman, as yet only half his victim, that the outward guise of purity was but a lie,

the children would pursue her with shrill cries, shouting a word that meant nothing to them but was terrible to her. Her shame was so public that it seemed all of nature knew about it. The children's shouts could have been no worse if they had been the whispers of the leaves, or the murmur of the summer breeze, or the shriek of the wintry wind! Another strange torture came from the gaze of unfamiliar eyes. When strangers peered at the scarlet letter—and they all did—they burned it fresh into Hester's soul. She often felt that she couldn't keep herself from covering the symbol with her hand, though she always restrained herself in the end. Familiar eyes brought their own kind of pain. Their cool stares of recognition were intolerable. In short, Hester Prynne always had the dreadful sense of human eyes upon the letter. No callus grew over the spot. Instead, the wound became more sensitive through her daily torture.

But once in a while, she felt an eye upon the mark that seemed to give her a moment's relief, as though half her agony were shared. The next instant, it all rushed back again, with a throb of deeper pain—for in that brief moment, she had sinned again. But had she sinned alone?

Hester's imagination was somewhat affected by the strange and lonely pain of her life. Walking here and there, with lonely footsteps, in the little world she was superficially connected to, it sometimes seemed to Hester that the scarlet letter had given her a new sense. It scared her, but she couldn't help believing that the letter gave her a sympathetic knowledge of the sin hidden in other people's hearts. She was terrified by the revelations that came to her this way. What were they? Could they be nothing more than the whispers of the Devil, who tried to convince Hester that the seeming purity of others was merely a lie, and that many breasts beside hers deserved a scarlet letter? Or was her awareness of the sins of others—so strange, and yet so clear—real? In all of her miserable experience, there was nothing so awful as this sensation. It struck her at the most inappropriate moments, shocking

and that, if truth were everywhere to be shown, a scarlet letter would blaze forth on many a bosom besides Hester Prynne's? Or, must she receive those intimations—so obscure, yet so distinct—as truth? In all her miserable experience, there was nothing else so awful and so loathsome as this sense. It perplexed, as well as shocked her, by the irreverent inopportuneness of the occasions that brought it into vivid action. Sometimes, the red infamy upon her breast would give a sympathetic throb, as she passed near a venerable minister or magistrate, the model of piety and justice, to whom that age of antique reverence looked up, as to a mortal man in fellowship with angels. "What evil thing is at hand?" would Hester say to herself. Lifting her reluctant eyes, there would be nothing human within the scope of view, save the form of this earthly saint! Again, a mystic sisterhood would contumaciously assert itself, as she met the sanctified frown of some matron, who, according to the rumor of all tongues, had kept cold snow within her bosom throughout life. That unsunned snow in the matron's bosom, and the burning shame on Hester Prynne's, what had the two in common? Or, once more, the electric thrill would give her warning,—"Behold, Hester, here is a companion!"—and, looking up, she would detect the eyes of a young maiden glancing at the scarlet letter, shyly and aside, and quickly averted, with a faint, chill crimson in her cheeks; as if her purity were somewhat sullied by that momentary glance. O Fiend, whose talisman was that fatal symbol, wouldst thou leave nothing, whether in youth or age, for this poor sinner to revere?—Such loss of faith is ever one of the saddest results of sin. Be it accepted as a proof that all was not corrupt in this poor victim of her own frailty, and man's hard law, that Hester Prynne yet struggled to believe that no fellow-mortal was guilty like herself.

The vulgar, who, in those dreary old times, were always contributing a grotesque horror to what interested their imaginations, had a story about the scarlet letter which we might readily work up into a terrific legend. They averred, that the symbol was not mere scarlet cloth, tinged in an earthly dye-pot, but was red-hot with infernal fire, and could be seen glowing all alight, whenever Hester Prynne walked abroad in the night-time. And we must needs say, it seared Hester's bosom so deeply, that perhaps there was more truth in the rumor than our modern incredulity may be inclined to admit.

and confusing her. Sometimes her red mark of shame would throb in sympathy as she passed a respected minister or magistrate, models of holiness and justice who were regarded as almost angelic in those days. "What evil thing is near?" Hester would ask herself. As she looked up reluctantly, she would find only this earthly saint! This same mystical sympathy would rudely assert itself when she met the frown of some older lady who was thought to have been pure and frigid her entire life. What could the coldness within that matron's breast have in common with the burning shame upon Hester Prynne's? Or, again, an electric shock would warn her: "Look, Hester, here is a companion." Looking up, she would find the eyes of a young maiden glancing shyly at the scarlet letter and turning quickly away with a faint blush, as though her purity were somehow spoiled by that brief glance. Oh Devil, whose symbol that scarlet letter was, would you leave nothing— young or old—for Hester to admire? Such loss of faith is always one of the saddest results of sin. Hester Prynne struggled to believe that no other person was guilty like her. Her struggle was proof that this victim of human weakness and man's strict law was not entirely corrupt.

In those dreary times, the common people were always adding some grotesque horror to whatever struck their imaginations. And so they created a story about the scarlet letter that we could easily build up into a terrific legend. They swore that the symbol was not mere scarlet cloth, dyed in a stone pot. It was red-hot with hellfire that could be seen glowing whenever Hester went walking in the nighttime. The letter burned Hester's breast so deeply that perhaps there was more truth in that story than we modern skeptics would care to admit.

Chapter 6: Pearl

We have as yet hardly spoken of the infant; that little creature, whose innocent life had sprung, by the inscrutable decree of Providence, a lovely and immortal flower, out of the rank luxuriance of a guilty passion. How strange it seemed to the sad woman, as she watched the growth, and the beauty that became every day more brilliant, and the intelligence that threw its quivering sunshine over the tiny features of this child! Her Pearl!—For so had Hester called her; not as a name expressive of her aspect, which had nothing of the calm, white, unimpassioned lustre that would be indicated by the comparison. But she named the infant "Pearl," as being of great price,—purchased with all she had,—her mother's only treasure! How strange, indeed! Man had marked this woman's sin by a scarlet letter, which had such potent and disastrous efficacy that no human sympathy could reach her, save it were sinful like herself. God, as a direct consequence of the sin which man thus punished, had given her a lovely child, whose place was on that same dishonored bosom, to connect her parent for ever with the race and descent of mortals, and to be finally a blessed soul in Heaven! Yet these thoughts affected Hester Prynne less with hope than apprehension. She knew that her deed had been evil; she could have no faith, therefore, that its result would be for good. Day after day, she looked fearfully into the child's expanding nature; ever dreading to detect some dark arid wild peculiarity, that should correspond with the guiltiness to which she owed her being.

Certainly, there was no physical defect. By its perfect shape, its vigor, and its natural dexterity in the use of all its untried limbs, the infant was worthy to have been brought forth in Eden; worthy to have been left there, to be the plaything of the angels, after the world's first parents were driven out. The child had a native grace which does not invariably coexist with faultless beauty; its attire, however simple, always impressed the beholder as if it were the very garb that precisely became it best. But little Pearl was not clad in rustic weeds. Her mother, with a morbid purpose that may be better understood hereafter, had bought the richest tissues that could be procured, and allowed her imaginative faculty its full play in the arrangement and decoration of the dresses which the child wore, before the public

Chapter 6: Pearl

We have hardly spoken about that innocent infant who happened to spring, like a beautiful, eternal flower, from the foul indulgence of her mother's guilty passion. How strange it seemed to Hester, as she watched her daughter grow more beautiful and more intelligent every day! Her Pearl! That's what Hester named her, not in reference to the child's appearance—which was neither calm nor pale, like a true pearl—but because she had come at a great price. Hester bought the child by parting with the only treasure she had: her virtue! How strange, indeed! Society had marked this woman's sin with a scarlet letter, which was so powerful that no human sympathy could reach her unless it was the sympathy of a fellow sinner. As the direct result of the sin that man had punished, God had given her a lovely child. Pearl's place was on Hester's dishonored bosom. She connected her mother to the rest of mankind, and she would eventually become a blessed soul in Heaven! Yet these thoughts gave Hester more fear than hope. She knew she had committed an evil act, so she had no faith that its result would be good. Day after day, she watched fearfully as the child grew, always dreading the emergence of some dark and wild trait derived from the guilt in which she was conceived.

Certainly, Pearl had no physical defect. The child was so perfectly formed, energetic, and coordinated that she could have been born in the Garden of Eden. And if she had been left there after Adam and Eve had been driven out, she could have been the playmate of the angels. The child had a natural grace, which doesn't always come with faultless beauty. Her clothes, no matter how simple, always seemed perfect. But little Pearl wasn't dressed shabbily. Her mother—with a dark purpose that will become clearer as the story goes on—had bought the most luxurious material she could find and allowed her imagination to run wild when she designed the dresses Pearl wore in public. She looked so magnificent when dressed up—her natural beauty made more stunning—that a circle of radiance glowed around her on

eye. So magnificent was the small figure, when thus arrayed, and such was the splendor of Pearl's own proper beauty, shining through the gorgeous robes which might have extinguished a paler loveliness, that there was an absolute circle of radiance around her, on the darksome cottage-floor. And yet a russet gown, torn and soiled with the child's rude play, made a picture of her just as perfect. Pearl's aspect was imbued with a spell of infinite variety; in this one child there were many children, comprehending the full scope between the wild-flower prettiness of a peasant-baby, and the pomp, in little, of an infant princess. Throughout all, however, there was a trait of passion, a certain depth of hue, which she never lost; and if, in any of her changes, she had grown fainter or paler, she would have ceased to be herself;—it would have been no longer Pearl!

This outward mutability indicated, and did not more than fairly express, the various properties of her inner life. Her nature appeared to possess depth, too, as well as variety; but—or else Hester's fears deceived her—it lacked reference and adaptation to the world into which she was born. The child could not be made amenable to rules. In giving her existence, a great law had been broken; and the result was a being, whose elements were perhaps beautiful and brilliant, but all in disorder; or with an order peculiar to themselves, amidst which the point of variety and arrangement was difficult or impossible to be discovered. Hester could only account for the child's character—and even then, most vaguely and imperfectly—by recalling what she herself had been, during that momentous period while Pearl was imbibing her soul from the spiritual world, and her bodily frame from its material of earth. The mother's impassioned state had been the medium through which were transmitted to the unborn infant the rays of its moral life; and, however white and clear originally, they had taken the deep stains of crimson and gold, the fiery lustre, the black shadow, and the untempered light, of the intervening substance. Above all, the warfare of Hester's spirit, at that epoch, was perpetuated in Pearl. She could recognize her wild, desperate, defiant mood, the flightiness of her temper, and even some of the very cloud-shapes of gloom and despondency that had brooded in her heart. They were now illuminated by the morning radiance of a young child's disposition, but, later in the day of earthly existence, might be prolific of the storm and whirlwind.

the cottage floor. A lesser beauty would have faded under such gorgeous garments. But a plain gown, torn and dirty from play, looked just as perfect on Pearl. Her features were ever-changing, as though enchanted. In this one child there were many children, ranging from the wild prettiness of a peasant baby to the miniature magnificence of an infant princess. Yet there was always a hint of passion, a certain color, which she never lost. If, in any of her changes, she had lost this color and grown paler, she would have ceased to be herself. She would no longer have been Pearl!

This outward changeability hinted at the nature of Pearl's inner life. Her personality seemed to be both deep and varied, but—unless Hester's fears fooled her—it was poorly adapted to the world she was born into. The child could not be made to follow rules. A great law had been broken to bring her into the world; the result was a creature whose traits were beautiful and brilliant but disordered. Or perhaps those traits had an order of their own, and one that was almost impossible to figure out. Hester could only make the vaguest sense of the child's personality by remembering what state she herself had been in when Pearl was conceived. Hester's passion had been passed on to the unborn infant. No matter how clean and clear Pearl's moral life had originally been, it had been dyed crimson and gold, with a fiery luster, black shadows, and the intense light of Hester's passion. Above all, the conflicted nature of Hester's spirit at that time had been passed on to Pearl. Hester recognized in her child her own wild, desperate defiance, her quick temper, and even some of the melancholy that had brooded in her heart. Those clouds of sadness were now illuminated by the morning light of Pearl's cheerful disposition, but later in her life they might produce a great storm.

The discipline of the family, in those days, was of a far more rigid kind than now. The frown, the harsh rebuke, the frequent application of the rod, enjoined by Scriptural authority, were used, not merely in the way of punishment for actual offences, but as a wholesome regimen for the growth and promotion of all childish virtues. Hester Prynne, nevertheless, the lonely mother of this one child, ran little risk of erring on the side of undue severity. Mindful, however, of her own errors and misfortunes, she early sought to impose a tender, but strict, control over the infant immortality that was committed to her charge. But the task was beyond her skill. After testing both smiles and frowns, and proving that neither mode of treatment possessed any calculable influence, Hester was ultimately compelled to stand aside, and permit the child to be swayed by her own impulses. Physical compulsion or restraint was effectual, of course, while it lasted. As to any other kind of discipline, whether addressed to her mind or heart, little Pearl might or might not be within its reach, in accordance with the caprice that ruled the moment. Her mother, while Pearl was yet an infant, grew acquainted with a certain peculiar look, that warned her when it would be labor thrown away to insist, persuade, or plead. It was a look so intelligent, yet inexplicable, so perverse, sometimes so malicious, but generally accompanied by a wild flow of spirits, that Hester could not help questioning, at such moments, whether Pearl was a human child. She seemed rather an airy sprite, which, after playing its fantastic sports for a little while upon the cottage-floor, would flit away with a mocking smile. Whenever that look appeared in her wild, bright, deeply black eyes, it invested her with a strange remoteness and intangibility; it was as if she were hovering in the air and might vanish, like a glimmering light that comes we know not whence, and goes we know not whither. Beholding it, Hester was constrained to rush towards the child,—to pursue the little elf in the flight which she invariably began,—to snatch her to her bosom, with a close pressure and earnest kisses,—not so much from overflowing love, as to assure herself that Pearl was flesh and blood, and not utterly delusive. But Pearl's laugh, when she was caught, though full of merriment and music, made her mother more doubtful than before.

Heart-smitten at this bewildering and baffling spell, that so often came between herself and her sole treasure, whom she had bought

NO FEAR

Parents disciplined their children much more harshly then than they do now. The Bible seemed to require frowns, harsh words, and beatings, and these techniques were used both to punish actual offenses and simply to promote the development of virtue. But Hester Prynne, the loving mother of this only child, was in no danger of being too harsh. Fully aware of her own errors and misdeeds, she tried from the first to impose a tender but firm control over the soul of her daughter. But that task was more than she could manage. After trying both smiles and frowns, and finding that neither had any real effect, Hester was forced to stand aside and let the child do as she pleased. She could physically handle her daughter, of course. As to any other kind of discipline, however, little Pearl might obey—or she might not. It depended on her whims at that moment. Since the time Pearl was a baby, Hester came to recognize a certain odd look that warned her when the child simply would not be persuaded. It was a strange but intelligent look: contrary, sometimes malicious, but generally accompanied by high spirits. At such moments, Hester could not help but wonder whether Pearl were really human. She seemed like a fairy that, after playing its tricks for a while on the cottage floor, would flit away with a mocking smile. Whenever that look appeared in Pearl's wild, bright, deeply black eyes, it made her seem remote and elusive. It was as though she were hovering in the air and might vanish at any moment, like a glimmering light from out of nowhere. Seeing that look, Hester felt compelled to rush over to her child, hold her tightly to her chest, and kiss her earnestly. She did this not from an excess of love so much as to assure herself that Pearl was flesh and blood and not a delusion. But when she was caught, Pearl's laugh, though full of joy and music, made her mother more doubtful than before.

Sometimes Hester burst into tears when swept up by this strange spell that so often came between herself and her one treasure, paid

so dear, and who was all her world, Hester sometimes burst into passionate tears. Then, perhaps,—for there was no foreseeing how it might affect her,—Pearl would frown, and clench her little fist, and harden her small features into a stern, unsympathizing look of discontent. Not seldom, she would laugh anew, and louder than before, like a thing incapable and unintelligent of human sorrow. Or—but this more rarely happened—she would be convulsed with a rage of grief, and sob out her love for her mother, in broken words, and seem intent on proving that she had a heart, by breaking it. Yet Hester was hardly safe in confiding herself to that gusty tenderness; it passed, as suddenly as it came. Brooding over all these matters, the mother felt like one who has evoked a spirit, but, by some irregularity in the process of conjuration, has failed to win the master-word that should control this new and incomprehensible intelligence. Her only real comfort was when the child lay in the placidity of sleep. Then she was sure of her, and tasted hours of quiet, sad, delicious happiness; until—perhaps with that perverse expression glimmering from beneath her opening lids—little Pearl awoke!

How soon—with what strange rapidity, indeed!—did Pearl arrive at an age that was capable of social intercourse, beyond the mother's ever-ready smile and nonsense-words! And then what a happiness would it have been, could Hester Prynne have heard her clear, bird-like voice mingling with the uproar of other childish voices, and have distinguished and unravelled her own darling's tones, amid all the entangled outcry of a group of sportive children! But this could never be. Pearl was a born outcast of the infantile world. An imp of evil, emblem and product of sin, she had no right among christened infants. Nothing was more remarkable than the instinct, as it seemed, with which the child comprehended her loneliness; the destiny that had drawn an inviolable circle round about her; the whole peculiarity, in short, of her position in respect to other children. Never, since her release from prison, had Hester met the public gaze without her. In all her walks about the town, Pearl, too, was there; first as the babe in arms, and afterwards as the little girl, small companion of her mother, holding a forefinger with her whole grasp, and tripping along at the rate of three or four footsteps to one of Hester's. She saw the children of the settlement, on the grassy margin of the street, or at the domestic thresholds, disporting them-

for at such a cost. Sometimes Pearl would frown and clench her fists and harden her tiny features into a stern and unhappy expression. Often she would laugh again, louder than before, as if she were incapable of understanding or feeling human sorrow. Sometimes—though this happened less often—Pearl would be overcome with grief and cry out in broken words with love for her mother, as though to prove she had a heart by breaking it. But Hester could not trust in that stormy show of affection: It passed as quickly as it came. Hester dwelled on all of this and felt like someone who has conjured up a spirit but, by some defect in the spell, couldn't control it. Her only real comfort came when the child lay peacefully asleep. Then she enjoyed hours of quiet, sad, delicious happiness, until (perhaps with that perverse expression glowing in her opening eyes) little Pearl woke up!

Pearl learned to speak at a very young age, moving quickly beyond her mother's loving nonsense words. It would have made Hester Prynne so happy to hear her daughter's clear, birdlike voice mixing with the voices of other children at play—untangling her daughter's voice from the energetic group. But this could never be! Pearl was born an outcast from that world. As an evil sprite, a symbol and product of sin, she was not allowed to mingle with the baptized children. Nothing was more remarkable than the instinctual way Pearl seemed to understand her place among other children. Since the time Hester had been released from prison, she had never walked in public without Pearl. Pearl was with her on every trip into town: first as a babe in her mother's arms, and later as her mother's tiny companion, holding onto a forefinger with her entire hand and taking three or four steps for every one of Hester's. She saw the town's children in the grass by the street or in the doorways of houses. They played whatever dull games their Puritan upbringing allowed: pretending to go to church, taunting Quakers, taking scalps in an imaginary fight against the Indians, or scaring one another with make-believe witchcraft. Pearl stared intently at them, but she never tried to introduce herself. She would not reply if spo-

selves in such grim fashion as the Puritanic nurture would permit; playing at going to church, perchance; or at scourging Quakers; or taking scalps in a sham-fight with the Indians; or scaring one another with freaks of imitative witchcraft. Pearl saw, and gazed intently, but never sought to make acquaintance. If spoken to, she would not speak again. If the children gathered about her, as they sometimes did, Pearl would grow positively terrible in her puny wrath, snatching up stones to fling at them, with shrill, incoherent exclamations that made her mother tremble, because they had so much the sound of a witch's anathemas in some unknown tongue.

The truth was, that the little Puritans, being of the most intolerant brood that ever lived, had got a vague idea of something outlandish, unearthly, or at variance with ordinary fashions, in the mother and child; and therefore scorned them in their hearts, and not unfrequently reviled them with their tongues. Pearl felt the sentiment, and requited it with the bitterest hatred that can be supposed to rankle in a childish bosom. These outbreaks of a fierce temper had a kind of value, and even comfort, for her mother; because there was at least an intelligible earnestness in the mood, instead of the fitful caprice that so often thwarted her in the child's manifestations. It appalled her, nevertheless, to discern here, again, a shadowy reflection of the evil that had existed in herself. All this enmity and passion had Pearl inherited, by inalienable right, out of Hester's heart. Mother and daughter stood together in the same circle of seclusion from human society; and in the nature of the child seemed to be perpetuated those unquiet elements that had distracted Hester Prynne before Pearl's birth, but had since begun to be soothed away by the softening influences of maternity.

At home, within and around her mother's cottage, Pearl wanted not a wide and various circle of acquaintance. The spell of life went forth from her ever creative spirit, and communicated itself to a thousand objects, as a torch kindles a flame wherever it may be applied. The unlikeliest materials, a stick, a bunch of rags, a flower, were the puppets of Pearl's witchcraft, and, without undergoing any outward change, became spiritually adapted to whatever drama occupied the stage of her inner world. Her one baby-voice served a multitude of imaginary personages, old and young, to talk withal. The pine-trees, aged, black, and solemn, and flinging groans and

ken to. And if the children gathered around her, as they sometimes did, Pearl would become absolutely terrifying in her puny wrath. She would pick up stones to throw at them and make incomprehensible shrieks that made her mother tremble because they sounded like the curses of some alien witch.

In truth, the little Puritans—some of the least tolerant children who ever lived—had gotten a vague idea that there was something bizarre and unnatural about this mother and child. The children felt scorn in their hearts for the two and often mocked them out loud. Pearl felt their scorn and often repaid it with the bitterest hatred that a child can muster. These fierce outbursts gave Hester a strange comfort because at least she knew that her daughter was acting and speaking in earnest. So much of the time, Pearl's moods were contrary and perverse and frustrated her mother. But even so, Hester was appalled to detect in her daughter a reflection of the evil that had existed in herself. Pearl had inherited all of this hatred and passion, as if by right, directly from Hester's heart. Mother and daughter stood together, excluded from human society. Pearl exhibited the same wild nature that had distracted Hester Prynne before her daughter's birth but that motherhood had begun to soften away.

At home, Pearl did not need a wide and varied circle of friends. The magic of life sprung out from her spirit, communicating with a thousand things around her like a torch igniting everything it touches. The most unlikely materials—a stick, a bunch of rags, a flower— became the objects of Pearl's witchcraft. Without undergoing any visible change, the things around her became puppets in Pearl's inner drama. Her single child's voice created entire conversations with hosts of imaginary people, young and old. It took only the slightest bit of imagination to transform the pine trees—old, black, and serious, and groaning as the wind blew through their branches—into

other melancholy utterances on the breeze, needed little transformation to figure as Puritan elders; the ugliest weeds of the garden were their children, whom Pearl smote down and uprooted, most unmercifully. It was wonderful, the vast variety of forms into which she threw her intellect, with no continuity, indeed, but darting up and dancing, always in a state of preternatural activity,—soon sinking down, as if exhausted by so rapid and feverish a tide of life,— and succeeded by other shapes of a similar wild energy. It was like nothing so much as the phantasmagoric play of the northern lights. In the mere exercise of the fancy, however, and the sportiveness of a growing mind, there might be little more than was observable in other children of bright faculties; except as Pearl, in the dearth of human playmates, was thrown more upon the visionary throng which she created. The singularity lay in the hostile feelings with which the child regarded all these offspring of her own heart and mind. She never created a friend, but seemed always to be sowing broadcast the dragon's teeth, whence sprung a harvest of armed enemies, against whom she rushed to battle. It was inexpressibly sad— then what depth of sorrow to a mother, who felt in her own heart the cause!—to observe, in one so young, this constant recognition of an adverse world, and so fierce a training of the energies that were to make good her cause, in the contest that must ensue.

Gazing at Pearl, Hester Prynne often dropped her work upon her knees, and cried out, with an agony which she would fain have hidden, but which made utterance for itself, betwixt speech and a groan,—"O Father in Heaven,—if Thou art still my Father,—what is this being which I have brought into the world!" And Pearl, overhearing the ejaculation, or aware, through some more subtile channel, of those throbs of anguish, would turn her vivid and beautiful little face upon her mother, smile with sprite-like intelligence, and resume her play.

One peculiarity of the child's deportment remains yet to be told. The very first thing which she had noticed, in her life, was— what?—not the mother's smile, responding to it, as other babies do, by that faint, embryo smile of the little mouth, remembered so doubtfully afterwards, and with such fond discussion whether it were indeed a smile. By no means! But that first object of which Pearl seemed to become aware was,—shall we say it?—the scarlet

Puritan elders. The ugliest weeds of the garden were their children, and Pearl mercilessly cut them down and uprooted them. The wide variety of ways she used her imagination was remarkable and truly random. She was almost unnaturally active, jumping up and dancing about, then sinking down, exhausted by such rapid, fevered imaginings until others took their place. Watching her play was like seeing the ghostly play of the northern lights. In her playfulness, Pearl was not that different from other bright children. But Pearl, with no other children to play with, relied far more on the hordes she imagined. And the truly unique thing was the hostile way she regarded the creations of her own heart and mind. She never created an imaginary friend. Instead, she always seemed to be planting dragons' teeth out of which would grow a crop of armed enemies for her to battle. It was unspeakably sad—and sadder still for the mother who blamed herself for it—to see the knowledge of the world's cruelty in someone so young. Pearl already understood that she would need to be well trained if she were to win in her fight against the world.

Gazing at Pearl, Hester Prynne often let her needlework fall from her lap and cried out with an agony she would have rather hidden: "Oh Father in Heaven, if You are still my Father, who is this person I have brought into the world!" And Pearl, either overhearing her mother's cries or somehow aware of them, would turn her rosy, beautiful little face to Hester, smile with fairylike intelligence, and resume her play.

I have left out one odd aspect of the child's personality. The very first thing she noticed in her life was not her mother's smile, as it is for so many babies. Most babies return that smile with a faint smile in their little mouths, while their parents debate whether it was really a smile at all. But not Pearl. The first thing she noticed was the scarlet letter on Hester's bosom! One day, as her mother stooped over the cradle, the infant's eyes seized upon the glimmering of the

letter on Hester's bosom! One day, as her mother stooped over the cradle, the infant's eyes had been caught by the glimmering of the gold embroidery about the letter; and, putting up her little hand, she grasped at it, smiling, not doubtfully, but with a decided gleam that gave her face the look of a much older child. Then, gasping for breath, did Hester Prynne clutch the fatal token, instinctively endeavouring to tear it away; so infinite was the torture inflicted by the intelligent touch of Pearl's baby-hand. Again, as if her mother's agonized gesture were meant only to make sport for her, did little Pearl look into her eyes, and smile! From that epoch, except when the child was asleep, Hester had never felt a moment's safety; not a moment's calm enjoyment of her. Weeks, it is true, would sometimes elapse, during which Pearl's gaze might never once be fixed upon the scarlet letter; but then, again, it would come at unawares, like the stroke of sudden death, and always with that peculiar smile, and odd expression of the eyes.

Once, this freakish, elvish cast came into the child's eyes, while Hester was looking at her own image in them, as mothers are fond of doing; and, suddenly,—for women in solitude, and with troubled hearts, are pestered with unaccountable delusions,—she fancied that she beheld, not her own miniature portrait, but another face in the small black mirror of Pearl's eye. It was a face, fiend-like, full of smiling malice, yet bearing the semblance of features that she had known full well, though seldom with a smile, and never with malice, in them. It was as if an evil spirit possessed the child, and had just then peeped forth in mockery. Many a time afterwards had Hester been tortured, though less vividly, by the same illusion.

In the afternoon of a certain summer's day, after Pearl grew big enough to run about, she amused herself with gathering handfuls of wild-flowers, and flinging them, one by one, at her mother's bosom; dancing up and down, like a little elf, whenever she hit the scarlet letter. Hester's first motion had been to cover her bosom with her clasped hands. But, whether from pride or resignation, or a feeling that her penance might best be wrought out by this unutterable pain, she resisted the impulse, and sat erect, pale as death, looking sadly into little Pearl's wild eyes. Still came the battery of flowers, almost invariably hitting the mark, and covering the mother's breast with hurts for which she could find no balm in this world, nor knew

gold embroidery around the letter. Reaching up with her little hand, she grasped at it and smiled with a certain gleam that made her look like a much older child. Gasping for breath, Hester Prynne clutched the sinful symbol, instinctively trying to move it away. The seemingly knowing touch of Pearl's baby hand was an incredible torture to her. Pearl looked into Hester's eyes again and smiled, as if her mother's agony were meant to amuse her. From that moment on, Hester never felt a moment of safety unless her child was asleep. She never enjoyed an instant of peace with her daughter. True, sometimes weeks would go by where Pearl didn't look at the scarlet letter. But then her gaze would fix on it unexpectedly, like the stroke of sudden death, and always with that strange smile and odd expression in her eyes.

Once, this strange, elfish look came into Pearl's eyes while Hester was gazing at her own image in them, as mothers are fond of doing. Lonely women, or those with troubled hearts, are pestered by delusions—so Hester imagined that she saw a face other than her own in the small black mirror of Pearl's eye. It was a demonic face, full of gleeful malice. It resembled a face she knew quite well, though that face rarely smiled, and it was never malicious. It was as if an evil spirit had possessed the child, and just then peeked out to mock Hester. After this, Hester was often tortured by a less-intense recurrence of the illusion.

One summer afternoon, after Pearl had grown big enough to run around, she was amusing herself by gathering handfuls of wild flowers and flinging them, one by one, at her mother's bosom. She danced like a little elf whenever a flower hit the scarlet letter. Hester's first instinct had been to cover her bosom with her hands, but, whether from pride, resignation, or a sense that this incredible pain might be penance for her sin, she resisted the impulse. She sat up straight, pale as death, and looked into little Pearl's wild eyes. The assault of flowers continued, almost always hitting the mark and covering Hester's breast with wounds that could not be healed. When Pearl was finally out of ammunition, she stood still and gazed at Hester.

how to seek it in another. At last, her shot being all expended, the child stood still and gazed at Hester, with that little, laughing image of a fiend peeping out—or, whether it peeped or no, her mother so imagined it—from the unsearchable abyss of her black eyes.

"Child, what art thou?" cried the mother.

"O, I am your little Pearl!" answered the child.

But, while she said it, Pearl laughed and began to dance up and down, with the humorsome gesticulation of a little imp, whose next freak might be to fly up the chimney.

"Art thou my child, in very truth?" asked Hester.

Nor did she put the question altogether idly, but, for the moment, with a portion of genuine earnestness; for, such was Pearl's wonderful intelligence, that her mother half-doubted whether she were not acquainted with the secret spell of her existence, and might not now reveal herself.

"Yes; I am little Pearl!" repeated the child, continuing her antics.

"Thou art not my child! Thou art no Pearl of mine!" said the mother, half-playfully; for it was often the case that a sportive impulse came over her, in the midst of her deepest suffering. "Tell me, then, what thou art, and who sent thee hither?"

"Tell me, mother!" said the child, seriously, coming up to Hester, and pressing herself close to her knees. "Do thou tell me!"

"Thy Heavenly Father sent thee!" answered Hester Prynne.

But she said it with a hesitation that did not escape the acuteness of the child. Whether moved only by her ordinary freakishness, or because an evil spirit prompted her, she put up her small forefinger, and touched the scarlet letter.

"He did not send me!" cried she, positively. "I have no Heavenly Father!"

"Hush, Pearl, hush! Thou must not talk so!" answered the mother, suppressing a groan. "He sent us all into this world. He sent even me, thy mother. Then, much more, thee! Or, if not, thou strange and elfish child, whence didst thou come?"

"Tell me! Tell me!" repeated Pearl, no longer seriously, but laughing, and capering about the floor. "It is thou that must tell me!"

But Hester could not resolve the query, being herself in a dismal labyrinth of doubt. She remembered—betwixt a smile and a shudder—the talk of the neighbouring townspeople; who, seeking

NO FEAR

That little laughing image of a demon peeped out from the deep abyss of Pearl's black eyes—or if it didn't, Hester imagined it did.

"What are you, child?" cried Hester.

"Oh, I am your little Pearl!" answered the child.

Pearl laughed while she spoke, and began to dance with the humorous motion of a little sprite whose next trick might be to fly up the chimney.

"Are you truly my child?" asked Hester.

The question was not entirely meaningless, but half in earnest at that moment. Pearl was so intelligent that her mother half-suspected she must be a magical spirit who was about to reveal herself.

"Yes, I am little Pearl!" repeated the child, continuing her antics.

"You are not my child! You are no Pearl of mine!" said the mother playfully, for she often felt playful in the midst of her deepest suffering. "Tell me, what are you and who sent you here?"

"You tell me, mother!" said the child, seriously, coming up to Hester and pressing herself close to her knees. "Do tell me that!"

"Your heavenly Father sent you!" answered Hester Prynne.

But she said it with a hesitation that the perceptive child noticed. Whether because of her own contrariness, or because an evil spirit prompted her, Pearl raised her small forefinger and touched the scarlet letter.

"He did not send me!" she cried with certainty. "I don't have a heavenly Father!"

"Hush, Pearl, hush! You must not talk like that!" answered the mother, stifling a groan. "He sent us all into the world. He even sent me, your mother—so of course he sent you! If he didn't, you strange, elfish child, where did you come from?"

"You tell me! You tell me!" repeated Pearl, no longer serious, but laughing and dancing about the floor. "It's you who must tell me!"

But Hester, lost in a dark maze of doubt, could not answer. She remembered, with a half-smile and half-shudder, the rumor the townspeople had spread that Pearl was the child of a demon. Since

vainly elsewhere for the child's paternity, and observing some of her odd attributes, had given out that poor little Pearl was a demon off-spring; such as, ever since old Catholic times, had occasionally been seen on earth, through the agency of their mothers' sin, and to promote some foul and wicked purpose. Luther, according to the scandal of his monkish enemies, was a brat of that hellish breed; nor was Pearl the only child to whom this inauspicious origin was assigned, among the New England Puritans.

NO FEAR

old Catholic times, people believed sinful mothers sometimes gave birth to demons who appeared on earth to carry out some wicked act. Luther's opponents, for example, spread the rumor that he was such a demon. Pearl was not the only child assumed by the New England Puritans to have such an unfortunate origin.

artin Luther: century monk tholic Church rmer credited with sparking he Protestant Reformation.

Chapter 7: The Governor's Hall

Hester Prynne went, one day, to the mansion of Governor Bellingham, with a pair of gloves, which she had fringed and embroidered to his order, and which were to be worn on some great occasion of state; for, though the chances of a popular election had caused this former ruler to descend a step or two from the highest rank, he still held an honorable and influential place among the colonial magistracy.

Another and far more important reason than the delivery of a pair of embroidered gloves impelled Hester, at this time, to seek an interview with a personage of so much power and activity in the affairs of the settlement. It had reached her ears, that there was a design on the part of some of the leading inhabitants, cherishing the more rigid order of principles in religion and government, to deprive her of her child. On the supposition that Pearl, as already hinted, was of demon origin, these good people not unreasonably argued that a Christian interest in the mother's soul required them to remove such a stumbling-block from her path. If the child, on the other hand, were really capable of moral and religious growth, and possessed the elements of ultimate salvation, then, surely, it would enjoy all the fairer prospect of these advantages by being transferred to wiser and better guardianship than Hester Prynne's. Among those who promoted the design, Governor Bellingham was said to be one of the most busy. It may appear singular, and, indeed, not a little ludicrous, that an affair of this kind, which, in later days, would have been referred to no higher jurisdiction than that of the selectmen of the town, should then have been a question publicly discussed, and on which statesmen of eminence took sides. At that epoch of pristine simplicity, however, matters of even slighter public interest, and of far less intrinsic weight than the welfare of Hester and her child, were strangely mixed up with the deliberations of legislators and acts of state. The period was hardly, if at all, earlier than that of our story, when a dispute concerning the right of property in a pig, not only caused a fierce and bitter contest in the legislative body of the colony, but resulted in an important modification of the framework itself of the legislature.

Full of concern, therefore,—but so conscious of her own right, that it seemed scarcely an unequal match between the public, on

Chapter 7: The Governor's Hall

One day, Hester Prynne brought a pair of gloves to the mansion of Governor Bellingham. She had fringed and embroidered the gloves, as he had ordered, for some important official occasion. Although this former ruler had lost the last election, he still held a place of honor and influence in colonial society.

There was another reason, more important than the delivery of his embroidered gloves, that Hester wanted to see this powerful man. She had learned that some of the leading townspeople, favoring stricter rules in religion and government, wanted to take Pearl away from her. These good people, believing Pearl to be demon child (and with good reason), argued that their concern for Hester's soul required them to remove this obstacle from her path to salvation. On the other hand, if the child really were capable of spiritual growth, they reasoned that its soul should have a better guardian than Hester Prynne. Governor Bellingham was said to be among the more prominent supporters of this plan. It may seem odd, perhaps even absurd, that a personal matter like this—which in later days would have been handled by the city council—would have been subject to public debate, with leading politicians taking sides. In that simpler time, though, legislators and statesman involved themselves in the slightest matters, even ones much less important than the fate of Hester and her child. Not long before the time of our story, a dispute over the ownership of a pig caused not only a bitter debate within the legislature but also led to an important change in the structure of the legislative body.

Hester was full of concern as she left her lonely cottage. And yet she was so confident of her own position that a match-up with the

the one side, and a lonely woman, backed by the sympathies of nature, on the other,—Hester Prynne set forth from her solitary cottage. Little Pearl, of course, was her companion. She was now of an age to run lightly along by her mother's side, and, constantly in motion from morn till sunset, could have accomplished a much longer journey than that before her. Often, nevertheless, more from caprice than necessity, she demanded to be taken up in arms, but was soon as imperious to be set down again, and frisked onward before Hester on the grassy pathway, with many a harmless trip and tumble. We have spoken of Pearl's rich and luxuriant beauty; a beauty that shone with deep and vivid tints; a bright complexion, eyes possessing intensity both of depth and glow, and hair already of a deep, glossy brown, and which, in after years, would be nearly akin to black. There was fire in her and throughout her; she seemed the unpremeditated offshoot of a passionate moment. Her mother, in contriving the child's garb, had allowed the gorgeous tendencies of her imagination their full play; arraying her in a crimson velvet tunic, of a peculiar cut, abundantly embroidered with fantasies and flourishes of gold thread. So much strength of coloring, which must have given a wan and pallid aspect to cheeks of a fainter bloom, was admirably adapted to Pearl's beauty, and made her the very brightest little jet of flame that ever danced upon the earth.

But it was a remarkable attribute of this garb, and, indeed, of the child's whole appearance, that it irresistibly and inevitably reminded the beholder of the token which Hester Prynne was doomed to wear upon her bosom. It was the scarlet letter in another form; the scarlet letter endowed with life! The mother herself—as if the red ignominy were so deeply scorched into her brain, that all her conceptions assumed its form—had carefully wrought out the similitude; lavishing many hours of morbid ingenuity, to create an analogy between the object of her affection, and the emblem of her guilt and torture. But, in truth, Pearl was the one, as well as the other; and only in consequence of that identity had Hester contrived so perfectly to represent the scarlet letter in her appearance.

As the two wayfarers came within the precincts of the town, the children of the Puritans looked up from their play,—or what passed for play with those sombre little urchins,—and spake gravely one to another:—

public on the one side and a single mother, backed by her maternal instincts, on the other almost seemed like an equal fight. Of course, little Pearl came along. She was now old enough to run along by her mother's side, and, as energetic as she was, she could have easily gone much farther than they were going that day. But, out of whim more than necessity, Pearl would often demand to be carried, only to demand to be let down again to run, tripping and falling harmlessly, on the grassy path ahead of Hester. I have described Pearl's rich, luxuriant beauty: vivid skin, a bright complexion, deep and lively eyes, and glossy brown hair that would look almost black in her later years. There was fire in and throughout her. She seemed like the unintended product of a passionate moment. In designing her child's clothing, Hester had allowed her imagination to run free, dressing her daughter in an oddly cut red velvet tunic, richly embroidered with gold thread. Such bold color, which would have made a fainter beauty look pale, suited Pearl very well. It made her look like the brightest flame ever to dance upon the earth.

But the strange effect of this outfit, and really of the child's whole appearance, is that it inevitably reminded the viewer of the symbol Hester Prynne was condemned to wear on her breast. Pearl was the scarlet letter in another form: the scarlet letter come to life! Hester herself had carefully crafted this likeness, as if the red shame were so deeply burned into her brain that all of her work resembled it. She spent many long, dark hours working to bring about this connection between the object of her affection and the symbol of her guilt. Of course, Pearl was both of these things, and in recognition of that fact, Hester worked to perfectly represent the scarlet letter in Pearl's appearance.

As the two travelers entered the town, the Puritan children looked up from their play—or what passed for play among those somber little kids—and spoke seriously to one another.

"Behold, verily, there is the woman of the scarlet letter; and, of a truth, moreover, there is the likeness of the scarlet letter running along by her side! Come, therefore, and let us fling mud at them!"

But Pearl, who was a dauntless child, after frowning, stamping her foot, and shaking her little hand with a variety of threatening gestures, suddenly made a rush at the knot of her enemies, and put them all to flight. She resembled, in her fierce pursuit of them, an infant pestilence,—the scarlet fever, or some such half-fledged angel of judgment,—whose mission was to punish the sins of the rising generation. She screamed and shouted, too, with a terrific volume of sound, which doubtless caused the hearts of the fugitives to quake within them. The victory accomplished, Pearl returned quietly to her mother, and looked up smiling into her face.

Without further adventure, they reached the dwelling of Governor Bellingham. This was a large wooden house, built in a fashion of which there are specimens still extant in the streets of our elder towns; now moss-grown, crumbling to decay, and melancholy at heart with the many sorrowful or joyful occurrences remembered or forgotten, that have happened, and passed away, within their dusky chambers. Then, however, there was the freshness of the passing year on its exterior, and the cheerfulness, gleaming forth from the sunny windows, of a human habitation into which death had never entered. It had indeed a very cheery aspect; the walls being overspread with a kind of stucco, in which fragments of broken glass were plentifully inter-mixed; so that, when the sunshine fell aslant-wise over the front of the edifice, it glittered and sparkled as if diamonds had been flung against it by the double handful. The brilliancy might have befitted Aladdin's palace, rather than the mansion of a grave old Puritan ruler. It was further decorated with strange and seemingly cabalistic figures and diagrams, suitable to the quaint taste of the age, which had been drawn in the stucco when newly laid on, and had now grown hard and durable, for the admiration of after times.

Pearl, looking at this bright wonder of a house, began to caper and dance, and imperatively required that the whole breadth of sunshine should be stripped off its front, and given her to play with.

"No, my little Pearl!" said her mother. "Thou must gather thine own sunshine. I have none to give thee!"

NO FEAR

"Look—there's the scarlet letter lady! And there's the little scarlet letter running alongside her! Let's throw mud at them!"

But Pearl was a fearless child. She frowned, stomped her foot, and shook her little hand in several threatening gestures. Then she suddenly charged at her enemies, sending them scattering away. Pursuing them, Pearl seemed like a baby pestilence: the scarlet fever, or some pint-sized angel of judgment sent to punish the sins of the young. She screamed and shouted so loud that the children's hearts must have quaked with fear. Victorious, Pearl returned quietly to her mother and looked up, smiling, into her face.

They reached Governor Bellingham's house without further incident. It was a large wooden structure, built in a style still found in some of the older towns today. These houses are now moss-covered, crumbling, and melancholy—filled with the many events of sorrow or celebration that have happened inside. But back then, the Governor's house looked fresh as a new year, with the sunny cheerfulness of a home that had never seen death. It was indeed cheerful: The walls were covered with stucco that was mixed with fragments of broken glass, so that when the sunshine came in at the right angle it glittered and sparkled as though studded with diamonds. This brilliance might have suited Aladdin's palace better than the mansion of a grave old Puritan ruler. Drawn into the stucco were strange, seemingly mystical figures and symbols, which suited the tastes of that quaint time.

Looking at this brilliant spectacle of a house, Pearl began to skip and dance. She ordered her mother to take the sunshine off the front and give it to her to play with.

"No, my little Pearl!" said Hester. "You have to gather your own sunshine. I don't have any to give you!"

They approached the door; which was of an arched form, and flanked on each side by a narrow tower or projection of the edifice, in both of which were lattice-windows, with wooden shutters to close over them at need. Lifting the iron hammer that hung at the portal, Hester Prynne gave a summons, which was answered by one of the Governor's bond-servants; a free-born Englishman, but now a seven years' slave. During that term he was to be the property of his master, and as much a commodity of bargain and sale as an ox, a joint-stool. The serf wore the blue coat, which was the customary garb of serving-men at that period, and long before, in the old hereditary halls of England.

"Is the worshipful Governor Bellingham within?" inquired Hester.

"Yea, forsooth," replied the bond-servant, staring with wide-open eyes at the scarlet letter, which, being a new-comer in the country, he had never before seen. "Yea, his honorable worship is within. But he hath a godly minister or two with him, and likewise a leech. Ye may not see his worship now."

"Nevertheless, I will enter," answered Hester Prynne; and the bond-servant, perhaps judging from the decision of her air and the glittering symbol in her bosom, that she was a great lady in the land, offered no opposition.

So the mother and little Pearl were admitted into the hall of entrance. With many variations, suggested by the nature of his building-materials, diversity of climate, and a different mode of social life, Governor Bellingham had planned his new habitation after the residences of gentlemen of fair estate in his native land. Here, then, was a wide and reasonably lofty hall, extending through the whole depth of the house, and forming a medium of general communication, more or less directly, with all the other apartments. At one extremity, this spacious room was lighted by the windows of the two towers, which formed a small recess on either side of the portal. At the other end, though partly muffled by a curtain, it was more powerfully illuminated by one of those embowed hall-windows which we read of in old books, and which was provided with a deep and cushioned seat. Here, on the cushion, lay a folio tome, probably of the *Chronicles of England*, or other such substantial literature; even as, in our own days, we scatter gilded volumes on the centre-table, to be turned over by the casual guest. The fur-

They approached the front door. The doorframe was arched, and on either side was a narrow tower-like projection for the windows and shutters. Hester gave a knock on the door's iron hammer. It was answered by one of the Governor's bond servants: a free-born Englishman who was now an indentured slave for the next seven years. During that time he was the property of his master, an object to be bargained over and sold, just like an ox or a stool. He wore the traditional clothing of a servant working in noble houses in England.

"Is the honorable Governor Bellingham in?" asked Hester.

"Certainly," the servant replied, staring wide-eyed at the scarlet letter. Being a newcomer in the country, he had never seen it before. "Yes, his right honorable self is in. But he has a reverend minister or two with him, and a doctor too. You can't see him now."

"No matter. I will enter," answered Hester Prynne. The servant did not stop her. Perhaps, based on the decisiveness in her speech and the symbol on her chest, he assumed she was a great lady.

The mother and little Pearl were admitted into the entryway. Governor Bellingham had designed his house after the wealthy gentlemen in his native England—though, of course, he had made many modifications to account for the differences in available building materials, climate, and social life in the colony. A wide and fairly high-ceilinged hall ran through the length of the house and opened into almost every other room. This hall was lit on one end by the windows of the two towers, which formed a little niche on either side of the door. The other end of the hall was lit by even stronger light from one of those large bay windows (the kind described in old books). The bay window was partly covered by a curtain and had a deep, cushioned seat below it. A large book—probably a *Chronicles of England* or some other serious work of literature—was sitting on the cushion. The volume was left there in the same way we scatter selected books on our living room tables for our guests to find. The furniture in the hall consisted of some heavy oak chairs, the backs of which were elaborately carved

Chronicles of [Engl]and, Scotland, [and] Ireland: Book [by] Raphael Holin[she]d, published in [la]te 16th century.

niture of the hall consisted of some ponderous chairs, the backs of which were elaborately carved with wreaths of oaken flowers; and likewise a table in the same taste; the whole being of the Elizabethan age, or perhaps earlier, and heirlooms, transferred hither from the Governor's paternal home. On the table—in token that the sentiment of old English hospitality had not been left behind—stood a large pewter tankard, at the bottom of which, had Hester or Pearl peeped into it, they might have seen the frothy remnant of a recent draught of ale.

On the wall hung a row of portraits, representing the forefathers of the Bellingham lineage, some with armour on their breasts, and others with stately ruffs and robes of peace. All were characterized by the sternness and severity which old portraits so invariably put on; as if they were the ghosts, rather than the pictures, of departed worthies, and were gazing with harsh and intolerant criticism at the pursuits and enjoyments of living men.

At about the centre of the oaken panels, that lined the hall, was suspended a suit of mail, not, like the pictures, an ancestral relic, but of the most modern date; for it had been manufactured by a skilful armorer in London, the same year in which Governor Bellingham came over to New England. There was a steel head-piece, a cuirass, a gorget, and greaves, with a pair of gauntlets and a sword hanging beneath; all, and especially the helmet and breastplate, so highly burnished as to glow with white radiance, and scatter an illumination everywhere about upon the floor. This bright panoply was not meant for mere idle show, but had been worn by the Governor on many a solemn muster and training field, and had glittered, moreover, at the head of a regiment in the Pequod war. For, though bred a lawyer, and accustomed to speak of Bacon, Coke, Noye, and Finch, as his professional associates, the exigencies of this new country had transformed Governor Bellingham into a soldier, as well as a statesman and ruler.

Little Pearl—who was as greatly pleased with the gleaming armour as she had been with the glittering frontispiece of the house—spent some time looking into the polished mirror of the breastplate.

"Mother," cried she, "I see you here. Look! Look!"

Hester looked, by way of humoring the child; and she saw that, owing to the peculiar effect of this convex mirror, the scarlet letter

with wreaths of flowers, and a matching table. All of the furnishings were heirlooms shipped over from the Governor's family home, and dating back to the Elizabethan age, or perhaps earlier. A large metal cup sat on the table, an indication that English hospitality had not been completely forgotten. Had Hester or Pearl looked into it, they might have seen the last drops of a recently poured glass of beer.

On the wall hung a row of portraits showing the Bellingham ancestors, some wearing armor and others wearing ceremonial collars and robes of peace. They all shared the stern character common to old portraits, looking more like ghosts peering down in judgment at the pursuits of the living than paintings of departed statesmen.

A suit of armor hung near the center of the oak panels lining the hall. Unlike the portraits, the armor was not a family heirloom. It was brand new, having been made by a skilled metalworker the same year Governor Bellingham arrived in New England. There was a steel headpiece, a breastplate, a collar, leggings, a pair of gloves, and a sword hanging beneath—all so highly polished, especially the headpiece and breastplate, that they shined white and scattered light across the floor. This bright gear was not merely for show. The Governor had worn it on several training fields, and when he sat at the front of a regiment in the war against the Pequot Indians. Though Governor Bellingham had been trained as a lawyer and was well versed in the works of the great legal minds of his day, the new country had transformed him into a soldier, as well as a statesman and ruler.

Little Pearl, who was as pleased by the gleaming armor as she had been by the glittering house, spent some time looking into the polished mirror of the breastplate.

"Mother," she cried, "I see you here. Look! Look!"

Hester looked, humoring the child. The large, curved mirror reflected the scarlet letter in huge, exaggerated proportions. It was

was represented in exaggerated and gigantic proportions, so as to be greatly the most prominent feature of her appearance. In truth, she seemed absolutely hidden behind it. Pearl pointed upward, also, at a similar picture in the head-piece; smiling at her mother, with the elf-ish intelligence that was so familiar an expression on her small physiognomy. That look of naughty merriment was likewise reflected in the mirror, with so much breadth and intensity of effect, that it made Hester Prynne feel as if it could not be the image of her own child, but of an imp who was seeking to mould itself into Pearl's shape.

"Come along, Pearl!" said she, drawing her away. "Come and look into this fair garden. It may be, we shall see flowers there; more beautiful ones than we find in the woods."

Pearl, accordingly, ran to the bow-window, at the farther end of the hall, and looked along the vista of a garden-walk, carpeted with closely shaven grass, and bordered with some rude and immature attempt at shrubbery. But the proprietor appeared already to have relinquished, as hopeless, the effort to perpetuate on this side of the Atlantic, in a hard soil and amid the close struggle for subsistence, the native English taste for ornamental gardening. Cabbages grew in plain sight; and a pumpkin vine, rooted at some distance, had run across the intervening space, and deposited one of its gigantic products directly beneath the hall-window; as if to warn the Governor that this great lump of vegetable gold was as rich an ornament as New England earth would offer him. There were a few rose-bushes, however, and a number of apple-trees, probably the descendants of those planted by the Reverend Mr. Blackstone, the first settler of the peninsula; that half-mythological personage who rides through our early annals, seated on the back of a bull.

Pearl, seeing the rose-bushes, began to cry for a red rose, and would not be pacified.

"Hush, child, hush!" said her mother earnestly. "Do not cry, dear little Pearl! I hear voices in the garden. The Governor is coming, and gentlemen along with him!"

In fact, adown the vista of the garden-avenue, a number of persons were seen approaching towards the house. Pearl, in utter scorn of her mother's attempt to quiet her, gave an eldritch scream, and then became silent; not from any notion of obedience, but because the quick and mobile curiosity of her disposition was excited by the appearance of these new personages.

easily Hester's most prominent feature: She seemed absolutely hidden behind it. Pearl pointed upwards to a similar reflection in the headpiece and smiled at her mother with her familiar elfish gleam. That look of naughty merriment was also reflected in the mirror, large and intense. Hester Prynne felt it couldn't be the image of her own child but rather that of an imp trying to mold itself into Pearl's shape.

"Come on, Pearl," she said, pulling her away. "Come and look at this lovely garden. Maybe we will see flowers there more beautiful than the ones we find in the woods."

Pearl ran to the bay window at the other end of the hall and looked along the garden path, which was carpeted with well-mowed grass and bordered with a crude attempt at shrubbery. It looked as though the Governor had already given up on replicating an English ornamental garden in this hard, unforgiving New England soil. Cabbages grew in plain sight, and a pumpkin-vine had stretched all the way across the path and dropped a pumpkin directly beneath the window—as if to warn the Governor that this great gold lump was the only ornament this land would offer him. Yet there were a few rose bushes and some apple trees, probably descended from the first trees planted by the Reverend Mr. Blackstone, the first settler in Massachusetts, who was rumored to have ridden around on a bull.

Upon seeing the rose bushes, Pearl demanded a red rose. She would not be quieted.

"Hush, child, hush!" her mother pleaded. "Don't call out, Pearl! I hear voices in the garden. The Governor is coming with some gentlemen."

In fact, a number of people could be seen walking down the path toward the house. Pearl, in defiance of her mother's attempt to quiet her, gave a loud shriek. Then she fell silent—not out of obedience, but because her curiosity was aroused by the appearance of these new people.

Chapter 8: The Elf-Child and the Minister

Governor Bellingham, in a loose gown and easy cap,—such as elderly gentlemen loved to indue themselves with, in their domestic privacy,—walked foremost, and appeared to be showing off his estate, and expatiating on his projected improvements. The wide circumference of an elaborate ruff, beneath his gray beard, in the antiquated fashion of King James's reign, caused his head to look not a little like that of John the Baptist in a charger. The impression made by his aspect, so rigid and severe, and frost-bitten with more than autumnal age, was hardly in keeping with the appliances of worldly enjoyment wherewith he had evidently done his utmost to surround himself. But it is an error to suppose that our grave forefathers—though accustomed to speak and think of human existence as a state merely of trial and warfare, and though unfeignedly prepared to sacrifice goods and life at the behest of duty—made it a matter of conscience to reject such means of comfort, or even luxury, as lay fairly within their grasp. This creed was never taught, for instance, by the venerable pastor, John Wilson, whose beard, white as a snow-drift, was seen over Governor Bellingham's shoulder; while its wearer suggested that pears and peaches might yet be naturalized in the New England climate, and that purple grapes might possibly be compelled to flourish, against the sunny garden-wall. The old clergyman, nurtured at the rich bosom of the English Church, had a long established and legitimate taste for all good and comfortable things; and however stern he might show himself in the pulpit, or in his public reproof of such transgressions as that of Hester Prynne, still, the genial benevolence of his private life had won him warmer affection than was accorded to any of his professional contemporaries.

Behind the Governor and Mr. Wilson came two other guests; one, the Reverend Arthur Dimmesdale, whom the reader may remember, as having taken a brief and reluctant part in the scene of Hester Prynne's disgrace; and, in close companionship with him, old Roger Chillingworth, a person of great skill in physic, who, for two or three years past, had been settled in the town. It was understood that this learned man was the physician as well as friend of the young minister, whose health had severely suffered, of late, by his too unreserved self-sacrifice to the labors and duties of the pastoral relation.

Chapter 8: The Elf-Child and the Minister

Governor Bellingham, in a loose gown and cap—the sort worn by elderly men in the comfort of their homes—walked in front of the group. He seemed to be showing off his home and explaining all the improvements he hoped to make. He wore a wide, ruffed collar beneath his gray beard, in the old fashion of King James's time, making his head look a little like John the Baptist's on a silver platter. The impression he made— stiff, harsh, and very old—seemed out of place with the worldly pleasures of his estate. But it would be wrong to assume that our great ancestors rejected comfort and luxury. True, they thought and spoke of human existence as a state of constant warfare and trial with temptation, and they were prepared to sacrifice their possessions and even their lives when duty called. But they still enjoyed what pleasures they could. Of course, this lesson was never taught by the wise, old pastor John Wilson, whose white beard could now be seen over Governor Bellingham's shoulder. Reverend Wilson was just then suggesting that pears and peaches might be transplanted to New England and grapes might grow well against the sunny garden wall. The old minister, who grew up in the wealthy Church of England, had a well-earned taste for all comforts. Despite how stern he might appear in the pulpit or in his public dealings with Hester Prynne, the warmth and goodwill displayed in his private life had made him more beloved than is typical for ministers.

g James: Ruler England, Scotnd, and Ireland (1603–1625).

John's beheading is described in Matthew 1:1–12.

Two other guests walked behind the Governor and Mr. Wilson. You may remember the Reverend Arthur Dimmesdale, who played a brief and reluctant role at the scene of Hester Prynne's public disgrace. Close beside him was old Roger Chillingworth, the skilled physician, who had been living in the town for the last two or three years. This wise man was well known as both doctor and friend to the young minister, whose health had recently suffered from his sacrificial devotion to his religious duties.

The Governor, in advance of his visitors, ascended one or two steps, and, throwing open the leaves of the great hall window, found himself close to little Pearl. The shadow of the curtain fell on Hester Prynne, and partially concealed her.

"What have we here?" said Governor Bellingham, looking with surprise at the scarlet little figure before him. "I profess, I have never seen the like, since my days of vanity, in old King James' time, when I was wont to esteem it a high favor to be admitted to a court mask! There used to be a swarm of these small apparitions, in holiday-time; and we called them children of the Lord of Misrule. But how gat such a guest into my hall?"

"Ay, indeed!" cried good old Mr. Wilson. "What little bird of scarlet plumage may this be? Methinks I have seen just such figures, when the sun has been shining through a richly painted window, and tracing out the golden and crimson images across the floor. But that was in the old land. Prithee, young one, who art thou, and what has ailed thy mother to bedizen thee in this strange fashion? Art thou a Christian child,—ha? Dost know thy catechism? Or art thou one of those naughty elfs or fairies, whom we thought to have left behind us, with other relics of Papistry, in merry old England?"

"I am mother's child," answered the scarlet vision, "and my name is Pearl!"

"Pearl?—Ruby, rather!—or Coral!—or Red Rose, at the very least, judging from thy hue!" responded the old minister, putting forth his hand in a vain attempt to pat little Pearl on the cheek. "But where is this mother of thine? Ah! I see," he added; and, turning to Governor Bellingham, whispered,—"This is the selfsame child of whom we have held speech together; and behold here the unhappy woman, Hester Prynne, her mother!"

"Sayest thou so?" cried the Governor. "Nay, we might have judged that such a child's mother must needs be a scarlet woman, and a worthy type of her Babylon! But she comes at a good time; and we will look into this matter forthwith."

Governor Bellingham stepped through the window into the hall, followed by his three guests.

"Hester Prynne," said he, fixing his naturally stern regard on the wearer of the scarlet letter, "there hath been much question concerning thee, of late. The point hath been weightily discussed, whether

Original Text

NO FEAR

The Governor, walking ahead of his visitors, climbed one or two steps and, throwing open the great hall window, found himself right in front of little Pearl. The shadow of the curtain fell on Hester Prynne, partially hiding her.

"What have we here?" said Governor Bellingham, looking surprised at the scarlet child in front of him. "I declare, I haven't seen something like this since my younger days, in old King James's time, when I used to go to masquerade parties at the court! There used to be a swarm of these little creatures at Christmastime. We called them the children of the Lord of Misrule. But how did this guest get into my hall?"

Lord of Misrule: Person appointed to preside over the Christmastime festivities in medieval England.

"Indeed!" cried good old Mr. Wilson. "What kind of little scarlet-feathered bird is this? I think I've seen these sorts of visions when the sun shines through a stained-glass window, casting gold and crimson pictures on the floor. But that was back in England. Tell me, young one, what are you, and what is wrong with your mother that she dresses you in such strange clothes? Are you a Christian child? Do you know your prayers? Or are you one of those elves or fairies we thought we had left behind us, along with all the other funny Catholic beliefs, in England?"

"I am my mother's child," answered the scarlet vision, "and my name is Pearl!"

"'Pearl?' No! You should be named 'Ruby,' or 'Coral,' or 'Red Rose' at least, judging by your color!" responded the old minister, stretching out his hand in a vain attempt to pat little Pearl on the cheek. "But where is this mother of yours? Ah, I see," he added. Turning to Governor Bellingham, he whispered, "This is the child we were talking about. And look, here is the unhappy woman, Hester Prynne, her mother!"

"Is it really?" cried the Governor. "Well, we should have figured the mother of such a child to be a scarlet woman, as that is the appropriate color for a whore! But she is here at a good time. We'll look into this matter immediately."

Governor Bellingham stepped through the window and into the hall. His three guests followed.

"Hester Prynne," he said, fixing his stern gaze on the wearer of the scarlet letter, "there has been a great debate concerning you. We have discussed whether we, who have the authority, are right to

we, that are of authority and influence, do well discharge our consciences by trusting an immortal soul, such as there is in yonder child, to the guidance of one who hath stumbled and fallen, amid the pitfalls of this world. Speak thou, the child's own mother! Were it not, thinkest thou, for thy little one's temporal and eternal welfare, that she be taken out of thy charge, and clad soberly, and disciplined strictly, and instructed in the truths of Heaven and earth? What canst thou do for the child, in this kind?"

"I can teach my little Pearl what I have learned from this!" answered Hester Prynne, laying her finger on the red token.

"Woman, it is thy badge of shame!" replied the stern magistrate. "It is because of the stain which that letter indicates, that we would transfer thy child to other hands."

"Nevertheless," said the mother calmly, though growing more pale, "this badge hath taught me,—it daily teaches me,—it is teaching me at this moment,—lessons whereof my child may be the wiser and better, albeit they can profit nothing to myself."

"We will judge warily," said Bellingham, "and look well what we are about to do. Good Master Wilson, I pray you, examine this Pearl,—since that is her name,—and see whether she hath had such Christian nurture as befits a child of her age."

The old minister seated himself in an arm-chair, and made an effort to draw Pearl betwixt his knees. But the child, unaccustomed to the touch or familiarity of any but her mother, escaped through the open window and stood on the upper step, looking like a wild, tropical bird, of rich plumage, ready to take flight into the upper air. Mr. Wilson, not a little astonished at this outbreak,—for he was a grandfatherly sort of personage, and usually a vast favorite with children,—essayed, however, to proceed with the examination.

"Pearl," said he, with great solemnity, "thou must take heed to instruction, that so, in due season, thou mayest wear in thy bosom the pearl of great price. Canst thou tell me, my child, who made thee?"

Now Pearl knew well enough who made her; for Hester Prynne, the daughter of a pious home, very soon after her talk with the child about her Heavenly Father, had begun to inform her of those truths which the human spirit, at whatever stage of immaturity, imbibes with such eager interest. Pearl, therefore, so large were the attain-

entrust the immortal soul of this child to your guidance. You have tripped and fallen amid the pitfalls of this world. Speak, mother of this child! Don't you think it would be best for your little one if she were taken from you, dressed conservatively, disciplined strictly, and taught the true way to live? What can you do for this child?"

"I can teach my little Pearl what I have learned from this!" answered Hester Prynne, placing her finger on the scarlet letter.

"Woman, that is your badge of shame!" replied the Governor. "It is because of the sin indicated by that letter that we want to place the child in other hands."

"Nonetheless," said Hester, calmly, though growing paler, "this badge has taught me—it teaches me every day, and it is teaching me right now—lessons that will make my child wiser and better, though they can do me no good."

"We will be cautious in our judgment," said Governor Bellingham, "and will think hard on the decision. Mister Wilson, please, examine this Pearl—since that is her name—and see if she's had the kind of Christian upbringing appropriate for her age."

The old minister sat down in an armchair and tried to set Pearl between his knees. But the child, who wasn't used to anyone but her mother, escaped through the open window and stood on the upper step outside. She looked like a wild tropical bird with colorful feathers, ready to take flight high into the sky. Mr. Wilson was quite surprised by her escape, for he was a grandfatherly type and children usually loved him. Still, he tried to continue with his examination.

"Pearl," he said, with great seriousness, "you must pay attention so that, in time, you can wear in your breast the pearl of great price. Can you tell me, my child, who made you?"

Pearl knew perfectly well who made her. Hester Prynne was herself raised in a pious home. She talked with Pearl about her heavenly Father and taught her those religious truths that young children intently absorb. In her three short years, Pearl had learned so much about religion that she could have passed any school examination

ments of her three years' lifetime, could have borne a fair examination in the New England Primer, or the first column of the Westminster Catechism, although unacquainted with the outward form of either of those celebrated works. But that perversity, which all children have more or less of, and of which little Pearl had a tenfold portion, now, at the most inopportune moment, took thorough possession of her, and closed her lips, or impelled her to speak words amiss. After putting her finger in her mouth, with many ungracious refusals to answer good Mr. Wilson's question, the child finally announced that she had not been made at all, but had been plucked by her mother off the bush of wild roses, that grew by the prison-door.

This fantasy was probably suggested by the near proximity of the Governor's red roses, as Pearl stood outside of the window; together with her recollection of the prison rose-bush, which she had passed in coming hither.

Old Roger Chillingworth, with a smile on his face, whispered something in the young clergyman's ear. Hester Prynne looked at the man of skill, and even then, with her fate hanging in the balance, was startled to perceive what a change had come over his features,—how much uglier they were,—how his dark complexion seemed to have grown duskier, and his figure more misshapen,—since the days when she had familiarly known him. She met his eyes for an instant, but was immediately constrained to give all her attention to the scene now going forward.

"This is awful!" cried the Governor, slowly recovering from the astonishment into which Pearl's response had thrown him. "Here is a child of three years old, and she cannot tell who made her! Without question, she is equally in the dark as to her soul, its present depravity, and future destiny! Methinks, gentlemen, we need inquire no further."

Hester caught hold of Pearl, and drew her forcibly into her arms, confronting the old Puritan magistrate with almost a fierce expression. Alone in the world, cast off by it, and with this sole treasure to keep her heart alive, she felt that she possessed indefeasible rights against the world, and was ready to defend them to the death.

"God gave me the child!" cried she. "He gave her, in requital of all things else, which ye had taken from me. She is my happiness!— she is my torture, none the less! Pearl keeps me here in life! Pearl

without having to study. But that same naughtiness present to some degree in all children existed ten-fold in Pearl. It seized her at this most inappropriate moment. She put her finger in her mouth and repeatedly refused Mr. Wilson's requests for an answer. Then the child finally announced that she had not been made at all but had been plucked by her mother off the wild rose bush that grew by the prison door.

Pearl probably concocted this story after seeing the Governor's red roses, which were right next to her by the window. She may have also remembered the prison rose bush she passed on the way to the Governor's house.

Old Roger Chillingworth, with a smile on his face, whispered something in the young minister's ear. Hester Prynne looked at the doctor. Even then, with her fate hanging in the balance, she was startled to see how much he had changed. His face was so much uglier, his dark complexion even darker, and his figure more misshapen since the days when she knew him well. She looked him in the eyes for an instant but immediately returned her full attention to the scene between Pearl and Mr. Wilson.

"This is awful!" cried the Governor, slowly recovering from his astonishment at Pearl's answer. "This three-year-old child cannot tell who made her! Without a doubt, she knows just as little about her soul, its present sinfulness, and its future destiny! Gentlemen, I think we know all we need to know."

Hester grabbed Pearl, held her strongly, and looked with an almost fierce expression at the Puritan magistrate. Hester was an outcast, alone in the world, with only this treasure to keep her heart alive. She felt that she had an absolute right to her daughter, and she was ready to defend that right to the death.

"God gave me the child!" she cried. "He gave her to me as compensation for everything that you had taken from me. She is my happiness. She is my torture—but still! Pearl keeps me alive! Pearl punishes me too! See ye not, she is the scarlet letter, only capable of being loved, and so endowed with a million-fold the power of retribution for my sin? Ye shall not take her! I will die first!"

"My poor woman," said the not unkind old minister, "the child shall be well cared for!—far better than thou canst do it."

"God gave her into my keeping," repeated Hester Prynne, raising her voice almost to a shriek. "I will not give her up!"—And here, by a sudden impulse, she turned to the young clergyman, Mr. Dimmesdale, at whom, up to this moment, she had seemed hardly so much as once to direct her eyes.—"Speak thou for me!" cried she. "Thou wast my pastor, and hadst charge of my soul, and knowest me better than these men can. I will not lose the child! Speak for me! Thou knowest,—for thou hast sympathies which these men lack!—thou knowest what is in my heart, and what are a mother's rights, and how much the stronger they are, when that mother has but her child and the scarlet letter! Look thou to it! I will not lose the child! Look to it!"

At this wild and singular appeal, which indicated that Hester Prynne's situation had provoked her to little less than madness, the young minister at once came forward, pale, and holding his hand over his heart, as was his custom whenever his peculiarly nervous temperament was thrown into agitation. He looked now more careworn and emaciated than as we described him at the scene of Hester's public ignominy; and whether it were his failing health, or whatever the cause might be, his large dark eyes had a world of pain in their troubled and melancholy depth.

"There is truth in what she says," began the minister, with a voice sweet, tremulous, but powerful, insomuch that the hall reëchoed, and the hollow armour rang with it,—"truth in what Hester says, and in the feeling which inspires her! God gave her the child, and gave her, too, an instinctive knowledge of its nature and requirements,—both seemingly so peculiar,—which no other mortal being can possess. And, more over, is there not a quality of awful sacredness in the relation between this mother and this child?"

"Ay!—how is that, good Master Dimmesdale?" interrupted the Governor. "Make that plain, I pray you!"

"It must be even so," resumed the minister. "For, if we deem it otherwise, do we not thereby say that the Heavenly Father, the

punishes me too! Don't you see that she is the scarlet letter? But I can love her, so she has the power to punish me for my sin a million times over. You will not take her! I will die first!"

"My poor woman," said the kind old minister, "the child will be well cared for, far better than you can care for her."

"God gave her to me to care for!" repeated Hester Prynne, raising her voice almost to a shriek. "I will not give her up!" Without a thought, she turned to the young minister, Mr. Dimmesdale. Until now, she had barely looked at him. "Speak up for me!" she cried. "You were my pastor and you cared for my soul. You know me better than these men do. I will not lose the child! Speak up for me! You know—you have understanding that these men lack—you know what is in my heart. You know a mother's rights and how strong they are when that mother has nothing but her child and this scarlet letter! Do something! I will not lose the child! Do something!"

After this wild and strange plea, which revealed that Hester Prynne's situation had driven her to the brink of madness, the young minister stepped forward. He was pale and he held his hand over his heart, as he did whenever circumstances agitated his unusually nervous disposition. He looked thinner and more worn down with worry than when he had spoken at Hester's public shaming. Either from his failing health or for some other reason, his large dark eyes had a world of pain in their troubled and melancholy depths.

"There is truth in what she says," began the minister. His voice was sweet and delicate, but so powerful that the room echoed and the hollow armor rang with his words. "There is truth in what Hester says, and in the feeling that inspires her! God gave the child to her, and He gave her an instinctive knowledge of the child's nature and needs. No other person could understand such a peculiar child. And doesn't a sacred relationship exist between this mother and her child?"

"How do you figure, good Master Dimmesdale?" interrupted the Governor. "Please, explain what you mean!"

"It has to be so," the minister continued. "If we say it isn't, doesn't that mean God Himself—creator of all flesh—allowed a sinful act to

Creator of all flesh, hath lightly recognized a deed of sin, and made of no account the distinction between unhallowed lust and holy love? This child of its father's guilt and its mother's shame hath come from the hand of God, to work in many ways upon her heart, who pleads so earnestly, and with such bitterness of spirit, the right to keep her. It was meant for a blessing; for the one blessing of her life! It was meant, doubtless, as the mother herself hath told us, for a retribution too; a torture, to be felt at many an unthought of moment; a pang, a sting, an ever-recurring agony, in the midst of a troubled joy! Hath she not expressed this thought in the garb of the poor child, so forcibly reminding us of that red symbol which sears her bosom?"

"Well said, again!" cried good Mr. Wilson. "I feared the woman had no better thought than to make a mountebank of her child!"

"O, not so!—not so!" continued Mr. Dimmesdale. "She recognizes, believe me, the solemn miracle which God hath wrought, in the existence of that child. And may she feel, too,—what, methinks, is the very truth,—that this boon was meant, above all things else, to keep the mother's soul alive, and to preserve her from blacker depths of sin into which Satan might else have sought to plunge her! Therefore it is good for this poor, sinful woman that she hath an infant immortality, a being capable of eternal joy or sorrow, confided to her care,—to be trained up by her to righteousness,—to remind her, at every moment, of her fall,—but yet to teach her, as it were by the Creator's sacred pledge, that, if she bring the child to Heaven, the child also will bring its parent thither! Herein is the sinful mother happier than the sinful father. For Hester Prynne's sake, then, and no less for the poor child's sake, let us leave them as Providence hath seen fit to place them!"

"You speak, my friend, with a strange earnestness," said old Roger Chillingworth, smiling at him.

"And there is weighty import in what my young brother hath spoken," added the Reverend Mr. Wilson. "What say you, worshipful Master Bellingham? Hath he not pleaded well for the poor woman?"

"Indeed hath he," answered the magistrate, "and hath adduced such arguments, that we will even leave the matter as it now stands; so long, at least, as there shall be no further scandal in the woman. Care must be had, nevertheless, to put the child to due and stated

happen without making a distinction between unholy lust and holy love? This child, born of its father's guilt and its mother's shame, came from the hand of God to work in many ways upon the mother's heart, which pleads so passionately to keep her. This girl was meant as a blessing—the one blessing in her mother's life! She was meant as a punishment too, just like her mother said. The girl is a torture in many idle moments: A pang, a sting, and a persistent agony in the midst of a troubled joy! Isn't this exactly what the mother is trying to express with the child's clothing? Isn't she consciously reminding us of the red symbol that burns her breast?"

"Well said again!" cried good Mr. Wilson. "I was worried that the woman was simply trying to make her child look like a clown!"

"Oh, no! Not at all!" continued Mr. Dimmesdale. "Believe me, she recognizes God's miracle in creating that child. And she may also feel—and I think this is the heart of the matter—this blessing was meant to keep her soul alive and out of the darker depths. Otherwise, Satan might have tried to plunge her deep in sin. So it is good for this poor, sinful woman that she has an infant soul entrusted to her care: to be raised by her in the path of virtue, to remind her constantly of her sin, but also to teach her that if she brings the child to Heaven, the child will bring its mother there. This is why the sinful mother is luckier than the sinful father. For Hester Prynne's sake and for the sake of the young child, let us leave them as God has seen fit to place them!"

"You speak with strange conviction, my friend," said old Roger Chillingworth, smiling at him.

"And there is deep meaning in what my young brother has said," added the Reverend Mr. Wilson. "What do you say, my honorable Master Bellingham? Hasn't he made a good case for the poor woman?"

"So he has," answered the magistrate. "He's convinced me that we should leave things as they are, at least as long as the woman causes no further scandals. Even so, we must take care to give the child

examination in the catechism at thy hands or Master Dimmesdale's. Moreover, at a proper season, the tithing-men must take heed that she go both to school and to meeting."

The young minister, on ceasing to speak, had withdrawn a few steps from the group, and stood with his face partially concealed in the heavy folds of the window-curtain; while the shadow of his figure, which the sunlight cast upon the floor, was tremulous with the vehemence of his appeal. Pearl, that wild and flighty little elf, stole softly towards him, and, taking his hand in the grasp of both her own, laid her cheek against it; a caress so tender, and withal so unobtrusive, that her mother, who was looking on, asked herself,—"Is that my Pearl?" Yet she knew that there was love in the child's heart, although it mostly revealed itself in passion, and hardly twice in her lifetime had been softened by such gentleness as now. The minister,—for, save the long-sought regards of woman, nothing is sweeter than these marks of childish preference, accorded spontaneously by a spiritual instinct, and therefore seeming to imply in us something truly worthy to be loved,—the minister looked round, laid his hand on the child's head, hesitated an instant, and then kissed her brow. Little Pearl's unwonted mood of sentiment lasted no longer; she laughed, and went capering down the hall, so airily, that old Mr. Wilson raised a question whether even her tiptoes touched the floor.

"The little baggage hath witchcraft in her, I profess," said he to Mr. Dimmesdale. "She needs no old woman's broomstick to fly withal!"

"A strange child!" remarked old Roger Chillingworth. "It is easy to see the mother's part in her. Would it be beyond a philosopher's research, think ye, gentlemen, to analyze that child's nature, and, from its make and mould, to give a shrewd guess at the father?"

"Nay; it would be sinful, in such a question, to follow the clew of profane philosophy," said Mr. Wilson. "Better to fast and pray upon it; and still better, it may be, to leave the mystery as we find it, unless Providence reveal it of its own accord. Thereby, every good Christian man hath a title to show a father's kindness towards the poor, deserted babe."

The affair being so satisfactorily concluded, Hester Prynne, with Pearl, departed from the house. As they descended the steps, it is averred that the lattice of a chamber-window was thrown open, and

a proper religious education, whether at your hands or at Master Dimmesdale's. And when she is old enough, the leaders of our congregation must see that she goes to both school and church."

After he finished speaking, the young minister withdrew a few steps from the group. He stood with his face half-hidden in the heavy folds of the window curtain. His shadow, thrown onto the floor by the sunlight, shook from the passion of his appeal. Pearl, that wild and unpredictable little elf, crept over to him. She took his hand in both of hers and laid her cheek against it. Her caress was so tender and gentle that her mother, watching this, asked herself, "Is that my Pearl?" She knew there was love in the child's heart, though it mostly exhibited wild passion. Hester had rarely seen Pearl's heart softened with such gentleness as it was now. Only the long-sought love of a woman is sweeter than the spontaneous, instinctual love of a child—a fact that seems to suggest there is something truly worthy of love in all of us. The minister looked around, laid his hand on the child's head, and, after hesitating for an instant, kissed her on the forehead. Little Pearl's unusually sweet mood came to an end: She laughed and went skipping down the hall so lightly that old Mr. Wilson wondered whether her toes even touched the floor.

"That little thing is bewitched, I swear," he said to Mr. Dimmesdale. "She doesn't need any broomstick to fly!"

"A strange child!" remarked old Roger Chillingworth. "It's easy to see her mother in her. Do you think, gentlemen, that some scientific research into that child's nature would allow us to make a shrewd guess at the identity of her father?"

"No—it would be sinful to use worldly science to answer such a question," said Mr. Wilson. "Better to fast and pray on it. Even better, perhaps, to leave the mystery be, unless God himself chooses to reveal it. That way, every good Christian will have the right to show a father's kindness to the poor, deserted child."

The matter being satisfactorily concluded, Hester Prynne and Pearl left the house. It is rumored that as they descended the steps, a window was thrown open and revealed the face of Mistress Hibbins,

forth into the sunny day was thrust the face of Mistress Hibbins, Governor Bellingham's bitter-tempered sister, and the same who, a few years later, was executed as a witch.

"Hist, hist!" said she, while her ill-omened physiognomy seemed to cast a shadow over the cheerful newness of the house. "Wilt thou go with us to-night? There will be a merry company in the forest; and I wellnigh promised the Black Man that comely Hester Prynne should make one."

"Make my excuse to him, so please you!" answered Hester, with a triumphant smile. "I must tarry at home, and keep watch over my little Pearl. Had they taken her from me, I would willingly have gone with thee into the forest, and signed my name in the Black Man's book too, and that with mine own blood!"

"We shall have thee there anon!" said the witch-lady, frowning, as she drew back her head.

But here—if we suppose this interview betwixt Mistress Hibbins and Hester Prynne to be authentic, and not a parable—was already an illustration of the young minister's argument against sundering the relation of a fallen mother to the offspring of her frailty. Even thus early had the child saved her from Satan's snare.

NO FEAR

Governor Bellingham's ill-tempered sister. This was the same sister who was executed as a witch a few years later.

"Psst—psst!" she said, while her ominous face seemed to cast a shadow over the bright and cheerful house. "Will you go with us tonight? There will be a party in the forest, and I promised the Devil that lovely Hester Prynne would join us."

"Send my regrets, if you like!" answered Hester, with a triumphant smile. "I must stay at home and take care of my little Pearl. If they had taken her from me, I would have gladly gone to the forest with you and signed my name in the Devil's book—with my own blood!"

"We'll have you there some day!" said the witch-lady, frowning, as she pulled her head back in.

Now, if we believe this encounter between Mistress Hibbins and Hester Prynne was authentic—not simply a fable—then we already have evidence supporting the young minister's argument against breaking the bond between the sinful mother and the fruit of her sin. Even this young, the child had saved the mother from Satan's snare.

Chapter 9: The Leech

Under the appellation of Roger Chillingworth, the reader will remember, was hidden another name, which its former wearer had resolved should never more be spoken. It has been related, how, in the crowd that witnessed Hester Prynne's ignominious exposure, stood a man, elderly, travel-worn, who, just emerging from the perilous wilderness, beheld the woman, in whom he hoped to find embodied the warmth and cheerfulness of home, set up as a type of sin before the people. Her matronly fame was trodden under all men's feet. Infamy was babbling around her in the public market-place. For her kindred, should the tidings ever reach them, and for the companions of her unspotted life, there remained nothing but the contagion of her dishonor; which would not fail to be distributed in strict accordance and proportion with the intimacy and sacredness of their previous relationship. Then why—since the choice was with himself—should the individual, whose connection with the fallen woman had been the most intimate and sacred of them all, come forward to vindicate his claim to an inheritance so little desirable? He resolved not to be pilloried beside her on her pedestal of shame. Unknown to all but Hester Prynne, and possessing the lock and key of her silence, he chose to withdraw his name from the roll of mankind, and, as regarded his former ties and interests, to vanish out of life as completely as if he indeed lay at the bottom of the ocean, whither rumor had long ago consigned him. This purpose once effected, new interests would immediately spring up, and likewise a new purpose; dark, it is true, if not guilty, but of force enough to engage the full strength of his faculties.

In pursuance of this resolve, he took up his residence in the Puritan town, as Roger Chillingworth, without other introduction than the learning and intelligence of which he possessed more than a common measure. As his studies, at a previous period of his life, had made him extensively acquainted with the medical science of the day, it was as a physician that he presented himself, and as such was cordially received. Skilful men, of the medical and chirurgical profession, were of rare occurrence in the colony. They seldom, it would appear, partook of the religious zeal that brought other emigrants across the Atlantic. In their researches into the human frame,

Chapter 9: The Leech

You will remember that the name Roger Chillingworth hid another name—one which its owner had resolved would never be spoken again. You have heard how, in the crowd that witnessed Hester Prynne's public shaming, there stood an elderly and travel-weary man. Right as he emerged from the hazardous wilderness, he saw the woman he had hoped would embody the warmth and cheerfulness of home instead embodying sin for all to see. Her reputation was trampled under the feet of all men. Everyone at the marketplace was discussing her wrongdoing. Her dishonor would spread like a contagious disease among her family—if the news reached them—and friends, according to their intimacy with Hester. Why would the man closest to that fallen woman willingly choose to come forward and claim his share of her dishonor? He resolved not to stand beside her on the pedestal of shame. He was unknown to all but Hester, and he had her promise to keep quiet. He chose to withdraw his name from the roll books of mankind. He allowed his old identity to vanish, as though his body actually lay at the bottom of the ocean, where rumor had long ago placed it. Having done this, new interests immediately sprang up and a new purpose presented itself. It was a dark, if not guilty, purpose, but one strong enough to consume his entire life.

To pursue this new purpose, he settled in the Puritan town as Roger Chillingworth. He had neither connections nor resources, other than his uncommon learning and intelligence. He presented himself as a doctor, drawing on his earlier studies of current medical practices. He was welcomed in the colony, since skilled doctors and surgeons rarely moved there. It seems these professionals seldom possessed the same religious zeal that brought other immigrants across the Atlantic. Perhaps in their studies, doctors became so enamored with the artful mechanics of the human body that they lost the desire to seek out life's mysteries in the spiritual realm. Whatever the

it may be that the higher and more subtile faculties of such men were materialized, and that they lost the spiritual view of existence amid the intricacies of that wondrous mechanism, which seemed to involve art enough to comprise all of life within itself. At all events, the health of the good town of Boston, so far as medicine had aught to do with it, had hitherto lain in the guardianship of an aged deacon and apothecary, whose piety and godly deportment were stronger testimonials in his favor, than any that he could have produced in the shape of a diploma. The only surgeon was one who combined the occasional exercise of that noble art with the daily and habitual flourish of a razor. To such a professional body Roger Chillingworth was a brilliant acquisition. He soon manifested his familiarity with the ponderous and imposing machinery of antique physic; in which every remedy contained a multitude of far-fetched and heterogeneous ingredients, as elaborately compounded as if the proposed result had been the Elixir of Life. In his Indian captivity, moreover, he had gained much knowledge of the properties of native herbs and roots; nor did he conceal from his patients, that these simple medicines, Nature's boon to the untutored savage, had quite as large a share of his own confidence as the European pharmacopœia, which so many learned doctors had spent centuries in elaborating.

This learned stranger was exemplary, as regarded at least the outward forms of a religious life, and, early after his arrival, had chosen for his spiritual guide the Reverend Mr. Dimmesdale. The young divine, whose scholar-like renown still lived in Oxford, was considered by his more fervent admirers as little less than a Heaven-ordained apostle, destined, should he live and labor for the ordinary term of life, to do as great deeds for the now feeble New England Church, as the early Fathers had achieved for the infancy of the Christian faith. About this period, however, the health of Mr. Dimmesdale had evidently begun to fail. By those best acquainted with his habits, the paleness of the young minister's cheek was accounted for by his too earnest devotion to study, his scrupulous fulfilment of parochial duty, and, more than all, by the fasts and vigils of which he made a frequent practices in order to keep the grossness of this earthly state from clogging and obscuring his spiritual lamp. Some declared, that, if Mr. Dimmesdale were really going to die, it was cause enough, that the world was not worthy to be any

reason, the physical health of the good town of Boston had up to that point been entrusted to an aged deacon and a pharmacist whose godliness was far greater than his learning. Their only surgeon doubled as a barber. Roger Chillingworth was a brilliant addition to that professional body. He soon demonstrated his familiarity with the ancient art of medicine, which combined a vast mixture of exotic ingredients in an intricate way that seemed more appropriate for an Elixir of Life. He had also learned a great deal about the native herbs and roots while imprisoned by the Indians. He recommended these simple, natural medicines to his patients with as much confidence as he had in prescribing European drugs that had been developed by learned doctors over centuries.

Elixir of Life: ...ry potion for ...ternal youth.

This learned stranger led an outwardly upright and religious life. Shortly after his arrival, he had chosen the Reverend Mr. Dimmesdale as his spiritual guide. The young minister, whose scholarly reputation still lived on back in Oxford, was considered by some of his greatest admirers to be almost a divinely chosen apostle. They were certain that, if he lived a full life, his deeds for the young New England church would be as great as those done by the first apostles for all of Christianity. Around this time, however, the health of Mr. Dimmesdale had clearly begun to fail. Those who knew him best attributed the paleness of the young minister's cheeks to his overly studious habits, his strict attention to his pastoral duties, and (more than anything) the fasts and vigils he often undertook in the hope of preventing his mortal frailty from dimming his spiritual light. Some said that if Mr. Dimmesdale were really going to die, it was because the world was no longer worthy of him. He, in characteristic humility, protested that if God should see fit to remove him, it would be because he was unfit to perform his humble mission on earth. But

longer trodden by his feet. He himself, on the other hand with characteristic humility, avowed his belief, that, if Providence should see fit to remove him, it would be because of his own unworthiness to perform its humblest mission here on earth. With all this difference of opinion as to the cause of his decline, there could be no question of the fact. His form grew emaciated; his voice, though still rich and sweet, had a certain melancholy prophecy of decay in it; he was often observed, on any slight alarm or other sudden accident, to put his hand over his heart, with first a flush and then a paleness, indicative of pain.

Such was the young clergyman's condition, and so imminent the prospect that his dawning light would be extinguished, all untimely, when Roger Chillingworth made his advent to the town. His first entry on the scene, few people could tell whence, dropping down, as it were, out of the sky, or starting from the nether earth, had an aspect of mystery, which was easily heightened to the miraculous. He was now known to be a man of skill; it was observed that he gathered herbs, and the blossoms of wild-flowers, and dug up roots and plucked off twigs from the forest-trees, like one acquainted with hidden virtues in what was value-less to common eyes. He was heard to speak of Sir Kenelm Digby, and other famous men,—whose scientific attainments were esteemed hardly less than supernatural,—as having been his correspondents or associates. Why, with such rank in the learned world, had he come hither? What could he, whose sphere was in great cities, be seeking in the wilderness? In answer to this query, a rumor gained ground,—and, however absurd, was entertained by some very sensible people,—that Heaven had wrought an absolute miracle, by transporting an eminent Doctor of Physic, from a German university, bodily through the air, and setting him down at the door of Mr. Dimmesdale's study! Individuals of wiser faith, indeed, who knew that Heaven promotes its purposes without aiming at the stage-effect of what is called miraculous interposition, were inclined to see a providential hand in Roger Chillingworth's so opportune arrival.

This idea was countenanced by the strong interest which the physician ever manifested in the young clergyman; he attached himself to him as a parishioner, and sought to win a friendly regard and confidence from his naturally reserved sensibility. He expressed

while there was some disagreement as to the cause, there could be no question that he was indeed ill. His body grew thin. His voice, though still rich and sweet, had a sad hint of decay in it. Often, at the slightest surprise, he would put his hand over his heart, first with a blush, then with a paleness that suggested pain.

This was the condition of the young clergyman, so close to an untimely death, when Roger Chillingworth appeared in town. Few people knew how he got there. To most, it seemed he had fallen out of the sky or risen up from the earth. It wasn't long before people came to see his presence as a miracle. He was known to be a skillful doctor. People noted that he gathered herbs and wildflowers, roots and twigs, as though he knew secrets hidden from the ordinary person's eyes. He spoke of associations with such notable men as Sir Kenelm Digby, and others whose scientific achievements tended toward the supernatural. Why, with such a reputation in the academic world, had he come here? What could this man, accustomed to the great cities, be seeking in the wilderness? It was rumored that a heavenly miracle transported this learned doctor, trained at a German university, through the air and set him down on Mr. Dimmesdale's doorstep. Absurd as this rumor sounds, it was believed by some of the more sensible people in the community. Even wiser people, who knew that Heaven accomplished its goals without the aid of elaborate miracles, were inclined to see the hand of God in Roger Chillingworth's timely arrival.

Kenelm Digby: century English teer and naval ficer known for ork in alchemy and astrology.

This idea was reinforced by the strong interest the physician paid to the young clergyman. He came to the minister as a church member and endeavored to make friends with the naturally reserved man. He expressed great concern at his pastor's poor health and

great alarm at his pastor's state of health, but was anxious to attempt the cure, and, if early undertaken, seemed not despondent of a favorable result. The elders, the deacons, the motherly dames, and the young and fair maidens, of Mr. Dimmesdale's flock, were alike importunate that he should make trial of the physician's frankly offered skill. Mr. Dimmesdale gently repelled their entreaties.

"I need no medicine," said he.

But how could the young minister say so, when, with every successive Sabbath, his cheek was paler and thinner, and his voice more tremulous than before,—when it had now become a constant habit, rather than a casual gesture, to press his hand over his heart? Was he weary of his labors? Did he wish to die? These questions were solemnly propounded to Mr. Dimmesdale by the elder ministers of Boston and the deacons of his church, who, to use their own phrase, "dealt with him" on the sin of rejecting the aid which Providence so manifestly held out. He listened in silence, and finally promised to confer with the physician.

"Were it God's will," said the Reverend Mr. Dimmesdale, when, in fulfilment of this pledge, he requested old Roger Chillingworth's professional advice, "I could be well content, that my labors, and my sorrows, and my sins, and my pains, should shortly end with me, and what is earthly of them be buried in my grave, and the spiritual go with me to my eternal state, rather than that you should put your skill to the proof in my behalf."

"Ah," replied Roger Chillingworth, with that quietness which, whether imposed or natural, marked all his deportment, "it is thus that a young clergyman is apt to speak. Youthful men, not having taken a deep root, give up their hold of life so easily! And saintly men, who walk with God on earth, would fain be away, to walk with him on the golden pavements of the New Jerusalem."

"Nay," rejoined the young minister, putting his hand to his heart, with a flush of pain flitting over his brow, "were I worthier to walk there, I could be better content to toil here."

"Good men ever interpret themselves too meanly," said the physician.

In this manner, the mysterious old Roger Chillingworth became the medical adviser of the Reverend Mr. Dimmesdale. As not only the disease interested the physician, but he was strongly moved to look into the character and qualities of the patient, these two men,

was anxious to attempt a cure. He believed that, if started soon, this treatment just might work. The elders, deacons, matrons, and young women of the congregation were all determined that Mr. Dimmesdale should try out the doctor's freely offered help. Mr. Dimmesdale gently refused.

"I need no medicine," he said.

But how could the young minister say no, when with every passing Sunday his face grew paler and thinner and his voice trembled more than it had before? How could he refuse when it had now become his constant habit to press his hand over his heart? Was he weary of his labors? Did he wish to die? The elder ministers of Boston and his own church deacons solemnly put these questions to Mr. Dimmesdale. To use their own phrase, they "dealt with him" concerning the sin of rejecting aid God had so clearly offered. He listened in silence, and finally promised to see the doctor.

"If it were God's will," said the Reverend Mr. Dimmesdale when, in honor of this pledge, he requested old Roger Chillingworth's professional advice, "I could be content that my labors and my sorrows, my sins and my pains, should soon end along with me. My earthly body could be buried in my grave, and the spiritual part could go with me into the afterlife. I would prefer for this to happen, rather than to have you test your skill on my behalf."

"Ah," replied Roger Chillingworth in that quiet way, whether real or pretend, he always carried himself. "Young clergymen often speak this way. Young men, not having rooted themselves, give up their hold on life so easily! And saintly men, who walk with God on earth, would rather depart, to walk with him on the golden streets of Heaven."

"No," replied the young minister, putting his hand to his heart as a flush of pain passed over his face, "if I were worthy to walk there, I could be happy to work here."

"Good men always think too little of themselves," said the doctor.

This is how the mysterious old Roger Chillingworth came to be medical adviser to Reverend Mr. Dimmesdale. Since the doctor was interested in the character of the patient as well as his disease, these two men, so different in age, gradually came to spend a great deal of

so different in age, came gradually to spend much time together. For the sake of the minister's health, and to enable the leech to gather plants with healing balm in them, they took long walks on the sea-shore, or in the forest; mingling various talk with the plash and murmur of the waves, and the solemn wind-anthem among the tree-tops. Often, likewise, one was the guest of the other, in his place of study and retirement. There was a fascination for the minister in the company of the man of science, in whom he recognized an intellectual cultivation of no moderate depth or scope; together with a range and freedom of ideas, that he would have vainly looked for among the members of his own profession. In truth, he was startled, if not shocked, to find this attribute in the physician. Mr. Dimmesdale was a true priest, a true religionist, with the reverential sentiment largely developed, and an order of mind that impelled itself powerfully along the track of a creed, and wore its passage continually deeper with the lapse of time. In no state of society would he have been what is called a man of liberal views; it would always be essential to his peace to feel the pressure of a faith about him, supporting, while it confined him within its iron framework. Not the less, however, though with a tremulous enjoyment, did he feel the occasional relief of looking at the universe through the medium of another kind of intellect than those with which he habitually held converse. It was as if a window were thrown open, admitting a freer atmosphere into the close and stifled study, where his life was wasting itself away, amid lamp-light, or obstructed day-beams, and the musty fragrance, be it sensual or moral, that exhales from books. But the air was too fresh and chill to be long breathed, with comfort. So the minister, and the physician with him, withdrew again within the limits of what their church defined as orthodox.

Thus Roger Chillingworth scrutinized his patient carefully, both as he saw him in his ordinary life, keeping an accustomed pathway in the range of thoughts familiar to him, and as he appeared when thrown amidst other moral scenery, the novelty of which might call out something new to the surface of his character. He deemed it essential, it would seem, to know the man, before attempting to do him good. Wherever there is a heart and an intellect, the diseases of the physical frame are tinged with the peculiarities of these. In Arthur Dimmesdale, thought and imagination were so active, and

time together. They took long walks by the seashore and in the forest, listening to the splash and murmur of the waves or the solemn song of the wind in the treetops. These walks were good for the minister's health, and they gave the doctor a chance to gather medicinal plants. They also spent time at each other's home. The minister was fascinated by this man of science. He recognized in him a sophisticated intellect and free-thinking and well-rounded mind not found among his fellow clergymen. He was actually a little startled, if not shocked, to find this quality in the doctor. Mr. Dimmesdale was a sincerely devoted priest—a true believer—with a carefully developed respect and focused commitment to religious practice, which had deepened in him with time. No one would have thought of him as a liberal-minded man. He needed to feel the constant pressure of faith around him, supporting him as it confined him within its rigid framework. Nonetheless, he occasionally, though hesitantly, enjoyed the relief that comes from hearing a different view of the world. It was like a window being opened, admitting fresh air into the stifling study where his life was wasting away amid lamplight or dim sunbeams and the musty odor of his books. But that air was too fresh and cold to be breathed with comfort for long. So the minister and the doctor would once again retreat into discussions that fell within the church's narrow view.

Through these methods, Roger Chillingworth examined his patient carefully, both in the familiar musings of his daily life and as he appeared in his moral surroundings, the novelty of which might bring out something new in his character. Chillingsworth seemed to feel it necessary to know the man before attempting to cure him. Bodily diseases are always tainted by the peculiar qualities of the heart and mind. Arthur Dimmesdale's thoughts and imagination were so active, and his spirit so sensitive, that his illness was likely grounded in these two organs. So Roger Chillingworth, the kindly

sensibility so intense, that the bodily infirmity would be likely to have its ground-work there. So Roger Chillingworth—the man of skill, the kind and friendly physician—strove to go deep into his patient's bosom, delving among his principles, prying into his recollections, and probing every thing with a cautious touch, like a treasure-seeker in a dark cavern. Few secrets can escape an investigator, who has opportunity and license to undertake such a quest, and skill to follow it up. A man burdened with a secret should especially avoid the intimacy of his physician. If the latter possess native sagacity, and a nameless something more,—let us call it intuition; if he show no intrusive egotism, nor disagreeably prominent characteristics of his own; if he have the power, which must be born with him, to bring his mind into such affinity with his patient's, that this last shall unawares have spoken what he imagines himself only to have thought; if such revelations be received without tumult, and acknowledged not so often by an uttered sympathy, as by silence, an inarticulate breath, and here and there a word, to indicate that all is understood; if, to these qualifications of a confidant be joined the advantages afforded by his recognized character as a physician;—then, at some inevitable moment, will the soul of the sufferer be dissolved, and flow forth in a dark, but transparent stream, bringing all its mysteries into the daylight.

Roger Chillingworth possessed all, or most, of the attributes above enumerated. Nevertheless, time went on; a kind of intimacy, as we have said, grew up between these two cultivated minds, which had as wide a field as the whole sphere of human thought and study, to meet upon; they discussed every topic of ethics and religion, of public affairs, and private character; they talked much, on both sides, of matters that seemed personal to themselves; and yet no secret, such as the physician fancied must exist there, ever stole out of the minister's consciousness into his companion's ear. The latter had his suspicions, indeed, that even the nature of Mr. Dimmesdale's bodily disease had never fairly revealed to him. It was a strange reserve!

After a time, at a hint from Roger Chillingworth, the friends of Mr. Dimmesdale effected an arrangement by which the two were lodged in the same house; so that every ebb and flow of the minister's life-tide might pass under the eye of his anxious and attached physician.

and skillful doctor, delved deep into his patient's heart, examining his principles, prying into his memories, and probing everything with a cautious touch, like a treasure hunter in a dark cave. Few secrets can escape an investigator who has the opportunity and skill to pursue them. A man with a secret shouldn't get too intimate with his doctor. If the doctor has natural wisdom along with intuition; if he doesn't have too big an ego, or any serious character flaws; if he has the innate power to become so intimate with his patient that the patient speaks what he imagines he has only thought; if the doctor receives these revelations calmly, acknowledging them only by silence, a small breath, and now and then a small word of understanding; if these qualities of a friend are joined with his status as a doctor, then, sure enough, the soul of the sufferer will reveal itself, like a dark, clear stream flowing into the daylight.

Roger Chillingwoth possessed most, if not all, of these qualities. As I mentioned before, an intimacy developed over time between these two learned men, whose minds could range over the whole of human thought. They discussed every topic of ethics and religion, of public affairs and private character. They both talked about personal matters. Yet the minister revealed no secret, such as the doctor imagined must be there. Indeed, the doctor suspected that he still hadn't truly discovered the nature of Mr. Dimmesdale's illness. The minister was so strangely private!

After a while, at the suggestion of Roger Chillingworth, the friends of Mr. Dimmesdale arranged for the two to live together, so that the anxious and attentive doctor could observe every aspect of the minister's life. The townspeople were very happy about this arrangement.

There was much joy throughout the town, when this greatly desirable object was attained. It was held to be the best possible measure for the young clergy-man's welfare; unless, indeed, as often urged by such as felt authorized to do so, he had selected some one of the many blooming damsels, spiritually devoted to him, to become his devoted wife. This latter step, however, there was no present prospect that Arthur Dimmesdale would be prevailed upon to take; he rejected all suggestions of the kind, as if priestly celibacy were one of his articles of church-discipline. Doomed by his own choice, therefore, as Mr. Dimmesdale so evidently was, to eat his unsavory morsel always at another's board, and endure the life-long chill which must be his lot who seeks to warm himself only at another's fireside, it truly seemed that this sagacious, experienced, benevolent, old physician, with his concord of paternal and reverential love for the young pastor, was the very man, of all mankind, to be constantly within reach of his voice.

The new abode of the two friends was with a pious widow, of good social rank, who dwelt in a house covering pretty nearly the site on which the venerable structure of King's Chapel has since been built. It had the grave-yard, originally Isaac Johnson's home-field, on one side, and so was well adapted to call up serious reflections, suited to their respective employments, in both minister and man of physic. The motherly care of the good widow assigned to Mr. Dimmesdale a front apartment, with a sunny exposure, and heavy window-curtains to create a noontide shadow, when desirable. The walls were hung round with tapestry, said to be from the Gobelin looms, and, at all events, representing the Scriptural story of David and Bathsheba, and Nathan the Prophet, in colors still unfaded, but which made the fair woman of the scene almost as grimly picturesque as the woe-denouncing seer. Here, the pale clergyman piled up his library, rich with parchment-bound folios of the Fathers, and the lore of Rabbis, and monkish erudition, of which the Protestant divines, even while they vilified and decried that class of writers, were yet constrained often to avail themselves. On the other side of the house, old Roger Chillingworth arranged his study and laboratory; not such as a modern man of science would reckon even tolerably complete, but provided with a distilling apparatus, and the means of compounding drugs and chemicals, which the practised alchemist knew well how to turn to purpose. With such

NO FEAR

They though it was the best possible thing for the young minister's health—that is, unless he was to select one of the town's many lovely young women to be his devoted wife. But there seemed to be no hope of Arthur Dimmesdale becoming convinced to take that step. He rejected all suggestions of that kind, as if his church, like the Catholics, required its ministers to remain celibate. So he doomed himself to always eat unfulfilling meals at someone else's table, to forever endure the unshakable chill that comes when warming yourself by someone else's fire. And so it truly seemed that this wise, experienced, benevolent old physician, who loved the young pastor like a son, was the very best man to be his constant companion.

The two friends lived with a pious widow of good social rank, whose house stood on almost the exact same spot where the cherished King's Chapel sits now. The graveyard—originally Isaac Johnson's yard—sat on one side, so it was well suited to inspire the sorts of serious reflections appropriate for a minister and a doctor. With a mother's consideration, the good widow gave Mr. Dimmesdale a front apartment that got lots of sunlight but also had heavy curtains to shade him when needed. Tapestries, said to be from the Gobelin looms, hung on the walls. They told the Biblical story of David and Bathsheba and Nathan the Prophet, in vivid colors that made the lovely woman look almost as grim as the disapproving prophet. The pale clergyman brought with him a library full of parchment-bound books containing the teachings of the apostles, the stories of the rabbis, and the knowledge of the monks. Even though Protestant ministers denounced those writers, they often felt compelled to resort to them. Old Roger Chillingworth set up his study and laboratory on the other side of the house. Chillingworth had a distilling apparatus and the means of mixing drugs and chemicals that a modern man of science might consider primitive but that the experienced alchemist knew how to use. These two learned men sat themselves down within their own comfortable space, though they often spent

Gobelin: Famous family of tapestry makers in France in the 15th and 16th centuries.

Biblical story: King David committed adultery with Bathsheba, the wife of his most trusted soldier, Uriah, whom he then had killed in battle. Nathan, David's prophet, admonished David for his actions.

commodiousness of situation, these two learned persons sat themselves down, each in his own domain, yet familiarly passing from one apartment to the other, and bestowing a mutual and not incurious inspection into one another's business.

And the Reverend Arthur Dimmesdale's best discerning friends, as we have intimated, very reasonably imagined that the hand of Providence had done all this, for the purpose,—besought in so many public, and domestic, and secret prayers—of restoring the young minister to health. But—it must now be said—another portion of the community had latterly begun to take its own view of the relation betwixt Mr. Dimmesdale and the mysterious old physician. When an uninstructed multitude attempts to see with its eyes, it is exceedingly apt to be deceived. When, however, it forms its judgment, as it usually does, on the intuitions of its great and warm heart, the conclusions thus attained are often so profound and so unerring, as to possess the character of truths supernaturally revealed. The people, in the case of which we speak, could justify its prejudice against Roger Chillingworth by no fact or argument worthy of serious refutation. There was an aged handicraftsman, it is true, who had been a citizen of London at the period of Sir Thomas Overbury's murder, now some thirty years agone; he testified to having seen the physician, under some other name, which the narrator of the story had now forgotten, in company with Doctor Forman, the famous old conjurer, who was implicated in the affair of Overbury. Two or three individuals hinted, that the man of skill, during his Indian captivity, had enlarged his medical attainments by joining in the incantations of the savage priests; who were universally acknowledged to be powerful enchanters, often performing seemingly miraculous cures by their skill in the black art. A large number—and many of these were persons of such sober sense and practical observation, that their opinions would have been valuable, in other matters—affirmed that Roger Chillingworth's aspect had undergone a remarkable change while he had dwelt in town, and especially since his abode with Mr. Dimmesdale. At first, his expression had been calm, meditative, scholar-like. Now, there was something ugly and evil in his face, which they had not previously noticed, and which grew still the more obvious to sight, the oftener they looked upon him. According to the vulgar idea, the fire in his

time in one another's apartment, showing a sincere interest in each other's business.

As I suggested, the Reverend Arthur Dimmesdale's most perceptive friends reasonably concluded that the hand of God arranged all of this for the benefit of the young minister's health. Many people had prayed for it in public, with their families, and in the privacy of their hearts. But, it must now be said, another part of the community began to take a different view of the relationship between Mr. Dimmesdale and the mysterious old doctor. An undisciplined public is likely to be fooled when looking at a situation on the surface. But when that group bases its judgment, as it usually does, on the intuitions of its great and warm heart, its conclusions are often so profoundly correct that they seem to be magically revealed truths. In this case, these individuals could not point to any significant fact or serious argument to justify their prejudice against Roger Chillingworth. True, there was an old handyman who had lived in London at the time of Sir Thomas Overbury's murder—some thirty years ago now—who remembered seeing the doctor in the company of Dr. Forman, the famous conjurer implicated in the crime. Chillingworth went by some other name then, though the handyman forgot what it was. Two or three people hinted that the doctor, during his captivity, had learned spells from the Indian priests. It was widely accepted that the Indians were powerful sorcerers, often achieving seemingly miraculous cures through their black magic. Many reasonable people, whose opinions were valued in the community, said that Roger Chillingworth had undergone a great physical change during his time in the town, particularly since he started rooming with Mr. Dimmesdale. At first, his expression had been calm, thoughtful, and studious. Now there was something ugly and evil in his face that those reasonable people hadn't noticed before. But the more they looked at him, the more obvious the deformity became. One popular rumor suggested the fire in his laboratory came from the underworld and was fed with demonic fuel, so it made sense that his face was growing darker from the smoke.

erbury: English
n of letters who
s poisoned for
position to the
erous relation-
ship, and later
rriage, between
unt of Roches-
nd Lady Essex.
Dr. Forman was
ted for his part
provider of the
poison.

laboratory had been brought from the lower regions, and was fed with infernal fuel; and so, as might be expected, his visage was getting sooty with the smoke.

To sum up the matter, it grew to be a widely diffused opinion, that the Reverend Arthur Dimmesdale, like many other personages of especial sanctity, in all ages of the Christian world, was haunted either by Satan himself, or Satan's emissary, in the guise of old Roger Chillingworth. This diabolical agent had the Divine permission, for a season, to burrow into the clergyman's intimacy, and plot against his soul. No sensible man, it was confessed, could doubt on which side the victory would turn. The people looked, with an unshaken hope, to see the minister come forth out of the conflict, transfigured with the glory which he would unquestionably win. Meanwhile, nevertheless, it was sad to think of the perchance mortal agony through which he must struggle towards his triumph.

Alas, to judge from the gloom and terror in the depths of the poor minister's eyes, the battle was a sore one, and the victory any thing but secure!

NO FEAR

To sum up, it came to be widely believed that the Reverend Arthur Dimmesdale, like other especially holy Christians throughout the ages, was haunted either by Satan himself or by Satan's messenger in the person of old Roger Chillingworth. For a period of time, God would allow this hellish agent to work his way into the minister's private life and plot against his soul. But no sensible man doubted who would triumph in the end. The townspeople had every faith that their minister would emerge from the conflict transformed by the glory of his spiritual victory. In the meantime, it was sad to think of the great pain he had to endure to achieve this triumph.

But to judge from the gloom and terror deep in the poor minister's eyes, the battle was a hard one, and his victory anything but certain.

Chapter 10: The Leech and His Patient

O ld Roger Chillingworth, throughout life, had been calm in temperament, kindly, though not of warm affections, but ever, and in all his relations with the world, a pure and upright man. He had begun an investigation, as he imagined, with the severe and equal integrity of a judge, desirous only of truth, even as if the question involved no more than the air-drawn lines and figures of a geometrical problem, instead of human passions, and wrongs inflicted on himself. But, as he proceeded, a terrible fascination, a kind of fierce, though still calm, necessity seized the old man within its gripe, and never set him free again, until he had done all its bidding. He now dug into the poor clergyman's heart, like a miner searching for gold; or, rather, like a sexton delving into a grave, possibly in quest of a jewel that had been buried on the dead man's bosom, but likely to find nothing save mortality and corruption. Alas for his own soul, if these were what he sought!

Sometimes, a light glimmered out of the physician's eyes, burning blue and ominous, like the reflection of a furnace, or, let us say, like one of those gleams of ghastly fire that darted from Bunyan's awful door-way in the hill-side, and quivered on the pilgrim's face. The soil where this dark miner was working had perchance shown indications that encouraged him.

"This man," said he, at one such moment, to himself, "pure as they deem him,—all spiritual as he seems,—hath inherited a strong animal nature from his father or his mother. Let us dig a little farther in the direction of this vein!"

Then, after long search into the minister's dim interior, and turning over many precious materials, in the shape of high aspirations for the welfare of his race, warm love of souls, pure sentiments, natural piety, strengthened by thought and study, and illuminated by revelation,—all of which invaluable gold was perhaps no better than rubbish to the seeker,—he would turn back, discouraged, and begin his quest towards another point. He groped along as stealthily, with as cautious a tread, and as wary an outlook, as a thief entering a chamber where a man lies only half asleep,—or, it may be, broad awake,—with purpose to steal the very treasure which this man guards as the apple of his eye. In spite of his premeditated careful-

Chapter 10: The Leech and His Patient

Old Roger Chillingworth had been a calm and kind man throughout his life. He may not have been warm, but he was always honest and upright in his dealings with the world. In his mind, he had begun his latest investigation with the stern but fair integrity of a judge, desiring only to find the truth. He figured he would approach the problem with the same dry logic and deductive reasoning that a mathematician brings to a geometrical question, rather than with the human emotions of someone wronged. But as he proceeded, a horrible fascination—a kind of fierce, though still calm, need to know—gripped the old man and would not let go. He now dug into the clergyman's heart like a miner searching for gold—or like a gravedigger digging into a grave with the hopes of stealing a jewel buried on the dead man's bosom, though he was likely to find nothing but death and decay. It's too bad for Chillingworth's soul that death and decay were all he sought!

At times, a light glimmered in the doctor's eyes, like the reflection of a furnace, or those terrifying lights that shined onto the pilgrim's face from Bunyan's awful hillside doorway. Perhaps the ground where that dark miner was digging provided some hint to encourage him.

hillside doorway: lighted doorway in Bunyan's work *Pilgrim's Progress* leads to the gates of Hell.

"This man," Chillingworth said to himself at one such moment, "though everyone thinks he is spiritual, has inherited a wild side from one of his parents. Let me dig a little further into that!"

Chillingworth would search long in the minister's psyche, as though it were a mine. He would rummage through the good things he found there as if they were trash, then he would turn back, discouraged, and resume his quest elsewhere in the minister's soul. The doctor groped along as carefully and quietly as a thief entering the room of a man half asleep—or perhaps only pretending to sleep—hoping to steal that man's most precious treasure. In spite of the doctor's care, Mr. Dimmesdale would sometimes become vaguely aware of the danger—as though the floor had creaked or the thief's clothes had rustled as his shadow fell across his sleeping victim. The minister's acute sensitivity often seemed like spiritual

ness, the floor would now and then creak; his garments would rustle; the shadow of his presence, in a forbidden proximity, would be thrown across his victim. In other words, Mr. Dimmesdale, whose sensibility of nerve often produced the effect of spiritual intuition, would become vaguely aware that something inimical to his peace had thrust itself into relation with him. But old Roger Chillingworth, too, had perceptions that were almost intuitive; and when the minister threw his startled eyes towards him, there the physician sat; his kind, watchful, sympathizing, but never intrusive friend.

Yet Mr. Dimmesdale would perhaps have seen this individual's character more perfectly, if a certain morbidness, to which sick hearts are liable, had not rendered him suspicious of all mankind. Trusting no man as his friend, he could not recognize his enemy when the latter actually appeared. He therefore still kept up a familiar intercourse with him, daily receiving the old physician in his study; or visiting the laboratory, and, for recreation's sake, watching the processes by which weeds were converted into drugs of potency.

One day, leaning his forehead on his hand, and his elbow on the sill of the open window, that looked towards the grave-yard, he talked with Roger Chillingworth, while the old man was examining a bundle of unsightly plants.

"Where," asked he, with a look askance at them,—for it was the clergyman's peculiarity that he seldom, now-a-days, looked straight-forth at any object, whether human or inanimate,—"where, my kind doctor, did you gather those herbs, with such a dark, flabby leaf?"

"Even in the grave-yard, here at hand," answered the physician, continuing his employment. "They are new to me. I found them growing on a grave, which bore no tombstone, nor other memorial of the dead man, save these ugly weeds that have taken upon themselves to keep him in remembrance. They grew out of his heart, and typify, it may be, some hideous secret that was buried with him, and which he had done better to confess during his lifetime."

"Perchance," said Mr. Dimmesdale, "he earnestly desired it, but could not."

"And wherefore?" rejoined the physician. "Wherefore not; since all the powers of nature call so earnestly for the confession of sin, that these black weeds have sprung up out of a buried heart, to make manifest an unspoken crime?"

intuition. He could sometimes sense when a threat was near. But old Roger Chillingworth's senses were also instinctive. When the minister looked with suspicion at the doctor, Chillingworth would sit there, seeming like a kind, observant, sympathetic, but never intrusive friend.

Mr. Dimmesdale might have seen the doctor's character more clearly if he had not become suspicious of the whole world. Sick hearts are prone to paranoia. Because he trusted no man as his friend, he could not recognize a real enemy when one appeared. So he kept up friendly relations with the doctor, receiving the old man in his study, or visiting the laboratory and watching him turn herbs into potent medicines.

One day the minister talked with Roger Chillingworth while the old man was examining a bundle of ugly plants. Mr. Dimmesdale sat with his forehead in his hand and his elbow resting on the sill of an open window that looked out on the graveyard.

"Where," he asked, with a sideways glance at the plants, for the minister had developed the odd habit of never looking straight at anything, "where, my kind doctor, did you gather herbs with such a dark, flabby leaf?"

"Why, right here in the graveyard," answered the doctor, continuing to examine them. "They are new to me. I found them growing on a grave that had no tombstone or other marker, except for these ugly weeds. It seems that they had taken it upon themselves to keep his memory. They grew out of his heart: Perhaps they reflect some hideous secret buried with him. He would have been better off had he confessed during his lifetime."

"Maybe," said Mr. Dimmesdale, "he truly wanted to confess but could not."

"And why?" replied the physician. "Why not, since all the powers of nature wanted the sin to be confessed, so much so that these black weeds sprung up out of a buried heart to reveal the hidden crime?"

"That, good Sir, is but a fantasy of yours," replied the minister. "There can be, if I forebode aright, no power, short of the Divine mercy, to disclose, whether by uttered words, or by type or emblem, the secrets that may be buried with a human heart. The heart, making itself guilty of such secrets, must perforce hold them, until the day when all hidden things shall be revealed. Nor have I so read or interpreted Holy Writ, as to understand that the disclosure of human thoughts and deeds, then to be made, is intended as a part of the retribution. That, surely, were a shallow view of it. No; these revelations, unless I greatly err, are meant merely to promote the intellectual satisfaction of all intelligent beings, who will stand waiting, on that day, to see the dark problem of this life made plain. A knowledge of men's hearts will be needful to the completest solution of that problem. And I conceive, moreover, that the hearts holding such miserable secrets as you speak of will yield them up, at that last day, not with reluctance, but with a joy unutterable."

"Then why not reveal them here?" asked Roger Chillingworth, glancing quietly aside at the minister. "Why should not the guilty ones sooner avail themselves of this unutterable solace?"

"They mostly do," said the clergyman, griping hard at his breast, as if afflicted with an importunate throb of pain. "Many, many a poor soul hath given its confidence to me, not only on the death-bed, but while strong in life, and fair in reputation. And ever, after such an outpouring, O, what a relief have I witnessed in those sinful brethren! even as in one who at last draws free air, after long stifling with his own polluted breath. How can it be otherwise? Why should a wretched man, guilty, we will say, of murder, prefer to keep the dead corpse buried in his own heart, rather than fling it forth at once, and let the universe take care of it!"

"Yet some men bury their secrets thus," observed the calm physician.

"True; there are such men," answered Mr. Dimmesdale. "But, not to suggest more obvious reasons, it may be that they are kept silent by the very constitution of their nature. Or,—can we not suppose it?—guilty as they may be, retaining, nevertheless, a zeal for God's glory and man's welfare, they shrink from displaying themselves black and filthy in the view of men; because, thenceforward, no good can be achieved by them; no evil of the past be redeemed by better service. So, to their own unutterable torment, they go about among

NO FEAR

"That, good sir, is only a fantasy of yours," replied the minister. "As far as I can tell, only divine mercy, either through spoken words or some kind of sign, can reveal the secrets buried in the human heart. The heart, once guilty of keeping such secrets, must hold them until the day when all that is hidden will be revealed. And, according to my reading and interpretation of Holy Scripture, the final disclosure of such thoughts and deeds is not going to be part of our punishment. Surely, that would be a shallow way to look at it. No, these revelations, unless I am quite mistaken, are merely meant to satisfy the minds of the intelligent beings who will watch on that final day to see the problems of this earthly life made plain. These beings will need to know men's hearts so that they can completely understand this world. And furthermore, I believe that the hearts holding such miserable secrets won't be reluctant to give them up on the last day, but will do so with unspeakable joy."

"Then why not reveal it here?" asked Roger Chillingworth, glancing quietly at the minister. "Why shouldn't the guilty ones enjoy this unspeakable relief sooner?"

"Most of them do," said the minister, gripping his breast hard as though suffering a sharp pain. "Many poor souls have confided in me—not just the ones on their deathbeds, but also those in the prime of life and enjoying a good reputation. And always, after a great outpouring, those sinful brothers are so relieved! It's as if they're finally able to breathe fresh air after having suffocated on their own polluted breath. How could it be any other way? Why would a sick man—someone guilty of murder, for example—prefer to keep the dead corpse buried in his own heart, rather than tossing it out for the universe to care for?"

"And still, some men do bury their secrets," observed the calm doctor.

"True, there are such men," answered Mr. Dimmesdale. "Not to be too obvious, but maybe it's in their very natures to remain silent. Or suppose that, guilty as they are, they still possess a zeal for God's glory and the well-being of mankind. Perhaps they don't wish to appear dirty in the eyes of men, so that they can continue to do good and redeem their past sins with future service. So, to their own unspeakable torture, they walk among their fellow creatures looking as pure as the new-fallen snow. And all the

their fellow-creatures, looking pure as new-fallen snow; while their hearts are all speckled and spotted with iniquity of which they cannot rid themselves."

"These men deceive themselves," said Roger Chillingworth, with somewhat more emphasis than usual, and making a slight gesture with his forefinger. "They fear to take up the shame that rightfully belongs to them. Their love for man, their zeal for God's service,—these holy impulses may or may not coexist in their hearts with the evil inmates to which their guilt has unbarred the door, and which must needs propagate a hellish breed within them. But, if they seek to glorify God, let them not lift heavenward their unclean hands! If they would serve their fellow-men, let them do it by making manifest the power and reality of conscience, in constraining them to penitential self-abasement! Wouldst thou have me to believe, O wise and pious friend, that a false show can be better—can be more for God's glory, or man's welfare—than God's own truth? Trust me, such men deceive themselves!"

"It may be so," said the young clergyman indifferently, as waiving a discussion that he considered irrelevant or unseasonable. He had a ready faculty, indeed, of escaping from any topic that agitated his too sensitive and nervous temperament.—"But, now, I would ask of my well-skilled physician, whether, in good sooth, he deems me to have profited by his kindly care of this weak frame of mine?"

Before Roger Chillingworth could answer, they heard the clear, wild laughter of a young child's voice, proceeding from the adjacent burial-ground. Looking instinctively from the open window,—for it was summer-time,—the minister beheld Hester Prynne and little Pearl passing along the footpath that traversed the inclosure. Pearl looked as beautiful as the day, but was in one of those moods of perverse merriment which, whenever they occurred, seemed to remove her entirely out of the sphere of sympathy or human contact. She now skipped irreverently from one grave to another; until, coming to the broad flat, armorial tombstone of a departed worthy,—perhaps of Isaac Johnson himself,—she began to dance upon it. In reply to her mother's command and entreaty that she would behave more decorously, little Pearl paused to gather the prickly burrs from a tall burdock, which grew beside the tomb. Taking a handful of these, she arranged them along the lines of the scarlet letter that

while, their hearts are spotted and stained with a sin they can't get rid of."

"These men are fooling themselves," said Roger Chillingworth, using a little more emphasis than usual and making a slight gesture with his index finger. "They are afraid to own up to the shame that is rightfully theirs. They may possess a holy love for mankind and keep a desire to serve God in their hearts, but their hearts might also invite evil impulses that breed hellish thoughts. If they seek to glorify God, don't let them lift their unclean hands to Heaven! If they wish to serve their fellow men, let them do it by demonstrating the power of conscience, which forces them to shamefully repent! Would you have me believe, my wise and pious friend, that a false act is better—can do more for God's glory, or the welfare of mankind—than God's own truth? Believe me, men who say that are fooling themselves!"

"That may be so," said the young minister, indifferently, as though dismissing a discussion he felt was irrelevant or inappropriate. He could skillfully avoid any topic that bothered his nervous temperament. "But now I would ask, my skillful doctor, whether you truly think my weak body has benefited from your kind care?"

Before Roger Chillingworth could answer, they heard the distinct, wild laughter of a young child coming from the nearby graveyard. The minister looked instinctively out the window—it was summer, so the window was open—and saw Hester Prynne and little Pearl passing along the footpath that surrounded the yard. Pearl looked as lovely as the day itself. But she was in one of her perverse moods that seemed to remove her entirely from the world of human sympathy. She skipped irreverently from one grave to another until she came to the broad, flat tombstone of an eminent man—perhaps Isaac Johnson himself! She began to dance on top of it. Her mother told her to behave respectfully. In response, little Pearl stopped to pick the prickly burrs from a plant that grew beside the grave. She took a handful and arranged them around the scarlet letter that decorated her mother's bosom. The burrs, as is their nature, held fast. Hester did not pluck them off.

decorated the maternal bosom, to which the burrs, as their nature was, tenaciously adhered. Hester did not pluck them off.

Roger Chillingworth had by this time approached the window, and smiled grimly down.

"There is no law, nor reverence for authority, no regard for human ordinances or opinions, right or wrong, mixed up with that child's composition," remarked he, as much to himself as to his companion. "I saw her, the other day, bespatter the Governor himself with water, at the cattle-trough in Spring Lane. What, in Heaven's name, is she? Is the imp altogether evil? Hath she affections? Hath she any discoverable principle of being?"

"None,—save the freedom of a broken law," answered Mr. Dimmesdale, in a quiet way, as if he had been discussing the point within himself. "Whether capable of good, I know not."

The child probably overheard their voices; for, looking up to the window, with a bright, but naughty smile of mirth and intelligence, she threw one of the prickly burrs at the Reverend Mr. Dimmesdale. The sensitive clergyman shrunk, with nervous dread, from the light missile. Detecting his emotion, Pearl clapped her little hands in the most extravagant ecstasy. Hester Prynne, likewise, had involuntarily looked up; and all these four persons, old and young, regarded one another in silence, till the child laughed aloud, and shouted,—"Come away, mother! Come away, or yonder old Black Man will catch you! He hath got hold of the minister already. Come away, mother, or he will catch you! But he cannot catch little Pearl!"

So she drew her mother away, skipping, dancing, and frisking fantastically among the hillocks of the dead people, like a creature that had nothing in common with a bygone and buried generation, nor owned herself akin to it. It was as if she had been made afresh, out of new elements, and must perforce be permitted to live her own life, and be a law unto herself, without her eccentricities being reckoned to her for a crime.

"There goes a woman," resumed Roger Chillingworth, after a pause, "who, be her demerits what they may, hath none of that mystery of hidden sinfulness which you deem so grievous to be borne. Is Hester Prynne the less miserable, think you, for that scarlet letter on her breast?"

NO FEAR

By this time, Roger Chillingworth had approached the window and was smiling down grimly.

"That child doesn't care about the law, authority, or public opinion, whether right or wrong," he remarked, as much to himself as to his companion. "The other day, I saw her spray the Governor himself with water at the cattle trough on Spring Lane. What, in Heaven's name, is she? Is that imp altogether evil? Does she have any feelings? Any governing principles?"

"None, except the freedom of a broken law," answered Mr. Dimmesdale, in a quiet way, as if he had been discussing the point with himself. "I don't know whether she is capable of good."

The girl likely overheard their voices. Looking up to the window with a bright but naughty smile full of delight and intelligence, she threw one of the prickly burrs at the Rev. Mr. Dimmesdale. The nervous clergyman cringed at the little missile. Seeing that she had gotten a reaction, Pearl clapped her little hands in extravagant joy. Hester Prynne had involuntarily looked up, and these four people, old and young, stared at one another in silence until the child laughed aloud. "Come away, mother!" she shouted. "Come away, or that old Devil will catch you! He's caught the minister already. Come away, mother, or he'll catch you! But he can't catch little Pearl!"

So she pulled her mother away, skipping and dancing ridiculously around the mounds of dead people, as though she was some little creature who had nothing in common with past generations and wanted nothing to do with them. It was as if she had been made out of a completely new substance and must be allowed to live her life by her own rules.

"There goes a woman," said Roger Chillingworth, after a pause, "who, though her faults are what they are, has none of that mystery of hidden sinfulness you say is so painful for people to bear. Is Hester Prynne less miserable, do you think, because of the scarlet letter on her breast?"

"I do verily believe it," answered the clergyman. "Nevertheless, I cannot answer for her. There was a look of pain in her face, which I would gladly have been spared the sight of. But still, methinks, it must needs be better for the sufferer to be free to show his pain, as this poor woman Hester is, than to cover it all up in his heart."

There was another pause; and the physician began anew to examine and arrange the plants which he had gathered.

"You inquired of me, a little time agone," said he, at length, "my judgment as touching your health."

"I did," answered the clergyman, "and would gladly learn it. Speak frankly, I pray you, be it for life or death."

"Freely, then, and plainly," said the physician, still busy with his plants, but keeping a wary eye on Mr. Dimmesdale, "the disorder is a strange one; not so much in itself, nor as outwardly manifested—in so far, at least, as the symptoms have been laid open to my observation. Looking daily at you, my good Sir, and watching the tokens of your aspect, now for months gone by, I should deem you a man sore sick, it may be, yet not so sick but that an instructed and watchful physician might well hope to cure you. But—I know not what to say—the disease is what I seem to know, yet know it not."

"You speak in riddles, learned Sir," said the pale minister, glancing aside out of the window.

"Then, to speak more plainly," continued the physician, "and I crave pardon, Sir,—should it seem to require pardon,—for this needful plainness of my speech. Let me ask,—as your friend,—as one having charge, under Providence, of your life and physical well-being,—hath all the operation of this disorder been fairly laid open and recounted to me?"

"How can you question it?" asked the minister. "Surely, it were child's play to call in a physician, and then hide the sore!"

"You would tell me, then, that I know all?" said Chillingworth, deliberately, and fixing an eye, bright with intense and concentrated intelligence, on the minister's face. "Be it so! But, again! He to whom only the outward and physical evil is laid open knoweth, oftentimes, but half the evil which he is called upon to cure. A bodily disease, which we look upon as whole and entire within itself, may, after all, be but a symptom of some ailment in the spiritual part. Your pardon, once again, good Sir, if my speech give the shadow of

"I truly believe it," answered the clergyman, "though I can't speak for her. There was a look of pain in her face that I would have rather not seen. But, I still think it must be better for the sufferer to be free to show his pain, as this poor woman Hester is free to show hers, than to cover it up in his heart."

There was another pause, and the physician again began to examine and arrange his new plants.

"You asked me, a little while ago," he said, after some time, "for my judgment about your health."

"I did," answered the clergyman, "and would be glad to hear it. Tell me honestly, please, whether you think I will live or die."

"I'll be straight with you," said the doctor, still busy with his plants but keeping a watchful eye on Mr. Dimmesdale, "the disease is strange. I don't mean the symptoms, at least as far as you have revealed them to me. Seeing you every day, my good sir, for many months now, I would think you were a very sick man—though not too sick for an educated and observant physician to cure you. I'm not sure what to say: It seems I know the disease, but at the same time, I don't."

"You speak in riddles, my learned sir," said the pale minister, glancing out the window.

"I'll be more plain," continued the doctor, "and I beg your pardon, sir, for being direct. Let me ask, as your friend, as one in charge of your life and bodily health: Have you told me all the symptoms of this disorder?"

"How can you doubt that?" asked the minister. "It would be childish to call for a physician and then conceal the illness!"

"So you're telling me that I know everything?" said Roger Chillingworth deliberately, staring the minister full in the face with intense and concentrated intelligence. "So be it! But let me say again that one who knows only the physical symptoms often knows only half of what he is asked to cure. A bodily disease, which we think of as self-contained, may after all be merely a symptom of some spiritual ailment. I beg your pardon, again, if my words give the slightest offense. Of all the men I have known,

offence. You, Sir, of all men whom I have known, are he whose body is the closest conjoined, and imbued, and identified, so to speak, with the spirit whereof it is the instrument."

"Then I need ask no further," said the clergyman, somewhat hastily rising from his chair. "You deal not, I take it, in medicine for the soul!"

"Thus, a sickness," continued Roger Chillingworth, going on, in an unaltered tone, without heeding the interruption,—but standing up, and confronting the emaciated and white-cheeked minister with his low, dark, and misshapen figure,—"a sickness, a sore place, if we may so call it, in your spirit, hath immediately its appropriate manifestation in your bodily frame. Would you, therefore, that your physician heal the bodily evil? How may this be, unless you first lay open to him the wound or trouble in your soul?"

"No!—not to thee!—not to an earthly physician!" cried Mr. Dimmesdale, passionately, and turning his eyes, full and bright, and with a kind of fierceness, on old Roger Chillingworth. "Not to thee! But, if it be the soul's disease, then do I commit myself to the one Physician of the soul! He, if it stand with his good pleasure, can cure; or he can kill! Let him do with me as, in his justice and wisdom, he shall see good. But who art thou, that meddlest in this matter?—that dares thrust himself between the sufferer and his God?"

With a frantic gesture, he rushed out of the room.

"It is as well, to have made this step," said Roger Chillingworth to himself, looking after the minister with a grave smile. "There is nothing lost. We shall be friends again anon. But see, now, how passion takes hold upon this man, and hurrieth him out of himself! As with one passion, so with another! He hath done a wild thing ere now, this pious Master Dimmesdale, in the hot passion of his heart!"

It proved not difficult to reëstablish the intimacy of the two companions, on the same footing and in the same degree as heretofore. The young clergyman, after a few hours of privacy, was sensible that the disorder of his nerves had hurried him into an unseemly outbreak of temper, which there had been nothing in the physician's words to excuse or palliate. He marvelled, indeed, at the violence with which he had thrust back the kind old man, when merely proffering the advice which it was his duty to bestow, and which the minister himself had expressly sought. With these remorseful feelings, he lost no time in making the amplest apologies, and besought his friend still to

you, sir, are the one whose body is most closely connected to the spirit inside."

"Then I will ask no more," said the minister, rising somewhat abruptly from his chair. "You do not, I assume, deal in medicines for the soul!"

"A sickness," continued Roger Chillingworth in the same tone, paying no mind to the interruption, but rather standing and confronting the thin, pale-faced minister with his small, dark and deformed figure, "a sickness—a sore spot, if we can call it that—in your spirit manifests itself in your body. Do you want your doctor to heal that bodily illness? How can he unless you first reveal the wound in your soul?"

"Not to you! Not to an earthly doctor!" cried Mr. Dimmesdale passionately, turning his eyes, fierce and bright, on old Roger Chillingworth. "Not to you! But if my soul is diseased, then I commit myself to the only doctor of the soul! He can cure or kill as He pleases. Let Him with do me as He, in His justice and wisdom, sees fit. Who are you to meddle in this? To thrust yourself between a sinner and his God?"

He rushed out of the room with a frantic gesture.

"It's good to have made this step," Roger Chillingworth said to himself, watching the minister go with a grave smile. "Nothing is lost. We'll soon be friends again. But look how passion takes hold of this man and causes him to lose control of himself! Other passions could also make him lose control. The pious Master Dimmesdale has done something wild before this, in the hot passion of his heart."

It was not difficult for the two companions to reestablish their intimacy, just as it had been before. After a few hours alone, the young minister realized that his nerves had led him to an inappropriate outburst, uncalled for by anything the doctor had said or done. Indeed, the minister was amazed at the violent way he had repelled the kind old man, who was dutifully giving advice he had expressly asked for. With these feelings of regret, the minister quickly and profusely apologized. He asked his friend to continue the care which, though it had not restored his health, had probably prolonged his feeble existence. Roger Chillingworth read-

continue the care, which, if not successful in restoring him to health, had, in all probability, been the means of prolonging his feeble existence to that hour. Roger Chillingworth readily assented, and went on with his medical supervision of the minister; doing his best for him, in all good faith, but always quitting the patient's apartment, at the close of a professional interview, with a mysterious and puzzled smile upon his lips. This expression was invisible in Mr. Dimmesdale's presence, but grew strongly evident as the physician crossed the threshold.

"A rare case!" he muttered. "I must needs look deeper into it. A strange sympathy betwixt soul and body! Were it only for the art's sake, I must search this matter to the bottom!"

It came to pass, not long after the scene above recorded, that the Reverend Mr. Dimmesdale, at noon-day, and entirely unawares, fell into a deep, deep slumber, sitting in his chair, with a large black-letter volume open before him on the table. It must have been a work of vast ability in the somniferous school of literature. The profound depth of the minister's repose was the more remarkable; inasmuch as he was one of those persons whose sleep, ordinarily, is as light, as fitful, and as easily scared away, as a small bird hopping on a twig. To such an unwonted remoteness, however, had his spirit now withdrawn into itself, that he stirred not in his chair, when old Roger Chillingworth, without any extraordinary precaution, came into the room. The physician advanced directly in front of his patient, laid his hand upon his bosom, and thrust aside the vestment, that, hitherto, had always covered it even from the professional eye.

Then, indeed, Mr. Dimmesdale shuddered, and slightly stirred.

After a brief pause, the physician turned away.

But with what a wild look of wonder, joy, and horror! With what a ghastly rapture, as it were, too mighty to be expressed only by the eye and features, and therefore bursting forth through the whole ugliness of his figure, and making itself even riotously manifest by the extravagant gestures with which he threw up his arms towards the ceiling, and stamped his foot upon the floor! Had a man seen old Roger Chillingworth, at that moment of his ecstasy, he would have had no need to ask how Satan comports himself, when a precious human soul is lost to Heaven, and won into his kingdom.

But what distinguished the physician's ecstasy from Satan's was the trait of wonder in it!

ily agreed and continued his medical supervision. He did his best for his patient but always left the room at the end of their consultations with a mysterious and puzzled smile on his lips. He concealed the expression while in Mr. Dimmesdale's presence, but it revealed itself fully as soon as the doctor left the room.

"A unique case," he muttered. "I need to look into it more deeply. There exists a strange bond between his soul and his body! I must get to the bottom of it, if only out of professional curiosity."

Not long after the scene described above, the Reverend Mr. Dimmesdale fell into a deep midday sleep while sitting in his chair. A large old book was open on the table in front of him. It must have been one of the great works from the school of boring literature. The overwhelming depth of the minister's sleep was even more remarkable because he was an incredibly light sleeper, as easily disturbed as a bird on a twig. But his soul had fallen into such an unusual slumber that he did not stir when old Roger Chillingworth, with no special care, came into the room. The doctor walked right up to his patient, laid his hand on his breast, and pushed aside the robe that had always hid his chest from the doctor's eye.

Mr. Dimmesdale shuddered and stirred slightly.

After a brief pause, the doctor turned away.

But what a look of wonder, joy, and horror was on the doctor's face! What terrible ecstasy, too intense to be expressed by only the eye and face, burst through the whole ugliness of his body! He threw his arms up to the ceiling and stamped his foot on the floor with emphatic gestures. If someone had seen old Roger Chillingworth at that instant of joy, they would have known what Satan looks like when a precious human soul is lost to Heaven and won for Hell instead.

But what distinguished the doctor's joy from Satan's was the quality of wonder in it!

Chapter 11: Inside a Heart

After the incident last described, the intercourse between the clergyman and the physician, though externally the same, was really of another character than it had previously been. The intellect of Roger Chillingworth had now a sufficiently plain path before it. It was not, indeed, precisely that which he had laid out for himself to tread. Calm, gentle, passionless, as he appeared, there was yet, we fear, a quiet depth of malice, hitherto latent, but active now, in this unfortunate old man, which led him to imagine a more intimate revenge than any mortal had ever wreaked upon an enemy. To make himself the one trusted friend, to whom should be confided all the fear, the remorse, the agony, the ineffectual repentance, the backward rush of sinful thoughts, expelled in vain! All that guilty sorrow, hidden from the world, whose great heart would have pitied and forgiven, to be revealed to him, the Pitiless, to him, the Unforgiving! All that dark treasure to be lavished on the very man, to whom nothing else could so adequately pay the debt of vengeance!

The clergyman's shy and sensitive reserve had balked this scheme. Roger Chillingworth, however, was inclined to be hardly, if at all, less satisfied with the aspect of affairs, which Providence—using the avenger and his victim for its own purposes, and, perchance, pardoning, where it seemed most to punish—had substituted for his black devices. A revelation, he could almost say, had been granted to him. It mattered little, for his object, whether celestial, or from what other region. By its aid, in all the subsequent relations betwixt him and Mr. Dimmesdale, not merely the external presence, but the very inmost soul of the latter seemed to be brought out before his eyes, so that he could see and comprehend its every movement. He became, thenceforth, not a spectator only, but a chief actor, in the poor minister's interior world. He could play upon him as he chose. Would he arouse him with a throb of agony? The victim was for ever on the rack; it needed only to know the spring that controlled the engine;—and the physician knew it well! Would he startle him with sudden fear? As at the waving of a magician's wand, uprose a grisly phantom,—uprose a thousand phantoms,—in many shapes, of death, or more awful shame, all flocking round about the clergyman, and pointing with their fingers at his breast!

Chapter 11: Inside a Heart

Following the incident just described, the relationship between the minister and the doctor changed substantially, though it outwardly appeared the same. Roger Chillingworth now had a clear path in front of him, even if it was not quite the one he had meant to take. And although he seemed calm, gentle, and reasonable, I am afraid there was a hidden well of malice that stirred from inside this poor old man and allowed him to conceive a more personal revenge than anyone else ever could. He had made himself the minister's one trusted friend—the person in whom Mr. Dimmesdale confided all the fear, remorse, agony, ineffective repentance, and sinful thoughts he struggled to keep away! The world would have pitied and forgiven him for all that guilty sorrow. But instead he only revealed himself to the pitiless and unforgiving doctor! All that dark treasure was lavished on the one man who sought to use it for vengeance!

The minister's shy and sensitive nature had foiled the doctor's plan for revenge. Yet Roger Chillingworth was no less satisfied with this turn of events that chance had substituted for his own wicked schemes. Fate would use both avenger and victim for its own purposes, perhaps pardoning where it seemed fit to punish. Roger Chillingworth could almost believe that he had been granted a revelation. It mattered little to him whether the revelation came from Heaven or from Hell: With its aid, he seemed to see deep into the soul of Mr. Dimmesdale. From then on, the doctor became not just an observer of the minister's life but a chief actor in it. He could manipulate the minister as he chose. Would he inspire a throb of agony? The minister was always on the rack. One only had to know how to turn the gears—and the doctor knew this well! Would he startle the minister with sudden fear? The minister imagined phantoms of awful shame flocking around him—as though these horrific forms were conjured by the wand of a magician—all pointing their fingers at his breast!

All this was accomplished with a subtlety so perfect, that the minister, though he had constantly a dim perception of some evil influence watching over him, could never gain a knowledge of its actual nature. True, he looked doubtfully, fearfully,—even, at times, with horror and the bitterness of hatred,—at the deformed figure of the old physician. His gestures, his gait, his grizzled beard, his slightest and most indifferent acts, the very fashion of his garments, were odious in the clergyman's sight; a token, implicitly to be relied on, of a deeper antipathy in the breast of the latter than he was willing to acknowledge to himself. For, as it was impossible to assign a reason for such distrust and abhorrence, so Mr. Dimmesdale, conscious that the poison of one morbid spot was infecting his heart's entire substance, attributed all his presentiments to no other cause. He took himself to task for his bad sympathies in reference to Roger Chillingworth, disregarded the lesson that he should have drawn from them, and did his best to root them out. Unable to accomplish this, he nevertheless, as a matter of principle, continued his habits of social familiarity with the old man, and thus gave him constant opportunities for perfecting the purpose to which—poor, forlorn creature that he was, and more wretched than his victim—the avenger had devoted himself.

While thus suffering under bodily disease, and gnawed and tortured by some black trouble of the soul, and given over to the machinations of his deadliest enemy, the Reverend Mr. Dimmesdale had achieved a brilliant popularity in his sacred office. He won it, indeed, in great part, by his sorrows. His intellectual gifts, his moral perceptions, his power of experiencing and communicating emotion, were kept in a state of preternatural activity by the prick and anguish of his daily life. His fame, though still on its upward slope, already overshadowed the soberer reputations of his fellow-clergymen, eminent as several of them were. There were scholars among them, who had spent more years in acquiring abstruse lore, connected with the divine profession, than Mr. Dimmesdale had lived; and who might well, therefore, be more profoundly versed in such solid and valuable attainments than their youthful brother. There were men, too, of a sturdier texture of mind than his, and endowed with a far greater share of shrewd, hard, iron or granite understanding; which, duly mingled with a fair proportion of doctrinal ingredient, constitutes

NO FEAR

Chillingworth accomplished all of his plans with such great subtlety that the minister could never identify it, though he was always dimly aware of some evil influence watching over him. True, he looked suspiciously, fearfully—sometimes even with horror and bitter hatred—at the deformed figure of the old doctor. Everything about him—his face, his walk, his grizzly beard, his clothes—was revolting to the minister, evidence of a deeper dislike than the minister was willing to admit to himself. But he had no reason for his distrust and hatred. So Mr. Dimmesdale, knowing that one poisonous stain was infecting his entire heart, attributed his feelings to the disease. He scolded himself for his bad feelings toward Roger Chillingworth. Rather than heed any lesson from these suspicions, he did his best to root them out. And though he was unable to get rid of them, he—as a matter of principle—continued his old friendship with the old man. This gave the doctor endless opportunities to wreak his vengeance. Poor, abandoned creature that he was, the doctor was even more miserable than his victim.

The Reverend Mr. Dimmesdale actually attained great popularity through his ministry while suffering with his bodily disease—a disease made all the more torturous by the dark trouble in his soul and the scheming of his deadliest enemy. To be honest, his popularity was due in great part to his sorrows. The pain endured through his daily life had made his mind, spirit, and sense of empathy almost supernaturally acute. His growing fame already overshadowed the somber reputations of even his most well-regarded fellow ministers. Some of these men were scholars who had been engaged in their obscure theological studies for longer than Mr. Dimmesdale had been alive. Others possessed stronger minds than Mr. Dimmesdale's, full of a shrewd and rigid understanding of the world. Such strict discipline, when mixed with the right amount of religious doctrine, makes for a respectable, effective, and unwelcoming clergyman. Still others were truly saintly men whose minds had been expanded by weary hours of patient thought with their books. They had been made even holier by their communications with Heaven, achieving almost divine purity

a highly respectable, efficacious, and unamiable variety of the clerical species. There were others, again, true saintly fathers, whose faculties had been elaborated by weary toil among their books, and by patient thought, and etherealized, moreover, by spiritual communications with the better world, into which their purity of life had almost introduced these holy personages, with their garments of mortality still clinging to them. All that they lacked was the gift that descended upon the chosen disciples, at Pentecost, in tongues of flame; symbolizing, it would seem, not the power of speech in foreign and unknown languages, but that of addressing the whole human brotherhood in the heart's native language. These fathers, otherwise so apostolic, lacked Heaven's last and rarest attestation of their office, the Tongue of Flame. They would have vainly sought—had they ever dreamed of seeking—to express the highest truths through the humblest medium of familiar words and images. Their voices came down, afar and indistinctly, from the upper heights where they habitually dwelt.

Not improbably, it was to this latter class of men that Mr. Dimmesdale, by many of his traits of character, naturally belonged. To their high mountain-peaks of faith and sanctity he would have climbed, had not the tendency been thwarted by the burden, whatever it might be, of crime or anguish, beneath which it was his doom to totter. It kept him down, on a level with the lowest; him, the man of ethereal attributes, whose voice the angels might else have listened to and answered! But this very burden it was, that gave him sympathies so intimate with the sinful brotherhood of mankind; so that his heart vibrated in unison with theirs, and received their pain into itself, and sent its own throb of pain through a thousand other hearts, in gushes of sad, persuasive eloquence. Oftenest persuasive, but sometimes terrible! The people knew not the power that moved them thus. They deemed the young clergyman a miracle of holiness. They fancied him the mouth-piece of Heaven's messages of wisdom, and rebuke, and love. In their eyes, the very ground on which he trod was sanctified. The virgins of his church grew pale around him, victims of a passion so imbued with religious sentiment that they imagined it to be all religion, and brought it openly, in their white bosoms, as their most acceptable sacrifice before the altar. The aged members of his flock, beholding Mr. Dimmesdale's frame so feeble,

NO FEAR

while still in their earthly bodies. All they lacked was the apostle's tongue of fire granting them the power to speak to every man's heart. These men would have tried in vain to express their high ideals in humble words and images—that is, if they had ever dreamed of trying! Instead, their voices had become distorted on their way down from these great heights.

es of fire: Ability that God granted to the apostles, ng their speech be understood all men in their language. Acts 2:6–12.

Mr. Dimmesdale would normally have belonged in this group of exceptionally spiritual ministers. He would have achieved their lofty heights of faith and holiness had he not been thwarted by the burden of whatever crime or suffering he struggled under. That burden kept this spiritual man—whose voice the angels might have answered!—down among the lowest of the low. But it also gave him an intimate understanding of the sinful brotherhood of mankind. His heart beat in unison with a thousand other hearts, taking in their pain and sending out its own beat in waves of sad, touching eloquence. Often touching, but sometimes terrible! The congregation did not understand the power that moved them so. They saw the young clergyman as a true miracle of holiness. They imagined him to be the spokesman of Heaven delivering messages of wisdom, rebuke, and love. In their eyes, the ground he walked on was holy. The young women in his church swooned when he came near, struck with a passion they imagined to be inspired by religious zeal. Believing their feelings entirely pure, they carried them openly in their breasts and offered them at the altar as their most valuable sacrifice. The elderly church members, seeing that Mr. Dimmesdale was even weaker than they and figuring he would ascend to Heaven first, asked their children to bury them

while they were themselves so rugged in their infirmity, believed that he would go heavenward before them, and enjoined it upon their children, that their old bones should be buried close to their young pastor's holy grave. And, all this time, perchance, when poor Mr. Dimmesdale was thinking of his grave, he questioned with himself whether the grass would ever grow on it, because an accursed thing must there be buried!

It is inconceivable, the agony with which this public veneration tortured him! It was his genuine impulse to adore the truth, and to reckon all things shadow-like, and utterly devoid of weight or value, that had not its divine essence as the life within their life. Then, what was he?—a substance?—or the dimmest of all shadows? He longed to speak out, from his own pulpit, at the full height of his voice, and tell the people what he was. "I, whom you behold in these black garments of the priesthood,—I, who ascend the sacred desk, and turn my pale face heavenward, taking upon myself to hold communion, in your behalf, with the Most High Omniscience,—I, in whose daily life you discern the sanctity of Enoch,—I, whose footsteps, as you suppose, leave a gleam along my earthly track, whereby the pilgrims that shall come after me may be guided to the regions of the blest,—I, who have laid the hand of baptism upon your children,—I, who have breathed the parting prayer over your dying friends, to whom the Amen sounded faintly from a world which they had quitted,—I, your pastor, whom you so reverence and trust, am utterly a pollution and a lie!"

More than once, Mr. Dimmesdale had gone into the pulpit, with a purpose never to come down its steps, until he should have spoken words like the above. More than once, he had cleared his throat, and drawn in the long, deep, and tremulous breath, which, when sent forth again, would come burdened with the black secret of his soul. More than once—nay, more than a hundred times—he had actually spoken! Spoken! But how? He had told his hearers that he was altogether vile, a viler companion of the vilest, the worst of sinners, an abomination, a thing of unimaginable iniquity; and that the only wonder was, that they did not see his wretched body shrivelled up before their eyes, by the burning wrath of the Almighty! Could there be plainer speech than this? Would not the people start up in their seats, by a simultaneous impulse, and tear him down

near the young pastor's grave. And the whole time, whenever poor Mr. Dimmesdale happened to think of his grave, he wondered whether grass would ever grow upon such a cursed burial mound!

This public admiration tortured Mr. Dimmesdale! His instinct was to adore the truth, and to think anything not filled with the divine essence of truth to be completely insignificant and worthless. But if that were the case, then what significance could he have? He longed to speak out from his own pulpit with the full weight of his voice and tell the people what he was. "I, whom you see dressed in these black robes of the priesthood . . . I, who ascend to the altar and turn my face upward to pray on your behalf . . . I, whose daily life you assume to be as holy as Enoch . . . I, whose footsteps you believe mark the pathway to Heaven . . . I, who have baptized your children . . . I, who have prayed over your dying friends . . . I, your pastor, whom you revere and trust, am a completely corrupt fraud!"

ch: Old Testament figure who, because of his righteousness, God allowed to ascend to Heaven before dying.

More than once, Mr. Dimmesdale had gone up to the pulpit thinking he would not come down until he had spoken these words. More than once he had cleared his throat and taken a long, deep, wavering breath, meant to deliver the black secret of his soul. More than once—no, more than a hundred times—he had actually spoken! But how? He had told his listeners that he was totally vile, the lowest companion of the low, the worst of sinners, a thing of unimaginable depravity. He said it was a wonder God did not torch his wretched body before their very eyes. Could he say it any more plainly? Wouldn't the people rise from their seats at once and tear him out of the pulpit he was defiling? No, indeed! They heard it all, and it only increased their admiration. They never imagined the true meaning lurking behind his words of self-condemnation. "The

out of the pulpit which he defiled? Not so, indeed! They heard it all, and did but reverence him the more. They little guessed what deadly purport lurked in those self-condemning words. "The godly youth!" said they among themselves. "The saint on earth! Alas, if he discern such sinfulness in his own white soul, what horrid spectacle would he behold in thine or mine!" The minister well knew—subtle, but remorseful hypocrite that he was!—the light in which his vague confession would be viewed. He had striven to put a cheat upon himself by making the avowal of a guilty conscience, but had gained only one other sin, and a self-acknowledged shame, without the momentary relief of being self-deceived. He had spoken the very truth, and transformed it into the veriest falsehood. And yet, by the constitution of his nature, he loved the truth, and loathed the lie, as few men ever did. Therefore, above all things else, he loathed his miserable self!

His inward trouble drove him to practices, more in accordance with the old, corrupted faith of Rome, than with the better light of the church in which he had been born and bred. In Mr. Dimmesdale's secret closet, under lock and key, there was a bloody scourge. Oftentimes, this Protestant and Puritan divine had plied it on his own shoulders; laughing bitterly at himself the while, and smiting so much the more pitilessly, because of that bitter laugh. It was his custom, too, as it has been that of many other pious Puritans, to fast,—not, however, like them, in order to purify the body and render it the fitter medium of celestial illumination,—but rigorously, and until his knees trembled beneath him, as an act of penance. He kept vigils, likewise, night after night, sometimes in utter darkness; sometimes with a glimmering lamp; and sometimes, viewing his own face in a looking-glass, by the most powerful light which he could throw upon it. He thus typified the constant introspection wherewith he tortured, but could not purify, himself. In these lengthened vigils, his brain often reeled, and visions seemed to flit before him; perhaps seen doubtfully, and by a faint light of their own, in the remote dimness of the chamber, or more vividly, and close beside him, within the looking-glass. Now it was a herd of diabolic shapes, that grinned and mocked at the pale minister, and beckoned him away with them; now a group of shining angels, who flew upward heavily, as sorrow-laden, but grew more ethereal

NO FEAR

godly young man!" they said to themselves. "He is a saint on earth! If he has such sinfulness in his own pure soul, what horrors must he see in yours or mine?" Subtle but remorseful hypocrite that he was, the minister knew they would interpret his vague confession this way. He tried to deceive himself by confessing a guilty conscience, but this only compounded the sin—and without even giving him the momentary relief of self-delusion. He had spoken the very truth but transformed it into the purest falsehood. And yet in his nature he loved the truth and hated lies as few men ever did. So he hated his miserable self above all else!

His inner turmoil drove him to practices more familiar to the corrupted old Catholic Church than the reformed faith in which he had been raised. Locked away in Mr. Dimmesdale's secret closet was a bloody whip. This Puritan had often whipped himself with it, laughing bitterly while he did, and then beating himself more brutally for his bitter laughter. He also fasted, as did other pious Puritans. But unlike these others, he did not fast to purify his body and make it a fitter vessel for holy inspiration. He fasted as an act of penance, until his knees trembled beneath him. He kept vigils night after night, sometimes in utter darkness, sometimes by a flickering light, and sometimes staring into a mirror while the light glared bright around him. These scenes symbolize the constant introspection through which he tortured, without purifying, himself. Visions often seemed to flit before him during these long vigils. Sometimes, these visions flickered vaguely in the dim corners of his room; sometimes they appeared more clearly, right beside him in the mirror. Now, devilish hordes grinned and mocked the pale minister, beckoning him to follow them. Now, a group of shining angels flew upward slowly, as though weighed down by their sorrow for him but growing lighter as they rose. Dead friends from his youth appeared, along with his white-bearded father with a saintlike frown and his mother, turning her face away as she passed. Though she was only a ghost, it would have been nice if she would throw her son a pitying glance! And

as they rose. Now came the dead friends of his youth, and his white-bearded father, with a saint-like frown, and his mother, turning her face away as she passed by. Ghost of a mother,—thinnest fantasy of a mother,—methinks she might yet have thrown a pitying glance towards her son! And now, through the chamber which these spectral thoughts had made so ghastly, glided Hester Prynne, leading along little Pearl, in her scarlet garb, and pointing her forefinger, first, at the scarlet letter on her bosom, and then at the clergyman's own breast.

None of these visions ever quite deluded him. At any moment, by an effort of his will, he could discern substances through their misty lack of substance, and convince himself that they were not solid in their nature, like yonder table of carved oak, or that big, square, leathern-bound and brazen-clasped volume of divinity. But, for all that, they were, in one sense, the truest and most substantial things which the poor minister now dealt with. It is the unspeakable misery of a life so false as his, that it steals the pith and substance out of whatever realities there are around us, and which were meant by Heaven to be the spirit's joy and nutriment. To the untrue man, the whole universe is false,—it is impalpable,—it shrinks to nothing within his grasp. And he himself, in so far as he shows himself in a false light, becomes a shadow, or, indeed, ceases to exist. The only truth, that continued to give Mr. Dimmesdale a real existence on this earth, was the anguish in his inmost soul, and the undissembled expression of it in his aspect. Had he once found power to smile, and wear a face of gayety, there would have been no such man!

On one of those ugly nights, which we have faintly hinted at, but forborne to picture forth, the minister started from his chair. A new thought had struck him. There might be a moment's peace in it. Attiring himself with as much care as if it had been for public worship, and precisely in the same manner, he stole softly down the staircase, undid the door, and issued forth.

now, across the terrible, ghost-filled room, glided Hester Prynne. She was leading her little Pearl in scarlet clothes and pointing her forefinger first at the scarlet letter on her own bosom and then at the clergyman's breast.

These visions never completely fooled him. At any time, by concentrating, he could make out objects—such as a carved oak table, or a large, leather-bound and bronze-clasped book of divinity—which convinced him that the visions were not real. But in a way the visions were the truest and most solid things the poor minister now dealt with. The most unspeakably tragic thing about a false life like his is that it sucks the substance from the reality around us, robbing the meaning from all the things that Heaven intended as nourishment to enrich the spirit. To the false man, the whole universe is false, unreal. It shrinks to nothing in his hands. And this man, as long as he walks in the false light, becomes a shadow and ceases to exist. The only truth that continued to give Mr. Dimmesdale a real existence on this earth was the anguish deep in his soul and the clear expression of its pain on his face. Had he found the power to force a smile—to pretend to be happy—he might have vanished forever!

On one of those ugly nights, which I have hinted at but have hesitated to fully describe, the minister leapt from his chair. Something occurred to him which just might provide him a moment of peace. He dressed himself as carefully as if he were going to lead a public worship, crept softly down the staircase, unlatched the door, and walked out.

Chapter 12: The Minister's Vigil

Walking in the shadow of a dream, as it were, and perhaps actually under the influence of a species of somnambulism, Mr. Dimmesdale reached the spot, where, now so long since, Hester Prynne had lived through her first hour of public ignominy. The same platform or scaffold, black and weather-stained with the storm or sunshine of seven long years, and foot-worn, too, with the tread of many culprits who had since ascended it, remained standing beneath the balcony of the meeting-house. The minister went up the steps.

It was an obscure night of early May. An unvaried pall of cloud muffled the whole expanse of sky from zenith to horizon. If the same multitude which had stood as eyewitnesses while Hester Prynne sustained her punishment could now have been summoned forth, they would have discerned no face above the platform, nor hardly the outline of a human shape, in the dark gray of the midnight. But the town was all asleep. There was no peril of discovery. The minister might stand there, if it so pleased him, until morning should redden in the east, without other risk than that the dank and chill night-air would creep into his frame, and stiffen his joints with rheumatism, and clog his throat with catarrh and cough; thereby defrauding the expectant audience of to-morrow's prayer and sermon. No eye could see him, save that ever-wakeful one which had seen him in his closet, wielding the bloody scourge. Why, then, had he come hither? Was it but the mockery of penitence? A mockery, indeed, but in which his soul trifled with itself! A mockery at which angels blushed and wept, while fiends rejoiced, with jeering laughter! He had been driven hither by the impulse of that Remorse which dogged him everywhere, and whose own sister and closely linked companion was that Cowardice which invariably drew him back, with her tremulous gripe, just when the other impulse had hurried him to the verge of a disclosure. Poor, miserable man! what right had infirmity like his to burden itself with crime? Crime is for the iron-nerved, who have their choice either to endure it, or, if it press too hard, to exert their fierce and savage strength for a good purpose, and fling it off at once! This feeble and most sensitive of spirits could do neither, yet continually did one thing or another, which intertwined, in the same inextricable knot, the agony of Heaven-defying guilt and vain repentance.

Chapter 12: The Minister's Vigil

Walking, as if in a dream—perhaps actually sleep-walking—Mr. Dimmesdale reached the spot where long ago Hester Prynne had first been publicly shamed. The same platform was there, black and weather-stained after seven long years. It was worn, too, from the feet of the many guilty people who had ascended it since. The minister went up the steps.

It was a dark night in early May. A thick layer of clouds covered the sky. If the same crowd that witnessed Hester Prynne's punishment could have been summoned, they would barely have been able to see the outline of a human shape, much less a face above the platform, in the gray dark of midnight. But the town was asleep. There was no danger of discovery. If the minister wished to stand there until the sun rose in the east, the only risk he would face is the damp, cold night air creeping into his body, stiffening his joints with arthritis and making his throat sore. His congregation might be cheated of their morning prayers and sermon, but that would be the worst of it. The only eye that would see him was God's, just as when he whipped himself in his closet. So why had he come there? Was it only to pretend to be sorry? Of course, that's the same game his soul always played! And angels blushed and cried at this masquerade, while demons rejoiced with jeering laughter! He had been led there by the same feeling of remorse that followed him everywhere. But cowardice—the sister and close companion of remorse—drew him back with her trembling grip just as he was on the verge of confession. Poor, miserable man! Why should his weak spirit burden itself with crime? Crime is for the iron-nerved—those who can either endure the guilt or use their strength to confess and bring an end to their pain! This weak and sensitive spirit could do neither. But he always went back and forth, weaving Heaven-defying guilt and vain remorse into an unbreakable knot.

And thus, while standing on the scaffold, in this vain show of expiation, Mr. Dimmesdale was overcome with a great horror of mind, as if the universe were gazing at a scarlet token on his naked breast, right over his heart. On that spot, in very truth, there was, and there had long been, the gnawing and poisonous tooth of bodily pain. Without any effort of his will, or power to restrain himself, he shrieked aloud; an outcry that went pealing through the night, and was beaten back from one house to another, and reverberated from the hills in the background; as if a company of devils detecting so much misery and terror in it, had made a plaything of the sound, and were bandying it to and fro.

"It is done!" muttered the minister, covering his face with his hands. "The whole town will awake and hurry forth, and find me here!"

But it was not so. The shriek had perhaps sounded with a far greater power, to his own startled ears, than it actually possessed. The town did not awake; or, if it did, the drowsy slumberers mistook the cry either for something frightful in a dream, or for the noise of witches; whose voices, at that period, were often heard to pass over the settlements or lonely cottages, as they rode with Satan through the air. The clergyman therefore, hearing no symptoms of disturbance, uncovered his eyes and looked about him. At one of the chamber-windows of Governor Bellingham's mansion which stood at some distance, on the line of another street, he beheld the appearance of the old magistrate himself, with a lamp in his hand, a white night-cap on his head, and a long white gown enveloping his figure. He looked like a ghost, evoked unseasonably from the grave. The cry had evidently startled him. At another window of the same house, moreover, appeared old Mistress Hibbins, the Governor's sister, also with her a lamp, which, even thus far off, revealed the expression of her sour and discontented face. She thrust forth her head from the lattice, and looked anxiously upward. Beyond the shadow of a doubt, this venerable witch-lady had heard Mr. Dimmesdale's outcry, and interpreted it, with its multitudinous echoes and reverberations, as the clamor of the fiends and night-hags, with whom she was well known to make excursions into the forest.

Detecting the gleam of Governor Bellingham's lamp, the old lady quickly extinguished her own, and vanished. Possibly, she went up among the clouds. The minister saw nothing further of her motions.

NO FEAR

While standing on the platform in this futile charade of repentance, Mr. Dimmesdale was overcome with horror, as though the universe were staring at a scarlet mark on his breast, right over his heart. To tell the truth, there had long been a gnawing, poisonous pain in that spot. Without the will or power to restrain himself, he cried aloud. The cry rang out through the night, bouncing from one house to another and echoing off the distant hills. It was as though a horde of devils had made a toy out of the horrible, miserable outcry and were tossing it back and forth.

"It is done!" muttered the minister, covering his face with his hands. "The whole town will awake and rush out to find me here!"

But this didn't happen. Perhaps the shriek sounded louder to him than it actually was. The town did not awake—or, if it did, the drowsy sleepers mistook the cry for a nightmare, or the sound of witches. At that time, witches were often heard as they rode with Satan above the settlements or lonely cottages. The minister, hearing no one stirring, uncovered his eyes and looked around. At one of the bedroom windows of Governor Bellingham's mansion, some distance away, he saw the old magistrate himself with a lamp in his hand and nightcap on his head. He wore a long white gown that made him look like a ghost rising suddenly from the grave. The cry had evidently startled him. Old Mistress Hibbins, the Governor's sister, appeared at another window of the same house. She also had a lamp. Even this far away, its light revealed her sour, unhappy face. She stuck her head out and looked anxiously upward. Without a doubt, this old witch-lady had heard Mr. Dimmesdale's cry and interpreted it as the sound of the demons and witches she was known to spend time with in the forest.

Seeing the light of Governor Bellingham's lamp, the old lady quickly extinguished her own and vanished. Maybe she flew up to the clouds. The minister didn't see her again that night. The magis-

The magistrate, after a wary observation of the darkness—into which, nevertheless, he could see but little farther than he might into a mill-stone—retired from the window.

The minister grew comparatively calm. His eyes, however, were soon greeted by a little, glimmering light, which, at first a long way off, was approaching up the street. It threw a gleam of recognition on here a post, and there a garden-fence, and here a latticed window-pane, and there a pump, with its full trough of water, and here, again, an arched door of oak, with an iron knocker, and a rough log for the door-step. The Reverend Mr. Dimmesdale noted all these minute particulars, even while firmly convinced that the doom of his existence was stealing onward, in the footsteps which he now heard; and that the gleam of the lantern would fall upon him, in a few moments more, and reveal his long-hidden secret. As the light drew nearer, he beheld, within its illuminated circle, his brother clergyman,—or, to speak more accurately, his professional father, as well as highly valued friend,—the Reverend Mr. Wilson; who, as Mr. Dimmesdale now conjectured, had been praying at the bedside of some dying man. And so he had. The good old minister came freshly from the death-chamber of Governor Winthrop, who had passed from earth to Heaven within that very hour. And now, surrounded, like the saint-like personages of olden times, with a radiant halo, that glorified him amid this gloomy night of sin,—as if the departed Governor had left him an inheritance of his glory, or as if he had caught upon himself the distant shine of the celestial city, while looking thitherward to see the triumphant pilgrim pass within its gates,—now, in short, good Father Wilson was moving homeward, aiding his footsteps with a lighted lantern! The glimmer of this luminary suggested the above conceits to Mr. Dimmesdale, who smiled,—nay, almost laughed at them,—and then wondered if he were going mad.

As the Reverend Mr. Wilson passed beside the scaffold, closely muffling his Geneva cloak about him with one arm, and holding the lantern before his breast with the other, the minister could hardly restrain himself from speaking.

"A good evening to you, venerable Father Wilson! Come up hither, I pray you, and pass a pleasant hour with me!"

trate, after cautiously surveying the darkness—which he could see into about as good as if he were looking through stone—drew back from the window.

The minister calmed down a bit, but his eyes soon detected a small glimmering light approaching from way up the street. It briefly illuminated nearby objects as it made its way: a post here, a garden fence there; a window, a water pump and trough; and that oak door, iron knocker, and wooden step of the prison house. The Reverend Mr. Dimmesdale noticed all of these details, even as he became convinced that the light was his doom drawing near. In a few moments, the lantern's beam would fall on him, revealing his long-hidden secret. As the light came closer he saw his fellow clergyman within its circle. To be more precise, it was his mentor and good friend, the Reverend Mr. Wilson. Mr. Dimmesdale assumed he had been praying at the bedside of some dying man. In fact, he had. The good old minister came from the death chamber of Governor Winthrop, who had passed to Heaven that very hour. Good Father Wilson was making his way home, his footsteps aided by a lantern's light which surrounded him with a radiant halo, like the saints of old. He seemed glorified on this gloomy, sin-filled night, as if the dead Governor had bequeathed to him his brilliance, or as if he had caught the shine from the heavenly city as he watched the Governor make his way there. These are the images that occurred to Mr. Dimmesdale. He smiled and almost laughed at the extravagant metaphors, and then he wondered if he were going mad.

The Reverend Mr. Wilson passed by the platform, holding his ministerial cloak about him with one arm and the lantern in front of him with the other. Dimmesdale could hardly keep from speaking:

"Good evening to you, Reverend Father Wilson. Come up here, please, and spend a fine hour with me!"

Good heavens! Had Mr. Dimmesdale actually spoken? For one instant, he believed that these words had passed his lips. But they were uttered only within his imagination. The venerable Father Wilson continued to step slowly onward, looking carefully at the muddy pathway before his feet, and never once turning his head towards the guilty platform. When the light of the glimmering lantern had faded quite away, the minister discovered, by the faintness which came over him, that the last few moments had been a crisis of terrible anxiety; although his mind had made an involuntary effort to relieve itself by a kind of lurid playfulness.

Shortly afterwards, the like grisly sense of the humorous again stole in among the solemn phantoms of his thought. He felt his limbs growing stiff with the unaccustomed chilliness of the night, and doubted whether he should be able to descend the steps of the scaffold. Morning would break, and find him there. The neighbourhood would begin to rouse itself. The earliest riser, coming forth in the dim twilight, would perceive a vaguely defined figure aloft on the place of shame; and, half-crazed betwixt alarm and curiosity, would go, knocking from door to door, summoning all the people to behold the ghost—as he needs must think it—of some defunct transgressor. A dusky tumult would flap its wings from one house to another. Then—the morning light still waxing stronger— old patriarchs would rise up in great haste, each in his flannel gown, and matronly dames, without pausing to put off their night-gear. The whole tribe of decorous personages, who had never heretofore been seen with a single hair of their heads awry, would start into public view, with the disorder of a nightmare in their aspects. Old Governor Bellingham would come grimly forth, with his King James's ruff fastened askew; and Mistress Hibbins, with some twigs of the forest clinging to her skirts, and looking sourer than ever, as having hardly got a wink of sleep after her night ride; and good Father Wilson, too, after spending half the night at death-bed, and liking ill to be disturbed, thus early, out of his dreams about the glorified saints. Hither, likewise, would come the elders and deacons of Mr. Dimmesdale's church, and the young virgins who so idolized their minister, and had made a shrine for him in their white bosoms; which, now, by the by, in their hurry and confusion, they would scantly have given themselves time to cover with their kerchiefs.

Good heavens! Had Mr. Dimmesdale actually spoken? For a moment, he believed that he had. But he only said those words in his mind. Old Father Wilson continued to walk slowly onward, looking carefully at the muddy path before him, and never once turning his head toward the guilty platform. After the light of the glimmering lantern had faded away entirely, the minister realized that even though his mind had tried to relieve itself through this elaborate game, the terrible tension of the last few minutes had left him weak.

Shortly afterward, this morbid humor again invaded his serious thoughts. He felt his limbs growing stiff with the chill of night. He wasn't sure whether he would be able to climb down from the platform. Morning would find him still sitting there. The neighborhood would begin to stir. The earliest riser, walking out into the dim twilight, would see a hazy figure on the platform. Caught between fear and curiosity, he would knock on every door, calling everyone to come and see the ghost—as he would surely think it was—of some dead sinner. The morning's commotion would spread from one house to another. Then, as the daylight grew stronger, respectable old men in their flannel nightgowns would quickly rise. Proud old women would get up without pausing to change out of their nightclothes. All of the town's most important people, who were never seen with a hair out of place, would hurry into public view with the disorder of a nightmare in their faces. Old Governor Bellingham would appear, his ruffled collar wrongly fastened. Mistress Hibbins would come out, twigs clinging to her skirt and her face looking more sour than ever after having spent all night riding with the witches. And good Father Wilson, unhappy to be woken from his dreams of the saints after spending half the night at a deathbed, would make his way there. So too would the elders of Mr. Dimmesdale's church, and the young women who had idolized their minister and made a place for him in their white bosoms, which they would barely have had time to cover with their handkerchiefs amid the chaos and confusion. In a word, everyone would come stumbling out of their doors. They would turn their amazed and horrified faces to the platform. Who would they see sitting there, the red rising sun shining on his face? Who but Arthur Dimmesdale, half-frozen to death, overcome with shame, and standing where Hester Prynne had stood!

All people, in a word, would come stumbling over their thresholds, and turning up their amazed and horror-stricken visages around the scaffold. Whom would they discern there, with the red eastern light upon his brow? Whom, but the Reverend Arthur Dimmesdale, half-frozen to death, overwhelmed with shame, and standing where Hester Prynne had stood!

Carried away by the grotesque horror of this picture, the minister, unawares, and to his own infinite alarm, burst into a great peal of laughter. It was immediately responded to by a light, airy, childish laugh, in which, with a thrill of the heart,—but he knew not whether of exquisite pain, or pleasure as acute—he recognized the tones of little Pearl.

"Pearl! Little Pearl!" cried he, after a moment's pause; then, suppressing his voice,—"Hester! Hester Prynne! Are you there?"

"Yes; it is Hester Prynne!" she replied, in a tone of surprise; and the minister heard her footsteps approaching from the sidewalk, along which she had been passing.—"It is I, and my little Pearl."

"Whence come you, Hester?" asked the minister. "What sent you hither?"

"I have been watching at a death-bed," answered Hester Prynne;—"at Governor Winthrop's death-bed, and have taken his measure for a robe, and am now going homeward to my dwelling."

"Come up hither, Hester, thou and little Pearl," said the Reverend Mr. Dimmesdale. "Ye have both been here before, but I was not with you. Come up hither once again, and we will stand all three together!"

She silently ascended the steps, and stood on the platform, holding little Pearl by the hand. The minister felt for the child's other hand, and took it. The moment that he did so, there came what seemed a tumultuous rush of new life, other life than his own, pouring like a torrent into his heart, and hurrying through all his veins, as if the mother and the child were communicating their vital warmth to his half-torpid system. The three formed an electric chain.

"Minister!" whispered little Pearl.

"What wouldst thou say, child?" asked Mr. Dimmesdale.

"Wilt thou stand here with mother and me, to-morrow noontide?" inquired Pearl.

The minister was carried away by the horror of this fantasy. Unconsciously, and to his great alarm, he burst into uncontrollable laughter. A light, airy, childish laugh responded immediately. With a pang in his heart—whether of pain or pleasure, he could not tell—he recognized the sound of little Pearl.

"Pearl! Little Pearl!" he cried, after a moment. Then, in a quieter voice, "Hester! Hester Prynne! Are you there?"

"Yes, it is Hester Prynne!" she replied, with a tone of surprise. The minister heard her footsteps approaching from the sidewalk. "It's me and my little Pearl."

"Where are you coming from, Hester?" asked the minister. "What's brought you here?"

"I have been at a deathbed," answered Hester Prynne. "Governor Winthrop's deathbed. I had to measure him for a burial robe, and now I'm heading home."

"Come up here, Hester, you and little Pearl," said the Reverend Mr. Dimmesdale. "You have been here before, but I was not with you. Come up here once more, and we will stand all three together."

She silently climbed the steps and stood on the platform, holding little Pearl by the hand. The minister felt for the child's other hand and took it. As soon as he did, a rush of new life poured through him. The energy poured into his heart and sped through his veins, as though the mother and child had sent their warmth through his half-dead body. The three formed an electric chain.

"Minister!" whispered little Pearl.

"What it is, child?" asked Mr. Dimmesdale.

"Will you stand here with mother and me at noontime tomorrow?" asked Pearl.

"Nay; not so, my little Pearl!" answered the minister; for, with the new energy of the moment, all the dread of public exposure, that had so long been the anguish of his life, had returned upon him; and he was already trembling at the conjunction in which—with a strange joy, nevertheless—he now found himself. "Not so, my child. I shall, indeed, stand with thy mother and thee one other day, but not to-morrow!"

Pearl laughed, and attempted to pull away her hand. But the minister held it fast.

"A moment longer, my child!" said he.

"But wilt thou promise," asked Pearl, "to take my hand, and mother's hand, to-morrow noontide?"

"Not then, Pearl," said the minister, "but another time!"

"And what other time?" persisted the child.

"At the great judgment day!" whispered the minister,—and, strangely enough, the sense that he was a professional teacher of the truth impelled him to answer the child so. "Then, and there, before the judgment-seat, thy mother, and thou, and I, must stand together! But the daylight of this world shall not see our meeting!"

Pearl laughed again.

But, before Mr. Dimmesdale had done speaking, a light gleamed far and wide over all the muffled sky. It was doubtless caused by one of those meteors, which the night-watcher may so often observe burning out to waste, in the vacant regions of the atmosphere. So powerful was its radiance, that it thoroughly illuminated the dense medium of cloud betwixt the sky and earth. The great vault brightened, like the dome of an immense lamp. It showed the familiar scene of the street, with the distinctness of mid-day, but also with the awfulness that is always imparted to familiar objects by an unaccustomed light. The wooden houses, with their jutting stories and quaint gable-peaks; the door-steps and thresholds, with the early grass springing up about them; the garden-plots, black with freshly turned earth; the wheel-track, little worn, and, even in the market-place, margined with green on either side;—all were visible, but with a singularity of aspect that seemed to give another moral interpretation to the things of this world than they had ever borne before. And there stood the minister, with his hand over his heart; and Hester Prynne, with the embroidered letter glimmering on her

"I'm afraid not, my little Pearl," answered the minister. With the new energy of the moment, all the dread of public exposure had returned. He was already trembling at the position in which he now found himself, though it also brought a strange joy. "No, my child. I promise to stand with your mother and you one day, but not tomorrow."

Pearl laughed and tried to pull her hand away. But the minister held it tight.

"One moment more, my child!" he said.

"But will you promise," asked Pearl, "to take my hand, and mother's hand, tomorrow at noon?"

"Not then, Pearl," said the minister, "but another time."

"What other time?" the child asked persistently.

"At the great judgment day," whispered the minister. Oddly enough, his sense of obligation as a teacher of the truth compelled him to give that answer. "Then and there, before the throne of judgment, your mother, you, and I must stand together. But the light of this world will not see us as one!"

Pearl laughed again.

But before Mr. Dimmesdale had finished speaking, a light gleamed over the clouded sky. It was probably caused by one of those meteors that stargazers so often see burning in the blank areas of the sky. The light was so powerful that it completely illuminated the dense layer of cloud between Heaven and earth. The dome of the sky brightened like a giant lamp. It illuminated the familiar scene of the street as clearly as the midday sun, but in the bizarre way that a strange light gives to well-known objects. It lit up the wooden houses, with their uneven stories and quaint peaks; the front doors, with their young grass growing before them; the gardens, black with newly turned soil; the wagon road, lightly worn and bordered with green. All of this was visible, but with a unique appearance that seemed to assign to the world a deeper meaning. And there stood the minister, with his hand over his heart, and Hester Prynne, with the embroidered letter shimmering on her bosom. Little Pearl, herself a symbol, stood between the two like a link connecting them. They stood in the noon-like light of that strange and solemn splendor, as though it would reveal all their secrets—like a dawn that will unite those who belong to each another.

bosom; and little Pearl, herself a symbol, and the connecting link between those two. They stood in the noon of that strange and solemn splendor, as if it were the light that is to reveal all secrets, and the daybreak that shall unite all who belong to one another.

There was witchcraft in little Pearl's eyes; and her face, as she glanced upward at the minister, wore that naughty smile which made its expression frequently so elvish. She withdrew her hand from Mr. Dimmesdale's, and pointed across the street. But he clasped both his hands over his breast, and cast his eyes towards the zenith.

Nothing was more common, in those days, than to interpret all meteoric appearances, and other natural phenomena, that occurred with less regularity than the rise and set of sun and moon, as so many revelations from a supernatural source. Thus, a blazing spear, a sword of flame, a bow, or a sheaf of arrows, seen in the midnight sky, prefigured Indian warfare. Pestilence was known to have been foreboded by a shower of crimson light. We doubt whether any marked event, for good or evil, ever befell New England, from its settlement down to Revolutionary times, of which the inhabitants had not been previously warned by some spectacle of this nature. Not seldom, it had been seen by multitudes. Oftener, however, its credibility rested on the faith of some lonely eyewitness, who beheld the wonder through the colored, magnifying, and distorting medium of his imagination, and shaped it more distinctly in his after-thought. It was, indeed, a majestic idea, that the destiny of nations should be revealed, in these awful hieroglyphics, on the cope of Heaven. A scroll so wide might not be deemed too expansive for Providence to write a people's doom upon. The belief was a favorite one with our forefathers, as betokening that their infant commonwealth was under a celestial guardianship of peculiar intimacy and strictness. But what shall we say, when an individual discovers a revelation, addressed to himself alone, on the same vast sheet of record! In such a case, it could only be the symptom of a highly disordered mental state, when a man, rendered morbidly self-contemplative by long, intense, and secret pain, had extended his egotism over the whole expanse of nature, until the firmament itself should appear no more than a fitting page for his soul's history and fate.

We impute it, therefore, solely to the disease in his own eye and heart, that the minister, looking upward to the zenith, beheld there the appearance of an immense letter,—the letter A,—marked out in

NO FEAR

Little Pearl's eyes took on a bewitched look. As she glanced up at the minister, her face wore that naughty, elfish smile. She pulled her hand back from Mr. Dimmesdale's and pointed across the street. But he clasped both his hands over his breast and looked up at the sky.

It was common in those days for people to interpret meteors and other natural phenomena as divine revelation. If something like a blazing spear, sword of flame, bow, or sheaf of arrows was seen in the midnight sky, it foretold war with the Indians. A shower of crimson light meant disease was coming. I doubt that any significant event, whether good or bad, ever occurred in New England without the inhabitants claiming they had been warned by some sort of sign. Many times, multitudes claimed to have seen the spectacle. More often, though, evidence rested with a single, lonely eyewitness, who viewed the event through the distortions of his imagination then shaped it more clearly afterward. What a magnificent idea that the fates of nations should be written in these heavenly symbols. God must not have thought such a wide scroll as the sky was too big to use for writing down a people's destiny. This belief was a favorite of our forefathers, since it suggested that God kept a close watch over their young commonwealth. But what can we say when a revelation addressed to just one person is written on that same giant scroll? That discovery could only be the symptom of insanity. It would show that the individual, so self-absorbed after a long, intense, and secret pain, had extended his egotism a step further, until the sky itself appeared nothing more than a record of his own history and fate.

So when the minister, looking up toward the meteor, thought he saw a vast letter A drawn in lines of dull red light, it had to be his self-absorbed heart playing tricks on his eyes. Not that the meteor

lines of dull red light. Not but the meteor may have shown itself at that point, burning duskily through a veil of cloud; but with no such shape as his guilty imagination gave it; or, at least, with so little definiteness, that another's guilt might have seen another symbol in it.

There was a singular circumstance that characterized Mr. Dimmesdale's psychological state, at this moment. All the time that he gazed upward to the zenith, he was, nevertheless, perfectly aware that little Pearl was pointing her finger towards old Roger Chillingworth, who stood at no great distance from the scaffold. The minister appeared to see him, with the same glance that discerned the miraculous letter. To his features, as to all other objects, the meteoric light imparted a new expression; or it might well be that the physician was not careful then, as at all other times, to hide the malevolence with which he looked upon his victim. Certainly, if the meteor kindled up the sky, and disclosed the earth, with an awfulness that admonished Hester Prynne and the clergyman of the day of judgment, then might Roger Chillingworth have passed with them for the arch-fiend, standing there, with a smile and scowl, to claim his own. So vivid was the expression, or so intense the minister's perception of it, that it seemed still to remain painted on the darkness, after the meteor had vanished, with an effect as if the street and all things else were at once annihilated.

"Who is that man, Hester?" gasped Mr. Dimmesdale, overcome with terror. "I shiver at him! Dost thou know the man? I hate him, Hester!"

She remembered her oath, and was silent.

"I tell thee, my soul shivers at him," muttered the minister again. "Who is he? Who is he? Canst thou do nothing for me? I have a nameless horror of the man."

"Minister," said little Pearl, "I can tell thee who he is!"

"Quickly, then, child!" said the minister, bending his ear close to her lips. "Quickly!—and as low as thou canst whisper."

Pearl mumbled something into his ear, that sounded, indeed, like human language, but was only such gibberish as children may be heard amusing themselves with, by the hour together. At all events, if it involved any secret information in regard to old Roger Chillingworth, it was in a tongue unknown to the erudite clergyman,

was not visible at the time, burning behind a cloudy veil. But some-one else's imagination could have easily seen in it the image of his own guilt, and not the minister's.

There was one thing on Mr. Dimmesdale's mind just then. All the while that he stared up at the meteor, he knew that little Pearl was pointing toward old Roger Chillingworth standing near the plat-form. The minister seemed to see him at the same time that he saw the miraculous letter in the sky. The meteor cast Roger Chillingworth in a new light, as it did the rest of the world—or perhaps the doctor was simply less careful than usual to mask his hatred for the minis-ter. If the meteor lit up the sky with a horror suggesting Judgment Day, then Roger Chillingworth might have stood in for the Devil himself, smiling as souls were cast into Hell. His expression—or at least the minister's perception of it—was so intense that it seemed to glow even after the light from the meteor had faded and left the rest of the scene in darkness.

"Who is that man, Hester?" gasped Mr. Dimmesdale, overcome with terror. "The sight of him makes me shiver! Do you know who he is? I hate him, Hester!"

She remembered her vow and remained silent.

"I tell you, the sight of him makes my soul shiver!" the minister muttered once again. "Who is he? Who is he? Can't you help me? I am terribly afraid of the man!"

"Minister," said little Pearl, "I can tell you who he is!"

"Quickly then, child!" said the minister, bending his ear close to her lips. "Quickly!—and as soft as you can whisper."

Pearl mumbled something into his ear. It sounded like a human language but was only the sort of gibberish that children often use when playing together. In any case, if her babbling con-tained any secret information about old Roger Chillingworth, it was spoken in a language the learned clergyman didn't under-

and did but increase the bewilderment of his mind. The elvish child then laughed aloud.

"Dost thou mock me now?" said the minister.

"Thou wast not bold!—thou wast not true!" answered the child. "Thou wouldst not promise to take my hand, and mother's hand, to-morrow noontide!"

"Worthy Sir," said the physician, who had now advanced to the foot of the platform. "Pious Master Dimmesdale! can this be you? Well, well, indeed! We men of study, whose heads are in our books, have need to be straitly looked after! We dream in our waking moments, and walk in our sleep. Come, good Sir, and my dear friend, I pray you, let me lead you home!"

"How knewest thou that I was here?" asked the minister, fearfully.

"Verily, and in good faith," answered Roger Chillingworth, "I knew nothing of the matter. I had spent the better part of the night at the bedside of the worshipful Governor Winthrop, doing what my poor skill might to give him ease. He going home to a better world, I, likewise, was on my way homeward, when this strange light shone out. Come with me, I beseech you, Reverend Sir; else you will be poorly able to do Sabbath duty to-morrow. Aha! see now, how they trouble the brain,—these books!—these books! You should study less, good Sir, and take a little pastime; or these night-whimseys will grow upon you!"

"I will go home with you," said Mr. Dimmesdale.

With a chill despondency, like one awaking, all nerveless, from an ugly dream, he yielded himself to the physician, and was led away.

The next day, however, being the Sabbath, he preached a discourse which was held to be the richest and most powerful, and the most replete with heavenly influences, that had ever proceeded from his lips. Souls, it is said, more souls than one, were brought to the truth by the efficacy of that sermon, and vowed within themselves to cherish a holy gratitude towards Mr. Dimmesdale throughout the long hereafter. But, as he came down the pulpit-steps, the gray-bearded sexton met him, holding up a black glove, which the minister recognized as his own.

"It was found," said the sexton, "this morning, on the scaffold, where evil-doers are set up to public shame. Satan dropped it there,

stand. This only made him more confused. The elf-child laughed out loud.

"Are you mocking me?" asked the minister.

"You weren't brave! You weren't honest!" answered the child. "You wouldn't promise to take my hand, and my mother's hand, tomorrow at noon!"

"My good man," said the doctor, who had advanced to the foot of the platform, "pious Mr. Dimmesdale! Is that you? Well, well! Scholars like us, whose heads are in our books, must be looked after quite closely! We daydream when awake, and we walk in our sleep. Come, good sir and dear friend, please, let me walk you home."

"How did you know I was here?" asked the minister, fearfully.

"Honestly," answered Roger Chillingworth, "I didn't know. I spent most of the night at the bedside of Governor Winthrop, doing what little I could to comfort him. He went home to a better a world. I was on my way home, too, when this light appeared. Come with me now, please, I beg you, good sir. Or you won't give a very good sermon tomorrow. Ah, I see now how much books can trouble the brain. You should study less, good sir, and relax more often, or these nighttime fantasies will only increase."

"I'll go home with you," said Mr. Dimmesdale.

With a chilling hopelessness, like one who wakes up trembling after a nightmare, he let the doctor lead him away.

The next day, he preached a sermon considered the most powerful and inspired he had ever given. It is said that many souls were saved by the strength of that sermon, vowing to remain grateful to Mr. Dimmesdale even in Heaven. But as he descended from the pulpit, the gray-bearded sexton met him, holding up a black glove. The minister recognized it as his own.

Sexton: Minor church officer [char]ed with main[taining] the grounds.

"It was found this morning," said the sexton, "on the platform where sinners are exhibited to public shame. Satan dropped it there, I

I take it, intending a scurrilous jest against your reverence. But, indeed, he was blind and foolish, as he ever and always is. A pure hand needs no glove to cover it!"

"Thank you, my good friend," said the minister gravely, but startled at heart; for, so confused was his remembrance, that he had almost brought himself to look at the events of the past night as visionary. "Yes, it seems to be my glove indeed!"

"And, since Satan saw fit to steal it, your reverence must needs handle him without gloves, henceforward," remarked the old sexton, grimly smiling. "But did your reverence hear of the portent that was seen last night? A great red letter in the sky,—the letter A,—which we interpret to stand for Angel. For, as our good Governor Winthrop was made an angel this past night, it was doubtless held fit that there should be some notice thereof!"

"No," answered the minister. "I had not heard of it."

presume, in a despicable joke against you. But the Devil was blind and foolish, as he always is. A pure hand needs no glove to cover it!"

"Thank you, my good friend," said the minister, sounding calm and serious, though fear was in his heart. His memory of the previous night was so muddled, he had nearly convinced himself it was all in his imagination. "Yes, this does seem to be my glove!"

"And, since Satan saw fit to steal it, from now on the gloves must come off when you fight with him," the old sexton said, smiling grimly. "But did you hear of the sign that was seen last night? A great red letter appeared in the sky—the letter A—which we take to stand for 'Angel.' Since our good Governor Winthrop became an angel last night, it is fitting that there should be some sign to mark the event."

"No," the minister answered, "I had not heard about that."

Chapter 13: Another View of Hester

In her late singular interview with Mr. Dimmesdale, Hester Prynne was shocked at the condition to which she found the clergyman reduced. His nerve seemed absolutely destroyed. His moral force was abased into more than childish weakness. It grovelled helpless on the ground, even while his intellectual faculties retained their pristine strength, or had perhaps acquired a morbid energy, which disease only could have given them. With her knowledge of a train of circumstances hidden from all others, she could readily infer, that, besides the legitimate action of his own conscience, a terrible machinery had been brought to bear, and was still operating, on Mr. Dimmesdale's well-being and repose. Knowing what this poor, fallen man had once been, her whole soul was moved by the shuddering terror with which he had appealed to her,—the outcast woman,—for support against his instinctively discovered enemy. She decided, moreover, that he had a right to her utmost aid. Little accustomed, in her long seclusion from society, to measure her ideas of right and wrong by any standard external to herself, Hester saw—or seemed to see—that there lay a responsibility upon her, in reference to the clergyman, which she owed to no other, nor to the whole world besides. The links that united her to the rest of human kind—links of flowers, or silk, or gold, or whatever the material—had all been broken. Here was the iron link of mutual crime, which neither he nor she could break. Like all other ties, it brought with it its obligations.

Hester Prynne did not now occupy precisely the same position in which we beheld her during the earlier periods of her ignominy. Years had come, and gone. Pearl was now seven years old. Her mother, with the scarlet letter on her breast, glittering in its fantastic embroidery, had long been a familiar object to the townspeople. As is apt to be the case when a person stands out in any prominence before the community, and, at the same time, interferes neither with public nor individual interests and convenience, a species of general regard had ultimately grown up in reference to Hester Prynne. It is to the credit of human nature, that, except where its selfishness is brought into play, it loves more readily than it hates. Hatred, by a gradual and quiet process, will even be transformed to love, unless the change be impeded by a continually new irritation of the orig-

Chapter 13: Another View of Hester

Hester Prynne was shocked by how different the clergyman had seemed in her recent encounter with him. He had lost his nerve almost completely. His moral strength had been reduced to that of a child, begging and crawling around on the ground. At the same time, his mind was as strong as ever, perhaps even energized by the sickness of his soul. Hester, with the knowledge of certain secret circumstances, could easily guess what had happened to him. In addition to the deserved pain his own conscience caused him, a terrible machine had been set to work on Mr. Dimmesdale. That machine was destroying his well-being and good health. Knowing what this poor, diminished man had once been, Hester's soul was moved by the desperate way he had begged her—her, the outcast!—for aid against the enemy he had instinctually discovered. She decided he had a right to her help. In her long isolation, Hester had come to measure right and wrong by her own standards, rather than those of the world. She saw that she had a responsibility to the minister that she did not have to anyone else. The links that bound her to the rest of humankind had been broken—whether they be links of flowers, silk, gold, or some other material. But her link to the minister was the iron link of a shared crime, and neither he nor she could break it. And like all other ties, it came with obligations.

Hester Prynne was not in quite the same position as she had been in the earlier years of her shame. Years had passed. Pearl was now seven years old. Hester, with the scarlet letter glittering on her breast, had long been a familiar sight. The townspeople now thought of her with the sort of respect afforded prominent people who do not interfere with either public or private affairs. It is a credit to human nature that it is quicker to love than hate, unless its selfishness is provoked. Even hatred itself will gradually give way to love, unless that original hatred is continually irritated. But Hester Prynne didn't irritate or irk anyone. She never fought against public opinion. Instead, she submitted without complaint to the worst it could offer. She did not claim that the public owed her any compensation for her suffering. She never begged for sympathy. And she

inal feeling of hostility. In this matter of Hester Prynne, there was neither irritation nor irksomeness. She never battled with the public, but submitted uncomplainingly to its worst usage; she made no claim upon it, in requital for what she suffered; she did not weigh upon its sympathies. Then, also, the blameless purity of her life, during all these years in which she had been set apart to infamy, was reckoned largely in her favor. With nothing now to lose, in the sight of mankind, and with no hope, and seemingly no wish, of gaining any thing, it could only be a genuine regard for virtue that had brought back the poor wanderer to its paths.

It was perceived, too, that, while Hester never put forward even the humblest title to share in the world's privileges,—farther than to breathe the common air, and earn daily bread for little Pearl and herself by the faithful labor of her hands,—she was quick to acknowledge her sisterhood with the race of man, whenever benefits were to be conferred. None so ready as she to give of her little substance to every demand of poverty; even though the bitter-hearted pauper threw back a gibe in requital of the food brought regularly to his door, or the garments wrought for him by the fingers that could have embroidered a monarch's robe. None so self-devoted as Hester, when pestilence stalked through the town. In all seasons of calamity, indeed, whether general or of individuals, the outcast of society at once found her place. She came, not as a guest, but as a rightful inmate, into the household that was darkened by trouble; as if its gloomy twilight were a medium in which she was entitled to hold intercourse with her fellow-creatures. There glimmered the embroidered letter, with comfort in its unearthly ray. Elsewhere the token of sin, it was the taper of the sick-chamber. It had even thrown its gleam, in the sufferer's hard extremity, across the verge of time. It had shown him where to set his foot, while the light of earth was fast becoming dim, and ere the light of futurity could reach him. In such emergencies, Hester's nature showed itself warm and rich; a wellspring of human tenderness, unfailing to every real demand, and inexhaustible by the largest. Her breast, with its badge of shame, was but the softer pillow for the head that needed one. She was self-ordained a Sister of Mercy; or, we may rather say, the world's heavy hand had so ordained her, when neither the world nor she looked forward to this result. The letter was the symbol of her calling. Such

was widely admired for the sinless purity of her life during the many years of her public shame. With nothing to lose in the eyes of the public—and nothing, it seemed, to gain either—it must have been a genuine desire for virtue that had altered her life's path.

It was noted, too, that Hester never claimed even the smallest share of worldly privileges. She worked for her freedom and the daily earnings for little Pearl and herself, and that was all she asked for. And she readily acknowledged her kinship with all of human kind when it came to public service. No one was as willing as she to give what little she had to the poor, even though the needy would often mock the woman who brought food to their door or made them plain clothes with hands skilled enough to stitch for kings. When disease swept through the town, no one was more devoted to the sick than Hester. Indeed, whenever disaster struck, whether it was widespread or fell on one individual, the outcast found her rightful place. It was as though times of sadness and turmoil provided the only means for Hester to commune with the rest of society. In that gloomy twilight, the unearthly glow of the embroidered letter was a comfort. It may be the token of sin in most places, but it shined like a candle in the homes of the sick. There, Hester was able to show her rich and warm nature. She was a wellspring of human tenderness, never failing to meet every real demand no matter how large. Her badge of shame only made her bosom softer for the head that needed rest. She had ordained herself a Sister of Mercy. Or perhaps I should say that the world's heavy hand had ordained her, when neither she nor the world expected it. The scarlet letter became the symbol of her calling. She was so helpful, with so much power to aid and to sympathize, that many refused to recognize the A for its original meaning. They said that it stood for "able," so strong a woman was Hester Prynne.

helpfulness was found in her,—so much power to do, and power to sympathize,—that many people refused to interpret the scarlet A by its original signification. They said that it meant Able; so strong was Hester Prynne, with a woman's strength.

It was only the darkened house that could contain her. When sunshine came again, she was not there. Her shadow had faded across the threshold. The helpful inmate had departed, without one backward glance to gather up the meed of gratitude, if any were in hearts of those whom she had served so zealously. Meeting them in the street, she never raised her head to receive their greeting. If they were resolute to accost her, she laid her finger on the scarlet letter, and passed on. This might be pride, but was so like humility, that it produced all the softening influence of the latter quality on the public mind. The public is despotic in its temper; it is capable of denying common justice, when too strenuously demanded as a right; but quite as frequently it awards more than justice, when the appeal is made, as despots love to have it made, entirely to its generosity. Interpreting Hester Prynne's deportment as an appeal of this nature, society was inclined to show its former victim a more benign countenance than she cared to be favored with, or, perchance, than she deserved.

The rulers, and the wise and learned men of the community, were longer in acknowledging the influence of Hester's good qualities than the people. The prejudices which they shared in common with the latter were fortified in themselves by an iron framework of reasoning, that made it a far tougher labor to expel them. Day by day, nevertheless, their sour and rigid wrinkles were relaxing into something which, in the due course of years, might grow to be an expression of almost benevolence. Thus it was with the men of rank, on whom their eminent position imposed the guardianship of the public morals. Individuals in private life, meanwhile, had quite forgiven Hester Prynne for her frailty; nay, more, they had begun to look upon the scarlet letter as the token, not of that one sin, for which she had borne so long and dreary a penance, but of her many good deeds since. "Do you see that woman with the embroidered badge?" they would say to strangers. "It is our Hester,—the town's own Hester,—who is so kind to the poor, so helpful to the sick, so comfortable to the afflicted!" Then, it is true, the propensity

NO FEAR

But only a house of sickness or sadness could hold her. When life brightened again, she was no longer there. Her shadow faded from the doorway. The helper departed without looking back for any sign of gratitude in the hearts of those she had served. When she passed them on the street, she never raised her head to greet them. If they persisted in approaching her, she pointed to the scarlet letter and walked on by. Hester may have been acting this way out of pride, but it seemed so much like humility that the public reacted as though it truly were. The public often acts like a fickle king. When justice is called for too aggressively, the public will often deny it. But that same public often goes overboard—just as a king would—in granting justice when the appeal is made to its generosity. Thinking that Hester Prynne's actions were an appeal to its generous nature, society was inclined to be more kind than she wanted, or perhaps than she even deserved.

The rulers—the wise and learned men of the community—took longer than the common people to acknowledge Hester's good qualities. They shared the same prejudices as the rest of the community, and their rigorous reasoning worked to hold those prejudices firmly in place. Yet, day by day, their sour faces relaxed into something that might eventually become a kind expression. The same was true for the men of high status, whose lofty positions made them the guardians of public virtue. But almost everyone had privately forgiven Hester Prynne for her human weakness. Even more than that, they had begun to look at the scarlet letter not as the symbol of one sin but as a symbol of the many good deeds she had done since. "Do you see that woman with the embroidered badge?" they would ask strangers. "That's our Hester—our own Hester—who is so kind to the poor, so helpful to the sick, so generous to the troubled!" Truly, the same human tendency to proclaim the worst when embodied in others also restrains them to only whisper about the scandals of the past. Nonetheless, even in the eyes of the very same men who talk

of human nature to tell the very worst of itself, when embodied in the person of another, would constrain them to whisper the black scandal of bygone years. It was none the less a fact, however, that, in the eyes of the very men who spoke thus, the scarlet letter had the effect of the cross on a nun's bosom. It imparted to the wearer a kind of sacredness, which enabled her to walk securely amid all peril. Had she fallen among thieves, it would have kept her safe. It was reported, and believed by many, that an Indian had drawn his arrow against the badge, and that the missile struck it, but fell harmless to the ground.

The effect of the symbol—or rather, of the position in respect to society that was indicated by it—on the mind of Hester Prynne herself, was powerful and peculiar. All the light and graceful foliage of her character had been withered up by this red-hot brand, and had long ago fallen away, leaving a bare and harsh outline, which might have been repulsive, had she possessed friends or companions to be repelled by it. Even the attractiveness of her person had undergone a similar change. It might be partly owing to the studied austerity of her dress, and partly to the lack of demonstration in her manners. It was a sad transformation, too, that her rich and luxuriant hair had either been cut off, or was so completely hidden by a cap, that not a shining lock of it ever once gushed into the sunshine. It was due in part to all these causes, but still more to something else, that there seemed to be no longer any thing in Hester's face for Love to dwell upon; nothing in Hester's form, though majestic and statue-like, that Passion would ever dream of clasping in its embrace; nothing in Hester's bosom, to make it ever again the pillow of Affection. Some attribute had departed from her, the permanence of which had been essential to keep her a woman. Such is frequently the fate, and such the stern development, of the feminine character and person, when the woman has encountered, and lived through, an experience of peculiar severity. If she be all tenderness, she will die. If she survive, the tenderness will either be crushed out of her, or—and the outward semblance is the same—crushed so deeply into her heart that it can never show itself more. The latter is perhaps the truest theory. She who has once been woman, and ceased to be so, might at any moment become a woman again, if there were only the magic touch to effect the transfiguration. We shall see whether Hester Prynne were ever afterwards so touched, and so transfigured.

about the sins of others, the scarlet letter had the effect of a cross on a nun's bosom. It gave the wearer a kind of holiness, enabling her to walk safely though all kinds of danger. It would have kept her safe if she had fallen prey to thieves. It was rumored—and many believed it—that an Indian's arrow had struck the letter and fallen harmlessly to the ground.

The symbol—or, rather of the position in society that it signaled—had a powerful and strange effect on the mind of Hester Prynne. All the light and graceful aspects of her character had been burned away by this flame-colored letter. Only a bare, harsh outline remained, like a tree that has lost its leaves. If she'd had any friends or companions, they might have been repelled by it. Even her lovely features had changed. The change might be partly due to the deliberate plainness of her clothing, and to her reserved manners. Her luxurious hair had been sadly transformed, as well: either cut off or so completely hidden beneath her cap that net even a lock of it ever saw the sun. Partly for these reasons, though more so for another reason, it seemed that there was no longer anything lovely in Hester's face. Her form, though majestic and statuesque, evoked no passion. Her bosom incited no thoughts of affection. Something had left her—some essential womanly quality. This stern change is often what happens when a woman lives through a tough time. She won't survive the experience if she is too tender. But if she does survive, any tenderness will either be crushed out of her or—what is essentially the same—buried so deeply inside her that it can never be seen again. Most often, it is buried. It would take a miracle for a woman who has been hardened in this way to become womanly once again. We'll see whether Hester ever received such a miracle, such a transformation.

Much of the marble coldness of Hester's impression was to be attributed to the circumstance that her life had turned, in a great measure, from passion and feeling, to thought. Standing alone in the world,—alone, as to any dependence on society, and with little Pearl to be guided and protected—alone, and hopeless of retrieving her position, even had she not scorned to consider it desirable,—she cast away the fragments of a broken chain. The world's law was no law for her mind. It was an age in which the human intellect, newly emancipated, had taken a more active and a wider range than for many centuries before. Men of the sword had overthrown nobles and kings. Men bolder than these had overthrown and rearranged—not actually, but within the sphere of theory, which was their most real abode—the whole system of ancient prejudice, wherewith was linked much of ancient principle. Hester Prynne imbibed this spirit. She assumed a freedom of speculation, then common enough on the other side of the Atlantic, but which our forefathers, had they known of it, would have held to be a deadlier crime than that stigmatized by the scarlet letter. In her lonesome cottage, by the sea-shore, thoughts visited her, such as dared to enter no other dwelling in New England; shadowy guests, that would have been as perilous as demons to their entertainer, could they have been seen so much as knocking at her door.

It is remarkable, that persons who speculate the most boldly often conform with the most perfect quietude to the external regulations of society. The thought suffices them, without investing itself in the flesh and blood of action. So it seemed to be with Hester. Yet, had little Pearl never come to her from the spiritual world, it might have been far otherwise. Then, she might have come down to us in history, hand in hand with Ann Hutchinson, as the foundress of a religious sect. She might, in one of her phases, have been a prophetess. She might, and not improbably would, have suffered death from the stern tribunals of the period, for attempting to undermine the foundations of the Puritan establishment. But, in the education of her child, the mother's enthusiasm of thought had something to wreak itself upon. Providence, in the person of this little girl, had assigned to Hester's charge the germ and blossom of womanhood, to be cherished and developed amid a host of difficulties. Every thing was against her. The world was hostile. The child's own nature had

NO FEAR

Much of the stone-like coldness of Hester's appearance could be attributed to the fact that she had gone from a life of passion and feeling to one of quiet thought. She stood alone in the world. She had little Pearl to guide and protect, without the help of the society around her. She had no hope of recovering her former social status, even if she had wanted to. She had cast aside her link to society like pieces of a broken chain. The world's law did not restrict her mind. This was an age when men had freed the mind from many centuries of tradition. Kings and nobility had been overthrown by revolution. Bolder men than the revolutionary soldiers had, in their writings at least, overthrown the entire system of ancient philosophy and its ancient prejudices. Hester had immersed herself in this spirit. She assumed a freedom of thought that was typical enough for Europe at the time but one that our Puritan forefathers would have considered a crime deadlier than the one marked by the scarlet letter. The thoughts that visited Hester in her lonely cottage by the seashore would not have dared to visit any other New England home. These shadowy guests would have been as dangerous to Hester as demons, if others could have seen them knocking at her door.

It's remarkable that the most freethinking people are often perfectly happy to conform to the various social conventions. Thought gives them their freedom, without converting it into physical action. This seemed to be the way with Hester. But this might not have been the case, if little Pearl had not descended from Heaven to join her. Otherwise, Hester might have gone down in history as the founder of religious sect, just like Ann Hutchinson. She might have become a prophet. More likely, church leaders would have executed her for undermining their Puritan establishment. But instead Hester's enthusiasm was expressed in the education of her child. God had placed this bud of womanhood in Hester's care, to be cherished and nurtured through life's many difficulties. Everything was against her. The world was a hostile place. The child's own perverse nature constantly hinted that she had been conceived in a fit of her mother's lawless passion. Hester would often bitterly ask whether it was for good or bad that the little creature had been born.

something wrong in it, which continually betokened that she had been born amiss,—the effluence of her mother's lawless passion,—and often impelled Hester to ask, in bitterness of heart, whether it were for ill or good that the poor little creature had been born at all.

Indeed, the same dark question often rose into her mind, with reference to the whole race of womanhood. Was existence worth accepting, even to the happiest among them? As concerned her own individual existence, she had long ago decided in the negative, and dismissed the point as settled. A tendency to speculation, though it may keep woman quiet, as it does man, yet makes her sad. She discerns, it may be, such a hopeless task before her. As a first step, the whole system of society is to be torn down, and built up anew. Then, the very nature of the opposite sex, or its long hereditary habit, which has become like nature, is to be essentially modified, before woman can be allowed to assume what seems a fair and suitable position. Finally, all other difficulties being obviated, woman cannot take advantage of these preliminary reforms, until she herself shall have undergone a still mightier change; in which, perhaps, the ethereal essence, wherein she has her truest life, will be found to have evaporated. A woman never overcomes these problems by any exercise of thought. They are not to be solved, or only in one way. If her heart chance to come upper-most, they vanish. Thus, Hester Prynne, whose heart had lost its regular and healthy throb, wandered without a clew in the dark labyrinth of mind; now turned aside by an insurmountable precipice; now starting back from a deep chasm. There was wild and ghastly scenery all around her, and a home and comfort nowhere. At times, a fearful doubt strove to possess her soul, whether it were not better to send Pearl at once to Heaven, and go herself to such futurity as Eternal Justice should provide.

The scarlet letter had not done its office.

Now, however, her interview with the Reverend Mr. Dimmesdale, on the night of his vigil, had given her a new theme of reflection, and held up to her an object that appeared worthy of any exertion and sacrifice for its attainment. She had witnessed the intense misery beneath which the minister struggled, or, to speak more accurately, had ceased to struggle. She saw that he stood on the verge of lunacy, if he had not already stepped across it. It was impossi-

NO FEAR

Hester asked the same question about all women. Was life worth the trouble to even the happiest woman? As for herself, she had decided long ago that it was not. Though the tendency to think too much may keep a woman quiet as it does so many men, it also makes her sad. Perhaps she understands the hopeless task ahead of her. First, the whole system of society must be torn down and built again. Then, the very nature of the opposite sex—or at least the habit passed down from generations—must be modified so that women can assume a fair position in society. And once all of these barriers have been lifted, a woman cannot take advantage of the reforms unless she herself has undergone an even greater change in the core of her being. A woman cannot overcome these problems through thought alone. They are not to be solved—or perhaps they have only one solution. If a woman's heart can rise above them, the problems vanish. So Hester Prynne, whose heart had lost its regular, healthy beat, wandered without purpose through the dark maze of her mind, thwarted by tall mountains and deep pitfalls. The scenery around her was wild and terrifying, and comfort was nowhere to be found. At times, a fearful doubt griped her: Would it be better to send Pearl immediately to Heaven, and go herself to whatever fate eternity had in store for her?

The scarlet letter had not done its job.

But her recent encounter with the Reverend Mr. Dimmesdale had given her something new to think about. It had given her a goal to work and sacrifice for. She had seen the intense misery the minister struggled against—or, rather, the misery he had stopped struggling against. She saw that he stood at the edge of madness, if indeed he had not already stepped across that edge. The secret sting of remorse could be painful. But without a doubt, the very hand that offered to

ble to doubt, that, whatever painful efficacy there might be in the secret sting of remorse, a deadlier venom had been infused into it by the hand that proffered relief. A secret enemy had been continually by his side, under the semblance of a friend and helper, and had availed himself of the opportunities thus afforded for tampering with the delicate springs of Mr. Dimmesdale's nature. Hester could not but ask herself, whether there had not originally been a defect of truth, courage, and loyalty, on her own part, in allowing the minister to be thrown into a position where so much evil was to be foreboded, and nothing auspicious to be hoped. Her only justification lay in the fact, that she had been able to discern no method of rescuing him from a blacker ruin than had overwhelmed herself, except by acquiescing in Roger Chillingworth's scheme of disguise. Under that impulse, she had made her choice, and had chosen, as it now appeared, the more wretched alternative of the two. She determined to redeem her error, so far as it might yet be possible. Strengthened by years of hard and solemn trial, she felt herself no longer so inadequate to cope with Roger Chillingworth as on that night, abased by sin, and half-maddened by the ignominy that was still new, when they had talked together in the prison-chamber. She had climbed her way, since then, to a higher point. The old man, on the other hand, had brought himself nearer to her level, or perhaps below it, by the revenge which he had stooped for.

In fine, Hester Prynne resolved to meet her former husband, and do what might be in her power for the rescue of the victim on whom he had so evidently set his gripe. The occasion was not long to seek. One afternoon, walking with Pearl in a retired part of the peninsula, she beheld the old physician, with a basket on one arm, and a staff in the other hand, stooping along the ground, in quest of roots and herbs to concoct his medicines withal.

help had made that stinging poisonous. A secret enemy had been constantly by the minister's side, disguised as a friend and helper. This enemy had taken advantage of the many opportunities to disturb Mr. Dimmesdale's delicate nature. Hester couldn't help but ask herself whether some defect of her own character—of her truth, or courage, or loyalty—had helped put the minister in this position. There was a lot to be afraid of, and little to hope for. Her only excuse was that agreeing to Roger Chillingworth's scheme was the only way she could think of to save him from an even greater public shame than her own. She had made her choice with that in mind. But now it seemed that she had chosen poorly. She decided to correct her error, to whatever extent she could. Strengthened by years of hard testing, she no longer felt herself unequal to a fight against Roger Chillingworth. She had climbed her way to a much higher place since that night when, defeated by her sins and her still-new shame, she had spoken with him in the prison chamber. On the other hand, revenge had lowered the old man closer down to her level—perhaps even below it.

In conclusion, Hester Prynne decided to meet her former husband, and to do what she could to rescue his victim from his grasp. She did not have to wait long. One afternoon, while walking with Pearl in an isolated part of the peninsula, she came upon the old doctor. With a basket on one arm and a staff in the other hand, he stooped along the ground, searching for roots and herbs with which to make his medicines.

Chapter 14: Hester and the Doctor

Hester bade little Pearl run down to the margin of the water, and play with the shells and tangled seaweed, until she should have talked awhile with yonder gatherer of herbs. So the child flew away like a bird, and, making bare her small white feet, went pattering along the moist margin of the sea. Here and there, she came to a full stop, and peeped curiously into a pool, left by the retiring tide as a mirror for Pearl to see her face in. Forth peeped at her, out of the pool, with dark, glistening curls around her head, and an elf-smile in her eyes, the image of a little maid, whom Pearl, having no other playmate, invited to take her hand and run a race with her. But the visionary little maid, on her part, beckoned likewise, as if to say,— "This is a better place! Come thou into the pool!" And Pearl, stepping in, mid-leg deep, beheld her own white feet at the bottom; while, out of a still lower depth, came the gleam of a kind of fragmentary smile, floating to and fro in the agitated water.

Meanwhile, her mother had accosted the physician.

"I would speak a word with you," said she,—"a word that concerns us much."

"Aha! And is it Mistress Hester that has a word for old Roger Chillingworth?" answered he, raising himself from his stooping posture. "With all my heart! Why, Mistress, I hear good tidings of you on all hands! No longer ago than yester-eve, a magistrate, a wise and godly man, was discoursing of your affairs, Mistress Hester, and whispered me that there had been question concerning you in the council. It was debated whether or no, with safety to the common weal, yonder scarlet letter might be taken off your bosom. On my life, Hester, I made my entreaty to the worshipful magistrate that it might be done forthwith!"

"It lies not in the pleasure of the magistrates to take off this badge," calmly replied Hester. "Were I worthy to be quit of it, it would fall away of its own nature, or be transformed into something that should speak a different purport."

"Nay, then, wear it, if it suit you better," rejoined he. "A woman must needs follow her own fancy, touching the adornment of her person. The letter is gayly embroidered, and shows right bravely on your bosom!"

Chapter 14: Hester and the Doctor

Hester told little Pearl to run down and play by the shore while she talked with the man gathering the herbs. The child flew away like a bird. She kicked off her shoes and went pattering along the water's edge in her bare white feet. Now and then she stopped and peered into a pool left by the receding water, which formed a mirror for Pearl to see her face in. Staring back at her from the water was a little girl with dark, shiny curls and an elflike smile in her eyes. Pearl, having no other playmate, invited the girl to take her hand and run a race with her. But the image of the girl also beckoned, as if to say, "This is a better place! Come into the pool with me!" Pearl stepped into the pool up to her knees and saw her own white feet at the bottom. Deeper down, she could see the gleam of a sort of broken smile, floating here and there in the stirred-up water.

Meanwhile, her mother had approached the doctor.

"I would like to talk with you," she said, "about a matter that concerns us both."

"Ah! Mistress Hester would like to talk with old Roger Chillingworth?" he answered, raising himself from his stooping position. "Well, my word! I say, Mistress, I hear many good things about you! As recently as last night a magistrate, a wise and godly man, was talking about you, Mistress Hester. He whispered to me that the council had been debating whether, without endangering public morality, that scarlet letter might be taken off your bosom. I swear to you, Hester, I asked that magistrate to see it done immediately!"

"The power of the magistrates cannot take off this symbol," Hester replied calmly. "If I were worthy to have it removed, it would simply fall away—or be transformed into something that would convey a different message."

"So wear it, if it suits you best," he replied. "A woman must, of course, follow her own whims when it comes to dressing herself. The letter is beautifully embroidered, and it sure looks fine on your bosom!"

All this while, Hester had been looking steadily at the old man, and was shocked, as well as wonder-smitten, to discern what a change had been wrought upon him within the past seven years. It was not so much that he had grown older; for though the traces of advancing life were visible, he bore his age well, and seemed to retain a wiry vigor and alertness. But the former aspect of an intellectual and studious man, calm and quiet, which was what she best remembered in him, had altogether vanished, and been succeeded by an eager, searching, almost fierce, yet carefully guarded look. It seemed to be his wish and purpose to mask this expression with a smile; but the latter played him false, and flickered over his visage so derisively, that the spectator could see his blackness all the better for it. Ever and anon, too, there came a glare of red light out of his eyes; as if the old man's soul were on fire, and kept on smouldering duskily within his breast, until, by some casual puff of passion, it was blown into a momentary flame. This he repressed as speedily as possible, and strove to look as if nothing of the kind had happened.

In a word, old Roger Chillingworth was a striking evidence of man's faculty of transforming himself into a Devil, if he will only, for a reasonable space of time, undertake a Devil's office. This unhappy person had effected such a transformation by devoting himself, for seven years, to the constant analysis of a heart full of torture, and deriving his enjoyment thence, and adding fuel to those fiery tortures which he analyzed and gloated over.

The scarlet letter burned on Hester Prynne's bosom. Here was another ruin, the responsibility of which came partly home to her.

"What see you in my face," asked the physician, "that you look at it so earnestly?"

"Something that would make me weep, if there were any tears bitter enough for it," answered she. "But let it pass! It is of yonder miserable man that I would speak."

"And what of him?" cried Roger Chillingworth eagerly, as if he loved the topic, and were glad of an opportunity to discuss it with the only person of whom he could make a confidant. "Not to hide the truth, Mistress Hester, my thoughts happen just now to be busy with the gentleman. So speak freely; and I will make answer."

"When we last spake together," said Hester, "now seven years ago, it was your pleasure to extort a promise of secrecy, as touching

While they were talking, Hester had been looking steadily at the old man. She was shocked and bewildered to see how much he had changed in the last seven years. It was not so much that he had grown older. There were signs of advancing age, but he had aged well, retaining his lean strength and alertness. But he no longer seemed like the intellectual and studious man, calm and quiet, that she remembered. That man had been replaced by a man who looked eager, inquisitive, almost fierce—yet carefully guarded. He tried to mask this expression with a smile, but he wore it so badly that it revealed his blackness even more. And there was a constant red light in his eyes, as if the old man's soul was on fire. It seemed to smolder and smoke in his breast until some passing wind of passion ignited it into a brief flame. He would put out that fire as quickly as possible and attempt to look as though nothing had happened.

In short, old Roger Chillingworth presented a striking example of how a man who spends enough time doing the Devil's work can actually transform himself into a Devil. This sad person had brought about this change by devoting himself, for seven full years, to the analysis of a tortured heart. He derived his enjoyment from this task, which only added fuel to those fiery tortures.

The scarlet letter burned on Hester Prynne's bosom. She felt partly responsible for this other ruined life.

"What do you see in my face," asked the doctor, "that makes you look at it so intently?"

"I see something that would make me weep, if tears were bitter enough for the sadness," she answered. "But let it pass. I would like to talk about that miserable man from the other night."

"What of him?" answered Roger Chillingworth eagerly, as though he loved the topic and was glad to discuss it with the only person he could confide in. "In all honesty, Mistress Hester, I was just now thinking of the gentleman. Speak freely, and I will answer you."

"When we last spoke," said Hester, "some seven years ago, you made me promise to keep our former relationship a secret. Since

the former relation betwixt yourself and me. As the life and good fame of yonder man were in your hands, there seemed no choice to me, save to be silent, in accordance with your behest. Yet it was not without heavy misgivings that I thus bound myself; for, having cast off all duty towards other human beings, there remained a duty towards him; and something whispered me that I was betraying it, in pledging myself to keep your counsel. Since that day, no man is so near to him as you. You tread behind his every footstep. You are beside him, sleeping and waking. You search his thoughts. You burrow and rankle in his heart! Your clutch is on his life, and you cause him to die daily a living death; and still he knows you not. In permitting this, I have surely acted a false part by the only man to whom the power was left me to be true!"

"What choice had you?" asked Roger Chillingworth. "My finger, pointed at this man, would have hurled him from his pulpit into a dungeon,—thence, peradventure, to the gallows!"

"It had been better so!" said Hester Prynne.

"What evil have I done the man?" asked Roger Chillingworth again. "I tell thee, Hester Prynne, the richest fee that ever physician earned from monarch could not have bought such care as I have wasted on this miserable priest! But for my aid, his life would have burned away in torments, within the first two years after the perpetration of his crime and thine. For, Hester, his spirit lacked the strength that could have borne up, as thine has, beneath a burden like thy scarlet letter. O, I could reveal a goodly secret! But enough! What art can do, I have exhausted on him. That he now breathes, and creeps about on earth, is owing all to me!"

"Better he had died at once!" said Hester Prynne.

"Yea, woman, thou sayest truly!" cried old Roger Chillingworth, letting the lurid fire of his heart blaze out before her eyes. "Better had he died at once! Never did mortal suffer what this man has suffered. And all, all, in the sight of his worst enemy! He has been conscious of me. He has felt an influence dwelling always upon him like a curse. He knew, by some spiritual sense,—for the Creator never made another being so sensitive as this,—he knew that no friendly hand was pulling at his heart-strings, and that an eye was looking curiously into him, which sought only evil, and found it. But

the life and reputation of that man were in your hands, I seemed to have no choice but to keep the secret as you asked. But I made that promise with great fear. Though I had renounced all duty toward other human beings, I still had a duty towards him. Something told me that I was betraying that duty by pledging to keep your secret. Since that day, no one has been as close to him as you. You follow his every footstep. You are beside him when he sleeps and when he is awake. You search his thoughts. You dig into his heart and make it sore! You have a grip on his life that causes him to die a living death every day. And yet he does not know the real you. By allowing this to happen, I have surely been untrue to the only man that I have the power to be true to!"

"What choice did you have?" asked Roger Chillingworth. "If I had pointed my finger at this man, he would have been thrown from his pulpit into prison—and perhaps from there to the gallows!"

"It would have been better that way!" said Hester Prynne.

"What evil have I done to this man?" asked Roger Chillingworth again. "I tell you, Hester Prynne, the richest king could not have bought the care that I have wasted on this miserable priest! If not for my help, his life would have been consumed by his torments within two years of your mutual crime. His spirit was not strong enough to bear a burden like your scarlet letter, Hester. Oh, I could have revealed the secret! But enough of that! I have done for him all that medicine can do. I am the only reason that he still breathes and crawls this earth!"

"It would have been better if he had died at once!" said Hester Prynne.

"Yes, woman, you speak the truth!" cried old Roger Chillingworth, letting the fire in his heart blaze in front of her eyes. "It would have been better if he had died at once! No man has ever suffered what this man has suffered. And all of it in the sight of his worst enemy! He has been aware of me. He has felt a pressure hanging over him like a curse. He knew, by some spiritual sense—for God has never made a being as sensitive as him—that an unfriendly hand was pulling at his heartstrings. He knew that an eye was peering intently into him, searching for evil—and finding it. But he did not know that he knew not that the eye and hand were mine! With the superstition common to his brotherhood, he fancied himself given over to a fiend, to be tortured with frightful dreams, and desperate thoughts, the sting of remorse, and despair of pardon; as a foretaste of what awaits him beyond the grave. But it was the constant shadow of my presence!—the closest propinquity of the man whom he had most vilely wronged!—and who had grown to exist only by this perpetual poison of the direst revenge! Yea, indeed!—he did not err!—there was a fiend at his elbow! A mortal man, with once a human heart, has become a fiend for his especial torment!"

The unfortunate physician, while uttering these words, lifted his hands with a look of horror, as if he had beheld some frightful shape, which he could not recognize, usurping the place of his own image in a glass. It was one of those moments—which sometimes occur only at the interval of years—when a man's moral aspect is faithfully revealed to his mind's eye. Not improbably, he had never before viewed himself as he did now.

"Hast thou not tortured him enough?" said Hester, noticing the old man's look. "Has he not paid thee all?"

"No!—no!—He has but increased the debt!" answered the physician; and, as he proceeded, his manner lost its fiercer characteristics, and subsided into gloom. "Dost thou remember me, Hester, as I was nine years agone? Even then, I was in the autumn of my days, nor was it the early autumn. But all my life had been made up of earnest, studious, thoughtful, quiet years, bestowed faithfully for the increase of mine own knowledge, and faithfully, too, though this latter object was but casual to the other,—faithfully for the advancement of human welfare. No life had been more peaceful and innocent than mine; few lives so rich with benefits conferred. Dost thou remember me? Was I not, though you might deem cold, nevertheless a man thoughtful for others, craving little for himself,—kind, true, just, and of constant, if not warm affections? Was I not all this?"

"All this, and more," said Hester.

"And what am I now?" demanded he, looking into her face, and permitting the whole evil within him to be written on his features. "I have already told thee what I am! A fiend! Who made me so?"

"It was myself!" cried Hester, shuddering. "It was I, not less than he. Why hast thou not avenged thyself on me?"

the eye and hand were mine! With the superstition common among ministers, he imagined himself handed over to a demon, to be tortured with terrible nightmares and desperate thoughts—the sting of remorse and the despair of pardon—as a taste of what waits for him in Hell. But it was my constant presence! The proximity of the man he had wronged the most! The man created by the poisonous drug of revenge! Yes, indeed! He was not wrong: There was a demon at his side! A mortal man, whose heart had once been human, but who has become a demon devoted to his torment!"

As the unfortunate doctor uttered these words, he raised his hands with a look of horror, as though he had looked into a mirror and seen a frightful, unrecognizable shape instead of his own image. It was one of those rare moments, which come only once every few years, in which a man sees his true character in his mind's eye. He had probably never seen himself as he did now.

"Haven't you tortured him enough?" said Hester, noticing the old man's look. "Hasn't he repaid you completely?"

"No! No! He has only increased the debt!" the doctor answered. As he went on, his manner lost some of its fierceness and became gloomy. "Hester, do you remember me as I was nine years ago? Even then, I was in the autumn of my life—and it was not early autumn. My life had consisted of earnest, studious, thoughtful, quiet years. I spent my time increasing my own knowledge and—though this was only a secondary goal—advancing human welfare. No life had been more peaceful and innocent than mine, and few lives had been so rich. Do you remember me? Wasn't I a man who thought of others and asked little for himself? Wasn't I a kind, faithful, just, and loyal—if not necessarily warm—man? Wasn't I all of this?"

"All of that, and more," said Hester.

"And what am I now?" he demanded, looking into her face and allowing all the evil inside him to appear on his own. "I have already told you what I am! A demon! Who made me into this?"

"It was me!" cried Hester, shuddering. "It was me as much as him. Why haven't you taken your revenge on me?"

"I have left thee to the scarlet letter," replied Roger Chillingworth. "If that have not avenged me, I can do no more!"

He laid his finger on it, with a smile.

"It has avenged thee!" answered Hester Prynne.

"I judged no less," said the physician. "And now, what wouldst thou with me touching this man?"

"I must reveal the secret," answered Hester, firmly. "He must discern thee in thy true character. What may be the result, I know not. But this long debt of confidence, due from me to him, whose bane and ruin I have been, shall at length be paid. So far as concerns the overthrow or preservation of his fair fame and his earthly state, and perchance his life, he is in thy hands. Nor do I,—whom the scarlet letter has disciplined to truth, though it be the truth of red-hot iron, entering into the soul,—nor do I perceive such advantage in his living any longer a life of ghastly emptiness, that I shall stoop to implore thy mercy. Do with him as thou wilt! There is no good for him,—no good for me,—no good for thee! There is no good for little Pearl! There is no path to guide us out of this dismal maze!"

"Woman, I could wellnigh pity thee!" said Roger Chillingworth, unable to restrain a thrill of admiration too; for there was a quality almost majestic in the despair which she expressed. "Thou hadst great elements. Peradventure, hadst thou met earlier with a better love than mine, this evil had not been. I pity thee, for the good that has been wasted in thy nature!"

"And I thee," answered Hester Prynne, "for the hatred that has transformed a wise and just man to a fiend! Wilt thou yet purge it out of thee, and be once more human? If not for his sake, then doubly for thine own! Forgive, and leave his further retribution to the Power that claims it! I said, but now, that there could be no good event for him, or thee, or me, who are here wandering together in this gloomy maze of evil, and stumbling, at every step, over the guilt wherewith we have strewn our path. It is not so! There might be good for thee, and thee alone, since thou hast been deeply wronged, and hast it at thy will to pardon. Wilt thou give up that only privilege? Wilt thou reject that priceless benefit?"

"Peace, Hester, peace!" replied the old man, with gloomy sternness. "It is not granted me to pardon. I have no such power as thou tellest me of. My old faith, long forgotten, comes back to me, and

"I have left you to the scarlet letter," replied Roger Chillingworth. "If that has not avenged me, I cannot do anything else."

He laid his finger on it, with a smile.

"It has avenged you!" Hester Prynne replied.

"I thought as much," said the doctor. "And now, what would you say to me about this man?"

"I must reveal the secret," answered Hester, firmly. "He must see your true character. I don't know what the result will be. But I have been the poison that has caused his ruin, and I will pay the debt that I have long owed him. His worldly reputation, his place in society, and perhaps his life are in your hands. I will not stoop to beg you for mercy: I do not see the advantage in his living a life of such awful emptiness. The scarlet letter has taught me the virtue of truth, even truth that burns the soul like a red-hot iron. Do what you will with him! There is no good in the world for him, no good for me, no good for you! There is no good for little Pearl! There is no path to guide us out of this grim maze!"

"Woman, I could almost pity you!" said Roger Chillingworth, unable to restrain a spark of admiration. There was almost a majestic quality in the despair that she expressed. "You had great qualities. Perhaps, if you had earlier found a better love than mine, all of this evil would not have come about. I pity you, for the good in your nature that has been wasted!"

"And I pity you," answered Hester Prynne, "for the hatred that has transformed a wise and just man into a demon! Will you purge it out of yourself, and become human once again? If not for his sake, then for your own! Forgive, and leave his further punishment to the Judgment Day! I said, moments ago, that there could be no good for him, or you, or me, who are wandering together in this gloomy maze of evil, stumbling with each step over the guilt we have placed in our path. But that wasn't true! There might be good for you—and only you. You have been deeply wronged and you have the power to pardon it. Will you give up that only power? Will you reject that priceless benefit?"

"Enough, Hester, enough!" replied the old man, with gloomy sternness. "It is not in my power to pardon. I do not have the power you speak of. My old faith, which I abandoned long ago, comes

explains all that we do, and all we suffer. By thy first step awry, thou didst plant the germ of evil; but, since that moment, it has all been a dark necessity. Ye that have wronged me are not sinful, save in a kind of typical illusion; neither am I fiend-like, who have snatched a fiend's office from his hands. It is our fate. Let the black flower blossom as it may! Now go thy ways, and deal as thou wilt with yonder man."

He waved his hand, and betook himself again to his employment of gathering herbs.

back to me. It explains all that we do and all we suffer. You planted the seed of evil when you stumbled. But since that moment, it has all been the hand of fate. You that have wronged me, but you're no more sinful than most people. And though I have done the work of a demon, I am not a demon. It is our fate. Let that black flower blossom as it pleases! Now go on your way, and do what you will with that man."

He waved his hand and began to gather herbs once again.

Chapter 15: Hester and Pearl

So Roger Chillingworth—a deformed old figure, with a face that haunted men's memories longer than they liked!—took leave of Hester Prynne, and went stooping away along the earth. He gathered here and there an herb, or grubbed up a root, and put it into the basket on his arm. His gray beard almost touched the ground, as he crept onward. Hester gazed after him a little while, looking with a half-fantastic curiosity to see whether the tender grass of early spring would not be blighted beneath him, and show the wavering track of his footsteps, sere and brown, across its cheerful verdure. She wondered what sort of herbs they were, which the old man was so sedulous to gather. Would not the earth, quickened to an evil purpose by the sympathy of his eye, greet him with poisonous shrubs, of species hitherto unknown, that would start up under his fingers? Or might it suffice him, that every wholesome growth should be converted into something deleterious and malignant at his touch? Did the sun, which shone so brightly everywhere else, really fall upon him? Or was there, as it rather seemed, a circle of ominous shadow moving along with his deformity, whichever way he turned himself? And whither was he now going? Would he not suddenly sink into the earth, leaving a barren and blasted spot, where, in due course of time, would be seen deadly nightshade, dogwood, henbane, and whatever else of vegetable wickedness the climate could produce, all flourishing with hideous luxuriance? Or would he spread bat's wings and flee away, looking so much the uglier, the higher he rose towards Heaven?

"Be it sin or no," said Hester Prynne bitterly, as she still gazed after him, "I hate the man!"

She upbraided herself for the sentiment, but could not overcome or lessen it. Attempting to do so, she thought of those long-past days, in a distant land, when he used to emerge at eventide from the seclusion of his study, and sit down in the fire-light of their home, and in the light of her nuptial smile. He needed to bask himself in that smile, he said, in order that the chill of so many lonely hours among his books might be taken off the scholar's heart. Such scenes had once appeared not otherwise than happy, but now, as viewed through the dismal medium of her subsequent life, they classed themselves among her ugliest remembrances. She marvelled how

Chapter 15: Hester and Pearl

oger Chillingworth took his leave of Hester Prynne. He was a deformed old figure, with a face that lingered unpleasantly in people's memories. As he stooped away, he gathered an herb here, dug up a root there, and put them into the basket on his arm. His gray beard almost touched the ground as he crept along. Hester stared after him for a while, half-imagining that his feet might burn the early spring grass on which he walked. She wondered what sort of herbs the old man was gathering so purposefully. Wouldn't the earth, awakened to his evil purpose, send poisonous shrubs growing up beneath his fingers? Wouldn't it suit him if his touch converted every good and wholesome thing into something diseased and harmful? Did the sun, which shined so brightly everywhere else, really fall on him? Or was there, as it seemed, a circle of ominous shadow following him wherever he turned? And where was he going now? Would he suddenly sink into the earth, leaving barren ground behind? Would poisonous plants grow up where he had vanished? Or would he spread bat's wings and fly away, looking uglier the closer he came to Heaven?

"Whether or not it's a sin," said Hester bitterly, as she stared after him, "I hate the man!"

She blamed herself for the feeling, but she could neither conquer it nor reduce it. Trying nonetheless to do so, she thought of days long past, in a distant land. He would emerge from his study at the end of the day and enjoy the firelight of their home, and the light of her newlywed's smile. He said that he needed to bask in that smile in order to warm his heart after so many cold and lonely hours among his books. Such scenes had seemed happy. But now, looking back at them through the lens of what followed, Hester considered them some of her ugliest memories. She was amazed that such scenes could have occurred! She wondered how she could ever have been

such scenes could have been! She marvelled how she could ever have been wrought upon to marry him! She deemed it her crime most to be repented of, that she had ever endured, and reciprocated, the lukewarm grasp of his hand, and had suffered the smile of her lips and eyes to mingle and melt into his own. And it seemed a fouler offence committed by Roger Chillingworth, than any which had since been done him, that, in the time when her heart knew no better, he had persuaded her to fancy herself happy by his side.

"Yes, I hate him!" repeated Hester, more bitterly than before. "He betrayed me! He has done me worse wrong than I did him!"

Let men tremble to win the hand of woman, unless they win along with it the utmost passion of her heart! Else it may be their miserable fortune, as it was Roger Chillingworth's, when some mightier touch than their own may have awakened all her sensibilities, to be reproached even for the calm content, the marble image of happiness, which they will have imposed upon her as the warm reality. But Hester ought long ago to have done with this injustice. What did it betoken? Had seven long years, under the torture of the scarlet letter, inflicted so much of misery, and wrought out no repentance?

The emotions of that brief space, while she stood gazing after the crooked figure of old Roger Chillingworth, threw a dark light on Hester's state of mind, revealing much that she might not otherwise have acknowledged to herself.

He being gone, she summoned back her child.

"Pearl! Little Pearl! Where are you?"

Pearl, whose activity of spirit never flagged, had been at no loss for amusement while her mother talked with the old gatherer of herbs. At first, as already told, she had flirted fancifully with her own image in a pool of water, beckoning the phantom forth, and—as it declined to venture—seeking a passage for herself into its sphere of impalpable earth and unattainable sky. Soon finding, however, that either she or the image was unreal, she turned elsewhere for better pastime. She made little boats out of birch-bark, and freighted them with snail-shells, and sent out more ventures on the mighty deep than any merchant in New England; but the larger part of them foundered near the shore. She seized a live horseshoe by the tail, and made prize of several five-fingers, and laid out a jelly-fish to melt

convinced to marry him! She considered it her worst crime that she had endured—and even returned—the lukewarm grasp of his hand, had allowed her smile to melt into his own. She certainly repented that misdeed. And it seemed that when Roger Chillingworth convinced her to believe herself happy by his side, at a time when her heart knew no better, he committed a graver offense than any that was later committed against him.

"Yes, I hate him!" repeated Hester, more bitterly than before. "He betrayed me! He has done worse to me than I ever did to him!"

Men should be afraid to win a woman's hand in marriage unless they win her complete heart and passion along with it! Otherwise it may be their misfortune, as it was Roger Chillingworth's, that when another man awakens the woman's feelings more powerfully, she reproaches her husband for the false image of happiness and contentment that he has passed off on her as the real thing. But Hester should have made peace with this injustice long ago. What did her outburst mean? Had seven long years under the torture of the scarlet letter inflicted so much misery without moving her to repentance?

The emotions of that brief time in which she stood staring after the crooked figure of old Roger Chillingworth shower Hester's state of mind in a dark light, revealing a great deal that she might otherwise have denied even to herself.

When he was gone, she summoned her child back.

"Pearl! Little Pearl! Where are you?"

Pearl, whose active spirit never tired, had amused herself while her mother talked with the old doctor. At first, as already described, she flirted with her own image in a pool of water, beckoning the phantom in the water to come out and play, and trying to join the girl when she saw that she would not leave her pool. When Pearl discovered that either she or the image was unreal, she turned elsewhere for better amusement. She made little boats out of birch bark, placed snail shells upon them, and sent more vessels into the mighty ocean than any merchant in New England. Most of them sank near the shore. She grabbed a horseshoe crab by the tail, collected several starfish, and laid a jellyfish out to melt in the warm sun. Then she took the white foam, which streaked along the advancing tide, and

in the warm sun. Then she took up the white foam, that streaked the line of the advancing tide, and threw it upon the breeze, scampering after it with winged footsteps, to catch the great snow-flakes ere they fell. Perceiving a flock of beach-birds, that fed and fluttered along the shore, the naughty child picked up her apron full of pebbles, and, creeping from rock to rock after these small sea-fowl, displayed remarkable dexterity in pelting them. One little gray bird, with a white breast, Pearl was almost sure, had been hit by a pebble and fluttered away with a broken wing. But then the elf-child sighed, and gave up her sport; because it grieved her to have done harm to a little being that was as wild as the sea-breeze, or as wild as Pearl herself.

Her final employment was to gather sea-weed, of various kinds, and make herself a scarf, or mantle, and a head-dress, and thus assume the aspect of a little mermaid. She inherited her mother's gift for devising drapery and costume. As the last touch to her mermaid's garb, Pearl took some eel-grass, and imitated, as best she could, on her own bosom, the decoration with which she was so familiar on her mother's. A letter,—the letter A,—but freshly green, instead of scarlet! The child bent her chin upon her breast, and contemplated this device with strange interest; even as if the one only thing for which she had been sent into the world was to make out its hidden import.

"I wonder if mother will ask me what it means!" thought Pearl.

Just then, she heard her mother's voice, and, flitting along as lightly as one of the little sea-birds, appeared, before Hester Prynne, dancing, laughing, and pointing her finger to the ornament upon her bosom.

"My little Pearl," said Hester, after a moment's silence, "the green letter, and on thy childish bosom, has no purport. But dost thou know, my child, what this letter means which thy mother is doomed to wear?"

"Yes, mother," said the child. "It is the great letter A. Thou hast taught it me in the horn-book."

Hester looked steadily into her little face; but, though there was that singular expression which she had so often remarked in her black eyes, she could not satisfy herself whether Pearl really attached any meaning to the symbol. She felt a morbid desire to ascertain the point.

threw it into the breeze. She scampered after the foam snowflakes, trying to catch them before they fell. Seeing a flock of seabirds feeding and fluttering along the shore, the naughty child gathered pebbles in her apron and, creeping from rock to rock as she stalked the small birds, showed remarkable ability in hitting them. Pearl was almost certain that one little gray bird with a white breast had been hit by a pebble and fluttered away with a broken wing. But then the elflike child gave up her amusement because it saddened her to have harmed a little being that was as wild as the sea breeze, as wild as Pearl herself.

Her final occupation was to gather seaweed of various sorts. She made herself a scarf and a headdress and dressed up like a little mermaid. She had her mother's gift for devising drapery and costume. As the final touch to her mermaid costume, Pearl took some eelgrass and imitated on her bosom, as best she could, the decoration that she was so used to seeing on her mother's. A letter—the letter A—but green instead of scarlet. The child lowered her chin to her breast and contemplated this design with great interest, as if deciphering the letter were the only thing she had been sent into the world to do.

"I wonder if mother will ask me what it means!" thought Pearl.

Just then she heard her mother's voice. Flitting along as lightly as one of the seabirds, she appeared before Hester Prynne, dancing, laughing, and pointing her finger to the symbol upon her bosom.

"My little Pearl," said Hester, after a moment's silence, "the green letter on your childish breast has no meaning. Do you know, my child, what this letter means, which your mother is condemned to wear?"

"Yes, mother," said the child. "It is capital A. You taught me to read it in the alphabet book."

Hester looked steadily into her little face. Though there was that odd expression that she so often saw in her black eyes, Hester could not decide whether Pearl really attached any meaning to the symbol. She felt a strange urge to settle the point.

"Dost thou know, child, wherefore thy mother wears this letter?"

"Truly do I!" answered Pearl, looking brightly into her mother's face. "It is for the same reason that the minister keeps his hand over his heart!"

"And what reason is that?" asked Hester, half-smiling at the absurd incongruity of the child's observation; but, on second thoughts, turning pale. "What has the letter to do with any heart, save mine?"

"Nay, mother, I have told all I know," said Pearl, more seriously than she was wont to speak. "Ask yonder old man whom thou hast been talking with! It may be he can tell. But in good earnest now, mother dear, what does this scarlet letter mean?—and why dost thou wear it on thy bosom?—and why does the minister keep his hand over his heart?"

She took her mother's hand in both her own, and gazed into her eyes with an earnestness that was seldom seen in her wild and capricious character. The thought occurred to Hester, that the child might really be seeking to approach her with childlike confidence, and doing what she could, and as intelligently as she knew how, to establish a meeting-point of sympathy. It showed Pearl in an unwonted aspect. Heretofore, the mother, while loving her child with the intensity of a sole affection, had schooled herself to hope for little other return than the waywardness of an April breeze; which spends its time in airy sport, and has its gusts of inexplicable passion, and is petulant in its best of moods, and chills oftener than caresses you, when you take it to your bosom; in requital of which misdemeanours, it will sometimes, of its own vague purpose, kiss your cheek with a kind of doubtful tenderness, and play gently with your hair, and then begone about its other idle business, leaving a dreamy pleasure at your heart. And this, moreover, was a mother's estimate of the child's disposition. Any other observer might have seen few but unamiable traits, and have given them a far darker coloring. But now the idea came strongly into Hester's mind, that Pearl, with her remarkable precocity and acuteness, might already have approached the age when she could be made a friend, and intrusted with as much of her mother's sorrows as could be imparted, without irreverence either to the parent or the child. In the little chaos of Pearl's character, there might be seen emerging—and could have been, from the very first—the stedfast principles of an unflinch-

"Do you know, child, why your mother wears this letter?"

"Truly I do!" answered Pearl, looking brightly into her mother's face. "It is for the same reason that the minister keeps his hand over his heart!"

"And what reason is that?" asked Hester, half-smiling at the absurd coincidence of the child's observation, but on second thought turning pale. "What does the letter have to do with any heart but mine?"

"I have told all that I know, mother," said Pearl, more seriously than she usually spoke. "Ask that old man over there who you have been talking with! Maybe he knows. But seriously, no, mother dear, what does this scarlet letter mean? Why do you wear it on your bosom? And why does the minister keep his hand over his heart?"

She took her mother's hand in both of her own and gazed into her eyes with a seriousness that she rarely showed. It occurred to Hester that the child might really be trying to enter into her confidence, doing what she could as intelligently as she could to establish a rapport with her mother. This thought revealed Pearl in a new light. Until now the mother, though she loved her child with the intensity of an only love, had forced herself to hope for little in return except the unruliness of an April breeze. Such a breeze spends its time playing breeze-games, sometimes gusting passionately for no good reason, behaving uncooperatively even in its best moods, and chills you more often than it caresses you when you try to hug it. To pay you back for these small offenses, the breeze will sometimes, for its own obscure reasons, kiss your cheek with a questionable tenderness, play gently with your hair, and go about its other pointless business, leaving a dreamy pleasure in your heart. And this was how the child's own mother saw her. Any other observer might have seen almost entirely undesirable traits and have viewed them far more harshly. But now the idea came into Hester's mind that Pearl, with her precocious awareness, might already be growing old enough to be treated as a friend. Hester might entrust Pearl with as many of her sorrows as could be shared between a mother and daughter. In the little chaos of Pearl's character, good traits might be seen emerging. Perhaps they had been there all along: unflinching courage, an unbreakable will, a sturdy pride that could be disciplined into self-respect, and a bitter distaste for hypocrisy. She had feelings too.

ing courage,—an uncontrollable will,—a sturdy pride, which might be disciplined into self-respect—and a bitter scorn of many things, which, when examined, might be found to have the taint of falsehood in them. She possessed affections, too, though hitherto acrid and disagreeable, as are the richest flavors of unripe fruit. With all these sterling attributes, thought Hester, the evil which she inherited from her mother must be great indeed, if a noble woman do not grow out of this elfish child.

Pearl's inevitable tendency to hover about the enigma of the scarlet letter seemed an innate quality of her being. From the earliest epoch of her conscious life, she had entered upon this as her appointed mission. Hester had often fancied that Providence had a design of justice and retribution, in endowing the child with this marked propensity; but never, until now, had she bethought herself to ask, whether, linked with that design, there might not likewise be a purpose of mercy and beneficence. If little Pearl were entertained with faith and trust, as a spirit-messenger no less than an earthly child, might it not be her errand to soothe away the sorrow that lay cold in her mother's heart, and converted it into a tomb?—and to help her to overcome the passion, once so wild, and even yet neither dead nor asleep, but only imprisoned within the same tomb-like heart?

Such were some of the thoughts that now stirred in Hester's mind, with as much vivacity of impression as if they had actually been whispered into her ear. And there was little Pearl, all this while, holding her mother's hand in both her own, and turning her face upward, while she put these searching questions, once and again, and still a third time.

"What does the letter mean, mother?—and why dost thou wear it?—and why does the minister keep his hand over his heart?"

"What shall I say?" thought Hester to herself.—"No! If this be the price of the child's sympathy, I cannot pay it!"

Then she spoke aloud.

"Silly Pearl," said she, "what questions are these? There are many things in this world that a child must not ask about. What know I of the minister's heart? And as for the scarlet letter, I wear it for the sake of its gold thread!"

In all the seven bygone years, Hester Prynne had never before been false to the symbol on her bosom. It may be that it was the

NO FEAR

They had been bitter and disagreeable until now, but so are the richest flavors of unripe fruit. With all of these excellent traits, thought Hester, if Pearl doesn't grow into a noble woman, she must have inherited an awful lot of evil from her mother.

Pearl's constant curiosity about the mystery of the scarlet letter seemed an essential part of her character. From the time Pearl had first been aware of it, she had been on a mission to discover its meaning. Hester had often imagined that God had given her daughter this interest to make her an instrument of justice and punishment. But now Hester wondered for the first time whether there might also be a divine purpose of mercy and kindness at work. If Hester put her faith and trust in Pearl, treating her as both a messenger sent from Heaven and an earthly child, could it be the daughter's purpose to soothe away the sorrow in her mother's heart? Was the girl meant to help her overcome the wild passion Hester had buried in her heart?

These thoughts ran through Hester's mind as clearly as if they had actually been whispered into her ear. Meanwhile, little Pearl kept holding her mother's hand in both her own and turning her face upward. She asked these searching questions again and again.

"What does the letter mean, mother? And why do you wear it? And why does the minister keep his hand over his heart?"

"What should I say?" thought Hester to herself. "No! If this is what I must pay to win the child's friendship, the price is too high!"

The she spoke aloud.

"Silly Pearl," she said, "what kind of questions are these? There are many things that a child must not ask about. What do I know about the minister's heart? And as for the scarlet letter, I wear it for the sake of its gold thread!"

In the past seven years, Hester Prynne had never lied about the symbol on her bosom. Perhaps the letter was the mark of a guardian

talisman of a stern and severe, but yet a guardian spirit, who now forsook her; as recognizing that, in spite of his strict watch over her heart, some new evil had crept into it, or some old one had never been expelled. As for little Pearl, the earnestness soon passed out of her face.

But the child did not see fit to let the matter drop. Two or three times, as her mother and she went homeward, and as often at sup-per-time, and while Hester was putting her to bed, and once after she seemed to be fairly asleep, Pearl looked up, with mischief gleaming in her black eyes.

"Mother," said she, "what does the scarlet letter mean?"

And the next morning, the first indication the child gave of being awake was by popping up her head from the pillow, and making that other inquiry, which she had so unaccountably connected with her investigations about the scarlet letter:—

"Mother!—Mother!—Why does the minister keep his hand over his heart?"

"Hold thy tongue, naughty child!" answered her mother, with an asperity that she had never permitted to herself before. "Do not tease me; else I shall shut thee into the dark closet!"

NO FEAR

spirit—stern and severe, but yet watchful—that left her as she said this. Perhaps the spirit recognized that some new evil had crept into her heart despite his watchfulness, or some old evil had always lingered there. As for little Pearl, the seriousness soon left her face.

But the child did not let the matter drop. Pearl asked again two or three times as they walked home, and then at dinner, and while Hester was putting her to bed. Even after she seemed to be fast asleep, Pearl looked up once with mischief gleaming in her black eyes.

"Mother," she said, "what does the scarlet letter mean?"

And the next morning, the first sign that the child was awake came when she popped her head up from her pillow and asked that other question, which she had inexplicably connected with her questions about the scarlet letter:

"Mother! Mother! Why does the minister keep his hand over his heart?"

"Silence, naughty child!" answered her mother, with a harshness she had never allowed herself before. "Do not tease me, or I will shut you away in the dark closet!"

Chapter 16: A Forest Walk

Hester Prynne remained constant in her resolve to make known to Mr. Dimmesdale, at whatever risk of present pain or ulterior consequences, the true character of the man who had crept into his intimacy. For several days, however, she vainly sought an opportunity of addressing him in some of the meditative walks which she knew him to be in the habit of taking, along the shores of the peninsula, or on the wooded hills of the neighboring country. There would have been no scandal, indeed, nor peril to the holy whiteness of the clergyman's good fame, had she visited him in his own study; where many a penitent, ere now, had confessed sins of perhaps as deep a die as the one betokened by the scarlet letter. But, partly that she dreaded the secret or undisguised interference of old Roger Chillingworth, and partly that her conscious heart imputed suspicion where none could have been felt, and partly that both the minister and she would need the whole wide world to breathe in, while they talked together,—for all these reasons, Hester never thought of meeting him in any narrower privacy than beneath the open sky.

At last, while attending in a sick-chamber, whither the Reverend Mr. Dimmesdale had been summoned to make a prayer, she learnt that he had gone, the day before, to visit the Apostle Eliot, among his Indian converts. He would probably return, by a certain hour, in the afternoon of the morrow. Betimes, therefore, the next day, Hester took little Pearl,—who was necessarily the companion of all her mother's expeditions, however inconvenient her presence,—and set forth.

The road, after the two wayfarers had crossed from the peninsula to the mainland, was no other than a footpath. It straggled onward into the mystery of the primeval forest. This hemmed it in so narrowly, and stood so black and dense on either side, and disclosed such imperfect glimpses of the sky above, that, to Hester's mind, it imaged not amiss the moral wilderness in which she had so long been wandering. The day was chill and sombre. Overhead was a gray expanse of cloud, slightly stirred, however, by a breeze; so that a gleam of flickering sunshine might now and then be seen at its solitary play along the path. This flitting cheerfulness was always at the farther extremity of some long vista through the forest. The sportive sunlight—feebly sportive, at best, in the predominant pensiveness

Chapter 16: A Forest Walk

Hester Prynne maintained her resolve to reveal to Mr. Dimmesdale the true character of the man who posed as his friend, no matter the consequences. Yet for several days she tried in vain to meet him on one of the long walks he often took along the seashore or in the wooded hills of the surrounding country. She could have visited him in his study, where many before had confessed sins perhaps as deep as that signified by the scarlet letter. There would have been no scandal in such a visit, nor danger to the minister's reputation. But she feared the interference of old Roger Chillingworth, and her guilty heart imagined that others would be suspicious even where this was impossible. Moreover, she and the minister would need the whole wide world to breathe in when they talked together. For all of these reasons, Hester never thought of meeting him anywhere more confined than under the open sky.

At last, while tending to a sick man whom Mr. Dimmesdale had recently visited and prayed over, she learned that Mr. Dimmedale had just gone to visit the Apostle Eliot among his Indian converts. He would probably return by a certain hour in the afternoon on the next day. So at the proper time, Hester set out with little Pearl, who had come on all of her mother's expeditions, whether convenient or not.

The Apostle
:: John Eliot, a
⸱ minister who
⸱d to the Mas-
⸱ssett tribe and
⸱ted the Bible
⸱eir language.

After Hester and Pearl had walked some way, the road became a mere footpath straggling on into the mysterious forest, which hemmed it in on all sides. The forest was so black and dense, admitting so little light, that it seemed to Hester to represent the moral wilderness in which she had been wandering. The day was cold and grim. Gray clouds hung overhead, stirred occasionally by a breeze. Flickering sunshine played now and then along the path, though this cheerfulness was always at the very edge of sight, never close by. The playful sunlight would retreat as they approached, leaving the spots where it had danced that much drearier, because they had hoped to find them bright.

of the day and scene—withdrew itself as they came nigh, and left the spots where it had danced the drearier, because they had hoped to find them bright.

"Mother," said little Pearl, "the sunshine does not love you. It runs away and hides itself, because it is afraid of something on your bosom. Now, see! There it is, playing, a good way off. Stand you here, and let me run and catch it. I am but a child. It will not flee from me; for I wear nothing on my bosom yet!"

"Nor ever will, my child, I hope," said Hester.

"And why not, mother?" asked Pearl, stopping short, just at the beginning of her race. "Will not it come of its own accord, when I am a woman grown?"

"Run away, child," answered her mother, "and catch the sunshine! It will soon be gone."

Pearl set forth, at a great pace, and, as Hester smiled to perceive, did actually catch the sunshine, and stood laughing in the midst of it, all brightened by its splendor, and scintillating with the vivacity excited by rapid motion. The light lingered about the lonely child, as if glad of such a playmate, until her mother had drawn almost nigh enough to step into the magic circle too.

"It will go now!" said Pearl, shaking her head.

"See!" answered Hester, smiling. "Now I can stretch out my hand, and grasp some of it."

As she attempted to do so, the sunshine vanished; or, to judge from the bright expression that was dancing on Pearl's features, her mother could have fancied that the child had absorbed it into herself, and would give it forth again, with a gleam about her path, as they should plunge into some gloomier shade. There was no other attribute that so much impressed her with a sense of new and untransmitted vigor in Pearl's nature, as this never-failing vivacity of spirits; she had not the disease of sadness, which almost all children, in these latter days, inherit, with the scrofula, from the troubles of their ancestors. Perhaps this too was a disease, and but the reflex of the wild energy with which Hester had fought against her sorrows, before Pearl's birth. It was certainly a doubtful charm, imparting a hard, metallic lustre to the child's character. She wanted—what some people want throughout life—a grief that should deeply touch her, and thus humanize and make her capable of sympathy. But there was time enough yet for little Pearl!

NO FEAR

"Mother," said little Pearl, "the sunshine does not love you. It runs away and hides itself because it is afraid of something on your chest. See! There it is, playing in the distance. Stay here and let me run and catch it. I am only a child. It will not flee from me, for I wear nothing on my chest yet!"

"And never shall, my child, I hope," said Hester.

"And why not, mother?" asked Pearl, stopping short just as she began to run off. "Won't that come of its own accord when I am grown into a woman?"

"Run away, child," her mother answered, "and catch the sunshine. It will soon be gone."

Pearl set off at a great pace. Hester smiled to see that she did actually catch the sunshine and stood laughing in the midst of it, brightened by its splendor and glowing with the liveliness of rapid motion. The light lingered around the lonely child as if glad to have such a playmate. Her mother drew almost close enough to step into the magic circle too.

"It will go now," said Pearl, shaking her head.

"See!" replied Hester, smiling, "now I can stretch out my hand and touch some of it."

As she tried to do so, the sunshine vanished. To judge from the bright expression that played across Pearl's face, her mother could have thought that the child had absorbed the sunlight into herself. Perhaps Pearl would send it forth again, to throw a gleam along her path as they plunged into the gloomy shade. No other trait drove home to Hester the vigor of Pearl's nature as much as the never-failing liveliness of her spirits. She did not have the disease of sadness that almost all children in these fallen days inherit from the their ancestors, along with the usual maladies. Perhaps this lack was itself a disease, the result of the wild energy with which Hester had fought against her sorrows before Pearl's birth. It was a dubious charm, giving a hard, metallic luster to the child's character. She lacked—as some people lack throughout their lives—a grief that would deeply touch her, making her capable of sympathy with others' grief. But there was time enough yet for little Pearl.

"Come, my child!" said Hester, looking about her, from the spot where Pearl had stood still in the sunshine. "We will sit down a little way within the wood, and rest ourselves."

"I am not aweary, mother," replied the little girl. "But you may sit down, if you will tell me a story meanwhile."

"A story, child!" said Hester. "And about what?"

"O, a story about the Black Man!" answered Pearl, taking hold of her mother's gown, and looking up, half-earnestly, half-mischievously, into her face. "How he haunts this forest, and carries a book with him,—a big, heavy book, with iron clasps; and how this ugly Black Man offers his book and an iron pen to every body that meets him here among the trees; and they are to write their names with their own blood. And then he sets his mark on their bosoms! Didst thou ever meet the Black Man, mother?"

"And who told you this story, Pearl?" asked her mother, recognizing a common superstition of the period.

"It was the old dame in the chimney-corner, at the house where you watched last night," said the child. "But she fancied me asleep while she was talking of it. She said that a thousand and a thousand people had met him here, and had written in his book, and have his mark on them. And that ugly-tempered lady, old Mistress Hibbins, was one. And, mother, the old dame said that this scarlet letter was the Black Man's mark on thee, and that it glows like a red flame when thou meetest him at midnight, here in the dark wood. Is it true, mother? And dost thou go to meet him in the night-time?"

"Didst thou ever awake, and find thy mother gone?" asked Hester.

"Not that I remember," said the child. "If thou fearest to leave me in our cottage, thou mightest take me along with thee. I would very gladly go! But, mother, tell me now! Is there such a Black Man? And didst thou ever meet him? And is this his mark?"

"Wilt thou let me be at peace, if I once tell thee?" asked her mother.

"Yes, if thou tellest me all," answered Pearl.

"Once in my life I met the Black Man!" said her mother. "This scarlet letter is his mark!"

Thus conversing, they entered sufficiently deep into the wood to secure themselves from the observation of any casual passenger along the forest-track. Here they sat down on a luxuriant heap of moss; which, at some epoch of the preceding century, had been a

NO FEAR

"Come, my child!" said Hester, looking around her from the spot where Pearl had stood in the sunshine, "we will sit down a little farther in the woods and rest ourselves."

"I am not tired, mother," replied the little girl. "But you may sit down, if you will tell me a story while you rest."

"A story, child!" said Hester. "A story about what?"

"Oh, a story about the Black Man," answered Pearl, grasping her mother's gown and looking up, half earnestly and half mischievously, into her face. "Tell me how he haunts this forest, carrying a big, heavy book, with iron clasps. Tell how this ugly Black Man offers his book and an iron pen to everyone who meets him here among the trees. Tell how they write their names with their own blood, and then he sets his mark on their chests. Did you ever meet the Black Man, mother?"

"And who told you this story, Pearl?" asked her mother, recognizing a superstition common in those days.

"It was the old woman in the chimney corner, at the sick house where you watched last night," said the child. "But she thought I was asleep when she spoke of it. She said that thousands of people had met him here, and had written in his book, and have his mark on them. She said that ugly old lady, Mistress Hibbins, was one of them. And, mother, the old woman said that this scarlet letter was the Black Man's mark on you, and that it glows like a red flame when you meet him at midnight, here in this dark wood. Is it true, mother? Do you go to meet him in the nighttime?"

"Did you ever wake and find your mother gone?" asked Hester.

"Not that I remember," said the child. "If you're afraid to leave me in our cottage, you might take me along with you. I would very gladly go! But mother, tell me now! Is there such a Black Man? And did you ever meet him? And is this his mark?"

"Will you leave me alone, if I tell you once?" asked her mother.

"Yes, if you tell me everything," answered Pearl.

"Once in my life I met the Black Man!" said her mother. "This scarlet letter is his mark!"

Talking in this way, they walked deep enough into the wood to be invisible to any casual passerby along the forest path. They sat down on a luxurious pile of moss, which had once been a gigantic pine, with its roots and trunk in the shade of the forest and its head high

gigantic pine, with its roots and trunk in the darksome shade, and its head aloft in the upper atmosphere. It was a little dell where they had seated themselves, with a leaf-strewn bank rising gently on either side, and a brook flowing through the midst, over a bed of fallen and drowned leaves. The trees impending over it had flung down great branches, from time to time, which choked up the current, and compelled it to form eddies and black depths at some points; while, in its swifter and livelier passages, there appeared a channel-way of pebbles, and brown, sparkling sand. Letting the eyes follow along the course of the stream, they could catch the reflected light from its water, at some short distance within the forest, but soon lost all traces of it amid the bewilderment of tree-trunks and underbrush, and here and there a huge rock, covered over with gray lichens. All these giant trees and boulders of granite seemed intent on making a mystery of the course of this small brook; fearing, perhaps, that, with its never-ceasing loquacity, it should whisper tales out of the heart of the old forest whence it flowed, or mirror its revelations on the smooth surface of a pool. Continually, indeed, as it stole onward, the streamlet kept up a babble, kind, quiet, soothing, but melancholy, like the voice of a young child that was spending its infancy without playfulness, and knew not how to be merry among sad acquaintance and events of sombre hue.

"O brook! O foolish and tiresome little brook!" cried Pearl, after listening awhile to its talk. "Why art thou so sad? Pluck up a spirit, and do not be all the time sighing and murmuring!"

But the brook, in the course of its little lifetime among the forest-trees, had gone through so solemn an experience that it could not help talking about it, and seemed to have nothing else to say. Pearl resembled the brook, inasmuch as the current of her life gushed from a well-spring as mysterious, and had flowed through scenes shadowed as heavily with gloom. But, unlike the little stream, she danced and sparkled, and prattled airily along her course.

"What does this sad little brook say, mother?" inquired she.

"If thou hadst a sorrow of thine own, the brook might tell thee of it," answered her mother, "even as it is telling me of mine! But now, Pearl, I hear a footstep along the path, and the noise of one putting aside the branches. I would have thee betake thyself to play, and leave me to speak with him that comes yonder."

in the upper atmosphere. They had seated themselves in a little dell. The banks of a brook rose on either side of them, covered in leaves, and the brook itself flowed through their midst. The trees that over-hung it had thrown down great branches from time to time, dis-rupting the brook's current and causing it to form eddies and black pools in some places. In the brook's swifter passages were pebbles and brown, sparkling sand. Letting their eyes follow the course of the stream, they could see the light reflected off its water—but soon it disappeared among tree trunks and underbrush, and here and there a huge rock covered over with gray lichens. All these giant trees and boulders seemed intent on making a mystery of this small brook's course. Perhaps they feared that, with its constant babbling, the water would whisper tales from the heart of the old forest or show the forest's secrets on the smooth surface of a pool. As it crept onward, the little stream kept up quite a babble. It was kind, quiet, and soothing, but melancholy, like the voice of a young child who never played, and who does not know how to be among sad friends and serious events.

"Oh, brook! Oh, foolish and tiresome little brook!" cried Pearl, after listening awhile to its talk. "Why are you so sad? Pick up your spirits, and don't be sighing and murmuring all the time!"

But the brook, over its little lifetime among the forest trees, had had such sad experiences that it could not help talking about them. Indeed, the brook seemed to have nothing else to say. Pearl resem-bled the brook: Her life had sprung from a well as mysterious as the brook's and had flowed through scenes as heavily shadowed with gloom. But unlike the little stream, she danced and sparkled and chatted airily as she went on her way.

"What does the sad little brook say, mother?" she asked.

"If you had a sorrow of your own, the brook might speak about it," answered her mother, "even as it is speaking to me about mine. But I hear a footstep along the path, and the sound of someone pushing branches aside. Go play and leave me to speak with the man coming this way."

"Is it the Black Man?" asked Pearl.

"Wilt thou go and play, child?" repeated her mother. "But do not stray far into the wood. And take heed that thou come at my first call."

"Yes, mother," answered Pearl. "But, if it be the Black Man, wilt thou not let me stay a moment, and look at him, with his big book under his arm?"

"Go, silly child!" said her mother, impatiently. "It is no Black Man! Thou canst see him now through the trees. It is the minister!"

"And so it is!" said the child. "And, mother, he has his hand over his heart! Is it because, when the minister wrote his name in the book, the Black Man set his mark in that place? But why does he not wear it outside his bosom, as thou dost, mother?"

"Go now, child, and thou shalt tease me as thou wilt another time" cried Hester Prynne. "But do not stray far. Keep where thou canst hear the babble of the brook."

The child went singing away, following up the current of the brook, and striving to mingle a more lightsome cadence with its melancholy voice. But the little stream would not be comforted, and still kept telling its unintelligible secret of some very mournful mystery that had happened—or making a prophetic lamentation about something that was yet to happen—within the verge of the dismal forest. So Pearl, who had enough of shadow in her own little life, chose to break off all acquaintance with this repining brook. She set herself, therefore, to gathering violets and wood-anemones, and some scarlet columbines that she found growing in the crevices of a high rock.

When her elf-child had departed, Hester Prynne made a step or two towards the track that led through the forest, but still remained under the deep shadow of the trees. She beheld the minister advancing along the path, entirely alone, and leaning on a staff which he had cut by the way-side. He looked haggard and feeble, and betrayed a nerveless despondency in his air, which had never so remarkably characterized him in his walks about the settlement, nor in any other situation where he deemed himself liable to notice. Here it was wofully visible, in this intense seclusion of the forest, which of itself would have been a heavy trial to the spirits. There was a listlessness in his gait; as if he saw no reason for taking one step farther, nor felt any desire to do so, but would have been glad,

"Is it the Black Man?" asked Pearl.

"Will you go and play, child?" her mother repeated. "But don't wander far into the wood. And take care that you come at my first call."

"Yes, mother," answered Pearl. "But if it is the Black Man, would you let me stay a moment and look at him, with his big book under his arm?"

"Go, silly child," her mother said impatiently. "It's not the Black Man! You can see him now, through the trees. It is the minister!"

"Yes it is!" said the child. "And, mother, he has his hand over his heart! Did the Black Man make his mark there when the minister wrote his name in the book? And why doesn't he wear the mark outside his chest, as you do, mother?"

"Go, child, and tease me another time," cried Hester Prynne. "But do not go far. Stay where you can hear the babble of the brook."

The child went singing away, following the current of the brook and trying to mix a happier sound into its sad voice. But the little stream would not be comforted. It kept telling its garbled secret of some mournful mystery or making a sad prophecy about something that would happen within the dismal forest. So Pearl, who had enough sadness in her own little life, broke off her friendship with the brook. She went about gathering flowers that she found growing in the crack of a high rock.

When her elf-child had left, Hester Prynne took a few steps toward the forest path but remained under the deep shadow of the trees. She saw the minister walking alone on the path and leaning on a rough staff made from a branch he had cut along the way. He looked worn and weak. He gave an impression of nervous despair, which had never been apparent when he walked around the village, nor any other place where he thought he might be seen. In the intense isolation of the forest, which itself would have depressed the spirits, his despair was sadly visible. There was an exhausted quality to his steps, as though he saw no reason to take another, nor felt any desire to do so. It seemed that he would have been glad—had he been glad of anything—to throw himself down at the root of

could he be glad of any thing, to fling himself down at the root of the nearest tree, and lie there passive for evermore. The leaves might bestrew him, and the soil gradually accumulate and form a little hillock over his frame, no matter whether there were life in it or no. Death was too definite an object to be wished for, or avoided.

To Hester's eye, the Reverend Mr. Dimmesdale exhibited no symptom of positive and vivacious suffering, except that, as little Pearl had remarked, he kept his hand over his heart.

the nearest tree and lie there, motionless, forever. The leaves might cover him, and the soil gradually form a little hill over his body, whether there was life in it or not. Death was too concrete a goal to be either wished for or avoided.

To Hester's eye, the Reverend Mr. Dimmesdale showed no sign of active, lively suffering—except that, as little Pearl had noticed, he kept his hand over his heart.

Chapter 17: The Pastor and His Parishioner

Slowly as the minister walked, he had almost gone by, before Hester Prynne could gather voice enough to attract his observation. At length, she succeeded.

"Arthur Dimmesdale!" she said, faintly at first; then louder, but hoarsely. "Arthur Dimmesdale!"

"Who speaks?" answered the minister.

Gathering himself quickly up, he stood more erect, like a man taken by surprise in a mood to which he was reluctant to have witnesses. Throwing his eyes anxiously in the direction of the voice, he indistinctly beheld a form under the trees, clad in garments so sombre, and so little relieved from the gray twilight into which the clouded sky and the heavy foliage had darkened the noontide, that he knew not whether it were a woman or a shadow. It may be, that his path-way through life was haunted thus, by a spectre that had stolen out from among his thoughts.

He made a step nigher, and discovered the scarlet letter.

"Hester! Hester Prynne!" said he. "Is it thou? Art thou in life?"

"Even so!" she answered. "In such life as has been mine these seven years past! And thou, Arthur Dimmesdale, dost thou yet live?"

It was no wonder that they thus questioned one another's actual and bodily existence, and even doubted of their own. So strangely did they meet, in the dim wood, that it was like the first encounter, in the world beyond the grave, of two spirits who had been intimately connected in their former life, but now stood coldly shuddering, in mutual dread; as not yet familiar with their state, nor wonted to the companionship of disembodied beings. Each a ghost, and awe-stricken at the other ghost! They were awe-stricken likewise at themselves; because the crisis flung back to them their consciousness, and revealed to each heart its history and experience, as life never does, except at such breathless epochs. The soul beheld its features in the mirror of the passing moment. It was with fear, and tremulously, and, as it were, by a slow, reluctant necessity, that Arthur Dimmesdale put forth his hand, chill as death, and touched the chill hand of Hester Prynne. The grasp, cold as it was, took away what was dreariest in the interview. They now felt themselves, at least, inhabitants of the same sphere.

Chapter 17: The Pastor and His Parishioner

Though the minister walked slowly, he had almost passed before Hester Prynne could find her voice. But she finally did.

"Arthur Dimmesdale!" she said, faintly at first and then louder, but hoarsely: "Arthur Dimmesdale!"

"Who speaks?" answered the minister.

Pulling himself together quickly, he stood up straighter, like a man taken by surprise in a private mood. Looking anxiously in the direction of the voice, he saw a shadowy figure under the trees. It was dressed in garments so dour, so similar to the noontime twilight produced by the clouds and the heavy foliage, that he did not know whether the shape was a woman or a shadow. Perhaps his path through life was habitually haunted by a ghost like this figure, which had somehow escaped from his thoughts into the real world.

He took a step closer and saw the scarlet letter.

"Hester! Hester Prynne!" he said. "Is it you? Are you alive?"

"Yes," she answered, "Living the same life I've had the past seven years. And you, Arthur Dimmesdale, are you still alive as well?"

It was no wonder that they questioned each other's existence and even doubted their own. Their meeting in the dim wood was so strange that it was like a first encounter in the afterlife, when spirits who had been intimately connected while alive stand shuddering in mutual dread because they are not yet familiar with their new condition, nor accustomed to the company of other spirits. Each is a ghost and dumbstruck at the other ghost. The two were also dumbstruck at themselves. This meeting made each heart aware of its history and experience, as life only does at such moments of crisis. Each soul saw itself in the mirror of the passing moment. With fear, trembling, and as though forced by necessity, Arthur Dimmesdale reached out his hand, as cold as death, and touched the cold hand of Hester Prynne. This touch, cold as it was, removed the dreariest aspect of the encounter. Now they understood that they were both living beings.

Without a word more spoken,—neither he nor she assuming the guidance, but with an unexpressed consent,—they glided back into the shadow of the woods, whence Hester had emerged, and sat down on the heap of moss where she and Pearl had before been sitting. When they found voice to speak, it was, at first, only to utter remarks and inquiries such as any two acquaintances might have made, about the gloomy sky, the threatening storm, and, next, the health of each. Thus they went onward, not boldly, but step by step, into the themes that were brooding deepest in their hearts. So long estranged by fate and circumstances, they needed something slight and casual to run before, and throw open the doors of intercourse, so that their real thoughts might be led across the threshold.

After a while, the minister fixed his eyes on Hester Prynne's.

"Hester," said he, "hast thou found peace?"

She smiled drearily, looking down upon her bosom.

"Hast thou?" she asked.

"None!—nothing but despair!" he answered. "What else could I look for, being what I am, and leading such a life as mine? Were I an atheist,—a man devoid of conscience,—a wretch with coarse and brutal instincts,—I might have found peace, long ere now. Nay, I never should have lost it! But, as matters stand with my soul, whatever of good capacity there originally was in me, all of God's gifts that were the choicest have become the ministers of spiritual torment. Hester, I am most miserable!"

"The people reverence thee," said Hester. "And surely thou workest good among them! Doth this bring thee no comfort?"

"More misery, Hester!—only the more misery!" answered the clergyman, with a bitter smile. "As concerns the good which I may appear to do, I have no faith in it. It must needs be a delusion. What can a ruined soul, like mine, effect towards the redemption of other souls?—or a polluted soul, towards their purification? And as for the people's reverence, would that it were turned to scorn and hatred! Canst thou deem it, Hester, a consolation, that I must stand up in my pulpit, and meet so many eyes turned upward to my face, as if the light of Heaven were beaming from it!—must see my flock hungry for the truth, and listening to my words as if a tongue of Pentecost were speaking!—and then look inward, and discern the black reality of what they idolize? I have laughed, in bitterness and

Without speaking another word, they glided back into the shadow of the woods Hester had emerged from. Neither took the lead: They moved by an unspoken consent, sitting down on the heap of moss where Hester and Pearl had been sitting. When they found the voice to speak, they at first only made the sort of small talk that anyone would have made. They spoke of the gloomy sky and the threatening storm. Each asked about the health of the other. And so they proceeded onward, not boldly but one step at a time, into the subjects on which they brooded most deeply. Separated so long by fate and circumstances, they needed something small and casual to open the doors of conversation so that their real thoughts could be led through the doorway.

After a while, the minister looked into Hester Prynne's eyes.

"Hester," he said, "have you found peace?"

She gave a weary smile and looked down at her bosom.

"Have you?" she asked.

"None—nothing but despair!" he answered. "What else could I expect, being what I am and leading such a life as mine? If I were an atheist, with base instincts and no conscience, I might have found peace long ago. Indeed, I would never have lost it. But, as things stand with my soul, God's greatest gifts have become the means by which I am tortured. Hester, I am utterly miserable!"

"The people respect you," said Hester. "And surely you do good works among them! Doesn't this bring you any comfort?"

"Misery, Hester—only more misery!" answered the clergyman with a bitter smile. "As for the good that I seem to do, I have no faith in it. It must be a delusion. What can a ruined soul like mine do to aid in the redemption of other souls? Can a polluted soul assist in their purification? And as for the people's respect, I wish that it was turned to scorn and hatred! Do you think it is a consolation, Hester, that I must stand in my pulpit and see so many eyes looking up into my face as though the light of Heaven were beaming out of it? That I must see my parishioners hungry for the truth and listening to my words as though I spoke it? And then to look at myself and see the dark reality of the man they idolize? I have often laughed, with a bitter and a pained heart, at the contrast between what I seem and what I am! And Satan laughs, as well!"

agony of heart, at the contrast between what I seem and what I am! And Satan laughs at it!"

"You wrong yourself in this," said Hester, gently. "You have deeply and sorely repented. Your sin is left behind you, in the days long past. Your present life is not less holy, in very truth, than it seems in people's eyes. Is there no reality in the penitence thus sealed and witnessed by good works? And wherefore should it not bring you peace?"

"No, Hester, no!" replied the clergyman. "There is no substance in it! It is cold and dead, and can do nothing for me! Of penance I have had enough! Of penitence there has been none! Else, I should long ago have thrown off these garments of mock holiness, and have shown myself to mankind as they will see me at the judgment-seat. Happy are you, Hester, that wear the scarlet letter openly upon your bosom! Mine burns in secret! Thou little knowest what a relief it is, after the torment of a seven years' cheat, to look into an eye that recognizes me for what I am! Had I one friend,—or were it my worst enemy!—to whom, when sickened with the praises of all other men, I could daily betake myself, and be known as the vilest of all sinners, methinks my soul might keep itself alive thereby. Even thus much of truth would save me! But, now, it is all falsehood!—all emptiness!—all death!"

Hester Prynne looked into his face, but hesitated to speak. Yet, uttering his long-restrained emotions so vehemently as he did, his words here offered her the very point of circumstances in which to interpose what she came to say. She conquered her fears, and spoke.

"Such a friend as thou hast even now wished for," said she, "with whom to weep over thy sin, thou hast in me, the partner of it!"— Again she hesitated, but brought out the words with an effort.— "Thou hast long had such an enemy, and dwellest with him under the same roof!"

The minister started to his feet, gasping for breath, and clutching at his heart as if he would have torn it out of his bosom.

"Ha! What sayest thou?" cried he. "An enemy! And under mine own roof! What mean you?"

Hester Prynne was now fully sensible of the deep injury for which she was responsible to this unhappy man, in permitting him to lie for so many years, or, indeed, for a single moment, at the mercy of

NO FEAR

"You are too hard on yourself," said Hester gently. "You have deeply and seriously repented. You sin is long behind you. Your present life is no less holy than it seems in people's eyes. Is there no reality in repentance confirmed by good works? And why shouldn't that bring you peace?"

"No, Hester—no!" replied the clergyman. "There is no reality in it! It is cold and dead, and can do nothing for me! I have had plenty of penance—but no repentance at all! If I had, I would have long ago thrown off these robes of mock holiness and shown myself to mankind as they will see me on the Judgment Day. You are lucky, Hester, that you wear the scarlet letter openly on your bosom. Mine burns in secret! You have no idea what a relief it is, after the torture of lying for seven years, to look into an eye that sees me for what I am! If I had one friend—or even my worst enemy!—to whom I was known as the vilest of all sinners, to whom I could go when I was sick with the praises of all other men and be known for what I am, then I think I might keep my soul alive. Even that much truth would save me! But now, it is all lies! All emptiness! All death!"

Hester Prynne looked into his face but hesitated to speak. Yet his vehement words offered her the perfect opportunity to interject what she had come to say. She conquered her fears and spoke:

"You have such a friend as you wished for just now," she said, "with whom to weep over your sin. You have me, the partner of it!" Again she hesitated, but said with an effort: "You have long had such an enemy, and live with him, under the same roof!"

The minister leapt to his feet, gasping for breath and clutching at his heart, as though he would have ripped it out of his breast.
"Ha! What do you say!" he cried. "An enemy under my roof! What do you mean?"
Hester Prynne was now fully aware of the deep injury that she was responsible for giving to this man, having permitted him to lie for so many years—or even for one minute—at the mercy of

one, whose purposes could not be other than malevolent. The very contiguity of his enemy, beneath whatever mask the latter might conceal himself, was enough to disturb the magnetic sphere of a being so sensitive as Arthur Dimmesdale. There had been a period when Hester was less alive to this consideration; or, perhaps, in the misanthropy of her own trouble, she left the minister to bear what she might picture to herself as a more tolerable doom. But of late, since the night of his vigil, all her sympathies towards him had been both softened and invigorated. She now read his heart more accurately. She doubted not, that the continual presence of Roger Chillingworth,—the secret poison of his malignity, infecting all the air about him,—and his authorized interference, as a physician, with the minister's physical and spiritual infirmities,—that these bad opportunities had been turned to a cruel purpose. By means of them, the sufferer's conscience had been kept in an irritated state, the tendency of which was, not to cure by wholesome pain, but to disorganize and corrupt his spiritual being. Its result, on earth, could hardly fail to be insanity, and hereafter, that eternal alienation from the Good and True, of which madness is perhaps the earthly type.

Such was the ruin to which she had brought the man, once,— nay, why should we not speak it?—still so passionately loved! Hester felt that the sacrifice of the clergyman's good name, and death itself, as she had already told Roger Chillingworth, would have been infinitely preferable to the alternative which she had taken upon herself to choose. And now, rather than have had this grievous wrong to confess, she would gladly have lain down on the forest-leaves, and died there, at Arthur Dimmesdale's feet.

"O Arthur," cried she, "forgive me! In all things else, I have striven to be true! Truth was the one virtue which I might have held fast, and did hold fast through all extremity; save when thy good,—thy life,— thy fame,—were put in question! Then I consented to a deception. But a lie is never good, even though death threaten on the other side! Dost thou not see what I would say? That old man!—the physician!— he whom they call Roger Chillingworth!—he was my husband!"

The minister looked at her, for an instant, with all that violence of passion, which—intermixed, in more shapes than one, with his higher, purer, softer qualities—was, in fact, the portion of him

the malevolent doctor. The closeness of his enemy, no matter how well concealed, was enough to disturb a spirit as sensitive as Arthur Dimmesdale. There had been a time when Hester was less aware of this. Perhaps her own troubles hardened her to all others, and so she left the minister to bear what she could imagine as a more tolerable fate. But recently, since that night on the platform, her feelings toward him had been both softened and heightened. She now read his heart more accurately. She did not doubt that Roger Chillingworth had taken advantage of the minister's circumstances cruelly, infecting the very air around the minister with his evil influence and exploiting his authority as a physician to meddle with the minister's health. He had kept the minister's conscience in a perpetually irritated state, which corrupted his spirit rather than curing it through wholesome pain. The result in this life could only be to drive the minister insane and, in the afterlife, to permanently separate him from the Good and True—insanity being essentially the same thing as damnation.

This was the condition to which she had reduced the man whom she once—well, why not say it?—whom she still loved so passionately! Hester believed that the sacrifice of the clergyman's reputation, and even his life itself, would have been better than the alternative she had taken it upon herself to choose. Rather than having to confess such a terrible wrong, she would gladly have lain down on the forest leaves and died at Arthur Dimmesdale's feet.

"Oh, Arthur!" she cried, "forgive me! I have tried to be true in everything else! Truth was the one thing I could hold onto through all of the troubles—except when your life and your reputation were called into question! Then I agreed to a deception. But a lie is never good, even if the alternative is death! Don't you see what I am trying to say? That old man—the doctor they call Roger Chillingworth— he was my husband!"

The minister looked at her for a moment, with all the violence of his passion—the part of him that the Devil claimed. That passion was mixed with his higher, purer, and softer qualities: Through it

which the Devil claimed, and through which he sought to win the rest. Never was there a blacker or a fiercer frown, than Hester now encountered. For the brief space that it lasted, it was a dark transfiguration. But his character had been so much enfeebled by suffering, that even its lower energies were incapable of more than a temporary struggle. He sank down on the ground, and buried his face in his hands.

"I might have known it!" murmured he. "I did know it! Was not the secret told me in the natural recoil of my heart, at the first sight of him, and as often as I have seen him since? Why did I not understand? O Hester Prynne, thou little, little knowest all the horror of this thing! And the shame!—the indelicacy!—the horrible ugliness of this exposure of a sick and guilty heart to the very eye that would gloat over it! Woman, woman, thou art accountable for this! I cannot forgive thee!"

"Thou shalt forgive me!" cried Hester, flinging herself on the fallen leaves beside him. "Let God punish! Thou shalt forgive!"

With sudden and desperate tenderness, she threw her arms around him, and pressed his head against her bosom; little caring though his cheek rested on the scarlet letter. He would have released himself, but strove in vain to do so. Hester would not set him free, lest he should look her sternly in the face. All the world had frowned on her,—for seven long years had it frowned upon this lonely woman,—and still she bore it all, nor ever once turned away her firm, sad eyes. Heaven, likewise, had frowned upon her, and she had not died. But the frown of this pale, weak, sinful, and sorrow-stricken man was what Hester could not bear, and live!

"Wilt thou yet forgive me?" she repeated, over and over again. "Wilt thou not frown? Wilt thou forgive?"

"I do forgive you, Hester," replied the minister, at length, with a deep utterance out of an abyss of sadness, but no anger. "I freely forgive you now. May God forgive us both! We are not, Hester, the worst sinners in the world. There is one worse than even the polluted priest! That old man's revenge has been blacker than my sin. He has violated, in cold blood, the sanctity of a human heart. Thou and I, Hester, never did so!"

"Never, never!" whispered she. "What we did had a consecration of its own. We felt it so! We said so to each other! Hast thou forgotten it?"

the Devil sought to conquer them. Hester had never seen a darker or a fiercer frown. For the moment it lasted, it was a violent transformation. But the minister's character had been so weakened by suffering that it was incapable of more than a temporary struggle. He sank to the ground and buried his face in his hands.

"I should have known it," he murmured. "I did know it! Didn't my heart tell me this secret when I pulled back at the first sight of him, and every time I have seen him since? Why didn't I understand? Oh, Hester Prynne, you don't know the horror of this thing! And the shame, the horrible ugliness when a sick and guilty heart is exposed to the very eye that would gloat over it! Woman, woman, you are to blame for this! I cannot forgive you!"

"You *will* forgive me!" cried Hester, throwing herself in the fallen leaves beside him. "Let God punish! You will forgive!"

With a sudden and desperate tenderness, she threw her arms around him and pressed his head against her breast. She did not care that his cheek rested on the scarlet letter. He would have freed himself, but he could not. Hester would not set him free, lest he look at her with reproach. All the world had frowned at her—for seven long years it had frowned at this lonely woman—and she bore it all, never turning away her firm, sad eyes. Heaven had frowned at her, too, and she had not died. But the frown of this pale, weak, sinful, and sorrowful man was more than Hester could bear!

"Will you forgive me yet?" she repeated, over and over again. "Will you not frown? Will you forgive?"

"I do forgive you, Hester," the minister eventually replied. He spoke deeply, out of great depths of sadness, but no anger. "I freely forgive you now. May God forgive us both. We are not, Hester, the worst sinners in the world. There is a sinner even greater than this sinful priest! That old man's revenge has been blacker than my sin. He has violated, in cold blood, the holiness of a human heart. You and I, Hester, never did that!"

"Never, never!" she whispered. "What we did had a holiness of its own. We felt that! We told each other so. Have you forgotten that?"

"Hush, Hester!" said Arthur Dimmesdale, rising from the ground. "No; I have not forgotten!"

They sat down again, side by side, and hand clasped in hand, on the mossy trunk of the fallen tree. Life had never brought them a gloomier hour; it was the point whither their pathway had so long been tending, and darkening ever, as it stole along;—and yet it inclosed a charm that made them linger upon it, and claim another, and another, and, after all, another moment. The forest was obscure around them, and creaked with a blast that was passing through it. The boughs were tossing heavily above their heads; while one solemn old tree groaned dolefully to another, as if telling the sad story of the pair that sat beneath, or constrained to forebode evil to come.

And yet they lingered. How dreary looked the forest-track that led backward to the settlement, where Hester Prynne must take up again the burden of her ignominy, and the minister the hollow mockery of his good name! So they lingered an instant longer. No golden light had ever been so precious as the gloom of this dark forest. Here, seen only by his eyes, the scarlet letter need not burn into the bosom of the fallen woman! Here, seen only by her eyes, Arthur Dimmesdale, false to God and man, might be, for one moment, true!

He started at a thought that suddenly occurred to him.

"Hester," cried he, "here is a new horror! Roger Chillingworth knows your purpose to reveal his true character. Will he continue, then, to keep our secret? What will now be the course of his revenge?"

"There is a strange secrecy in his nature," replied Hester, thoughtfully; "and it has grown upon him by the hidden practices of his revenge. I deem it not likely that he will betray the secret. He will doubtless seek other means of satiating his dark passion."

"And I—how am I to live longer, breathing the same air with this deadly enemy?" exclaimed Arthur Dimmesdale, shrinking within himself, and pressing his hand nervously against his heart,—a gesture that had grown involuntary with him. "Think for me, Hester! Thou art strong. Resolve for me!"

"Thou must dwell no longer with this man," said Hester, slowly and firmly. "Thy heart must be no longer under his evil eye!"

"It were far worse than death!" replied the minister. "But how to avoid it? What choice remains to me? Shall I lie down again on these

"Hush, Hester!" said Arthur Dimmesdale, rising from the ground. "No, I have not forgotten!"

They sat down again, side by side and hand in hand, on the mossy trunk of the fallen tree. Life had never brought them a gloomier hour: This was the point to which their paths had been leading, darkening as they went along. And yet the moment revealed a charm that made them linger over it, and claim another moment, and another still—and yet one more moment. The forest was dark around them and creaked as the wind passed through it. As the branches were tossed back and forth overhead, one solemn old tree groaned sorrowfully to another. It was as though the trees were telling the sad story of the pair that sat beneath them or warning of evil still to come.

And yet they lingered. The forest path back to the settlement looked dreary: There Hester Prynne would once again take up the burden of her shame, and the minister the hollow mockery of his reputation! So they lingered another moment. No golden light was ever so precious as the gloom of this dark forest. Here, seen only by his eyes, the scarlet letter did not burn the bosom of the sinful woman! Here, seen only by her eyes, Arthur Dimmesdale—false to God and to man—might, for one moment, be true!

He started suddenly as a thought occurred to him.

"Hester!" he cried, "I have thought of a new horror! Roger Chillingworth knows that you intend to reveal his true character. Will he continue to keep our secret? What revenge will he take now?"

"There is a strange secrecy in his nature," Hester replied, thoughtfully. "And he has grown more secretive as he has taken his hidden revenge. I think it unlikely that he will betray our secret now—but he will certainly seek revenge by other means."

"And I—how am I to live, breathing the same air as this deadly enemy?" exclaimed Arthur Dimmesdale, shrinking into himself and pressing his hand nervously against his heart. The gesture had become involuntary for him. "Think for me, Hester! You are strong. Decide for me!"

"You must live with this man no longer," said Hester, slowly and firmly. "Your heart must be no longer under his evil eye!"

"That would be worse than death!" replied the minister. "But how can I avoid it? What choice do I have left? Should I lie down again

withered leaves, where I cast myself when thou didst tell me what he was? Must I sink down there, and die at once?"

"Alas, what a ruin has befallen thee!" said Hester, with the tears gushing into her eyes. "Wilt thou die for very weakness? There is no other cause!"

"The judgment of God is on me," answered the conscience-stricken priest. "It is too mighty for me to struggle with!"

"Heaven would show mercy," rejoined Hester "hadst thou but the strength to take advantage of it."

"Be thou strong for me!" answered he. "Advise me what to do."

"Is the world then so narrow?" exclaimed Hester Prynne, fixing her deep eyes on the minister's, and instinctively exercising a magnetic power over a spirit so shattered and subdued, that it could hardly hold itself erect. "Doth the universe lie within the compass of yonder town, which only a little time ago was but a leaf-strewn desert, as lonely as this around us? Whither leads yonder forest-track? Backward to the settlement, thou sayest! Yes; but onward, too! Deeper it goes, and deeper, into the wilderness, less plainly to be seen at every step; until, some few miles hence, the yellow leaves will show no vestige of the white man's tread. There thou art free! So brief a journey would bring thee from a world where thou hast been most wretched, to one where thou mayest still be happy! Is there not shade enough in all this boundless forest to hide thy heart from the gaze of Roger Chillingworth?"

"Yes, Hester; but only under the fallen leaves!" replied the minister, with a sad smile.

"Then there is the broad pathway of the sea!" continued Hester. "It brought thee hither. If thou so choose, it will bear thee back again. In our native land, whether in some remote rural village or in vast London,—or, surely, in Germany, in France, in pleasant Italy,—thou wouldst be beyond his power and knowledge! And what hast thou to do with all these iron men, and their opinions? They have kept thy better part in bondage too long already!"

"It cannot be!" answered the minister, listening as if he were called upon to realize a dream. "I am powerless to go. Wretched and sinful as I am, I have had no other thought than to drag on my earthly existence in the sphere where Providence hath placed me. Lost as my own soul is, I would still do what I may for other human

on these withered leaves, where I threw myself when you told me who he was? Must I fall down there and die at once?"

"Oh, what have you come to?" said Hester, with tears filling her eyes. "Will you die of weakness? There is no other reason!"

"The judgment of God is upon me," answered the guilty priest. "It is too strong for me to resist!"

"Heaven would be merciful," replied Hester, "if you had the strength to ask for mercy."

"Be strong for me!" he answered. "Advise me what to do."

"Is the world that small?" exclaimed Hester Prynne, looking at the minister with her deep eyes. Instinctively, she exercised her power over a spirit so broken and beaten down that it could hardly hold itself upright. "Is that town, which not that long ago was just part of the forest, the entire universe? Where does this forest path go? Back to the settlement, you say! Yes, but it goes onward too! It goes deeper and deeper into the wilderness, less visible with every step. A few miles from here, the yellow leaves show no trace of the white man's tracks. There you would be free! Such a brief journey would take you from a world where you have been miserable to one where you might still be happy! Isn't there enough shade in this vast forest to hide your heart from the gaze of Roger Chillingworth?"

"Yes, Hester, but only buried under the fallen leaves!" replied the minister, with a sad smile.

"Then there is the wide road of the sea!" continued Hester. "It brought you here. If you choose, it will bring you back again. There you would be beyond his power and his knowledge! You could live in our native land—in London, or some faraway rural village—or in Germany, France, or Italy. And what do you care for all of these magistrates and their opinions? They have kept your better part locked away for far too long!"

"It cannot be!" answered the minister, listening as though he were being encouraged to realize a dream. "I do not have the power to go. Miserable and sinful as I am, I have no desire to do anything but continue my earthly life where I have been placed. Although my own soul is lost, I would still do what I can for other souls! Though

souls! I dare not quit my post, though an unfaithful sentinel, whose sure reward is death and dishonor, when his dreary watch shall come to an end!"

"Thou art crushed under this seven years' weight of misery," replied Hester, fervently resolved to buoy him up with her own energy. "But thou shalt leave it all behind thee! It shall not cumber thy steps, as thou treadest along the forest-path; neither shalt thou freight the ship with it, if thou prefer to cross the sea. Leave this wreck and ruin here where it hath happened! Meddle no more with it! Begin all anew! Hast thou exhausted possibility in the failure of this one trial? Not so! The future is yet full of trial and success. There is happiness to be enjoyed! There is good to be done! Exchange this false life of thine for a true one. Be, if thy spirit summon thee to such a mission, the teacher and apostle of the red men. Or,—as is more thy nature,—be a scholar and a sage among the wisest and the most renowned of the cultivated world. Preach! Write! Act! Do anything, save to lie down and die! Give up this name of Arthur Dimmesdale, and make thyself another, and a high one, such as thou canst wear without fear or shame. Why shouldst thou tarry so much as one other day in the torments that have so gnawed into thy life!—that have made thee feeble to will and to do!—that will leave thee powerless even to repent! Up, and away!"

"O Hester!" cried Arthur Dimmesdale, in whose eyes a fitful light, kindled by her enthusiasm, flashed up and died away, "thou tellest of running a race to a man whose knees are tottering beneath him! I must die here. There is not the strength or courage left me to venture into the wide, strange, difficult world, alone!"

It was the last expression of the despondency of a broken spirit. He lacked energy to grasp the better fortune that seemed within his reach.

He repeated the word.

"Alone, Hester!"

"Thou shalt not go alone!" answered she, in a deep whisper.

Then, all was spoken!

NO FEAR

I am an unfaithful watchman, sure to be rewarded with death and dishonor when my dreary watch comes to an end, yet I dare not quit my post!"

"You are crushed under the weight of seven years' misery," replied Hester, determined to hold him up with her own energy. "But you will leave it all behind! It will not trip you up as you walk along the forest path. Your misery will not weigh the ship down, if you prefer to cross the sea. Leave this ruined life here. Begin anew! Have you exhausted every possibility in failing this one trial? No! The future is still full of trial and success. There is happiness to be enjoyed! There is good to be done! Trade this false life for a true one! Be a wise scholar in the company of the wisest, if your spirit calls you to it. Preach! Write! Act! Do anything except lie down and die! Throw off the name of Arthur Dimmesdale and make yourself another. Let it be a high name, which you can wear without fear or shame. Why remain here one more day, where torments have eaten away at your life? Where troubles have made you too weak to decide and to act? Where misery has left you powerless even to repent? Rise up and leave!"

"Oh, Hester," cried Arthur Dimmesdale. Her enthusiasm sparked a flickering light in his eyes: It flashed up and died away. "You talk of running a race to a man whose knees are wobbling beneath him! I must die here! I do not have the strength or the courage to venture into the wide, strange, difficult world alone!"

It was the last expression of the despair of a broken spirit. He lacked the energy to grab onto the better fortune that seemed within his reach.

He repeated the words: "Alone, Hester!"

"You will not go alone!" she answered, in a deep whisper.
And when she'd said that, she'd said everything there was to say.

Chapter 18: A Flood of Sunshine

Arthur Dimmesdale gazed into Hester's face with a look in which hope and joy shone out, indeed, but with fear betwixt them, and a kind of horror at her boldness, who had spoken what he vaguely hinted at, but dared not speak.

But Hester Prynne, with a mind of native courage and activity, and for so long a period not merely estranged, but outlawed, from society, had habituated herself to such latitude of speculation as was altogether foreign to the clergyman. She had wandered, without rule or guidance, in a moral wilderness; as vast, as intricate and shadowy, as the untamed forest, amid the gloom of which they were now holding a colloquy that was to decide their fate. Her intellect and heart had their home, as it were, in desert places, where she roamed as freely as the wild Indian in his woods. For years past she had looked from this estranged point of view at human institutions, and whatever priests or legislators had established; criticizing all with hardly more reverence than the Indian would feel for the clerical band, the judicial robe, the pillory, the gallows, the fireside, or the church. The tendency of her fate and fortunes had been to set her free. The scarlet letter was her passport into regions where other women dared not tread. Shame, Despair, Solitude! These had been her teachers,—stern and wild ones,—and they had made her strong, but taught her much amiss.

The minister, on the other hand, had never gone through an experience calculated to lead him beyond the scope of generally received laws; although, in a single instance, he had so fearfully transgressed one of the most sacred of them. But this had been a sin of passion, not of principle, nor even purpose. Since that wretched epoch, he had watched, with morbid zeal and minuteness, not his acts,—for those it was easy to arrange,—but each breath of emotion, and his every thought. At the head of the social system, as the clergymen of that day stood, he was only the more trammelled by its regulations, its principles, and even its prejudices. As a priest, the framework of his order inevitably hemmed him in. As a man who had once sinned, but who kept his conscience all alive and painfully sensitive by the fretting of an unhealed wound, he might have been supposed safer within the line of virtue, than if he had never sinned at all.

Chapter 18: A Flood of Sunshine

Arthur Dimmesdale gazed into Hester's face with a look of hope and joy—yet there was fear and a kind of shock at her boldness in speaking what he had hinted at but did not dare to say.

But Hester Prynne had a naturally active and courageous mind. She had been outlawed from society for so long that she had become used to a freedom of thought that was altogether foreign to the clergyman. She had wandered in a moral wilderness, without rule or guidance—a wilderness as vast, dark, and complex as the untamed forest in which they were now together. Her mind and heart were at home in uninhabited places, where she roamed as freely as the wild Indian in his woods. For many years now she had looked at human institutions from this isolated point of view. She criticized it all with almost as little reverence as an Indian would feel for the ministry or the judiciary, the many forms of ritual punishment, the fireside around which families gathered, or the church in which they prayed. Her fate had set her free from all. The scarlet letter was her passport into regions where other women dared not go. Shame, despair, and solitude had been her stern and wild teachers. They had made her strong, but they had often guided her poorly.

The minister, on the other hand, had never experienced anything to lead him beyond the scope of social authority—though he had once violated that authority quite gravely. But that had been a sin of passion, not a matter of choosing the wrong principle to follow or even of making a deliberate choice at all. Since that awful time, he had kept an obsessively close watch not only over his acts—for those were easy to control—but over each emotion and passing thought he experienced. In those days, the clergyman stood at the head of the social system. And so Mr. Dimmesdale was all the more trodden down by society's regulations, its principles, and even its prejudices. As a priest, the framework of order inevitably constrained him. As a man who had once sinned, and then kept his conscience alive and painfully sensitive by worrying over the unhealed spiritual wound, it might be the case the he was less likely to step out of line than if he had never sinned at all.

Thus, we seem to see that, as regarded Hester Prynne, the whole seven years of outlaw and ignominy had been little other than a preparation for this very hour. But Arthur Dimmesdale! Were such a man once more to fall, what plea could be urged in extenuation of his crime? None; unless it avail him somewhat, that he was broken down by long and exquisite suffering; that his mind was darkened and confused by the very remorse which harrowed it; that, between fleeing as an avowed criminal, and remaining as a hypocrite, conscience might find it hard to strike the balance; that it was human to avoid the peril of death and infamy, and the inscrutable machinations of an enemy; that, finally, to this poor pilgrim, on his dreary and desert path, faint, sick, miserable, there appeared a glimpse of human affection and sympathy, a new life, and a true one, in exchange for the heavy doom which he was now expiating. And be the stern and sad truth spoken, that the breach which guilt has once made into the human soul is never, in this mortal state, repaired. It may be watched and guarded; so that the enemy shall not force his way again into the citadel, and might even, in his subsequent assaults, select some other avenue, in preference to that where he had formerly succeeded. But there is still the ruined wall, and, near it, the stealthy tread of the foe that would win over again his unforgotten triumph.

The struggle, if there were one, need not be described. Let it suffice, that the clergyman resolved to flee, and not alone.

"If, in all these past seven years," thought he, "I could recall one instant of peace or hope, I would yet endure, for the sake of that earnest of Heaven's mercy. But now,—since I am irrevocably doomed,—wherefore should I not snatch the solace allowed to the condemned culprit before his execution? Or, if this be the path to a better life, as Hester would persuade me, I surely give up no fairer prospect by pursuing it! Neither can I any longer live without her companionship; so powerful is she to sustain,—so tender to soothe! O Thou to whom I dare not lift mine eyes, wilt Thou yet pardon me!"

"Thou wilt go!" said Hester calmly, as he met her glance.

The decision once made, a glow of strange enjoyment threw its flickering brightness over the trouble of his breast. It was the exhilarating effect—upon a prisoner just escaped from the dungeon of his own heart—of breathing the wild, free atmosphere of

NO FEAR

And so it seems that for Hester Prynne, her seven years of isolation and shame had only prepared her for this very moment. But Arthur Dimmesdale! If such a man were to sin again, what plea could be made to excuse his crime? None, except that he was broken down by long, intense suffering. Perhaps it could be said that any conscience would have trouble choosing between fleeing as a confessed criminal and remaining as a hypocrite. And it is only human to avoid the dangers of death and shame and the mysterious plotting of an enemy. Moreover, this poor man, wandering exhausted, sick, and miserable down his lonely, dreary path, this man had finally caught a glimpse of human affection and sympathy. He had seen a new life, a true one, which could be traded for the heavy sentence he was now serving. And, truth be told, a soul that guilt has entered can never be repaired in this life. It is like a defeated castle: It may be watched and guarded so that the enemy will not enter once again. But the ruined wall remains, and close by is the foe who wishes to triumph once again.

If there was a struggle in the clergyman's soul, it need not be described. Suffice it to say that he resolved to flee—and not alone.

"If in all these last seven years," he thought, "I could remember one instant of peace or hope, then I would remain here because of that sign of Heaven's mercy. But now, since I am doomed beyond salvation, why shouldn't I enjoy the relief allowed to the condemned criminal before he is put to death? Or if this is the path to a better life, as Hester says it is, then surely I am not giving anything up to pursue it! And I can no longer live without her companionship: Her power sustains me, and her tenderness soothes me! O God, to whom I dare not lift my eyes, will you pardon me?"

"You will go!" said Hester calmly, as he looked her in the eyes.

Now that the decision was made, a strange glow of pleasure entered his heart. It was the thrill of breathing the wild, free air of a region without God or rules. He felt like a prisoner escaped from a dungeon. His spirit leaped up and came nearer to the sky than it

an unredeemed, unchristianized, lawless region. His spirit rose, as it were, with a bound, and attained a nearer prospect of the sky, than throughout all the misery which had kept him grovelling on the earth. Of a deeply religious temperament, there was inevitably a tinge of the devotional in his mood.

"Do I feel joy again?" cried he, wondering at himself. "Methought the germ of it was dead in me! O Hester, thou art my better angel! I seem to have flung myself—sick, sin-stained, and sorrow-blackened—down upon these forest-leaves, and to have risen up all made anew, and with new powers to glorify Him that hath been merciful! This is already the better life! Why did we not find it sooner?"

"Let us not look back," answered Hester Prynne. "The past is gone! Wherefore should we linger upon it now? See! With this symbol, I undo it all, and make it as it had never been!"

So speaking, she undid the clasp that fastened the scarlet letter, and, taking it from her bosom, threw it to a distance among the withered leaves. The mystic token alighted on the hither verge of the stream. With a hand's breadth farther flight it would have fallen into the water, and have given the little brook another woe to carry onward, besides the unintelligible tale which it still kept murmuring about. But there lay the embroidered letter, glittering like a lost jewel, which some ill-fated wanderer might pick up, and thenceforth be haunted by strange phantoms of guilt, sinkings of the heart, and unaccountable misfortune.

The stigma gone, Hester heaved a long, deep sigh, in which the burden of shame and anguish departed from her spirit. O exquisite relief! She had not known the weight, until she felt the freedom! By another impulse, she took off the formal cap that confined her hair; and down it fell upon her shoulders, dark and rich, with at once a shadow and a light in its abundance, and imparting the charm of softness to her features. There played around her mouth, and beamed out of her eyes, a radiant and tender smile, that seemed gushing from the very heart of womanhood. A crimson flush was glowing on her cheek, that had been long so pale. Her sex, her youth, and the whole richness of her beauty, came back from what men call the irrevocable past, and clustered themselves, with her maiden hope, and a happiness before unknown, within the magic circle of this hour. And, as if the gloom of the earth and sky had been but the effluence of

had in all the years that his miserable guilt had kept him groveling on the earth. His temperament was deeply religious, and so there was an inevitable trace (but only a trace) of religious devotion in his mood.

"Is this joy I feel once again?" he cried, amazed at himself. "I thought that there was no joy left in me! Oh, Hester, you are my better angel! I have thrown myself—sick, sinful, and miserable—down on these forest leaves, and I have been made new, with no powers to glorify God, who has been merciful! I have already reached a better life! Why didn't we find it sooner?"

"Let's not look back now," answered Hester Prynne. "The past is gone! Why should we linger over it now? Look. With this symbol I undo everything and make it as though it had never been!"

Saying this, she undid the clasp that fastened the scarlet letter. Taking it from her breast, she threw it among the withered leaves. The mystic symbol landed on the near bank of the stream. Had it flown a little farther, it would have fallen into the water and given the little brook another woe to carry onward. But there lay the embroidered letter, glittering like a lost jewel for some cursed wanderer to pick up. That ill-fated person might then be haunted by strange, guilty spirits; sad emotions; and inexplicable misfortune.

With the symbol gone, Hester heaved a long, deep sigh. The burden of shame and anguish left her spirit. What a relief! She had not known the weight she carried until she felt herself free of it! With another whim, she took off the formal cap that had hidden her hair. Dark and rich, it fell down upon her shoulders, full of shadows and of light. A smile beamed out of her eyes, tender and radiant, which seemed to gush forth from the very heart of womanhood. A crimson blush glowed on her cheek, which had been pale for so long. Her sex, her youth, and the richness of her beauty came back from what men call the irretrievable past. Together with hope and a happiness she had never known, they gathered within the magic circle of this hour. The gloom of the earth and sky vanished with their sorrow, as though it had flowed from these two human hearts. All at once, as when Heaven smiles suddenly, the sunshine burst forth.

these two mortal hearts, it vanished with their sorrow. All at once, as with a sudden smile of Heaven, forth burst the sunshine, pouring a very flood into the obscure forest, gladdening each green leaf, transmuting the yellow fallen ones to gold, and gleaming adown the gray trunks of the solemn trees. The objects that had made a shadow hitherto, embodied the brightness now. The course of the little brook might be traced by its merry gleam afar into the wood's heart of mystery, which had become a mystery of joy.

Such was the sympathy of Nature—that wild, heathen Nature of the forest, never subjugated by human law, nor illumined by higher truth—with the bliss of these two spirits! Love, whether newly born, or aroused from a deathlike slumber, must always create a sunshine, filling the heart so full of radiance, that it overflows upon the outward world. Had the forest still kept its gloom, it would have been bright in Hester's eyes, and bright in Arthur Dimmesdale's!

Hester looked at him with the thrill of another joy. "Thou must know Pearl!" said she. "Our little Pearl! Thou hast seen her,—yes, I know it!—but thou wilt see her now with other eyes. She is a strange child! I hardly comprehend her! But thou wilt love her dearly, as I do, and wilt advise me how to deal with her."

"Dost thou think the child will be glad to know me?" asked the minister, somewhat uneasily. "I have long shrunk from children, because they often show a distrust,—a backwardness to be familiar with me. I have even been afraid of little Pearl!"

"Ah, that was sad!" answered the mother. "But she will love thee dearly, and thou her. She is not far off. I will call her! Pearl! Pearl!"

"I see the child," observed the minister. "Yonder she is, standing in a streak of sunshine, a good way off, on the other side of the brook. So thou thinkest the child will love me?"

Hester smiled, and again called to Pearl, who was visible, at some distance, as the minister had described her, like a bright-apparelled vision, in a sunbeam, which fell down upon her through an arch of boughs. The ray quivered to and fro, making her figure dim or distinct,—now like a real child, now like a child's spirit,—as the splendor went and came again. She heard her mother's voice, and approached slowly through the forest.

Pearl had not found the hour pass wearisomely, while her mother sat talking with the clergyman. The great black forest—stern as it

NO FEAR

It flooded into the dark forest, gladdening every green leaf, turning the fallen yellow ones into gold, and gleaming down the gray trunks of the solemn trees. The objects that had cast a shadow before now embodied the brightness. The course of the little brook could be traced by its merry gleam far into the heart of the forest's mystery, which was now a mystery of joy.

Nature itself—the wild, godless Nature of the forest, free from human law and ignorant of higher truth—acted in sympathy with the bliss of these two spirits! Love, whether newly born or awakened from a long slumber, always creates sunshine. It fills the heart so full of brightness that it spills over into the outside world. Even if the forest had remained gloomy, it would have seemed bright to Hester and Arthur Dimmesdale!

Hester looked at him with a thrill of another joy. "You must meet Pearl!" she said. "Our little Pearl! You have seen her—I know that—but now you will see her with other eyes. She is a strange child! I barely understand her! But you will love her dearly, as I do, and you'll tell me how to deal with her!"

"Do you think she will be glad to meet me?" asked the minister, somewhat uneasily. "I usually avoid children because they seem not to trust me. I have even been afraid of little Pearl!"

"That is sad," replied the mother. "But she will love you dearly, and you will love her. She isn't far from here. I will call her. Pearl! Pearl!"

"I see her," the minister said. "She's over there, standing in the sunbeams—a way off on the other side of the brook. So you think that she will love me?"

Hester smiled and called to Pearl again. She could be seen in the distance, as the minister had described her: a brightly dressed vision standing in a sunbeam, which fell down on her through the branches above. The sunbeam quivered here and there, making her form dim and then distinct. She looked first like a real child and then like a child's spirit as the light came and went. She heard her mother's voice and approached slowly through the forest.

Pearl had not been bored while her mother sat talking with the clergyman. The great black forest, which seemed stern to those who

showed itself to those who brought the guilt and troubles of the world into its bosom—became the playmate of the lonely infant, as well as it knew how. Sombre as it was, it put on the kindest of its moods to welcome her. It offered her the partridge-berries, the growth of the preceding autumn, but ripening only in the spring, and now red as drops of blood upon the withered leaves. These Pearl gathered, and was pleased with their wild flavor. The small denizens of the wilderness hardly took pains to move out of her path. A partridge, indeed, with a brood of ten behind her, ran forward threateningly, but soon repented of her fierceness, and clucked to her young ones not to be afraid. A pigeon, alone on a low branch, allowed Pearl to come beneath, and uttered a sound as much of greeting as alarm. A squirrel, from the lofty depths of his domestic tree, chattered either in anger or merriment,—for a squirrel is such a choleric and humorous little personage that it is hard to distinguish between his moods,—so he chattered at the child, and flung down a nut upon her head. It was a last year's nut, and already gnawed by his sharp tooth. A fox, startled from his sleep by her light foot-step on the leaves, looked inquisitively at Pearl, as doubting whether it were better to steal off, or renew his nap on the same spot. A wolf, it is said,—but here the tale has surely lapsed into the improbable,—came up, and smelt of Pearl's robe, and offered his savage head to be patted by her hand. The truth seems to be, however, that the mother-forest, and these wild things which it nourished, all recognized a kindred wildness in the human child.

And she was gentler here than in the grassy-margined streets of the settlement, or in her mother's cottage. The flowers appeared to know it; and one and another whispered, as she passed, "Adorn thyself with me, thou beautiful child, adorn thyself with me!"—and, to please them, Pearl gathered the violets, and anemones, and columbines, and some twigs of the freshest green, which the old trees held down before her eyes. With these she decorated her hair, and her young waist, and became a nymph-child, or an infant dryad, or whatever else was in closest sympathy with the antique wood. In such guise had Pearl adorned herself, when she heard her mother's voice, and came slowly back.

Slowly; for she saw the clergyman!

carried with them the guilt and troubles of the world, became the playmate of the lonely child, as best it knew how. Although it was grave, it welcomed her with the kindest of moods. It offered her partridgeberries, which grew in the autumn but only ripened in the spring. Now they were as red as drops of blood upon the withered leaves. Pearl gathered these berries and enjoyed their wild flavor. The small wood creatures hardly bothered to move out of her way. A partridge, with her brood of ten birds behind her, ran at Pearl threateningly but soon changed her mind. She clucked to her young ones not to be afraid. A pigeon, alone on a low branch, allowed Pearl to walk beneath her. The bird made a noise more welcoming than fearful. High up in his tree, a squirrel chattered at Pearl. He was either angry or merry. It was hard to tell which. The squirrel is such an angry and moody little creature that it is hard to tell what emotion he's expressing. Whatever mood he was in, the squirrel threw a nut down at Pearl's head. It was from the last year and already chewed by his sharp teeth. A fox, awoken by Pearl's light footsteps on the dry leaves, looked at her inquisitively. He seemed uncertain whether to run away or go back to sleep. People say—though it's hard to believe them—that a wolf came up and sniffed Pearl's clothing, then let her pat his head. The truth seems to be that the forest and all that lived in it recognized the natural wildness in the human child.

And she was gentler here than in the streets of the town or in her mother's cottage. The woods seemed to know that. As she passed, plants whispered to her: "Decorate yourself with me, you beautiful child! Decorate yourself with me!" To make them happy, Pearl gathered many flowers along with several green twigs, which the old trees held down before her eyes. She decorated her hair and her young waist with these, becoming a nymph or a young druid, or whatever else was close to the old forest. Pearl had decorated herself in this way when she heard her mother's voice and returned slowly.

Slowly—because she saw the minister!

Chapter 19: The Child at the Brookside

Thou wilt love her dearly," repeated Hester Prynne, as she and the minister sat watching little Pearl. "Dost thou not think her beautiful? And see with what natural skill she has made those simple flowers adorn her! Had she gathered pearls, and diamonds, and rubies, in the wood, they could not have become her better. She is a splendid child! But I know whose brow she has!"

"Dost thou know, Hester," said Arthur Dimmesdale, with an unquiet smile, "that this dear child, tripping about always at thy side, hath caused me many an alarm? Methought—O Hester, what a thought is that, and how terrible to dread it!—that my own features were partly repeated in her face, and so strikingly that the world might see them! But she is mostly thine!"

"No, no! Not mostly!" answered the mother with a tender smile. "A little longer, and thou needest not to be afraid to trace whose child she is. But how strangely beautiful she looks, with those wild flowers in her hair! It is as if one of the fairies, whom we left in our dear old England, had decked her out to meet us."

It was with a feeling which neither of them had ever before experienced, that they sat and watched Pearl's slow advance. In her was visible the tie that united them. She had been offered to the world, these seven years past, as the living hieroglyphic, in which was revealed the secret they so darkly sought to hide,—all written in this symbol,—all plainly manifest,—had there been a prophet or magician skilled to read the character of flame! And Pearl was the oneness of their being. Be the foregone evil what it might, how could they doubt that their earthly lives and future destinies were conjoined, when they beheld at once the material union, and the spiritual idea, in whom they met, and were to dwell immortally together? Thoughts like these—and perhaps other thoughts, which they did not acknowledge or define— threw an awe about the child, as she came onward.

"Let her see nothing strange,—no passion nor eagerness—in thy way of accosting her," whispered Hester. "Our Pearl is a fitful and fantastic little elf, sometimes. Especially, she is seldom tolerant of emotion, when she does not fully comprehend the why and wherefore. But the child hath strong affections! She loves me, and will love thee!"

Chapter 19: The Child at the Brookside

You will love her fondly," repeated Hester Prynne, as she and the minister sat watching little Pearl. "Isn't she beautiful? And look how she has adorned herself with such simple flowers! If she had gathered pearls, diamonds, and rubies instead, they could not have suited her better! She is a wonderful child! But I know whose forehead she has!"

"Do you know, Hester," said Arthur Dimmesdale, with an uneasy smile, "that this dear child, who is always at your side, has often alarmed me? I thought—oh, Hester, it is awful to dread such a thought!—that I could see my own features in her face, so clearly that the whole world would see them! But she is mostly yours!"

"No, no! Not mostly!" answered Hester, with a tender smile. "A little longer and you won't need to be afraid that others will learn whose child she is. She looks so strangely beautiful with those wild flowers in her hair! It's as if one of the fairies, whom we left behind in England, had dressed her to meet us."

They sat together, feeling something they had not felt before, and watched Pearl walk toward them slowly. She made visible the tie that bound them. For the past seven years, she had been offered to the world as a mysterious symbol, a clue to the secret that they sought to hide. Their secret had been revealed in Pearl, if only some prophet or magician had been skilled enough to see it. Pearl represented the oneness of their being. No matter what evil had come before, how could they doubt that their mortal lives and future destinies were linked? In Pearl's body, the two were joined. In her soul, they would be linked immortally. Thoughts like these, and perhaps others that went unacknowledged, cast awe around the child as she came toward them.

"Don't let her see anything strange in your approach: no passion or overeagerness," whispered Hester. "Our Pearl is a flighty little elf sometimes. She doesn't usually tolerate emotion when she doesn't understand why it has arisen. But she has strong emotions! She loves me and will love you!"

"Thou canst not think," said the minister, glancing aside at Hester Prynne, "how my heart dreads this interview, and yearns for it! But, in truth, as I already told thee, children are not readily won to be familiar with me. They will not climb my knee, nor prattle in my ear, nor answer to my smile; but stand apart, and eye me strangely. Even little babes, when I take them in my arms, weep bitterly. Yet Pearl, twice in her little lifetime, hath been kind to me! The first time,—thou knowest it well! The last was when thou ledst her with thee to the house of yonder stern old Governor."

"And thou didst plead so bravely in her behalf and mine!" answered the mother. "I remember it; and so shall little Pearl. Fear nothing! She may be strange and shy at first, but will soon learn to love thee!"

By this time Pearl had reached the margin of the brook, and stood on the farther side, gazing silently at Hester and the clergyman, who still sat together on the mossy tree-trunk, waiting to receive her. Just where she had paused the brook chanced to form a pool, so smooth and quiet that it reflected a perfect image of her little figure, with all the brilliant picturesqueness of her beauty, in its adornment of flowers and wreathed foliage, but more refined and spiritual-ized than the reality. This image, so nearly identical with the living Pearl, seemed to communicate somewhat of its own shadowy and intangible quality to the child herself. It was strange, the way in which Pearl stood, looking so stedfastly at them through the dim medium of the forest-gloom; herself, meanwhile, all glorified with a ray of sunshine, that was attracted thitherward as by a certain sympathy. In the brook beneath stood another child,—another and the same,—with likewise its ray of golden light. Hester felt herself, in some indistinct and tantalizing manner, estranged from Pearl; as if the child, in her lonely ramble through the forest, had strayed out of the sphere in which she and her mother dwelt together, and was now vainly seeking to return to it.

There was both truth and error in the impression; the child and mother were estranged, but through Hester's fault, not Pearl's. Since the latter rambled from her side, another inmate had been admitted within the circle of the mother's feelings, and so modified the aspect of them all, that Pearl, the returning wanderer, could not find her wonted place, and hardly knew where she was.

NO FEAR

"You cannot imagine," said the minister, glancing at Hester Prynne, "how my heart dreads this interview and how it desires it! But as I've already told you, children don't often like me. They will not sit in my lap, nor whisper in my ear, nor answer my smile. They stand far off and look at me strangely. Even little babies weep bitterly when I hold them. Yet Pearl, twice already, has been kind to me! The first time you remember well! The second was when you led her to the house of that stern old Governor."

"And you pleaded so bravely on her behalf and mine!" answered Hester. "I remember it, and so will little Pearl. Do not be afraid. She may be strange and shy at first, but she will soon learn to love you!"

By this time, Pearl had reached the edge of the brook. She stood on the far side, staring silently at Hester and the clergyman, who still sat together on the mossy tree trunk, waiting for her. Just where she was standing, the brook formed a pool so smooth and quiet that it reflected a perfect little image of her. The water showed all the brilliance of her beauty, decorated with flowers and wreathed with leaves, but the image was more refined and spiritual than the reality. This image, almost identical to the living Pearl, seemed to lend the child some of its shadowy, immaterial quality. Pearl stood looking at them through the dim forest gloom. It was strange, her looking through that gloom while she herself was brightened by a ray of sunshine that had been drawn to her. In the brook beneath her there appeared another child, with its own ray of golden light. Hester felt herself, in some strange way, isolated from Pearl. It was as though the child, in her lonely walk through the woods, had left the world in which she and her mother lived together and was now seeking in vain to return.

There was some truth in that impression. Mother and child were estranged—but it was Hester's fault, not Pearl's. Since the child had left her side, someone else had entered the circle of her mother's feelings. Those feeling had been so altered that Pearl, the returning wanderer, could not find her usual place there. She hardly knew where she was.

"I have a strange fancy," observed the sensitive minister, "that this brook is the boundary between two worlds, and that thou canst never meet thy Pearl again. Or is she an elfish spirit, who, as the legends of our childhood taught us, is forbidden to cross a running stream? Pray hasten her; for this delay has already imparted a tremor to my nerves."

"Come, dearest child!" said Hester encouragingly, and stretching out both her arms. "How slow thou art! When hast thou been so sluggish before now? Here is a friend of mine, who must be thy friend also. Thou wilt have twice as much love, henceforward, as thy mother alone could give thee! Leap across the brook and come to us. Thou canst leap like a young deer!"

Pearl, without responding in any manner to these honey-sweet expressions, remained on the other side of the brook. Now she fixed her bright, wild eyes on her mother, now on the minister, and now included them both in the same glance; as if to detect and explain to herself the relation which they bore to one another. For some unaccountable reason, as Arthur Dimmesdale felt the child's eyes upon himself, his hand,—with that gesture so habitual as to have become involuntary—stole over his heart. At length, assuming a singular air of authority, Pearl stretched out her hand, with the small forefinger extended, and pointing evidently towards her mother's breast. And beneath, in the mirror of the brook, there was the flower-girdled and sunny image of little Pearl, pointing her small forefinger too.

"Thou strange child, why dost thou not come to me?" exclaimed Hester.

Pearl still pointed with her forefinger; and a frown gathered on her brow; the more impressive from the childish, the almost baby-like aspect of the features that conveyed it. As her mother still kept beckoning to her, and arraying her face in a holiday suit of unaccustomed smiles, the child stamped her foot with a yet more imperious look and gesture. In the brook, again, was the fantastic beauty of the image, with its reflected frown, its pointed finger, and imperious gesture, giving emphasis to the aspect of little Pearl.

"Hasten, Pearl; or I shall be angry with thee!" cried Hester Prynne, who, however inured to such behaviour on the elf-child's part at other seasons, was naturally anxious for a more seemly deportment

"I have a strange notion," said the observant minister, "that this brook is the border between two worlds and that you will never meet your Pearl again. Or is she an elflike spirit? Our childhood tales taught us that elves are forbidden to cross a running stream. Tell her to hurry—this delay has already given a tremble to my nerves."

"Come, dear child!" Hester encouraged her, stretching out both arms. "You are so slow! When have you moved as slowly as this? There is a friend of mine here, who must be your friend as well. From now on, you will have twice as much love as I could give you alone! Leap across the brook and come to us. You can leap like a young deer!"

Pearl, without responding to these sweet expressions, remained on the other side of the brook. She looked at her mother with bright, wild eyes, and then at the minister. Then she looked at them both at once, as if to figure out how they were related to one another. For some inexplicable reason, as Arthur Dimmesdale felt the child's eyes upon him, he hand crept over his heart. The gesture was so habitual that it had become involuntary. After some time, and with an air of great authority, Pearl extended her hand. With her small index figure extended, she pointed toward her mother's breast. Below her, in the mirror of the brook, there was the flower-decorated and sunny image of little Pearl, pointing her index finger too.

"You strange child! Why don't you come to me?" said Hester.

Pearl still pointed, and a frown took shape on her brow. It was all the more impressive for the childish, almost babylike face that conveyed it. Her mother kept beckoning to her, with a face full of unusual smiles. The child stamped her foot with an even more demanding look and gesture. The brook reflected the fantastic beauty of the image, giving the frown and pointed finger and demanding gesture even greater emphasis.

"Hurry, Pearl, or I will be angry with you!" cried Hester Prynne. Though she was accustomed to the behavior of her elflike child, she was naturally anxious for her to act differently just now. "Leap across

now. "Leap across the brook, naughty child, and run hither! Else I must come to thee!"

But Pearl, not a whit startled at her mother's threats, any more than mollified by her entreaties, now suddenly burst into a fit of passion, gesticulating violently and throwing her small figure into the most extravagant contortions. She accompanied this wild outbreak with piercing shrieks, which the woods reverberated on all sides; so that, alone as she was in her childish and unreasonable wrath, it seemed as if a hidden multitude were lending her their sympathy and encouragement. Seen in the brook, once more, was the shadowy wrath of Pearl's image, crowned and girdled with flowers, but stamping its foot, wildly gesticulating, and, in the midst of all, still pointing its small forefinger at Hester's bosom!

"I see what ails the child," whispered Hester to the clergyman, and turning pale in spite of a strong effort to conceal her trouble and annoyance. "Children will not abide any, the slightest, change in the accustomed aspect of things that are daily before their eyes. Pearl misses something which she has always seen me wear!"

"I pray you," answered the minister, "if thou hast any means of pacifying the child, do it forthwith! Save it were the cankered wrath of an old witch, like Mistress Hibbins," added he, attempting to smile. "I know nothing that I would not sooner encounter than this passion in a child. In Pearl's young beauty, as in the wrinkled witch, it has a preternatural effect. Pacify her, if thou lovest me!"

Hester turned again towards Pearl, with a crimson blush upon her cheek, a conscious glance aside at the clergyman, and then a heavy sigh; while, even before she had time to speak, the blush yielded to a deadly pallor.

"Pearl," said she, sadly, "look down at thy feet! There!—before thee!—on the hither side of the brook!"

The child turned her eyes to the point indicated; and there lay the scarlet letter, so close upon the margin of the stream, that the gold embroidery was reflected in it.

"Bring it hither!" said Hester.

"Come thou and take it up!" answered Pearl.

"Was ever such a child!" observed Hester aside to the minister. "O, I have much to tell thee about her. But, in very truth, she is right as regards this hateful token. I must bear its torture yet a little longer,—

the brook, naughty child, and run over here! Otherwise I will cross over to you!"

But Pearl, no more startled by her mother's threats than she was calmed by her pleadings, suddenly burst into a fit of passion. She made violent gestures, twisting her small figure into the strangest shapes. Along with these wild gestures, she made piercing shrieks. The woods echoed all around her. Alone as she was in her childish and unreasonable anger, it seemed as though many hidden voices lent her sympathy and encouragement. Reflected in the brook once more was the shadowy anger of Pearl's image, crowned and encircled with flowers. The image was stamping its foot, gesturing wildly, and—in the midst of it all—still pointing its tiny index finger at Hester's bosom.

"I see what troubles the child," whispered Hester to the clergyman. She turned pale, despite her best efforts to hide her irritation. "Children will not tolerate even the slightest change in the things they are used to seeing every day. Pearl misses something that she has always seen me wear!"

"Please," replied the minister, "if you have any way of calming the child, do it now! Aside from the bitter anger of an old witch like Mistress Hibbins," he added, trying to smile, "I would rather be confronted with anything other than this passion in a child. It has a supernatural effect in Pearl's young beauty, as it does in the wrinkled witch. Calm her, if you love me!"

Hester turned toward Pearl again, blushing and glancing aside at the clergyman. She sighed heavily and, before she could speak, the blush faded. Hester looked deadly pale.

"Pearl," she said sadly, "look down at your feet! There—in front on you—on the other side of the brook!"

The child looked where her mother had indicated. The scarlet letter lay there, so close to the edge of the stream that the gold embroidery was reflected in the water.

"Bring it here!" said Hester.

"You come here and pick it up!" replied Pearl.

"Was there ever a child like this?" Hester asked the minister. "I have so much to tell you about her! But she is right about this hateful symbol. I must bear its torture a little longer—but only a few only a few days longer,—until we shall have left this region, and look back hither as to a land which we have dreamed of. The forest cannot hide it! The mid-ocean shall take it from my hand, and swallow it up for ever!"

With these words, she advanced to the margin of the brook, took up the scarlet letter, and fastened it again into her bosom. Hopefully, but a moment ago, as Hester had spoken of drowning it in the deep sea, there was a sense of inevitable doom upon her, as she thus received back this deadly symbol from the hand of fate. She had flung it into infinite space!—she had drawn an hour's free breath!—and here again was the scarlet misery, glittering on the old spot! So it ever is, whether thus typified or no, that an evil deed invests itself with the character of doom. Hester next gathered up the heavy tresses of her hair, and confined them beneath her cap. As if there were a withering spell in the sad letter, her beauty, the warmth and richness of her womanhood, departed, like fading sunshine; and a gray shadow seemed to fall across her.

When the dreary change was wrought, she extended her hand to Pearl.

"Dost thou know thy mother now, child?" asked she, reproachfully, but with a subdued tone. "Wilt thou come across the brook, and own thy mother, now that she has her shame upon her,—now that she is sad?"

"Yes; now I will!" answered the child, bounding across the brook, and clasping Hester in her arms. "Now thou art my mother indeed! And I am thy little Pearl!"

In a mood of tenderness that was not usual with her, she drew down her mother's head, and kissed her brow and both her cheeks. But then—by a kind of necessity that always impelled this child to alloy whatever comfort she might chance to give with a throb of anguish—Pearl put up her mouth, and kissed the scarlet letter too!

"That was not kind!" said Hester. "When thou hast shown me a little love, thou mockest me!"

"Why doth the minister sit yonder?" asked Pearl.

"He waits to welcome thee," replied her mother. "Come thou, and entreat his blessing! He loves thee, my little Pearl, and loves thy mother too. Wilt thou not love him? Come! he longs to greet thee!"

days longer. When we have left this region, we will look back on it as though it were a dream. The forest cannot hide the scarlet letter, but the ocean will take it from my hand and swallow it up forever!"

With these words, she walked to edge of the brook, picked up the scarlet letter, and fastened it again onto her bosom. Just a moment earlier, Hester had spoken hopefully of drowning the letter in the deep sea. But there was a sense of inevitable doom about her now, as though fate itself had returned the deadly symbol to her. She had thrown it off into the universe! She had breathed free for an hour! And now the scarlet misery was glittering once again, right in its old spot! It's always this way. An evil deed, whether symbolized or not, always takes on the appearance of fate. Hester gathered up the heavy locks of her hair and hid them beneath the cap. Her beauty, the warmth and richness of her womanhood, left her like fading sunshine. A gray shadow seemed to fall on her. It was as though there was a withering spell in the sad letter.

When the change was complete, she extended her hand to Pearl.

"Do you recognize your mother now, child?" she asked. There was a subdued reproach in her voice. "Will you come across the brook and acknowledge your mother, now that she has her shame upon her—now that she is sad?"

"Yes, now I will!" answered the child. She bounded across the brook and wrapped Hester in her arms. "Now you are my mother again, and I am your little Pearl!"

In a tender mood that was unusual for her, she lowered her mother's head and kissed her forehead and both cheeks. But then—as though the child needed to mix a throb of pain into any comfort she might give—Pearl kissed the scarlet letter too.

"That was not nice!" said Hester. "When you have shown me a little love, you mock me!"

"Why is the minister sitting over there?" asked Pearl.

"He's waiting to welcome you," replied her mother. "Come, and ask for his blessing! He loves you, my little Pearl, and he loves your mother too. Won't you love him? Come, he's waiting to greet you."

"Doth he love us?" said Pearl, looking up with acute intelligence into her mother's face. "Will he go back with us, hand in hand, we three together, into the town?"

"Not now, dear child," answered Hester. "But in days to come he will walk hand in hand with us. We will have a home and fireside of our own; and thou shalt sit upon his knee; and he will teach thee many things, and love thee dearly. Thou wilt love him; wilt thou not?"

"And will he always keep his hand over his heart?" inquired Pearl.

"Foolish child, what a question is that!" exclaimed her mother. "Come and ask his blessing!"

But, whether influenced by the jealousy that seems instinctive with every petted child towards a dangerous rival, or from whatever caprice of her freakish nature, Pearl would show no favor to the clergyman. It was only by an exertion of force that her mother brought her up to him, hanging back, and manifesting her reluctance by odd grimaces; of which, ever since her babyhood, she had possessed a singular variety, and could transform her mobile physiognomy into a series of different aspects, with a new mischief in them, each and all. The minister—painfully embarrassed, but hoping that a kiss might prove a talisman to admit him into the child's kindlier regards—bent forward, and impressed one on her brow. Hereupon, Pearl broke from her mother, and, running to the brook, stooped over it, and bathed her forehead, until the unwelcome kiss was quite washed off, and diffused through a long lapse of the gliding water. She then remained apart, silently watching Hester and the clergyman; while they talked together, and made such arrangements as were suggested by their new position, and the purposes soon to be fulfilled.

And now this fateful interview had come to a close. The dell was to be left a solitude among its dark, old trees, which, with their multitudinous tongues, would whisper long of what had passed there, and no mortal be the wiser. And the melancholy brook would add this other tale to the mystery with which its little heart was already overburdened, and whereof it still kept up a murmuring babble, with not a whit more cheerfulness of tone than for ages heretofore.

Original Text

NO FEAR

"Does he love us?" asked Pearl, looking into her mother's face with a sharp intelligence. "Will he go back into the town with us, hand in hand?"

"Not now, my child," answered Hester. "But soon he will walk hand in hand with us. We will have a home and a hearth of our own. You will sit upon his knee, and he will teach you many things and love you dearly. You will love him—won't you?"

"Will he always keep his hand over his heart?" asked Pearl.

"Silly child, what kind of question is that?" exclaimed her mother. "Come here and ask his blessing!"

But Pearl would not show any affection toward the clergyman. Perhaps she was jealous of the attention her mother paid to the minister, as parents' pets often are. Or perhaps it was another of her inexplicable whims. Whatever the reason, Pearl could only be brought over to the minister by force, hanging back and grimacing all the while. Ever since she had been a baby, she'd had an incredible array of grimaces. She could pull her face into many shapes, with a different mischief in each one. The minister was greatly embarrassed but hoped that a kiss might win him entrance into the child's good thoughts. He bent forward and placed one on her forehead—at which Pearl broke free of her mother and ran off to the brook. Stooping over the water, she washed her forehead until the unwelcome kiss was entirely gone, spread throughout the flowing brook. She stood alone, silently watching Hester and the clergyman as the two talked and planned.

And so the fateful encounter came to an end. The dell would be left alone with its dark, old trees, which could safely whisper of what had happened there. No one would ever hear. The melancholy brook would add this tale to the mystery, which it carried in its little heart. It would babble of what had happened on this day, no more cheerful for the addition.

Chapter 20: The Minister in a Maze

As the minister departed, in advance of Hester Prynne and little Pearl, he threw a backward glance; half-expecting that he should discover only some faintly traced features or outline of the mother and the child, slowly fading into the twilight of the woods. So great a vicissitude in his life could not at once be received as real. But there was Hester, clad in her gray robe, still standing beside the tree-trunk, which some blast had overthrown a long antiquity ago, and which time had ever since been covering with moss, so that these two fated ones, with earth's heaviest burden on them, might there sit down together, and find a single hour's rest and solace. And there was Pearl, too, lightly dancing from the margin of the brook,—now that the intrusive third person was gone,—and taking her old place by her mother's side. So the minister had not fallen asleep, and dreamed!

In order to free his mind from this indistinctness and duplicity of impression, which vexed it with a strange disquietude, he recalled and more thoroughly defined the plans which Hester and himself had sketched for their departure. It had been determined between them, that the Old World, with its crowds and cities, offered them a more eligible shelter and concealment than the wilds of New England, or all America, with its alternatives of an Indian wigwam, or the few settlements of Europeans, scattered thinly along the seaboard. Not to speak of the clergyman's health, so inadequate to sustain the hardships of a forest life, his native gifts, his culture, and his entire development would secure him a home only in the midst of civilization and refinement; the higher the state, the more delicately adapted to it the man. In furtherance of this choice, it so happened that a ship lay in the harbour; one of those questionable cruisers, frequent at that day, which, without being absolutely outlaws of the deep, yet roamed over its surface with a remarkable irresponsibility of character. This vessel had recently arrived from the Spanish Main, and, within three days' time, would sail for Bristol. Hester Prynne—whose vocation, as a self-enlisted Sister of Charity, had brought her acquainted with the captain and crew—could take upon herself to secure the passage of two individuals and a child, with all the secrecy which circumstances rendered more than desirable.

Chapter 20: The Minister in a Maze

The minister left before Hester Prynne and little Pearl. As he went, he looked backward, half expecting to see a faint outline of the mother and child fading into twilight of the woods. He could not believe that such a big change was actually real. But there was Hester, dressed in her gray robe, still standing beside the tree trunk. A storm had brought the trunk down many years ago, and moss had grown on it so that one day Hester and the minister could sit together and rest from their heavy burdens. Now Pearl was there, too, dancing lightly away from the brook's edge. When the minister was gone, she had taken her familiar place by her mother's side. The minister had not fallen asleep and dreamed after all!

To free his mind from the hazy impressions that troubled it, he reminded himself of the plans he and Hester had made for their departure. They had decided that Europe, with its crowds and cities, offered them a better home and hiding place than anywhere in America, with its choice between an Indian dwelling and a few settlements along the coast. Also, the minister's health could not endure the hardships of life in the woods. His gifts, his refinement, and his education meant he needed to live in a civilized place— the more civilized, the better. As fate would have it, there was a ship at harbor to help them carry out this plan. It was one of those dubious vessels that were common at that time. Without actually breaking laws, they sailed with remarkable irresponsibility. The ship had recently arrived from Spain and would sail for England in three days. Hester Prynne's self-appointed duties as a Sister of Charity had brought her into contact with the ship's crew and captain. She could therefore book spots on the ship for two adults and a child, with all the secrecy the circumstances required.

The minister had inquired of Hester, with no little interest, the precise time at which the vessel might be expected to depart. It would probably be on the fourth day from the present. "That is most fortunate!" he had then said to himself. Now, why the Reverend Mr. Dimmesdale considered it so very fortunate, we hesitate to reveal. Nevertheless,—to hold nothing back from the reader,—it was because, on the third day from the present, he was to preach the Election Sermon; and, as such an occasion formed an honorable epoch in the life of a New England clergyman, he could not have chanced upon a more suitable mode and time of terminating his professional career. "At least, they shall say of me," thought this exemplary man, "that I leave no public duty unperformed, nor ill performed!" Sad, indeed, that an introspection so profound and acute as this poor minister's should be so miserably deceived! We have had, and may still have, worse things to tell of him; but none, we apprehend, so pitiably weak; no evidence, at once so slight and irrefragable, of a subtle disease, that had long since begun to eat into the real substance of his character. No man, for any considerable period, can wear one face to himself, and another to the multitude, without finally getting bewildered as to which may be the true.

The excitement of Mr. Dimmesdale's feelings, as he returned from his interview with Hester, lent him unaccustomed physical energy, and hurried him townward at a rapid pace. The pathway among the woods seemed wilder, more uncouth with its rude natural obstacles, and less trodden by the foot of man, than he remembered it on his outward journey. But he leaped across the plashy places, thrust himself through the clinging underbrush, climbed the ascent, plunged into the hollow, and overcame, in short, all the difficulties of the track, with an unweariable activity that astonished him. He could not but recall how feebly, and with what frequent pauses for breath, he had toiled over the same ground only two days before. As he drew near the town, he took an impression of change from the series of familiar objects that presented themselves. It seemed not yesterday, not one, nor two, but many days, or even years ago, since he had quitted them. There, indeed, was each former trace of the street, as he remembered it, and all the peculiarities of the houses, with the due multitude of gable-peaks, and a weathercock at every point where his memory suggested one. Not the less, however,

NO FEAR

The minister had asked Hester, with great interest, the exact time at which the ship would sail. It would probably be four days from now. "That's very lucky!" he said to himself. I hesitate to reveal why the Reverend Mr. Dimmesdale thought it so lucky, but, to hold nothing back from the reader, it was because three days from now he was scheduled to preach the Election Sermon, an honor for any New England minister. He couldn't have lucked into a better way and time of ending his career. "At least they will say of me," thought this excellent minister, "that I leave no duty unfulfilled or badly performed!" It's sad that a mind as deep and as sharp as his could be so badly deceived! I've told you worse things about him and may speak of others even worse than those. But nothing could be as sadly weak as this remark. There was no better evidence—slight though it was, it was undeniable—of the subtle disease that had eaten away at his character for many years now. No man can long present one face to himself and another to the public without getting confused about which face is the true one.

The strength of Mr. Dimmesdale's emotions as he returned from his meeting with Hester gave him unusual physical energy. He walked quite quickly toward town. The path through the woods seemed wilder and less worn than he remembered it from his outgoing trip. But he leaped across the puddles, pushed through the underbrush, climbed the hill, and descended again. He overcame every obstacle with a tireless activeness that surprised him. He remembered how weakly, and with what frequent stops to catch his breath, he walked over that same ground only two days before. As he approached the town, it seemed that the familiar objects around him had changed. It felt like he'd been gone not for a day or two, but for many years. True, the streets were exactly as he remembered them, and the details of every house from gable to weathercock just as he recalled. Yet there remained a stubborn sense of change. The same was true of the people he met. They did not look any older or younger. The old men's beards were no whiter, nor could yesterday's crawling baby now walk. Although it was impossible to describe how, the minister had a deep sense that these people had changed.

came this importunately obtrusive sense of change. The same was true as regarded the acquaintances whom he met, and all the well-known shapes of human life, about the little town. They looked neither older nor younger, now; the beards of the aged were no whiter, nor could the creeping babe of yesterday walk on his feet today; it was impossible to describe in what respect they differed from the individuals on whom he had so recently bestowed a parting glance; and yet the minister's deepest sense seemed to inform him of their mutability. A similar impression struck him most remarkably, as he passed under the walls of his own church. The edifice had so very strange, and yet so familiar, an aspect, that Mr. Dimmesdale's mind vibrated between two ideas; either that he had seen it only in a dream hitherto, or that he was merely dreaming about it now.

This phenomenon, in the various shapes which it assumed, indicated no external change, but so sudden and important a change in the spectator of the familiar scene, that the intervening space of a single day had operated on his consciousness like the lapse of years. The minister's own will, and Hester's will, and the fate that grew between them, had wrought this transformation. It was the same town as heretofore; but the same minister returned not from the forest. He might have said to the friends who greeted him,—"I am not the man for whom you take me! I left him yonder in the forest, withdrawn into a secret dell, by a mossy tree-trunk, and near a melancholy brook! Go, seek your minister, and see if his emaciated figure, his thin cheek, his white, heavy, pain-wrinkled brow, be not flung down there like a cast-off garment!" His friends, no doubt, would still have insisted with him,—"Thou art thyself the man!"—but the error would have been their own, not his.

Before Mr. Dimmesdale reached home, his inner man gave him other evidences of a revolution in the sphere of thought and feeling. In truth, nothing short of a total change of dynasty and moral code, in that interior kingdom, was adequate to account for the impulses now communicated to the unfortunate and startled minister. At every step he was incited to do some strange, wild, wicked thing or other, with a sense that it would be at once involuntary and intentional; in spite of himself, yet growing out of a profounder self than that which opposed the impulse. For instance, he met one of his own deacons. The good old man addressed him with the paternal

NO FEAR

Something similar occurred to him as he walked by his church. The building was both familiar and strange. Mr. Dimmesdale could not decide whether he had only seen it in a dream before or whether he was now dreaming.

The town hadn't changed. Rather, there had been a sudden and important change in the viewer of this familiar scene. One day had worked on his mind like the passage of many years. The minister's will, and Hester's will, and the fate that bound them together had created this transformation. It was the same town as before, but not the same minister. He could have said to the friends who greeted him: "I am not the man you think I am! I left him back there in the forest, in a secret dell by a mossy tree trunk, near a melancholy brook! Go look for your minister there, and see if his emaciated body, his thin cheek, and his white brow, wrinkled in pain, aren't all left behind there, cast aside like old rags!" No doubt, his friends would have kept insisting: "You are the man yourself!" But the error would have been theirs, not his.

Before Mr. Dimmesdale reached home, his mind gave him more evidence of a revolution in his thoughts and feelings. Only a total change in his morals could explain the impulses that now startled the minister. At every turn, he was inclined to do something strange, or wild, or wicked—and he had the sense that doing these things would be both unintentional and intentional. He would be acting in spite of himself, yet in agreement with some deeper self. For instance, he met one of the deacons from his church. The good old man addressed Mr. Dimmesdale with the fatherly affection and privilege the deacon's age, character, and position gave him and with the

affection and patriarchal privilege, which his venerable age, his upright and holy character, and his station in the Church, entitled him to use; and, conjoined with this, the deep, almost worshipping respect, which the minister's professional and private claims alike demanded. Never was there a more beautiful example of how the majesty of age and wisdom may comport with the obeisance and respect enjoined upon it, as from a lower social rank and inferior order of endowment, towards a higher. Now, during a conversation of some two or three moments between the Reverend Mr. Dimmesdale and this excellent and hoary-bearded deacon, it was only by the most careful self-control that the former could refrain from uttering certain blasphemous suggestions that rose into his mind, respecting the communion-supper. He absolutely trembled and turned pale as ashes, lest his tongue should wag itself, in utterance of these horrible matters, and plead his own consent for so doing, without his having fairly given it. And, even with this terror in his heart, he could hardly avoid laughing to imagine how the sanctified old patriarchal deacon would have been petrified by his minister's impiety!

Again, another incident of the same nature. Hurrying along the street, the Reverend Mr. Dimmesdale encountered the eldest female member of his church; a most pious and exemplary old dame; poor, widowed, lonely, and with a heart as full of reminiscences about her dead husband and children, and her dead friends of long ago, as a burial-ground is full of storied gravestones. Yet all this, which would else have been such heavy sorrow, was made almost a solemn joy to her devout old soul by religious consolations and the truths of Scripture, wherewith she had fed herself continually for more than thirty years. And, since Mr. Dimmesdale had taken her in charge, the good grandam's chief earthly comfort—which, unless it had been likewise a heavenly comfort, could have been none at all—was to meet her pastor, whether casually, or of set purpose, and be refreshed with a word of warm, fragrant, Heaven-breathing Gospel truth from his beloved lips into her dulled, but rapturously attentive ear. But, on this occasion, up to the moment of putting his lips to the old woman's ear, Mr. Dimmesdale, as the great enemy of souls would have it, could recall no text of Scripture, nor aught else, except a brief, pithy, and, as it then appeared to him, unanswerable argument against the immortality of the human soul. The instilment thereof into her mind

graciousness and respect the minister's stature demanded. It was a beautiful example of how wise old age can pay its respects to a man of superior accomplishments. The two men talked for only a few moments, during which Mr. Dimmesdale could barely keep himself from shouting blasphemies at this excellent and gray-haired deacon. He trembled and turned pale, afraid that his tongue would speak his thoughts aloud and claim that he had consented to the speech. But even with this terror in his heart, he could hardly keep from laughing at the thought of how the holy old deacon would react to his minister's crude outburst.

And similar things kept happening. As he hurried along the street, the Reverend Mr. Dimmesdale ran into the eldest member of his church. She was a holy old woman, a poor lonely widow with a heart full of memories about her dead husband, her children, and friends of long ago. She could have been deeply sad, but her devotion turned her pain into solemn joy. For thirty years now, she had fed her soul with religious thoughts and the truths of Scripture. Since Mr. Dimmesdale had become her minister, the good old woman's chief comfort was to see him. Whenever they met, she felt refreshed by the warm words of the gospel that flowed from his lips into her attentive (though slightly deaf) ears. But this time, as he leaned in to speak into the old woman's ear, Mr. Dimmesdale could recall no word of Scripture, nor anything else—except a brief and seemingly unanswerable argument against life after death. If he had spoken this, the old woman would probably have dropped down dead, as though he'd poured poison in her ear. What he actually whispered, the minister could never recall. Perhaps he said something confusing that didn't make any real impression. Yet as the minister looked back at her, he saw an expression of holy joy and gratitude that seemed to shine like Heaven itself on her pale, wrinkled face.

would probably have caused this aged sister to drop down dead, at once, as by the effect of an intensely poisonous infusion. What he really did whisper, the minister could never afterwards recollect. There was, perhaps, a fortunate disorder in his utterance, which failed to impart any distinct idea to the good widow's comprehension, or which Providence interpreted after a method of its own. Assuredly, as the minister looked back, he beheld an expression of divine gratitude and ecstasy that seemed like the shine of the celestial city on her face, so wrinkled and ashy pale.

Again, a third instance. After parting from the old church-member, he met the youngest sister of them all. It was a maiden newly won—and won by the Reverend Mr. Dimmesdale's own sermon, on the Sabbath after his vigil—to barter the transitory pleasures of the world for the heavenly hope, that was to assume brighter substance as life grew dark around her, and which would gild the utter gloom with final glory. She was fair and pure as a lily that had bloomed in Paradise. The minister knew well that he was himself enshrined within the stainless sanctity of her heart, which hung its snowy curtains about his image, imparting to religion the warmth of love, and to love a religious purity. Satan, that afternoon, had surely led the poor young girl away from her mother's side, and thrown her into the pathway of this sorely tempted, or—shall we not rather say?—this lost and desperate man. As she drew nigh, the arch-fiend whispered him to condense into small compass and drop into her tender bosom a germ of evil that would be sure to blossom darkly soon, and bear black fruit betimes. Such was his sense of power over this virgin soul, trusting him as she did, that the minister felt potent to blight all the field of innocence with but one wicked look, and develop all its opposite with but a word. So—with a mightier struggle than he had yet sustained—he held his Geneva cloak before his face, and hurried onward, making no sign of recognition, and leaving the young sister to digest his rudeness as she might. She ransacked her conscience,—which was full of harmless little matters, like her pocket or her work-bag,—and took herself to task, poor thing, for a thousand imaginary faults; and went about her household duties with swollen eyelids the next morning.

Before the minister had time to celebrate his victory over this last temptation, he was conscious of another impulse, more ludicrous,

NO FEAR

And this happened a third time. After parting from that aged church member, he met the youngest of them all. It was a young woman newly claimed for God's kingdom, won over by Mr. Dimmesdale himself. The morning after he stood on the platform, the minister had convinced her to trade the fleeting pleasures of the world for the hope of an everlasting life to come. She was as lovely and as pure as a lily that had bloomed in Paradise. The minister knew she had enshrined him in her heart, where she hung pure white curtains around his image—giving religion the warmth of love, and love the purity of religion. That afternoon, Satan had surely led this poor young girl away from her mother and put her in the path of this tempted, lost, and desperate man. As she drew close, the Devil whispered to him that he should drop an evil seed in her heart and watch it blossom and bear black fruit. The minister felt such power over this pure soul, who trusted him so much. He could destroy her innocence with just one wicked look and develop her lust with only a word. After a great struggle, he covered his face with his cloak and hurried past the woman without greeting her, leaving her to interpret his rudeness however she wanted. She rifled through her conscience, which was as full of little nothings as her pocket. She took herself to task—poor thing!—for a thousand imaginary faults and cried herself to sleep that night.

Before the minister had time to celebrate his victory over this last temptation, he became aware of another impulse. It was more

and almost as horrible. It was,—we blush to tell it,—it was to stop short in the road, and teach some wicked words to a knot of little Puritan children who were playing there, and had but just begun to talk. Denying himself this freak, as unworthy of his cloth, he met a drunken seaman, one of the ship's crew from the Spanish Main. And, here, since he had so valiantly forborne all other wickedness, poor Mr. Dimmesdale longed, at least, to shake hands with the tarry blackguard, and recreate himself with a few improper jests, such as dissolute sailors so abound with, and a volley of good, round, solid, satisfactory, and Heaven-defying oaths! It was not so much a better principle, as partly his natural good taste, and still more his buck-ramed habit of clerical decorum, that carried him safely through the latter crisis.

"What is it that haunts and tempts me thus?" cried the minister to himself, at length, pausing in the street, and striking his hand against his forehead. "Am I mad? or am I given over utterly to the fiend? Did I make a contract with him in the forest, and sign it with my blood? And does he now summon me to its fulfilment, by suggesting the performance of every wickedness which his most foul imagination can conceive?"

At the moment when the Reverend Mr. Dimmesdale thus communed with himself, and struck his forehead with his hand, old Mistress Hibbins, the reputed witch-lady, is said to have been passing by. She made a very grand appearance; having on a high head-dress, a rich gown of velvet, and a ruff done up with the famous yellow starch, of which Ann Turner, her especial friend, had taught her the secret, before this last good lady had been hanged for Sir Thomas Overbury's murder. Whether the witch had read the minister's thoughts, or no, she came to a full stop, looked shrewdly into his face, smiled craftily, and—though little given to converse with clergymen—began a conversation.

"So, reverend Sir, you have made a visit into the forest," observed the witch-lady, nodding her high head-dress at him. "The next time, I pray you to allow me only a fair warning, and I shall be proud to bear you company. Without taking overmuch upon myself, my good word will go far towards gaining any strange gentleman a fair reception from yonder potentate you wot of!"

NO FEAR

absurd than what had come before and almost as horrible. It was (I blush to describe it) to teach some wicked words to a cluster of little Puritan children who were playing in the road. These kids had only just learned to talk. Restraining himself from this, he met a drunken sailor, a crewman from the Spanish ship. Since he had so courageously resisted all other wickedness, Mr. Dimmesdale longed to at least shake hands with the man. He would enjoy a few off-color jokes, which sailors are so full of, and a barrage of good, solid, anti-God curses! It was not exactly his better principles that kept him from doing so, as much as his natural good taste and habitual decorum.

"What is it that haunts and tempts me like this?" cried the minister to himself. He paused in the street and hit his hand against his forehead. "Have I gone crazy? Or have I given my soul to the Devil? Did I make a deal with him in the forest and sign it with my blood? And is he now demanding I hold up my end of the bargain by suggesting as many evil deeds as his hellish imagination can dream up?

At the moment when the Reverend Mr. Dimmesdale was speaking to himself in this way, and striking his forehead with his hand, it is said that old Mistress Hibbins, the rumored witch, passed by. She wore a large headdress, a rich velvet gown, and a heavily starched ruff. It was a special starch: Her friend Anne Turner taught her the trick before the good lady had been hanged for Sir Thomas Overbury's murder. Maybe the witch had read the minister's thoughts and maybe she hadn't, but either way she stopped, looked into his face, and smiled craftily. Though she didn't often speak to clergymen, she began a conversation.

"So, reverend sir, you have visited the forest," observed the witch-lady, nodding her high headdress at him. "The next time you go, let me know and I will be proud to keep you company. I don't mean to brag, but a good word from me will help you get in good with that powerful man of whom you know."

"I profess, madam," answered the clergyman, with a grave obeisance, such as the lady's rank demanded, and his own good-breeding made imperative,—"I profess, on my conscience and character, that I am utterly bewildered as touching the purport of your words! I went not into the forest to seek a potentate; neither do I, at any future time, design a visit thither, with a view to gaining the favor of such personage. My one sufficient object was to greet that pious friend of mine, the Apostle Eliot, and rejoice with him over the many precious souls he hath won from heathendom!"

"Ha, ha, ha!" cackled the old witch-lady, still nodding her high head-dress at the minister. "Well, well, we must needs talk thus in the daytime! You carry it off like an old hand! But at midnight, and in the forest, we shall have other talk together!"

She passed on with her aged stateliness, but often turning back her head and smiling at him, like one willing to recognize a secret intimacy of connection.

"Have I then sold myself," thought the minister, "to the fiend whom, if men say true, this yellow-starched and velveted old hag has chosen for her prince and master!"

The wretched minister! He had made a bargain very like it! Tempted by a dream of happiness, he had yielded himself with deliberate choice, as he had never done before, to what he knew was deadly sin. And the infectious poison of that sin had been thus rapidly diffused throughout his moral system. It had stupefied all blessed impulses, and awakened into vivid life the whole brotherhood of bad ones. Scorn, bitterness, unprovoked malignity, gratuitous desire of ill, ridicule of whatever was good and holy, all awoke, to tempt, even while they frightened him. And his encounter with old Mistress Hibbins, if it were a real incident, did but show his sympathy and fellowship with wicked mortals and the world of perverted spirits.

He had by this time reached his dwelling, on the edge of the burial-ground, and, hastening up the stairs, took refuge in his study. The minister was glad to have reached this shelter, without first betraying himself to the world by any of those strange and wicked eccentricities to which he had been continually impelled while passing through the streets. He entered the accustomed room, and looked around him on its books, its windows, its fireplace, and the

"Honestly, madam," answered the clergyman, with the serious bow that the lady's position and his own good breeding demanded, "on my conscience and my character, I am completely confused about the meaning of your words! I did not go the forest seeking to visit any man of power, nor do I intend to do so. My one and only purpose was to meet that holy friend of mine, the Apostle Eliot, and celebrate the many precious souls he has won over to the church!"

The old witch-lady cackled and nodded her headdress at the minister. "Well, well—we must say such things in the day time! You carry it off like an old hand! But at midnight, in the forest, we will have to talk honestly together!"

She walked off with the stateliness of her age, but often looked back and smiled at him, like one who acknowledges a secret, intimate connection.

"So have I sold myself," thought the minister, "to the Devil who they say this old woman has chosen for her lord and master?"

The miserable minister! He had made a very similar bargain! Tempted by a dream of happiness, he had deliberately given in to deadly sin, as he had never done before. And the poison of that sin had rapidly infected his entire moral system. It had deadened all of his holy impulses and awakened a whole host of bad ones. He was tempted and frightened by scorn, bitterness, malice, and a desire to ridicule everything good and holy. And his encounter with old Mistress Hibbins—if it happened in the first place—showed his sympathy and friendship with wicked mortals and the world of strange spirits.

By this time, he had reached his home by the edge of the burial ground. Hurrying up the stairs, he took shelter in his study. The minister was glad he'd made it home without revealing himself to the world with any of the strange and wicked actions he'd felt compelled to take. He entered the familiar room and looked around him at its books, its windows, its fireplace, and the tapestries that hung from its walls. The same sense of strangeness that haunted him

tapestried comfort of the walls, with the same perception of strangeness that had haunted him throughout his walk from the forest-dell into the town, and thitherward. Here he had studied and written; here, gone through fast and vigil, and come forth half alive; here, striven to pray; here, borne a hundred thousand agonies! There was the Bible, in its rich old Hebrew, with Moses and the Prophets speaking to him, and God's voice through all!

There, on the table, with the inky pen beside it, was an unfinished sermon, with a sentence broken in the midst, where his thoughts had ceased to gush out upon the page two days before. He knew that it was himself, the thin and white-cheeked minister, who had done and suffered these things, and written thus far into the Election Sermon! But he seemed to stand apart, and eye this former self with scornful, pitying, but half-envious curiosity. That self was gone! Another man had returned out of the forest; a wiser one; with a knowledge of hidden mysteries which the simplicity of the former never could have reached. A bitter kind of knowledge that!

While occupied with these reflections, a knock came at the door of the study, and the minister said, "Come in!"—not wholly devoid of an idea that he might behold an evil spirit. And so he did! It was old Roger Chillingworth that entered. The minister stood, white and speechless, with one hand on the Hebrew Scriptures, and the other spread upon his breast.

"Welcome home, reverend Sir!" said the physician. "And how found you that godly man, the Apostle Eliot? But methinks, dear Sir, you look pale; as if the travel through the wilderness had been too sore for you. Will not my aid be requisite to put you in heart and strength to preach your Election Sermon?"

"Nay, I think not so," rejoined the Reverend Mr. Dimmesdale. "My journey, and the sight of the holy Apostle yonder, and the free air which I have breathed, have done me good, after so long confinement in my study. I think to need no more of your drugs, my kind physician, good though they be, and administered by a friendly hand."

All this time, Roger Chillingworth was looking at the minister with the grave and intent regard of a physician towards his patient. But, in spite of this outward show, the latter was almost convinced of the old man's knowledge, or, at least, his confident suspicion,

throughout his walk from the forest had followed him home. He had studied and written here, fasted and tried to pray here, endured a hundred thousand agonies here! There was the Bible, in its rich old Hebrew, with Moses and the prophets speaking to him and God's voice through it all.

There on the table, with the pen beside it, was an unfinished sermon. He had stopped writing it two days ago, when his thoughts had broken off in the middle of a sentence. He knew that he himself, the thin and white-cheeked minister, who had done and suffered these things, and had written this much of the Election Sermon! But he seemed to stand apart from this former self, looking at him with a mix of scornful pity and half-envious curiosity. That old self was gone. Another man had returned from the forest, a wiser one. This new man had knowledge of hidden mysteries his former, simpler self could never have understood. It was truly a bitter knowledge!

While he was caught up in these thoughts, there was a knock on the door of the study. The minister said, "Come in!" half-thinking an evil spirit would enter. And then one did! It was old Roger Chillingworth. The minister stood there, pale and speechless, with one hand on the Holy Scriptures and the other on his chest.

"Welcome home, reverend sir," said the physician. "How was that holy man, the apostle Eliot? Dear sir, I think you look pale, as though travel through the wilderness has exhausted you. Won't you need my help to give you the spirit and strength to preach the Election Sermon?"

"No, I don't think so," replied the Reverend Mr. Dimmesdale. "My journey, my conversation with the holy Apostle, and the fresh air have all done me good, after being cooped up in my study for so long. I don't think I'll need any more of your drugs, my kind doctor, though they are good indeed—and dispensed by a friendly hand."

All the while, Roger Chillingworth looked at the minister with the serious intensity of a physician examining his patient. But in spite of this show, the minister was nearly certain that the old man knew—or at least strongly suspected—that he had spoken with

with respect to his own interview with Hester Prynne. The physician knew, then, that, in the minister's regard, he was no longer a trusted friend, but his bitterest enemy. So much being known, it would appear natural that a part of it should be expressed. It is singular, however, how long a time often passes before words embody things; and with what security two persons, who choose to avoid a certain subject, may approach its very verge, and retire without disturbing it. Thus, the minister felt no apprehension that Roger Chillingworth would touch, in express words, upon the real position which they sustained towards one another. Yet did the physician, in his dark way, creep frightfully near the secret.

"Were it not better," said he, "that you use my poor skill to-night? Verily, dear Sir, we must take pains to make you strong and vigorous for this occasion of the Election discourse. The people look for great things from you; apprehending that another year may come about, and find their pastor gone."

"Yea, to another world," replied the minister, with pious resignation. "Heaven grant it be a better one; for, in good sooth, I hardly think to tarry with my flock through the flitting seasons of another year! But, touching your medicine, kind Sir, in my present frame of body I need it not."

"I joy to hear it," answered the physician. "It may be that my remedies, so long administered in vain, begin now to take due effect. Happy man were I, and well deserving of New England's gratitude, could I achieve this cure!"

"I thank you from my heart, most watchful friend," said the Reverend Mr. Dimmesdale, with a solemn smile. "I thank you, and can but requite your good deeds with my prayers."

"A good man's prayers are golden recompense!" rejoined old Roger Chillingworth, as he took his leave. "Yea, they are the current gold coin of the New Jerusalem, with the King's own mint-mark on them!"

Left alone, the minister summoned a servant of the house, and requested food, which, being set before him, he ate with ravenous appetite. Then, flinging the already written pages of the Election Sermon into the fire, he forthwith began another, which he wrote with such an impulsive flow of thought and emotion, that he fancied himself inspired; and only wondered that Heaven should see fit to

Hester Prynne. The doctor knew that the minister no longer thought of him as a trusted friend but rather as a bitter enemy. It would seem natural that they'd talk about this change. But it's one of those interesting things—a long time can pass before you say aloud what you're both thinking. Two people who choose to avoid a certain subject may approach the very edge of it and then veer away. And so the minister was not concerned that Roger Chillingworth would say anything to hint at their real relationship to one another. Yet the doctor, in his dark way, came dreadfully close to the secret.

"Wouldn't it be better," he said, "for you to use my poor skills tonight? Dear sir, we must be sure to make you strong for the day of the Election Sermon. The people expect great things from you, since they know you might be gone next year."

"Yes, to another world," the minister replied with pious resignation. "May Heaven make it a better one! Truly, I don't expect that I will remain with my parishioners for another year! But, as for your medicine, kind sir, at the moment I do not need it."

"It brings me joy to hear it," replied the doctor. "Perhaps my remedies, which seemed to be in vain, have finally begun to take effect. I would be a happy man, and well deserving of New England's gratitude, if I could cure you!"

"Thanks from the bottom of my heart, my watchful friend," said the Reverend Mr. Dimmesdale with a solemn smile. "I thank you and can only repay your good deeds with my prayers."

"A good man's prayers are golden payment!" replied old Roger Chillingworth, as he took his leave. "Yes, they are the true currency of Heaven, with God's own stamp on them!"

Left to himself, the minister summoned a servant and asked for food. When it was brought to him, he ate ravenously. Then, throwing the already-written pages of his Election Sermon into the fire, he immediately began another, writing with such impulsive thought and emotion that he imagined himself to be inspired. He was amazed that Heaven could see fit to play the great music of prophecy on such a sin-

transmit the grand and solemn music of its oracles through so foul an organ-pipe as he. However, leaving that mystery to solve itself, or go unsolved for ever, he drove his task onward, with earnest haste and ecstasy. Thus the night fled away, as if it were a winged steed, and he careering on it; morning came, and peeped blushing through the curtains; and at last sunrise threw a golden beam into the study, and laid it right across the minister's bedazzled eyes. There he was, with the pen still between his fingers, and a vast, immeasurable tract of written space behind him!

ful instrument as him. Leaving that mystery to solve itself or remain forever unsolved, he kept on writing with earnest and ecstatic speed. And so the night flew by, as though it were a winged horse and he riding it. Morning came and peeped through the curtains. And then sunrise threw a golden beam into the study, laying it right across the minister's dazzled eyes. There he sat, with the pen still in his hand, and many, many pages in front of him!

Chapter 21: The New England Holiday

Betimes in the morning of the day on which the new Governor was to receive his office at the hands of the people, Hester Prynne and little Pearl came into the market-place. It was already thronged with the craftsmen and other plebeian inhabitants of the town, in considerable numbers; among whom, likewise, were many rough figures, whose attire of deer-skins marked them as belonging to some of the forest settlements, which surrounded the little metropolis of the colony.

On this public holiday, as on all other occasions, for seven years past, Hester was clad in a garment of coarse gray cloth. Not more by its hue than by some indescribable peculiarity in its fashion, it had the effect of making her fade personally out of sight and outline; while, again, the scarlet letter brought her back from this twilight indistinctness, and revealed her under the moral aspect of its own illumination. Her face, so long familiar to the townspeople, showed the marble quietude which they were accustomed to behold there. It was like a mask; or rather, like the frozen calmness of a dead woman's features; owing this dreary resemblance to the fact that Hester was actually dead, in respect to any claim of sympathy, and had departed out of the world with which she still seemed to mingle.

It might be, on this one day, that there was an expression unseen before, nor, indeed, vivid enough to be detected now; unless some preternaturally gifted observer should have first read the heart, and have afterwards sought a corresponding development in the countenance and mien. Such a spiritual seer might have conceived, that, after sustaining the gaze of the multitude through seven miserable years as a necessity, a penance, and something which it was a stern religion to endure, she now, for one last time more, encountered it freely and voluntarily, in order to convert what had so long been agony into a kind of triumph. "Look your last on the scarlet letter and its wearer!"—the people's victim and life-long bond-slave, as they fancied her, might say to them. "Yet a little while, and she will be beyond your reach! A few hours longer, and the deep, mysterious ocean will quench and hide for ever the symbol which ye have caused to burn upon her bosom!" Nor were it an inconsistency too improbable to be assigned to human nature, should we

Chapter 21: The New England Holiday

On the morning of the new Governor's inauguration, Hester Prynne and little Pearl entered the marketplace. It was already full of craftsmen and other common townspeople. There were a great many of them and many rougher figures too: people wearing the deerskin garments common in the forest settlements that surrounded the town.

On this public holiday, as on every day for the last seven years, Hester wore a garment of coarse gray cloth. Its color and its cut combined to make her fade from sight, until the scarlet letter brought her back into focus, revealing her in the light of its own moral judgment. Her face, which the townspeople knew well, showed the stony self-control they were used to seeing there. It was like a mask—or rather, like the frozen calm of a dead woman's face. The similarity stemmed from the fact that, as far as the town was concerned, Hester was as good as dead. She had left the world in which she still seemed to walk.

Perhaps, on this day, there was an expression on Hester's face that hadn't been seen there before. It was too subtle to be detected— unless a psychic could have read Hester's heart, then looked for a similar feeling in her face. Such a psychic might have sensed that Hester had endured the gaze of the crowd for several miserable years because she had to, because it was a penance, and because her religion demanded it—and now she was enduring it freely and voluntarily, for one last time. She was converting what had been an agony into a kind of triumph. "Take your last look at the scarlet letter and its wearer!" Hester, the public's victim and slave might say. "Just a little longer, and she will be beyond your reach! A few more hours and the deep, mysterious ocean will drown the symbol you have made to burn on her bosom!" And it would not be inconsistent with human nature to suppose that Hester felt some regret, too, at the very moment when she was about to be freed from the pain that had become such a part of her. She might feel a great desire to draw a

suppose a feeling of regret in Hester's mind, at the moment when she was about to win her freedom from the pain which had been thus deeply incorporated with her being. Might there not be an irresistible desire to quaff a last, long, breathless draught of the cup of wormwood and aloes, with which nearly all her years of womanhood had been perpetually flavored? The wine of life, henceforth to be presented to her lips, must be indeed rich, delicious, and exhilarating, in its chased and golden beaker; or else leave an inevitable and weary languor, after the lees of bitterness wherewith she had been drugged, as with a cordial of intensest potency.

Pearl was decked out with airy gayety. It would have been impossible to guess that this bright and sunny apparition owed its existence to the shape of gloomy gray; or that a fancy, at once so gorgeous and so delicate as must have been requisite to contrive the child's apparel, was the same that had achieved a task perhaps more difficult, in imparting so distinct a peculiarity to Hester's simple robe. The dress, so proper was it to little Pearl, seemed an effluence, or inevitable development and outward manifestation of her character, no more to be separated from her than the many-hued brilliancy from a butterfly's wing, or the painted glory from the leaf of a bright flower. As with these, so with the child; her garb was all of one idea with her nature. On this eventful day, moreover, there was a certain singular inquietude and excitement in her mood, resembling nothing so much as the shimmer of a diamond, that sparkles and flashes with the varied throbbings of the breast on which it is displayed. Children have always a sympathy in the agitations of those connected with them; always, especially, a sense of any trouble or impending revolution, of whatever kind, in domestic circumstances; and therefore Pearl, who was the gem on her mother's unquiet bosom, betrayed, by the very dance of her spirits, the emotions which none could detect in the marble passiveness of Hester's brow.

This effervescence made her flit with a bird-like movement, rather than walk by her mother's side. She broke continually into shouts of a wild, inarticulate, and sometimes piercing music. When they reached the market-place, she became still more restless, on perceiving the stir and bustle that enlivened the spot; for it was usually more like the broad and lonesome green before a village meeting-house, than the centre of a town's business.

last, long drink from the bitter cup that had flavored all the years of her adulthood. The wine of life she would drink from now on would be rich, delicious, and thrilling—or else leave her weary, after the intensity of the bitter drink she had drunk for so long.

Pearl was dressed in light and happy clothes. It would have been impossible to guess that this bright, sunny creature owed her existence to that gray, gloomy woman. Equally impossible to guess was that the imagination that had dreamed up Pearl's gorgeous and delicate outfit was the same that had achieved a possibly more difficult task: giving such a distinct peculiarity to Hester's simple robe. The dress suited little Pearl so well that it seemed like an extension of her character, as difficult to separate from her essence as the colors from a butterfly's wing or the leaf from a flower. Pearl's dress was one with her nature. And on this eventful day, there was a certain uneasiness and excitement in her mood. It was like the shimmer of a diamond that sparkles and flashes along with the throbs of the breast on which it is displayed. Children always have a sense of the upheavals that concern them: They are especially sensitive to any trouble or coming change in their home life. And so Pearl, who was the gem on her mother's uneasy bosom, betrayed in her sparkling and flickering spirits emotions that no one could see on the marble stillness of Hester's face.

Pearl's bubbliness made her move like a bird, flitting along rather than walking by her mother's side. She kept breaking into shouts of wild, inarticulate, and sometimes piercing music. When they reached the marketplace, she became even more restless, sensing the energy of the crowd. The spot was usually like a broad, lonely lawn in front of a meetinghouse. Today it was the center of the town's business.

"Why, what is this, mother?" cried she. "Wherefore have all the people left their work to-day? Is it a play-day for the whole world? See, there is the blacksmith! He has washed his sooty face, and put on his Sabbath-day clothes, and looks, as if he would gladly be merry, if any kind body would only teach him how! And there is Master Brackett, the old jailer, nodding and smiling at me. Why does he do so, mother?"

"He remembers thee a little babe, my child," answered Hester.

"He should not nod and smile at me, for all that,—the black, grim, ugly-eyed old man!" said Pearl. "He may nod at thee if he will; for thou art clad in gray, and wearest the scarlet letter. But, see, mother, how many faces of strange people, and Indians among them, and sailors! What have they all come to do here in the market-place?"

"They wait to see the procession pass," said Hester. "For the Governor and the magistrates are to go by, and the ministers, and all the great people and good people, with the music, and the soldiers marching before them."

"And will the minister be there?" asked Pearl. "And will he hold out both his hands to me, as when thou ledst me to him from the brook-side?"

"He will be there, child," answered her mother. "But he will not greet thee to-day; nor must thou greet him."

"What a strange, sad man is he!" said the child, as if speaking partly to herself. "In the dark night-time, he calls us to him, and holds thy hand and mine, as when we stood with him on the scaffold yonder! And in the deep forest, where only the old trees can hear, and the strip of sky see it, he talks with thee, sitting on a heap of moss! And he kisses my forehead, too, so that the little brook would hardly wash it off! But here in the sunny day, and among all the people, he knows us not; nor must we know him! A strange, sad man is he, with his hand always over his heart!"

"Be quiet, Pearl! Thou understandest not these things," said her mother. "Think not now of the minister, but look about thee, and see how cheery is every body's face to-day. The children have come from their schools, and the grown people from their workshops and their fields, on purpose to be happy. For, to-day, a new man is beginning to rule over them; and so—as has been the custom of mankind ever since a nation was first gathered—they make merry

NO FEAR

"Why, what's going on, mother?" Pearl cried. "Why have all these people left work today? Is it a playday for the whole world? Look, there's the blacksmith! He has washed his dirty face and put on his Sunday best. He looks as though he would be jolly, if someone could teach him how! And there's Master Brackett, the old jailer, nodding and smiling at me. Why is he doing that, mother?"

"He remembers you as a little baby, my child," answered Hester.

"He shouldn't nod and smile at me, the mean, grim, ugly-eyed old man!" said Pearl. "He can nod at you, if he likes, for you are dressed in gray and wearing the scarlet letter. But see, mother, how many strange faces there are: even Indians and sailors! What are they all doing here, in the marketplace?"

"They are waiting to see the procession," said Hester. "The Governor and the magistrates will pass by, and the ministers and all the great people and good people, with the band and the soldiers marching ahead of them."

"And will the minister be there?" asked Pearl. "And will he hold out his hands to me, as he did when you led me to him in the forest?"

"He will be there, child," answered her mother, "but he will not greet you today. And you must not greet him."

"What a strange, sad man he is!" said the child, as though speaking half to herself. "At night he calls us to him, and holds our hands, like that time when we stood on that platform over there! And in the deep forest, where only the old trees can hear and the strip of sky can see, he sits on a heap of moss and talks with you! And he kisses my forehead, too, so that the little brook would hardly wash it off! But here, in the sunny day and among all the people, he doesn't know us—and we can't know him! A strange, sad man he is, with his hand always over his heart!"

"Be quiet, Pearl—you do not understand these things," said her mother. "Do not think of the minister, but look around you and see how cheerful everyone's face is today. The children have left their schools. The adults have left their workshops and fields. They have come here to be happy because a new man is beginning to rule over them today. So they make merry and rejoice, as if the coming year will be a good and golden one!"

Modern Translation

363

and rejoice; as if a good and golden year were at length to pass over the poor old world!"

It was as Hester said, in regard to the unwonted jollity that brightened the faces of the people. Into this festal season of the year—as it already was, and continued to be during the greater part of two centuries—the Puritans compressed whatever mirth and public joy they deemed allowable to human infirmity; thereby so far dispelling the customary cloud, that, for the space of a single holiday, they appeared scarcely more grave than most other communities at a period of general affliction.

But we perhaps exaggerate the gray or sable tinge, which undoubtedly characterized the mood and manners of the age. The persons now in the market-place of Boston had not been born to an inheritance of Puritanic gloom. They were native Englishmen, whose fathers had lived in the sunny richness of the Elizabethan epoch; a time when the life of England, viewed as one great mass, would appear to have been as stately, magnificent, and joyous, as the world has ever witnessed. Had they followed their hereditary taste, the New England settlers would have illustrated all events of public importance by bonfires, banquets, pageantries, and processions. Nor would it have been impracticable, in the observance of majestic ceremonies, to combine mirthful recreation with solemnity, and give, as it were, a grotesque and brilliant embroidery to the great robe of state, which a nation, at such festivals, puts on. There was some shadow of an attempt of this kind in the mode of celebrating the day on which the political year of the colony commenced. The dim reflection of a remembered splendor, a colorless and manifold diluted repetition of what they had beheld in proud old London,— we will not say at a royal coronation, but at a Lord Mayor's show,— might be traced in the customs which our forefathers instituted, with reference to the annual installation of magistrates. The fathers and founders of the commonwealth—the statesman, the priest, and the soldier—deemed it a duty then to assume the outward state and majesty, which, in accordance with antique style, was looked upon as the proper garb of public or social eminence. All came forth, to move in procession before the people's eye, and thus impart a needed dignity to the single framework of a government so newly constructed.

NO FEAR

The scene was as Hester described it: The faces of the people were unusually bright and jolly. The Puritans compressed the small amount of permitted joy and happiness into the holiday season, which this was. On those days, the usual cloud was so completely dispelled that for one day the Puritans seemed no more serious than a normal community faced with a plague.

And then again, perhaps I'm exaggerating the darkness of the moods and manners of the day. The people who filled Boston's marketplace were not born to inherit the Puritan gloom. They were native Englishmen, whose fathers had lived in the sunny richness of Queen Elizabeth's reign. At that time, the life of England, viewed as a whole, seems to have been as grand, magnificent, and joyous as anything the world has ever witnessed. Had they followed in the steps of their ancestors, the New England settlers would have celebrated all events of public importance with bonfires, banquets, pageants, and processions. And it would have been possible, in performing these ceremonies, to combine joyful play with solemnity and give an eccentric, brilliant embroidery to the great robe of state that a nation puts on at such festivals. There was a hint of an attempt at this playfulness in the celebration of political inaugurations. A dim reflection of a half-remembered splendor, a gray and diluted version of what these settlers had seen in proud old London, could be observed in our forefathers' celebration of the annual installation of magistrates. The leaders of the community—politician, priest, and soldier—felt it was their duty to put on the older style of dress. They all moved in a procession before the eyes of the people, giving a needed dignity to a government so recently formed.

Then, too, the people were countenanced, if not encouraged, in relaxing the severe and close application to their various modes of rugged industry, which, at all other times, seemed of the same piece and material with their religion. Here, it is true, were none of the appliances which popular merriment would so readily have found in the England of Elizabeth's time, or that of James;—no rude shows of a theatrical kind; no minstrel with his harp and legendary ballad, nor gleeman, with an ape dancing to his music; no juggler, with his tricks of mimic witchcraft; no Merry Andrew, to stir up the multitude with jests, perhaps hundreds of years old, but still effective, by their appeals to the very broadest sources of mirthful sympathy. All such professors of the several branches of jocularity would have been sternly repressed, not only by the rigid discipline of law, but by the general sentiment which gives law its vitality. Not the less, however, the great, honest face of the people smiled, grimly, perhaps, but widely too. Nor were sports wanting, such as the colonists had witnessed, and shared in, long ago, at the country fairs and on the village-greens of England; and which it was thought well to keep alive on this new soil, for the sake of the courage and manliness that were essential in them. Wrestling-matches, in the differing fashions of Cornwall and Devonshire, were seen here and there about the market-place; in one corner, there was a friendly bout at quarter-staff; and—what attracted most interest of all—on the platform of the pillory, already so noted in our pages, two masters of defence were commencing an exhibition with the buckler and broadsword. But, much to the disappointment of the crowd, this latter business was broken off by the interposition of the town beadle, who had no idea of permitting the majesty of the law to be violated by such an abuse of one of its consecrated places.

It may not be too much to affirm, on the whole, (the people being then in the first stages of joyless deportment, and the offspring of sires who had known how to be merry, in their day,) that they would compare favorably, in point of holiday keeping, with their descendants, even at so long an interval as ourselves. Their immediate posterity, the generation next to the early emigrants, wore the blackest shade of Puritanism, and so darkened the national visage with it, that all the subsequent years have not sufficed to clear it up. We have yet to learn again the forgotten art of gayety.

NO FEAR

And the people were allowed, if not exactly encouraged, to relax the severe discipline of their work ethic, which so often seemed to be the same thing as their religion. True, there were none of the elements a public celebration would have had in Elizabethan England: no crude theatrical shows, no ballad-singing minstrel, no musician and dancing ape, no juggler, and no jester with his timeworn, well-loved jests. All such professors in the art of humor would have been repressed by both the rigid discipline of the law and by the general sentiment of the public. And yet nonetheless, the great, honest face of the people showed a smile—a grim smile, maybe, but a wide one. And there were games of the sort that the colonists had seen and taken part in long ago, at the county fairs and on the village greens of England. It was thought that keeping them alive in this new country would encourage courage and manliness. Wrestling matches were seen here and there in the marketplace. In one corner, there was a friendly fight with wooden staffs. But the pillory platform—already so well noted in these pages—attracted the greatest attention. There, two masters of defense were staging an exhibition with swords and shields. But, to the crowd's great disappointment, this last show was cut short by the town beadle, who would not permit the seriousness of the place to be violated.

These people were the sons and daughters of fathers who had known how to have a good time, in their day. It may not be exaggeration to say that these Puritans' celebrations would compare favorably with those of their descendants, even such distant descendants as us. The sons and daughters of those in the marketplace that day put on the blackest shade of Puritanism, so darkening the national character that it has never cleared up again. We have yet to relearn the forgotten art of joyfulness.

The picture of human life in the market-place, though its general tint was the sad gray, brown, or black of the English emigrants, was yet enlivened by some diversity of hue. A party of Indians—in their savage finery of curiously embroidered deer-skin robes, wampum-belts, red and yellow ochre, and feathers, and armed with the bow and arrow and stone-headed spear—stood apart, with countenances of inflexible gravity, beyond what even the Puritan aspect could attain. Nor, wild as were these painted barbarians, were they the wildest feature of the scene. This distinction could more justly be claimed by some mariners,—a part of the crew of the vessel from the Spanish Main,—who had come ashore to see the humors of Election Day. They were rough-looking desperadoes, with sun-blackened faces, and an immensity of beard; their wide, short trousers were confined about the waist by belts, often clasped with a rough plate of gold, and sustaining always a long knife, and, in some instances, a sword. From beneath their broad-brimmed hats of palm-leaf, gleamed eyes which, even in good nature and merriment, had a kind of animal ferocity. They transgressed, without fear or scruple, the rules of behaviour that were binding on all others; smoking tobacco under the beadle's very nose, although each whiff would have cost a townsman a shilling; and quaffing, at their pleasure, draughts of wine or aqua-vitae from pocket-flasks, which they freely tendered to the gaping crowd around them. It remarkably characterized the incomplete morality of the age, rigid as we call it, that a license was allowed the seafaring class, not merely for their freaks on shore, but for far more desperate deeds on their proper element. The sailor of that day would go near to be arraigned as a pirate in our own. There could be little doubt, for instance, that this very ship's crew, though no unfavorable specimens of the nautical brotherhood, had been guilty, as we should phrase it, of depredations on the Spanish commerce, such as would have perilled all their necks in a modern court of justice.

But the sea, in those old times, heaved, swelled, and foamed very much at its own will, or subject only to the tempestuous wind, with hardly any attempts at regulation by human law. The buccaneer on the wave might relinquish his calling, and become at once, if he chose, a man of probity and piety on land; nor, even in the full career of his reckless life, was he regarded as a personage with whom it

NO FEAR

Although the marketplace was full of sadly dressed English settlers, in grays and browns and blacks, there was some diversity to liven the scene. A group of Indians were dressed in their savage best: oddly embroidered deerskin robes, belts strung with beads, red and yellow body paint, and feathers. They were armed with bow and arrow and stone-tipped spear. They stood apart from the crowd, with faces of unmoving seriousness—beyond what even the Puritans could achieve. As wild as these painted barbarians were, they weren't the wildest aspect of the scene. That title could be justly claimed by a group of sailors: the crew of the Spanish ship, come ashore to see the festivities of Election Day. They were rough-looking adventurers with sun-blackened faces and immense beards. Their short pants were kept up by belts, often clasped with a rough plate of gold, and holding a long knife and sometimes even a sword. Under their broad, palm-leaf hats gleamed eyes that had an animal ferocity, even when good-natured and merry. Without fear or reservation, they broke the accepted rules of behavior. They smoked tobacco under the beadle's nose, which would have cost any townsman a fine. They drank wine or whisky from pocket flasks whenever they pleased, offering drinks to the shocked crowd that surrounded them. We think of the morality of that time as rigid, but it wasn't, really: Sailors were allowed a lot of leeway, not just for their hijinks on shore but also for far greater crimes at sea. The sailor of that day would be hunted as a pirate in our own. There could be little doubt, for instance, that the crew of this very ship had been guilty of stealing Spanish goods. Today, they would face hanging.

In those days, the sea moved with a will of its own or subject only to the wind. Human law hardly even attempted regulation. The sailor could give up his calling, if he chose, and instantly become a respected man on land. And even while he led his reckless life, it was not thought disrespectable to deal with him. And so the Puritan elders, in their black cloaks, ruffled collars, and pointed hats, smiled

was disreputable to traffic or casually associate. Thus, the Puritan elders, in their black cloaks, starched bands, and steeple-crowned hats, smiled not unbenignantly at the clamor and rude deportment of these jolly seafaring men; and it excited neither surprise nor animadversion when so reputable a citizen as old Roger Chillingworth, the physician, was seen to enter the market-place, in close and familiar talk with the commander of the questionable vessel.

The latter was by far the most showy and gallant figure, so far as apparel went, anywhere to be seen among the multitude. He wore a profusion of ribbons on his garment, and gold lace on his hat, which was also encircled by a gold chain, and surmounted with a feather. There was a sword at his side, and a sword-cut on his forehead, which, by the arrangement of his hair, he seemed anxious rather to display than hide. A landsman could hardly have worn this garb and shown this face, and worn and shown them both with such a galliard air, without undergoing stern question before a magistrate, and probably incurring fine or imprisonment, or perhaps an exhibition in the stocks. As regarded the shipmaster, however, all was looked upon as pertaining to the character, as to a fish his glistening scales.

After parting from the physician, the commander of the Bristol ship strolled idly through the market-place; until, happening to approach the spot where Hester Prynne was standing, he appeared to recognize, and did not hesitate to address her. As was usually the case wherever Hester stood, a small, vacant area—a sort of magic circle—had formed itself about her, into which, though the people were elbowing one another at a little distance, none ventured, or felt disposed to intrude. It was a forcible type of the moral solitude in which the scarlet letter enveloped its fated wearer; partly by her own reserve, and partly by the instinctive, though no longer so unkindly, withdrawal of her fellow-creatures. Now, if never before, it answered a good purpose, by enabling Hester and the seaman to speak together without risk of being overheard; and so changed was Hester Prynne's repute before the public, that the matron in town most eminent for rigid morality could not have held such intercourse with less result of scandal than herself.

"So, mistress," said the mariner, "I must bid the steward make ready one more berth than you bargained for! No fear of scurvy or

NO FEAR

at the noise and rudeness of these jolly sailors. It did not cause surprise or elicit rebuke when a respectable citizen such as Roger Chillingworth, the doctor, was seen to enter the marketplace talking in a familiar way with the commander of the dubious ship.

The commander was by far the most showily dressed figure to be seen anywhere in the crowd. He wore a great many ribbons on his coat and gold lace on his hat, which was encircled by a gold chain and topped with a feather. There was a sword at his side and sword-scar on his forehead. You could tell by his hairdo that he wanted to show off the scar, rather than hide it. A citizen of the land could not have worn this outfit and displayed this face, and done so with such a grand air, without facing stern questioning from a magistrate, a probable fine, and then possible shaming in the stocks. Yet because he was a shipmaster, this man's appearance looked as appropriate as a fish's glistening scales.

After parting from the doctor, the commander of the ship strolled idly through the marketplace. When he came upon the spot where Hester Prynne was standing, he seemed to recognize her. He did not hesitate to address her. As was usually the case wherever Hester stood, a small empty space—a sort of magic circle—had formed around her. Though people were elbowing one another and crammed together all around her, no one ventured into that space. It was a physical sign of the moral solitude in which the scarlet letter encircled its wearer, partly through her own reserve, and partly by the instinctive (though no longer unkind) withdrawal of her fellow citizens. Now, at least, it served a good purpose: Hester and the ship's commander could speak together without the risk of being overheard. Her reputation was so changed that she risked no scandal by this public conversation, no more than would the most well-respected matron in town, known for rigid morality.

"So, ma'am," said the captain, "I must instruct the steward to make room for one more passenger than you had bargained for! We

ship-fever, this voyage! What with the ship's surgeon and this other doctor, our only danger will be from drug or pill; more by token, as there is a lot of apothecary's stuff aboard, which I traded for with a Spanish vessel."

"What mean you?" inquired Hester, startled more than she permitted to appear. "Have you another passenger?"

"Why, know you not," cried the shipmaster, "that this physician here—Chillingworth, he calls himself—is minded to try my cabin-fare with you? Ay, ay, you must have known it; for he tells me he is of your party, and a close friend to the gentleman you spoke of,—he that is in peril from these sour old Puritan rulers!"

"They know each other well, indeed," replied Hester, with a mien of calmness, though in the utmost consternation. "They have long dwelt together."

Nothing further passed between the mariner and Hester Prynne. But, at that instant, she beheld old Roger Chillingworth himself, standing in the remotest corner of the market-place, and smiling on her; a smile which—across the wide and bustling square, and through all the talk and laughter, and various thoughts, moods, and interests of the crowd—conveyed secret and fearful meaning.

needn't fear any diseases on this voyage. With the ship's surgeon and this other doctor on board, our only danger will be from the drugs they prescribe—and I did trade with a Spanish ship for a great deal of medicine."

"What do you mean?" asked Hester, more startled than she allowed herself to show. "Do you have another passenger?"

"Don't you know," cried the ship's captain, "that this doctor here—he calls himself Chillingworth—has decided to try ship's cooking along with you? Yeah, sure, you must have known. He tells me that he is a member of your party and a close friend of the gentleman you spoke of—the one that is in danger from these sour old Puritans."

"They do know each other well," replied Hester, maintaining the appearance of calmness despite her great distress. "They have lived together for a long time."

The sailor and Hester Prynne spoke nothing more. But at that moment she saw old Roger Chillingworth himself, standing in the farthest corner of the marketplace and smiling at her. Even across the broad and busy square, through all the talk and laughter and various thoughts, moods, and interests of the crowd, that smile conveyed a secret and fearful meaning.

Chapter 22: The Procession

Before Hester Prynne could call together her thoughts, and consider what was practicable to be done in this new and startling aspect of affairs, the sound of military music was heard approaching along a contiguous street. It denoted the advance of the procession of magistrates and citizens, on its way towards the meeting-house; where, in compliance with a custom thus early established, and ever since observed, the Reverend Mr. Dimmesdale was to deliver an Election Sermon.

Soon the head of the procession showed itself, with a slow and stately march, turning a corner, and making its way across the market-place. First came the music. It comprised a variety of instruments, perhaps imperfectly adapted to one another, and played with no great skill, but yet attaining the great object for which the harmony of drum and clarion addresses itself to the multitude,—that of imparting a higher and more heroic air to the scene of life that passes before the eye. Little Pearl at first clapped her hands, but then lost, for an instant, the restless agitation that had kept her in a continual effervescence throughout the morning; she gazed silently, and seemed to be borne upward, like a floating sea-bird, on the long heaves and swells of sound. But she was brought back to her former mood by the shimmer of the sunshine on the weapons and bright armour of the military company, which followed after the music, and formed the honorary escort of the procession. This body of soldiery—which still sustains a corporate existence, and marches down from past ages with an ancient and honorable fame—was composed of no mercenary materials. Its ranks were filled with gentlemen, who felt the stirrings of martial impulse, and sought to establish a kind of College of Arms, where, as in an association of Knights Templars, they might learn the science, and, so far as peaceful exercise would teach them, the practices of war. The high estimation then placed upon the military character might be seen in the lofty port of each individual member of the company. Some of them, indeed, by their services in the Low Countries and on other fields of European warfare, had fairly won their title to assume the name and pomp of soldiership. The entire array, moreover, clad in burnished steel, and with plumage nodding over their bright morions, had a brilliancy of effect which no modern display can aspire to equal.

Chapter 22: The Procession

Before Hester could gather her thoughts and consider what she ought to do with this new and startling information, the sound of military music approached along a nearby street. It signaled the procession of magistrates and citizens on its way toward the meetinghouse. According to a custom established early and observed ever since, the Reverend Mr. Dimmesdale would there deliver an Election Sermon.

The front of the procession soon arrived with a slow and stately march. It turned a corner and made its way across the marketplace. The band came first. It contained a variety of instruments, poorly selected and badly played. Yet they achieved their objective, giving a higher and more heroic impression to the scene. Little Pearl clapped her hands at first but then for a moment lost the energy that had kept her in continual motion all morning. She gazed silently, seemingly carried on the waves of sound and as a seabird is carried on the wind. She was brought back to earth by the gleam of the sunshine on the weapons and bright armor of the military company. The soldiers followed the band as an honorary escort for the procession. The company, which still exists today, contained no mercenaries. Its ranks were filled with gentlemen who wished to be soldiers and sought to establish a sort of College of Arms where they might learn the theory and, as far as peaceful exercises could teach, practice of war. The pride each member of the company carried himself with testified to the great value placed on military character at that time. Some of them had served in European wars and could rightly claim the title and stature of a soldier. The entire company, dressed in polished steel with feathers topping their shining helmets, had a brilliant effect that no modern display can hope to equal.

And yet the men of civil eminence, who came immediately behind the military escort, were better worth a thoughtful observer's eye. Even in outward demeanour they showed a stamp of majesty that made the warrior's haughty stride look vulgar, if not absurd. It was an age when what we call talent had far less consideration than now, but the massive materials which produce stability and dignity of character a great deal more. The people possessed, by hereditary right, the quality of reverence; which, in their descendants, if it survive at all, exists in smaller proportion, and with a vastly diminished force in the selection and estimate of public men. The change may be for good or ill, and is partly, perhaps, for both. In that old day, the English settler on these rude shores,—having left king, nobles, and all degrees of awful rank behind, while still the faculty and necessity of reverence were strong in him,— bestowed it on the white hair and venerable brow of age; on long-tried integrity; on solid wisdom and sad-colored experience; on endowments of that grave and weighty order, which gives the idea of permanence, and comes under the general definition of respectability. These primitive statesmen, therefore,—Bradstreet, Endicott, Dudley, Bellingham, and their compeers,—who were elevated to power by the early choice of the people, seem to have been not often brilliant, but distinguished by a ponderous sobriety, rather than activity of intellect. They had fortitude and self-reliance, and, in time of difficulty or peril, stood up for the welfare of the state like a line of cliffs against a tempestuous tide. The traits of character here indicated were well represented in the square cast of countenance and large physical development of the new colonial magistrates. So far as a demeanour of natural authority was concerned, the mother country need not have been ashamed to see these foremost men of an actual democracy adopted into the House of Peers, or made the Privy Council of the sovereign.

Next in order to the magistrates came the young and eminently distinguished divine, from whose lips the religious discourse of the anniversary was expected. His was the profession, at that era, in which intellectual ability displayed itself far more than in political life; for—leaving a higher motive out of the question—it offered inducements powerful enough, in the almost worshipping respect of the community, to win the most aspiring ambition into its service. Even political power—as in the case of Increase Mather—was within the grasp of a successful priest.

NO FEAR

Still, it is the eminent statesmen following immediately after the military escort who deserve a more thoughtful observation. Even outwardly, they showed the mark of majesty that made the soldier's proud stride look cheap, if not absurd. This was an age when talent carried less weight than it does today. The burdensome materials that produce stability and dignity of character were much more important to the people. Our ancestors were more inclined to revere their superiors than we are in this day and age. Reverence is neither earned nor given today as it was then, and therefore it plays a much smaller role in political life. The change may be for good or ill—perhaps a bit of both. But in those bygone days the English settler on those uncultured shores, having left behind the king, noblemen, and all sorts of social hierarchy, still felt the urge to employ his sense of reverence. So he bestowed that reverence upon those whose white hair and wrinkled brow signified age, whose integrity had been tested and passed, who possess solid wisdom and sober experience, whose grave and stately attitude gives the impression of permanence, and generally passes for respectability. The early leaders elected to power by their people were rarely brilliant. They distinguished themselves by a thoughtful seriousness rather than an active intellect. They were strong and self-reliant. In difficult or dangerous times, they stood up for the good of the state like a line of cliffs against a stormy tide. These qualities were well represented in the square faces and large forms of the colonial magistrates taking office on that day. As far as the appearance of natural authority was concerned, these democratically elected leaders would have fit in perfectly at England's House of Lords or the king's Privy Council.

Following the magistrates came the young, distinguished minister expected to give a sermon that day. In that era, clergymen displayed more intellectual ability than politicians. Putting spiritual motivations aside, the ministry offered to an ambitious man many attractive incentives, notably the almost worshipping respect of the community. Even political power was within the grasp of a successful minister.

It was the observation of those who beheld him now, that never, since Mr. Dimmesdale first set his foot on the New England shore, had he exhibited such energy as was seen in the gait and air with which he kept his pace in the procession. There was no feebleness of step, as at other times; his frame was not bent; nor did his hand rest ominously upon his heart. Yet, if the clergyman were rightly viewed, his strength seemed not of the body. It might be spiritual, and imparted to him by angelic ministrations. It might be the exhilaration of that potent cordial, which is distilled only in the furnace-glow of earnest and long-continued thought. Or, perchance, his sensitive temperament was invigorated by the loud and piercing music, that swelled heavenward, and uplifted him on its ascending wave. Nevertheless, so abstracted was his look, it might be questioned whether Mr. Dimmesdale even heard the music. There was his body, moving onward, and with an unaccustomed force. But where was his mind? Far and deep in its own region, busying itself, with preternatural activity, to marshal a procession of stately thoughts that were soon to issue thence; and so he saw nothing, heard nothing, knew nothing, of what was around him; but the spiritual element took up the feeble frame, and carried it along, unconscious of the burden, and converting it to spirit like itself. Men of uncommon intellect, who have grown morbid, possess this occasional power of mighty effort, into which they throw the life of many days, and then are lifeless for as many more.

Hester Prynne, gazing steadfastly at the clergyman, felt a dreary influence come over her, but wherefore or whence she knew not; unless that he seemed so remote from her own sphere, and utterly beyond her reach. One glance of recognition, she had imagined, must needs pass between them. She thought of the dim forest, with its little dell of solitude, and love, and anguish, and the mossy tree-trunk, where, sitting hand in hand, they had mingled their sad and passionate talk with the melancholy murmur of the brook. How deeply had they known each other then! And was this the man? She hardly knew him now! He, moving proudly past, enveloped, as it were, in the rich music, with the procession of majestic and venerable fathers; he, so unattainable in his worldly position, and still more so in that far vista of his unsympathizing thoughts, through which she now beheld him! Her spirit sank with the idea that all must have

NO FEAR

Those who saw him felt that Mr. Dimmesdale had never walked with such energy as he did on that day. There was no feebleness in his step, as there had been at other times. His body was not stooped, nor did his hand rest ominously upon his heart. And yet, when properly observed, the minister's strength did not seem physical. Perhaps it was spiritual, a gift of the angels. Perhaps he was fortified by the liquor of the mind, distilled over a slow fire of serious thought. Or maybe his sensitive temperament was enlivened by the loud, piercing music that lifted him toward Heaven on its rising wave. Yet he wore a look so distant and removed that it was not clear that Mr. Dimmesdale even heard the music. His body was there, moving forward with an uncharacteristic force. But where was his mind? Deep within itself. His mind busied itself with otherworldly activity as it directed a procession of grand thoughts that would soon be marching out. He saw nothing, heard nothing, and was aware of nothing around him. But his spirit carried his feeble body along, unaware of the burden as it converted the body to spirit like itself. On occasion, men of great intellect who have grown sick can muster up a mighty effort. They throw several days' energies into that effort and then are left lifeless for several days after.

Hester Prynne felt an unsettling influence come over her as she gazed steadily at the minister. She didn't know where this feeling came from, though it may have been that the minister seemed distant from her, so completely beyond her reach. She had imagined that a fleeting glance of recognition would pass between them. She thought of the dim forest, with its little place of solitude and love and pain. She thought of the mossy tree trunk where, sitting hand in hand, their sad and passionate conversation mixed in with the sad babble of the brook. They had known each other so deeply then! Was this the same man? She hardly recognized him! He was moving proudly past her, surrounded by rich music and majestic old men. He seemed unattainable in his worldly position, but even more so in his self-contained thoughts! Hester's spirit sank at the feeling that it all must have been a delusion. Though she had dreamed it so viv-

been a delusion, and that, vividly as she had dreamed it, there could be no real bond betwixt the clergyman and herself. And thus much of woman was there in Hester, that she could scarcely forgive him,—least of all now, when the heavy foot-step of their approaching Fate might be heard, nearer, nearer!—for being able so completely to withdraw himself from their mutual world; while she groped darkly, and stretched forth her cold hands, and found him not.

Pearl either saw and responded to her mother's feelings, or herself felt the remoteness and intangibility that had fallen around the minister. While the procession passed, the child was uneasy, fluttering up and down, like a bird on the point of taking flight. When the whole had gone by, she looked up into Hester's face.

"Mother," said she, "was that the same minister that kissed me by the brook?"

"Hold thy peace, dear little Pearl!" whispered her mother. "We must not always talk in the market-place of what happens to us in the forest."

"I could not be sure that it was he; so strange he looked," continued the child. "Else I would have run to him, and bid him kiss me now, before all the people; even as he did yonder among the dark old trees. What would the minister have said, mother? Would he have clapped his hand over his heart, and scowled on and bid me begone?"

"What should he say, Pearl," answered Hester, "save that it was no time to kiss, and that kisses are not to be given in the market-place? Well for thee, foolish child, that thou didst not speak to him!"

Another shade of the same sentiment, in reference to Mr. Dimmesdale, was expressed by a person whose eccentricities—or insanity, as we should term it—led her to do what few of the towns-people would have ventured on; to begin a conversation with the wearer of the scarlet letter, in public. It was Mistress Hibbins, who, arrayed in great magnificence, with a triple ruff, a broidered stomacher, a gown of rich velvet, and a gold-headed cane, had come forth to see the procession. As this ancient lady had the renown (which subsequently cost her no less a price than her life) of being a principal actor in all the works of necromancy that were continually going forward, the crowd gave way before her, and seemed to fear the touch of her garment, as if it carried the plague among its gor-

idly, perhaps there could be no real connection between the minister and herself. Hester was enough of a woman that she could barely forgive him for being able to withdraw himself so completely from their mutual world—and now of all times, when fate was approaching with a heavy footstep. Hester groped in that dark world with her hands outstretched, but she did not find him.

Pearl either sensed her mother's feeling and responded to them or felt herself how distant the minister had become. The child was restless as the procession went by. She fluttered up and down like a bird about to take flight. When it had passed, she looked up into Hester's face.

"Mother," she said, "was that the same minister who kissed me by the brook?"

"Hush, my dear little Pearl," her mother whispered. "We cannot always talk in public about what happens to us in the privacy of the woods."

"He looked so different that I couldn't be sure it was him," the child went on. "I would have run to him and asked him to kiss me now, in front of all these people, just as did among those dark old trees. What would the minister have said, mother? Would he have put his hand over his heart, scowled at me, and told me to go away?"

"What would you expect him to say, Pearl," answered Hester, "except that it wasn't the proper time or place to kiss? Foolish child, it's a good thing you didn't speak to him!"

Mistress Hibbins felt the same way about Mr. Dimmesdale. Her eccentricities, which we would have called insanity, led her to do what few of the townspeople would have dared: She began a conversation with Hester in public. She had dressed magnificently, to the point of extravagance, to come see the procession. Since this old woman had the reputation for being a witch—a reputation that would later cost her life—the crowd parted before her. People seemed afraid of the touch of her clothes, as though they carried an infectious disease within their gorgeous folds. Though by this point many people felt warmly toward Hester Prynne, by standing next to Mistress Hibbins she had doubled the dread the old woman usually inspired. The crowd moved away from the area of the marketplace where the two women stood.

geous folds. Seen in conjunction with Hester Prynne,—kindly as so many now felt towards the latter,—the dread inspired by Mistress Hibbins was doubled, and caused a general movement from that part of the market-place in which the two women stood.

"Now, what mortal imagination could conceive it!" whispered the old lady confidentially to Hester. "Yonder divine man! That saint on earth, as the people uphold him to be, and as—I must needs say—he really looks! Who, now, that saw him pass in the procession, would think how little while it is since he went forth out of his study,—chewing a Hebrew text of Scripture in his mouth, I warrant,—to take an airing in the forest! Aha! we know what that means, Hester Prynne! But, truly, forsooth, I find it hard to believe him the same man. Many a church-member saw I, walking behind the music, that has danced in the same measure with me, when Somebody was fiddler, and, it might be, an Indian powwow or a Lapland wizard changing hands with us! That is but a trifle, when a woman knows the world. But this minister! Couldst thou surely tell, Hester, whether he was the same man that encountered thee on the forest-path!"

"Madam, I know not of what you speak," answered Hester Prynne, feeling Mistress Hibbins to be of infirm mind; yet strangely startled and awe-stricken by the confidence with which she affirmed a personal connection between so many persons (herself among them) and the Evil One. "It is not for me to talk lightly of a learned and pious minister of the Word, like the Reverend Mr. Dimmesdale!"

"Fie, woman, fie!" cried the old lady, shaking her finger at Hester. "Dost thou think I have been to the forest so many times, and have yet no skill to judge who else has been there? Yea; though no leaf of the wild garlands, which they wore while they danced, be left in their hair! I know thee, Hester; for I behold the token. We may all see it in the sunshine; and it glows like a red flame in the dark. Thou wearest it openly; so there need be no question about that. But this minister! Let me tell thee in thine ear! When the Black Man sees one of his own servants, signed and sealed, so shy of owning to the bond as is the Reverend Mr. Dimmesdale, he hath a way of ordering matters so that the mark shall be disclosed in open daylight to the eyes of all the world! What is it that the minister seeks to hide, with his hand always over his heart? Ha, Hester Prynne!"

"Who could have imagined?" the old lady whispered confidentially to Hester. "That holy man! People say that he is a saint on earth, and—I must say—he looks like one! Seeing him in the procession now, who would think that not long ago he left his study to breathe the fresh air of the forest! Well, we know what that means, Hester Prynne! But I find it truly hard to believe that he is the same man. Many church members walking in the procession have joined me in my witchcraft. That means little to a worldly woman. But this minister! Would you have known, Hester, that he was the same man who met you on the forest path?"

"Ma'am, I don't know what you're talking about," answered Hester Prynne, sensing that Mistress Hibbins was not in her right mind. Nonetheless, Hester was strangely affected by the bold manner with which she discussed the personal connection between so many people—herself included—and the Devil. "It is not my place to speak lightly of the wise and devout Reverend Dimmesdale."

"No, woman!" cried the old lady, shaking her finger at Hester. "Do you think that, having been to the forest as often as I have, I cannot tell who else has been there? Even though the flowers they wore in their hair while dancing are gone, I can still tell. I know you, Hester, because I see your symbol. We can all see it in the sunshine, and it glows like a red flame in the dark! You wear it openly, so no one can doubt it. But this minister! Let me whisper in your ear! The Black Man has a way of causing the truth to come to light when he sees one of his own sworn servants acting so shy about the bond they share, as the Reverend Mister Dimmesdale does. His mark will be revealed to the whole world. What is the minister trying to hide with his hand always over his heart? Ha, Hester Prynne!"

"What is it, good Mistress Hibbins?" eagerly asked little Pearl. "Hast thou seen it?"

"No matter, darling!" responded Mistress Hibbins, making Pearl a profound reverence. "Thou thyself wilt see it, one time or another. They say, child, thou art of the lineage of the Prince of the Air! Wilt thou ride with me, some fine night, to see thy father? Then thou shalt know wherefore the minister keeps his hand over his heart!"

Laughing so shrilly that all the market-place could hear her, the weird old gentlewoman took her departure.

By this time the preliminary prayer had been offered in the meeting-house, and the accents of the Reverend Mr. Dimmesdale were heard commencing his discourse. An irresistible feeling kept Hester near the spot. As the sacred edifice was too much thronged to admit another auditor, she took up her position close beside the scaffold of the pillory. It was in sufficient proximity to bring the whole sermon to her ears, in the shape of an indistinct, but varied, murmur and flow of the minister's very peculiar voice.

This vocal organ was in itself a rich endowment; insomuch that a listener, comprehending nothing of the language in which the preacher spoke, might still have been swayed to and fro by the mere tone and cadence. Like all other music, it breathed passion and pathos, and emotions high or tender, in a tongue native to the human heart, wherever educated. Muffled as the sound was by its passage through the church-walls, Hester Prynne listened with such intentness, and sympathized so intimately, that the sermon had throughout a meaning for her, entirely apart from its indistinguishable words. These, perhaps, if more distinctly heard, might have been only a grosser medium, and have clogged the spiritual sense. Now she caught the low undertone, as of the wind sinking down to repose itself; then ascended with it, as it rose through progressive gradations of sweetness and power, until its volume seemed to envelop her with an atmosphere of awe and solemn grandeur. And yet, majestic as the voice sometimes became, there was for ever in it an essential character of plaintiveness. A loud or low expression of anguish,—the whisper, or the shriek, as it might be conceived, of suffering humanity, that touched a sensibility in every bosom! At times this deep strain of pathos was all that could be heard, and scarcely heard, sighing amid a desolate silence. But even

NO FEAR

"What is it, Mistress Hibbins?" asked little Pearl eagerly. "Have you seen it?"

"It doesn't matter, darling!" answered Mistress Hibbins, bowing deeply to Pearl. "You will see it for yourself eventually. You know, child, they say that you are descended from the Prince of Air! Will you ride with me some lovely night to see your father? Then you will know why the minister keeps his hand over his heart!"

The strange woman left, laughing with such a shrill sound that the entire marketplace could hear her.

By this point, the introductory prayer had concluded in the meetinghouse and the voice of the Reverend Mr. Dimmesdale's could be heard beginning his sermon. An irresistible urge kept Hester close by. Since the meetinghouse was too crowded to admit another listener, she stood beside the scaffold of the pillory. It was close enough for her to hear the entire sermon, though she could not make out the words. Instead, she heard only the murmur and flow of the minister's peculiar voice.

His voice was a great gift. The tone and rhythm of his speech could move even a listener who spoke no English. Like all music, it conveyed emotion in a universal language. Although the sound was muffled by its passage through the church walls, Hester Prynne listened so intently and with such great feeling that the sermon held a meaning for her apart from its indistinguishable words. Had she been able to hear the words, their dull meaning might have diminished the sermon's spiritual significance. Now she heard low sounds, as though the wind was settling down to rest. Then the voice rose again with increasing sweetness and power until it seemed to envelop her in an atmosphere of awe and grandeur. But no matter how majestic the voice became, it always contained a hint of anguish. Shifting between a whisper and a shriek, the audible pain seemed to convey the human suffering felt in every breast. At times, this note of deep pain was all that could be heard—and barely heard at that. An attentive listener could detect this cry of pain even when the minister's voice grew loud and commanding, assuming all the power it could and nearly causing the church to burst with sound. What was it? The anguish of a human heart, heavy with sorrow and perhaps guilt, revealing its secret to the great heart of mankind and begging, not in vain, for sympathy or forgiveness! This profound and constant undertone gave the minister his great oratorical power.

when the minister's voice grew high and commanding,—when it gushed irrepressibly upward,—when it assumed its utmost breadth and power, so overfilling the church as to burst its way through the solid walls, and diffuse itself in the open air,—still, if the auditor listened intently, and for the purpose, he could detect the same cry of pain. What was it? The complaint of a human heart, sorrow-laden, perchance guilty, telling its secret, whether of guilt or sorrow, to the great heart of mankind; beseeching its sympathy or forgiveness,—at every moment,—in each accent,—and never in vain! It was this profound and continual undertone that gave the clergyman his most appropriate power.

During all this time Hester stood, statue-like, at the foot of the scaffold. If the minister's voice had not kept her there, there would nevertheless have been an inevitable magnetism in that spot, whence she dated the first hour of her life of ignominy. There was a sense within her,—too ill-defined to be made a thought, but weighing heavily on her mind,—that her whole orb of life, both before and after, was connected with this spot, as with the one point that gave it unity.

Little Pearl, meanwhile, had quitted her mother's side, and was playing at her own will about the market-place. She made the sombre crowd cheerful by her erratic and glistening ray; even as a bird of bright plumage illuminates a whole tree of dusky foliage by darting to and fro, half-seen and half-concealed, amid the twilight of the clustering leaves. She had an undulating, but, oftentimes, a sharp and irregular movement. It indicated the restless vivacity of her spirit which to-day was doubly indefatigable in its tiptoe dance, because it was played upon and vibrated with her mother's disquietude. Whenever Pearl saw any thing to excite her ever active and wandering curiosity she flew thitherward, and, as we might say, seized upon that man or thing as her own property, so far as she desired it; but without yielding the minutest degree of control over her motions in requital. The Puritans looked on, and, if they smiled, were none the less inclined to pronounce the child a demon offspring, from the indescribable charm of beauty and eccentricity that shone through her little figure, and sparkled with its activity. She ran and looked the wild Indian in the face; and he grew conscious of a nature wilder than his own. Thence, with native audacity, but still with a reserve as characteristic, she flew into the midst of a group

NO FEAR

All this while, Hester stood like a statue at the base of the plat-form. She would have been drawn to this spot where she spent the first hour of her public shame, even if the minister's voice had not held her there. She had a sense—not clear enough to be a thought, but still weighing heavily on her mind—that her entire life was con-nected to this one spot, the one unifying point.

Meanwhile, little Pearl had left her mother's side and gone off to play in the marketplace. She cheered up the serious crowd with the odd, glistening light of her presence, just as a brightly colored bird lights up a dark tree by darting back and forth among the darkly clustered leaves. She moved in a constantly changing, sometimes sharp manner that expressed the restless liveliness of her spirit. Never satisfied with the predictable or conventional, her spirit today was doubly excited by her mother's uneasiness, which it sensed and responded to. Whenever a person or thing drew Pearl's wandering curiosity, she flew straight to it and seized upon it as though it were her own. Yet she always maintained her freedom of movement. She was never possessed by what she sought to possess. The Puritans watched her. Even the ones who smiled at her were quite willing to believe that she was likely the child of a demon, judging by the strange, eccentric beauty that sparkled throughout her. She ran and stared into the face of the wild Indian, and he recognized a spirit more wild than his own. Then, with both audacity and a charac-teristic reserve, she flew into the middle of a group of sailors. The red-faced wild men of the ocean gazed at Pearl with wonder and amazement, as though a flake of sea foam had assumed the shape

of mariners, the swarthy-cheeked wild men of the ocean, as the Indians were of the land; and they gazed wonderingly and admiringly at Pearl, as if a flake of the sea-foam had taken the shape of a little maid, and were gifted with a soul of the sea-fire, that flashes beneath the prow in the night-time.

One of these seafaring men—the shipmaster, indeed, who had spoken to Hester Prynne—was so smitten with Pearl's aspect, that he attempted to lay hands upon her, with purpose to snatch a kiss. Finding it as impossible to touch her as to catch a humming-bird in the air, he took from his hat the gold chain that was twisted about it, and threw it to the child. Pearl immediately twined it around her neck and waist, with such happy skill, that, once seen there, it became a part of her, and it was difficult to imagine her without it.

"Thy mother is yonder woman with the scarlet letter," said the seaman. "Wilt thou carry her a message from me?"

"If the message pleases me I will," answered Pearl.

"Then tell her," rejoined he, "that I spake again with the black-a-visaged, hump-shouldered old doctor, and he engages to bring his friend, the gentleman she wots of, aboard with him. So let thy mother take no thought, save for herself and thee. Wilt thou tell her this, thou witch-baby?"

"Mistress Hibbins says my father is the Prince of the Air!" cried Pearl, with her naughty smile. "If thou callest me that ill name, I shall tell him of thee; and he will chase thy ship with a tempest!"

Pursuing a zigzag course across the market-place, the child returned to her mother, and communicated what the mariner had said. Hester's strong, calm, steadfastly enduring spirit almost sank, at last, on beholding this dark and grim countenance of an inevitable doom, which—at the moment when a passage seemed to open for the minister and herself out of their labyrinth of misery—showed itself, with an unrelenting smile, right in the midst of their path.

With her mind harassed by the terrible perplexity in which the shipmaster's intelligence involved her, she was also subjected to another trial. There were many people present, from the country roundabout, who had often heard of the scarlet letter, and to whom it had been made terrific by a hundred false or exaggerated rumors, but who had never beheld it with their own bodily eyes. These, after exhausting other modes of amusement, now thronged about

of a girl but retained the soul of the fire that sailors see in the deep water at night.

One of these sailors was the same commander who had spoken to Hester Prynne. He was so taken with Pearl that he tried to grab her, intending to steal a kiss. Realizing that he could no more touch her than catch a hummingbird, he removed the gold chain that was twisted around his hat and threw it to the child. Pearl immediately twisted it around her neck and waist with such skill that, once in place, the chain became a part of her, and it was hard to imagine her without it.

"Your mother is that woman with the scarlet letter," said the sailor. "Will you deliver a message to her from me?"

"If I like the message," answered Pearl.

"Then tell her," he responded, "that I spoke with the black-faced, hump-backed old doctor. He intends to bring his friend, the gentleman she knows about, aboard the ship with him. So your need not worry about him, only about herself and you. Will you tell her this, you witch-baby?"

"Mistress Hibbins says my father is the Prince of Air!" cried Pearl, with a naughty smile. "If you call me that name again, I will tell him, and he will send a storm to toss your ship at sea!"

Taking a zigzag path across the marketplace, the child returned to her mother and delivered the message. Hester's strong, calm, enduring spirit almost sank. Just when there seemed to be a way for the minister and her to escape their maze of misery, the path was blocked by the smiling face of grim and inevitable doom.

Just as her mind was grappling with the terrible confusion the commander's news had caused, Hester faced another assault. Many people from the surrounding countryside had heard something of the scarlet letter. They had heard a hundred rumors and exaggerations about it but had never actually seen it. Growing tired of other amusements, these people gathered around Hester Prynne and rudely intruded upon her. Yet as rude as they were, they would

Hester Prynne with rude and boorish intrusiveness. Unscrupulous as it was, however, it could not bring them nearer than a circuit of several yards. At that distance they accordingly stood, fixed there by the centrifugal force of the repugnance which the mystic symbol inspired. The whole gang of sailors, likewise, observing the press of spectators, and learning the purport of the scarlet letter, came and thrust their sunburnt and desperado-looking faces into the ring. Even the Indians were affected by a sort of cold shadow of the white man's curiosity, and, gliding through the crowd, fastened their snake-like black eyes on Hester's bosom; conceiving, perhaps, that the wearer of this brilliantly embroidered badge must needs be a personage of high dignity among her people. Lastly, the inhabitants of the town (their own interest in this worn-out subject languidly reviving itself, by sympathy with what they saw others feel) lounged idly to the same quarter, and tormented Hester Prynne, perhaps more than all the rest, with their cool, well-acquainted gaze at her familiar shame. Hester saw and recognized the selfsame faces of that group of matrons, who had awaited her forthcoming from the prison-door, seven years ago; all save one, the youngest and only compassionate among them, whose burial-robe she had since made. At the final hour, when she was so soon to fling aside the burning letter, it had strangely become the centre of more remark and excitement, and was thus made to sear her breast more painfully than at any time since the first day she put it on.

While Hester stood in that magic circle of ignominy, where the cunning cruelty of her sentence seemed to have fixed her for ever, the admirable preacher was looking down from the sacred pulpit upon an audience, whose very inmost spirits had yielded to his control. The sainted minister in the church! The woman of the scarlet letter in the market-place! What imagination would have been irreverent enough to surmise that the same scorching stigma was on them both?

not come closer than several yards—held at that distance by the repulsive force of that mystical symbol. The gang of sailors—seeing the crowd gather and learning the meaning of the scarlet letter—came over and stuck their sunburned faces into the ring around Hester. Even the Indians were affected by the white man's curiosity. Gliding through the crowd, they fixed their snakelike black eyes on Hester's bosom. Perhaps they imagined that the woman who wore such a brilliantly embroidered symbol must be someone of great stature among her people. Finally, the townspeople—whose interest in this tired subject was revived by the response they saw in the others—slowly wandered over. They tormented Hester Prynne, perhaps more than all the others, with their detached, knowing gaze at her familiar shame. Hester recognized in those faces the same scorn that she had seen in the faces of the women who had waited for her to emerge from the prison door seven years ago. She had since made burial robes for all but one, the youngest and only compassionate one among them. At this last moment, just as she was about to cast off the burning letter, it had strangely become the center of more attention—and therefore burned hotter—than at any time since she had first put it on.

While Hester stood in that magic circle of shame, where the clever cruelty of her sentence seemed destined to last forever, the admired minister was looking down from the sacred pulpit at the audience, whose innermost spirit had submitted to his control. The sainted minister in church! The woman of the scarlet letter in the marketplace! Who would have imagined that the same burning mark was on them both?

Chapter 23: The Revelation of the Scarlet Letter

The eloquent voice, on which the souls of the listening audience had been borne aloft, as on the swelling waves of the sea, at length came to a pause. There was a momentary silence, profound as what should follow the utterance of oracles. Then ensued a murmur and half-hushed tumult; as if the auditors, released from the high spell that had transported them into the region of another's mind, were returning into themselves, with all their awe and wonder still heavy on them. In a moment more, the crowd began to gush forth from the doors of the church. Now that there was an end, they needed other breath, more fit to support the gross and earthly life into which they relapsed, than that atmosphere which the preacher had converted into words of flame, and had burdened with the rich fragrance of his thought.

In the open air their rapture broke into speech. The street and the market-place absolutely babbled, from side to side, with applauses of the minister. His hearers could not rest until they had told one another of what each knew better than he could tell or hear. According to their united testimony, never had man spoken in so wise, so high, and so holy a spirit, as he that spake this day; nor had inspiration ever breathed through mortal lips more evidently than it did through his. Its influence could be seen, as it were, descending upon him, and possessing him, and continually lifting him out of the written discourse that lay before him, and filling him with ideas that must have been as marvellous to himself as to his audience. His subject, it appeared, had been the relation between the Deity and the communities of mankind, with a special reference to the New England which they were here planting in the wilderness. And, as he drew towards the close, a spirit as of prophecy had come upon him, constraining him to its purpose as mightily as the old prophets of Israel were constrained; only with this difference, that, whereas the Jewish seers had denounced judgments and ruin on their country, it was his mission to foretell a high and glorious destiny for the newly gathered people of the Lord. But, throughout it all, and through the whole discourse, there had been a certain deep, sad undertone of pathos, which could not be interpreted otherwise than as the natural regret of one soon to pass away. Yes; their

Chapter 23: The Revelation of the Scarlet Letter

The eloquent voice, which had moved the souls of the audience like waves on the sea, finally grew quiet. For a moment all was silent, as though prophecy had just been spoken. And then there was a murmur, a half-stifled clamor. The listeners, as if waking from a spell, returned to themselves with a mix of awe and wonder still weighing heavily upon them. After another moment, the crowd began to pour out of the church. Now that the sermon was over they needed fresh air, something to support the physical life they were reentering. They needed relief from the atmosphere of flame and deep perfume that the minister's words had created.

Once in the open air, the crowd burst into speech, filling the street and the marketplace with their praise of the minister. They could not rest until they had told each other about what had happened, which everyone already knew better than anyone could say. They all agreed that no one had ever spoken with such wisdom and great holiness as their minister had that day. Inspiration, they felt, had never filled human speech as much as it had filled his. It was as though the Holy Spirit had descended upon him, possessed him, and lifted him above the words written on the page. It filled him with ideas that must have been as marvelous to him as they were to his audience. His subject had been the relationship between God and human communities, with especial attention paid to the communities of New England founded in the wilderness. As he drew toward his conclusion, something like a prophetic spirit had come to him, bending him to its purpose just as it had used the old prophets of Israel. Only the Jewish prophets had predicted judgment and ruin for their country, but their minister spoke of the glorious destiny awaiting the newly gathered community of God. Yet throughout the whole sermon, there had been an undertone of deep sadness. It could only be interpreted as the natural regret of a man about to die. Yes, their minister, whom they loved so dearly—and who loved them so much that he could not depart for Heaven without a sigh—sensed that his death was approaching and that he would

minister whom they so loved—and who so loved them all, that he could not depart heavenward without a sigh—had the foreboding of untimely death upon him, and would soon leave them in their tears! This idea of his transitory stay on earth gave the last emphasis to the effect which the preacher had produced; it was as if an angel, in his passage to the skies, had shaken his bright wings over the people for an instant,—at once a shadow and a splendor,—and had shed down a shower of golden truths upon them.

Thus, there had come to the Reverend Mr. Dimmesdale—as to most men, in their various spheres, though seldom recognized until they see it far behind them—an epoch of life more brilliant and full of triumph than any previous one, or than any which could hereafter be. He stood, at this moment, on the very proudest eminence of superiority, to which the gifts of intellect, rich lore, prevailing eloquence, and a reputation of whitest sanctity, could exalt a clergyman in New England's earliest days, when the professional character was of itself a lofty pedestal. Such was the position which the minister occupied, as he bowed his head forward on the cushions of the pulpit, at the close of his Election Sermon. Meanwhile, Hester Prynne was standing beside the scaffold of the pillory, with the scarlet letter still burning on her breast!

Now was heard again the clangor of the music, and the measured tramp of the military escort, issuing from the church-door. The procession was to be marshalled thence to the town-hall, where a solemn banquet would complete the ceremonies of the day.

Once more, therefore, the train of venerable and majestic fathers was seen moving through a broad pathway of the people, who drew back reverently, on either side, as the Governor and magistrates, the old and wise men, the holy ministers, and all that were eminent and renowned, advanced into the midst of them. When they were fairly in the market-place, their presence was greeted by a shout. This—though doubtless it might acquire additional force and volume from the childlike loyalty which the age awarded to its rulers—was felt to be an irrepressible outburst of the enthusiasm kindled in the auditors by that high strain of eloquence which was yet reverberating in their ears. Each felt the impulse in himself, and, in the same breath, caught it from his neighbour. Within the church, it had hardly been kept down; beneath the sky, it pealed upward to the zenith. There

soon leave them in tears. The idea that the minister's time on earth would be short made the sermon's effect even stronger. It was as though an angel on his way to Heaven had shaken his bright wings over the people for a moment, sending a shower of golden truths down upon them.

And so there had come to the Reverend Mr. Dimmesdale—as there comes to most men, though they seldom recognize it until too late—a period of life more brilliant and full of triumph than any that had come before or would come after. At this moment he stood at the highest peak to which intellect, eloquence, and purity could elevate a clergyman in the early days of New England, when the profession of minister was already a lofty pedestal. This was the minister's position, as he bowed his head forward on the pulpit at the end of his Election Sermon. And meanwhile Hester Prynne was standing beside the scaffold of the pillory with the scarlet letter still burning on her breast!

The sound of the band was heard again, as were the rhythmic steps of the militia members as they walked out from the church door. The procession was to march from there to the town hall, where a great banquet would complete the day's ceremonies.

And so the parade of community elders moved along a broad path as the people cleared the way for them, drawing back with reverence as the Governor, magistrates, old and wise men, holy ministers, and all other powerful and well-regarded townsmen walked into the middle of the crowd. The procession was greeted by a shout as it reached the center of the marketplace. Those who had listened to the minister's eloquence speech, still ringing in their ears, felt an irrepressible outburst of enthusiasm, strengthened by their childlike loyalty to their leaders, which each person passed along to his neighbor. The feeling had barely been contained inside the church. Now, underneath the sky, it rang upward to the heights. There were enough people and enough great, harmonious feeling to produce a sound more impressive than the blast of the organ, the thunder, or

were human beings enough, and enough of highly wrought and symphonious feeling, to produce that more impressive sound than the organ-tones of the blast, or the thunder, or the roar of the sea; even that mighty swell of many voices, blended into one great voice by the universal impulse which makes likewise one vast heart out of the many. Never, from the soil of New England, had gone up such a shout! Never, on New England soil, had stood the man so honored by his mortal brethren as the preacher!

How fared it with him then? Were there not the brilliant particles of a halo in the air about his head? So etherealized by spirit as he was, and so apotheosized by worshipping admirers, did his footsteps in the procession really tread upon the dust of earth?

As the ranks of military men and civil fathers moved onward, all eyes were turned towards the point where the minister was seen to approach among them. The shout died into a murmur, as one portion of the crowd after another obtained a glimpse of him. How feeble and pale he looked amid all his triumph! The energy—or say, rather, the inspiration which had held him up, until he should have delivered the sacred message that brought its own strength along with it from Heaven—was withdrawn, now that it had so faithfully performed its office. The glow, which they had just before beheld burning on his cheek, was extinguished, like a flame that sinks down hopelessly among the late-decaying embers. It seemed hardly the face of a man alive, with such a deathlike hue; it was hardly a man with life in him, that tottered on his path so nervelessly, yet tottered, and did not fall!

One of his clerical brethren,—it was the venerable John Wilson,—observing the state in which Mr. Dimmesdale was left by the retiring wave of intellect and sensibility, stepped forward hastily to offer his support. The minister tremulously, but decidedly, repelled the old man's arm. He still walked onward, if that movement could be so described, which rather resembled the wavering effort of an infant, with its mother's arms in view, outstretched to tempt him forward. And now, almost imperceptible as were the latter steps of his progress, he had come opposite the well-remembered and weather-darkened scaffold, where, long since, with all that dreary lapse of time between, Hester Prynne had encountered the world's ignominious stare. There stood Hester, holding little Pearl by the hand! And there

the roar of the sea. Never before had a shout like this gone up from the soil of New England! Never had there been a New England man so honored by his fellow man as this preacher!

So what did he make of it? Wasn't there a sparkling halo floating above his head? Being so filled with spirit, and held up so high by his worshippers, did his footsteps really fall upon the dust of the earth?

As the military men and civic leaders moved past, all eyes turned toward the point where the minister could be seen drawing near. The shouts quieted to a murmur as one part of the crowd and then another caught a glimpse of him. How weak and pale he looked even in his triumph! The energy—or rather, the inspiration that had held him up to deliver the sacred message—had vanished now that it had performed it's mission. The fire that had glowed on his cheek was extinguished like a flame that sinks down into the dying embers. His face hardly seemed to belong to a living man—its color was so deathly. It was hardly a man with life in him who wobbled along his path—wobbled, but did not fall!

One of his fellow ministers—the great John Wilson—saw the condition in which the retreating wave of inspiration had left Mr. Dimmesdale and stepped quickly forward to offer his support. The minister refused his arm, though he trembled as he did so. He kept walking forward, if it could be described as walking. His movement more closely resembled those of an infant teetering toward its mother's arms as they were stretched out to coax him along. And now, although his last steps had been almost imperceptibly small, he arrived at the familiar and weather-beaten platform where Hester Prynne had long ago faced the world's shameful stare. There stood Hester, holding little Pearl by the hand! And there was the scarlet letter on her breast! The minister paused here, although the band

was the scarlet letter on her breast! The minister here made a pause; although the music still played the stately and rejoicing march to which the procession moved. It summoned him onward,—onward to the festival!—but here he made a pause.

Bellingham, for the last few moments, had kept an anxious eye upon him. He now left his own place in the procession, and advanced to give assistance; judging from Mr. Dimmesdale's aspect that he must otherwise inevitably fall. But there was something in the latter's expression that warned back the magistrate, although a man not readily obeying the vague intimations that pass from one spirit to another. The crowd, meanwhile, looked on with awe and wonder. This earthly faintness was, in their view, only another phase of the minister's celestial strength; nor would it have seemed a miracle too high to be wrought for one so holy, had he ascended before their eyes, waxing dimmer and brighter, and fading at last into the light of Heaven!

He turned towards the scaffold, and stretched forth his arms.

"Hester," said he, "come hither! Come, my little Pearl!"

It was a ghastly look with which he regarded them; but there was something at once tender and strangely triumphant in it. The child, with the bird-like motion which was one of her characteristics, flew to him, and clasped her arms about his knees. Hester Prynne—slowly, as if impelled by inevitable fate, and against her strongest will—likewise drew near, but paused before she reached him. At this instant old Roger Chillingworth thrust himself through the crowd,—or, perhaps, so dark, disturbed, and evil was his look, he rose up out of some nether region,—to snatch back his victim from what he sought to do! Be that as it might, the old man rushed forward and caught the minister by the arm.

"Madman, hold! What is your purpose?" whispered he. "Wave back that woman! Cast off this child! All shall be well! Do not blacken your fame, and perish in dishonor! I can yet save you! Would you bring infamy on your sacred profession?"

"Ha, tempter! Methinks thou art too late!" answered the minister, encountering his eye, fearfully, but firmly. "Thy power is not what it was! With God's help, I shall escape thee now!"

He again extended his hand to the woman of the scarlet letter.

still played its stately and joyful march and the procession moved forward. The music summoned him onward to the festival, but he paused here.

Bellingham had kept an anxious eye upon him for the last few moments. Now he left his own place in the procession to give assistance. From Mr. Dimmesdale's appearance, it seemed certain that he would fall. But there was something in the minister's expression that warned Bellingham to stay back, though he was not the sort of man to follow ambiguous signs. The crowd, meanwhile, looked on with awe and wonder. This mortal weakness was, in their eyes, just another indication of the minister's heavenly strength. It would not have seemed too great a miracle for one so holy to ascend right before their eyes, growing dimmer and yet brighter as he finally faded into the light of Heaven!

He turned toward the platform and extended his arms.

"Hester," he said, "come here! Come, my little Pearl!"

He gave them a ghastly look, but there was something both tender and strangely triumphant to it. The child, with her birdlike motion, flew to him and clasped her arms around his knees. Hester Prynne—slowly, as if moved against her will by an inevitable fate—also drew near, but paused before she reached him. At that moment old Roger Chillingworth broke through the crowd to stop his victim from what he was about to do. Or, perhaps, looking as dark, disturbed, and evil as he did, Chillingworth rose up from some corner of Hell. Whatever the case, the old man rushed forward and grabbed the minister by the arm.

"Stop, madman! What are you doing" he whispered. "Send that woman back! Push this child away! Everything will be fine! Don't ruin your fame and die dishonored! I can still save you! Do you want to bring shame to your sacred profession?"

"Ha, tempter! I think you are too late!" answered the minister, looking him in the eye fearfully but firmly. "Your power is not as strong as it was! With God's help, I will escape you now!"

Again he extended his hand to the woman with the scarlet letter.

"Hester Prynne," cried he, with a piercing earnestness, "in the name of Him, so terrible and so merciful, who gives me grace, at this last moment, to do what—for my own heavy sin and miserable agony—I withheld myself from doing seven years ago, come hither now, and twine thy strength about me! Thy strength, Hester; but let it be guided by the will which God hath granted me! This wretched and wronged old man is opposing it with all his might!—with all his own might and the fiend's! Come, Hester, come! Support me up yonder scaffold!"

The crowd was in a tumult. The men of rank and dignity, who stood more immediately around the clergyman, were so taken by surprise, and so perplexed as to the purport of what they saw,—unable to receive the explanation which most readily presented itself, or to imagine any other,—that they remained silent and inactive spectators of the judgment which Providence seemed about to work. They beheld the minister, leaning on Hester's shoulder and supported by her arm around him, approach the scaffold, and ascend its steps; while still the little hand of the sin-born child was clasped in his. Old Roger Chillingworth followed, as one intimately connected with the drama of guilt and sorrow in which they had all been actors, and well entitled, therefore, to be present at its closing scene.

"Hadst thou sought the whole earth over," said he, looking darkly at the clergyman, "there was no one place so secret,—no high place nor lowly place, where thou couldst have escaped me,—save on this very scaffold!"

"Thanks be to Him who hath led me hither!" answered the minister.

Yet he trembled, and turned to Hester with an expression of doubt and anxiety in his eyes, not the less evidently betrayed, that there was a feeble smile upon his lips.

"Is not this better," murmured he, "than what we dreamed of in the forest?"

"I know not! I know not!" she hurriedly replied. "Better? Yea; so we may both die, and little Pearl with us!"

"For thee and Pearl, be it as God shall order," said the minister; "and God is merciful! Let me now do the will which He hath made plain before my sight. For, Hester, I am a dying man. So let me make haste to take my shame upon me."

"Hester Prynne," he cried with an intense seriousness, "in the name of God, so terrible and so merciful, who gives me grace at this last moment to do what I kept myself from doing seven years ago, come here now and wrap your strength around me! Your strength, Hester, but let it be guided by the will that God has granted me! This old man, both sinful and sinned against, is opposing me with all his might! With all his might and with the Devil's too! Come here, Hester—come here! Help me up onto that platform!"

The crowd was frenzied. The men of rank and dignity who stood closest to the clergyman were surprised and confused by what they were seeing. They remained silent and passive observers of the judgment God seemed prepared to carry out, unwilling to accept the obvious explanation but unable to imagine any other. They saw the minister, leaning on Hester's shoulder and supported by her arm, approach the platform and climb its steps. The little hand of the sin-born child was held in his. Old Roger Chillingworth followed. He was intimately connected with the drama of guilt and sorrow in which they had all played a part, and therefore he was entitled to be present at its closing scene.

"Even if you had searched the whole world," he said, looking at the clergyman with malice, "there was no place so secret, high or low, where you could have escaped me—except on this very platform!"

"Thanks be to Him who has led me here!" replied the minister.

Yet he trembled and looked to Hester with doubt and anxiety in his eyes, though there was a feeble smile upon his lips.

"Isn't this better," he murmured, "than what we dreamed of in the forest?"

"I don't know! I don't know!" she quickly replied. "Better? I suppose, so we both can die, and little Pearl along with us!"

"May it be as God wishes for you and Pearl," said the minister, "and God is merciful! Let me now do what He has made clear to me. Hester, I am dying. Let me be quick to take on my shame!"

Partly supported by Hester Prynne, and holding one hand of little Pearl's, the Reverend Mr. Dimmesdale turned to the dignified and venerable rulers; to the holy ministers, who were his brethren; to the people, whose great heart was thoroughly appalled, yet overflowing with tearful sympathy, as knowing that some deep life-matter—which, if full of sin, was full of anguish and repentance likewise—was now to be laid open to them. The sun, but little past its meridian, shone down upon the clergyman, and gave a distinctness to his figure, as he stood out from all the earth to put in his plea of guilty at the bar of Eternal Justice.

"People of New England!" cried he, with a voice that rose over them, high, solemn, and majestic,—yet had always a tremor through it, and sometimes a shriek, struggling up out of a fathomless depth of remorse and woe,—"ye, that have loved me!—ye, that have deemed me holy!—behold me here, the one sinner of the world! At last!—at last!—I stand upon the spot where, seven years since, I should have stood; here, with this woman, whose arm, more than the little strength wherewith I have crept hitherward, sustains me, at this dreadful moment, from grovelling down upon my face! Lo, the scarlet letter which Hester wears! Ye have all shuddered at it! Wherever her walk hath been,—wherever, so miserably burdened, she may have hoped to find repose,—it hath cast a lurid gleam of awe and horrible repugnance round about her. But there stood one in the midst of you, at whose brand of sin and infamy ye have not shuddered!"

It seemed, at this point, as if the minister must leave the remainder of his secret undisclosed. But he fought back the bodily weakness,—and, still more, the faintness of heart,—that was striving for the mastery with him. He threw off all assistance, and stepped passionately forward a pace before the woman and the child.

"It was on him!" he continued, with a kind of fierceness; so determined was he to speak out the whole. "God's eye beheld it! The angels were for ever pointing at it! The Devil knew it well, and fretted it continually with the touch of his burning finger! But he hid it cunningly from men, and walked among you with the mien of a spirit, mournful, because so pure in a sinful world!—and sad, because he missed his heavenly kindred! Now, at the death-hour, he stands up before you! He bids you look again at Hester's scar-

NO FEAR

Partly supported by Hester Prynne and holding little Pearl's hand, the Reverend Mr. Dimmesdale turned to the community leaders, the fellow holy ministers, and the people. Deep down, the people were both shocked and truly sympathetic, sensing that some profound aspect of life—full of sin, but also full of repentance—was about to be revealed. The sun, a little past its highest point, shone down upon the minister, making his form distinct. He stood apart from all the earth, ready to plead guilty before the court of eternal justice.

"People of New England!" he cried, with a voice that rose over them. The voice was high, solemn, and majestic but with that familiar tremor and an occasional shriek that would struggle up from the bottomless depth of remorse and woe. "You people that have loved me! You that have thought me holy! Look at me, the one sinner in the world! At last, at last, I stand upon the spot where I should have stood seven years before. I stand here with this woman whose arm gives me more strength at this dreadful moment than the little strength I crept here with. If not for her, I would now be groveling on my face! See the scarlet letter Hester wears! You have all shuddered at it! Wherever she has walked, wherever she has hoped to find rest from this miserable burden, it has cast a glow of terror and disgust around her. But someone stood in your midst whose sin and shame you did not shudder at!"

It seemed, at this point, as though the minister would not live to reveal the rest of his secret. But he fought off the weak body and faint heart that was struggling to master him. He shook off all assistance and passionately stepped forward from the woman and their daughter.

"The mark of sin was upon him!" he continued, with a fierce determination to reveal the whole truth. "The eye of God saw it! The angels were constantly pointing at it! The Devil was well aware of it. He kept scratching it with his burning finger! But this man cleverly hid it from other men. He walked among you with the expression of one who mourned because his pure spirit was forced to live in such a sinful world. He looked sad, as though his missed the company of the angels among whom he belonged! Now, at the hour of his death,

let letter! He tells you, that, with all its mysterious horror, it is but the shadow of what he bears on his own breast, and that even this, his own red stigma, is no more than the type of what has seared his inmost heart! Stand any here that question God's judgment on a sinner? Behold! Behold a dreadful witness of it!"

With a convulsive motion he tore away the ministerial band from before his breast. It was revealed! But it were irreverent to describe that revelation. For an instant the gaze of the horror-stricken multitude was concentred on the ghastly miracle; while the minister stood with a flush of triumph in his face, as one who, in the crisis of acutest pain, had won a victory. Then, down he sank upon the scaffold! Hester partly raised him, and supported his head against her bosom. Old Roger Chillingworth knelt down beside him, with a blank, dull countenance, out of which the life seemed to have departed.

"Thou hast escaped me!" he repeated more than once. "Thou hast escaped me!"

"May God forgive thee!" said the minister. "Thou, too, hast deeply sinned!"

He withdrew his dying eyes from the old man, and fixed them on the woman and the child.

"My little Pearl," said he feebly,—and there was a sweet and gentle smile over his face, as of a spirit sinking into deep repose; nay, now that the burden was removed, it seemed almost as if he would be sportive with the child,—"dear little Pearl, wilt thou kiss me now? Thou wouldst not yonder, in the forest! But now thou wilt?"

Pearl kissed his lips. A spell was broken. The great scene of grief, in which the wild infant bore a part, had developed all her sympathies; and as her tears fell upon her father's cheek, they were the pledge that she would grow up amid human joy and sorrow, nor for ever do battle with the world, but be a woman in it. Towards her mother, too, Pearl's errand as a messenger of anguish was all fulfilled.

"Hester," said the clergyman, "farewell!"

"Shall we not meet again?" whispered she, bending her face down close to his. "Shall we not spend our immortal life together? Surely, surely, we have ransomed one another, with all this woe! Thou lookest far into eternity, with those bright dying eyes! Then tell me what thou seest?"

he stands before you! He asks you to look at Hester's scarlet letter once again! He tells you that, as mysterious and horrible as it is, it is only a shadow of what he wears on his own breast! Even his own red mark is nothing compared to what is burned deep into his heart! Does anyone here doubt that God punishes sinners? Look! Behold a terrible witness of his punishment!"

With a spasm, he tore his minister's robe away from his breast. It was revealed! But it would be pointless to describe that revelation. For an instant, the eyes of the horrified mass were focused on the dreadful miracle. The minister stood with a flush of triumph in his face, as though he had persevered in the midst of a great torment. Then he crumpled upon the platform! Hester raised him slightly, supporting his head against her bosom. Old Roger Chillingworth kneeled down next to him, his face blank and dull, as though the life had drained out of it.

"You have escaped me!" he said over and over. "You have escaped me!"

"May God forgive you!" said the minister. "You have sinned deeply too!"

His dying eyes turned away from the old man and looked instead at the woman and child.

"My little Pearl!" he said, weakly. There was a sweet and gentle smile on his face, as though his spirit was sinking into a deep rest. Now that his burden was lifted, it seemed almost as though he would play with the child. "Dear little Pearl, will you kiss me now? You wouldn't when we were in the forest! But will you now?"

Pearl kissed his lips. A spell was broken. The wild infant's sympathies had been developed by the enormous grief she had grown up around. Her tears that now fell upon her father's cheek were a pledge to open herself to human joy and sorrow. She would not fight constantly against the world but would be a woman in it. Pearl's role as a bringer of pain to her mother also came to an end.

"Hester," said the clergyman, "goodbye!"

"Won't we meet again?" she whispered, bending her face down close to his. "Won't we spend eternity together? Surely, surely, we have saved each other through all this misery! You see far into eternity now, with those bright dying eyes! Tell me what you see!"

"Hush, Hester, hush!" said he, with tremulous solemnity. "The law we broke!—the sin here so awfully revealed!—let these alone be in thy thoughts! I fear! I fear! It may be, that, when we forgot our God,—when we violated our reverence each for the other's soul,—it was thenceforth vain to hope that we could meet hereafter, in an everlasting and pure reunion. God knows; and He is merciful! He hath proved his mercy, most of all, in my afflictions. By giving me this burning torture to bear upon my breast! By sending yonder dark and terrible old man, to keep the torture always at red-heat! By bringing me hither, to die this death of triumphant ignominy before the people! Had either of these agonies been wanting, I had been lost for ever! Praised be his name! His will be done! Farewell!"

That final word came forth with the minister's expiring breath. The multitude, silent till then, broke out in a strange, deep voice of awe and wonder, which could not as yet find utterance, save in this murmur that rolled so heavily after the departed spirit.

NO FEAR

"Hush, Hester, hush!" he said, with trembling gravity. "Think only of the law that we broke and the sin that has been horribly revealed here! I am afraid! I am afraid! From the moment we forgot our God—when we forgot our love for each other's souls—it may have been vain to hope that we could have a pure and everlasting reunion in Heaven. God knows, and He is merciful. He has shown His mercy, above all, in my trials. He gave me this burning torture to bear on my breast! He sent that dark and terrible old man, to keep the torture always red-hot! He brought me here, to die in triumphant shame in front of all the people! Without either of these agonies, I would have been lost forever! Praised be His name! His will be done! Goodbye!"

That minister spoke that last word with his dying breath. The crowd, silent up to that point, erupted with a strange, deep sound of awe and wonder. Their reaction could only be expressed in this murmur, which rolled so heavily after the minister's departing soul.

Chapter 24: Conclusion

A fter many days, when time sufficed for the people to arrange their thoughts in reference to the foregoing scene, there was more than one account of what had been witnessed on the scaffold.

Most of the spectators testified to having seen, on the breast of the unhappy minister, a scarlet letter—the very semblance of that worn by Hester Prynne—imprinted in the flesh. As regarded its origin, there were various explanations, all of which must necessarily have been conjectural. Some affirmed that the Reverend Mr. Dimmesdale, on the very day when Hester Prynne first wore her ignominious badge, had begun a course of penance,—which he afterwards, in so many futile methods, followed out,—by inflicting hideous torture on himself. Others contended that the stigma had not been produced until a long time subsequent, when old Roger Chillingworth, being a potent necromancer, had caused it to appear, through the agency of magic and poisonous drugs. Others, again— and those best able to appreciate the minister's peculiar sensibility, and the wonderful operation of his spirit upon the body,—whispered their belief, that the awful symbol was the effect of the ever active tooth of remorse, gnawing from the inmost heart outwardly, and at last manifesting Heaven's dreadful judgment by the visible presence of the letter. The reader may choose among these theories. We have thrown all the light we could acquire upon the portent, and would gladly, now that it has done its office, erase its deep print out of our own brain; where long meditation has fixed it in very undesirable distinctness.

It is singular, nevertheless, that certain persons, who were spectators of the whole scene, and professed never once to have removed their eyes from the Reverend Mr. Dimmesdale, denied that there was any mark whatever on his breast, more than on a new-born infant's. Neither, by their report, had his dying words acknowledged, nor even remotely implied, any, the slightest connection, on his part, with the guilt for which Hester Prynne had so long worn the scarlet letter. According to these highly respectable witnesses, the minister, conscious that he was dying,—conscious, also, that the reverence of the multitude placed him already among saints and angels,—had

Chapter 24: Conclusion

After several days, when enough time had passed for people to gather their thoughts, there was more than one account of what they had seen on the platform.

Most of the crowd claimed to have seen a scarlet letter on the breast of the sorrowful minister—looking exactly the same as the one worn by Hester Prynne—imprinted in his flesh. There were many explanations for it, none better than a guess. Some said that the Reverend Mr. Dimmesdale, on the very day when Hester Prynne first wore her badge of shame, had begun a regimen of penance by inflicting a series of hideous tortures upon himself. Others said that the mark appeared much later, when old Roger Chillingworth—a powerful sorcerer—produced it with his magic drugs. Others, who could best appreciate the minister's peculiar sensitivity and the way his spirit worked on his body, whispered that the awful symbol was the effect of his constant remorse. They said the remorse had gnawed outward from his heart until finally the letter rendered Heaven's dreadful judgment visible upon his breast. You are free to choose among these stories. I have learned all that I could about the symbol. Now that it has had its effect, I would be glad to erase its deep mark from my own brain. I have thought about the sign for so long that it is now uncomfortably distinct in my mind.

Still, it is curious that several people who witnessed the whole scene, and claimed to have never taken their eyes off the Reverend Mr. Dimmesdale, denied that there was a mark at all on his breast. They said he was as bare as a newborn. They also said his dying words never acknowledged, nor even implied, any connection with the guilty act for which Hester Prynne had worn the scarlet letter all this time. These highly respectable witnesses said that the minister, knowing that he was dying and that the people thought him the equal of saints and angels, had breathed his last in the arms of that sinful woman as a way of expressing the futility of human righ-

desired, by yielding up his breath in the arms of that fallen woman, to express to the world how utterly nugatory is the choicest of man's own righteousness. After exhausting life in his efforts for mankind's spiritual good, he had made the manner of his death a parable, in order to impress on his admirers the mighty and mournful lesson, that, in the view of Infinite Purity, we are sinners all alike. It was to teach them, that the holiest among us has but attained so far above his fellows as to discern more clearly the Mercy which looks down, and repudiate more utterly the phantom of human merit, which would look aspiringly upward. Without disputing a truth so momentous, we must be allowed to consider this version of Mr. Dimmesdale's story as only an instance of that stubborn fidelity with which a man's friends—and especially a clergyman's—will sometimes uphold his character; when proofs, clear as the mid-day sunshine on the scarlet letter, establish him a false and sin-stained creature of the dust.

The authority which we have chiefly followed—a manuscript of old date, drawn up from the verbal testimony of individuals, some of whom had known Hester Prynne, while others had heard the tale from contemporary witnesses—fully confirms the view taken in the foregoing pages. Among many morals which press upon us from the poor minister's miserable experience, we put only this into a sentence:—"Be true! Be true! Be true! Show freely to the world, if not your worst, yet some trait whereby the worst may be inferred!"

Nothing was more remarkable than the change which took place, almost immediately after Mr. Dimmesdale's death, in the appearance and demeanour of the old man known as Roger Chillingworth. All his strength and energy—all his vital and intellectual force—seemed at once to desert him; insomuch that he positively withered up, shrivelled away, and almost vanished from mortal sight, like an uprooted weed that lies wilting in the sun. This unhappy man had made the very principle of his life to consist in the pursuit and systematic exercise of revenge; and when, by its completest triumph and consummation, that evil principle was left with no further material to support it,—when, in short, there was no more Devil's work on earth for him to do, it only remained for the unhumanized mortal to betake himself whither his Master would find him tasks enough, and pay him his wages duly. But, to all these

teousness. After spending his life working for mankind's spiritual good, he had made his death into a parable. He wished to impress upon his admirers the strong, sorrowful message that, in the view of the pure God, we are all equally sinners. He tried to teach them that even the holiest among us has only learned enough to understand more clearly the scope of divine mercy and to completely abandon the illusion of human goodness in the eyes of God. While I don't want to dispute the truth of such a powerful lesson, more than anything that version of Mr. Dimmesdale's story provides evidence of the stubborn lengths to which a man's friends—and especially a clergyman's friends—will sometimes go to defend his character against even the clearest proofs that he is a deceitful, sinful man.

In telling this story, I have mostly relied on an old manuscript drawn from the testimony of individuals. Some of these people had known Hester Prynne, while others had heard the story from contemporary witnesses. The document fully confirms the view that I have taken in these pages. Among many morals that I could draw from the tale, I choose this: "Be true! Be true! If you will not show the world your worst, at least show some quality that suggests to others the worst in you!"

After Mr. Dimmesdale's death, a remarkable change took place in the appearance and personality of the old man known as Roger Chillingworth. All his strength and energy, all his physical and intellectual force, seemed to leave him at once. He withered up, shriveled away, and almost vanished from human sight, like an uprooted weed that wilts in the sun. This sad man had made the pursuit of revenge the one mission in his life. When that evil aim had achieved its ultimate end—when there was no more Devil's work left for him on earth—there was nothing for that inhuman man to do but return to his master. But I would like show some mercy to Roger Chillingworth, as I would to all of these characters that I have known for so long now. The question of whether hatred and love are not, in the end, the same is worth investigation. Each requires a great deal of intimacy to reach full development. Each requires that

shadowy beings, so long our near acquaintances,—as well Roger Chillingworth as his companions—we would fain be merciful. It is a curious subject of observation and inquiry, whether hatred and love be not the same thing at bottom. Each, in its utmost development, supposes a high degree of intimacy and heart-knowledge; each renders one individual dependent for the food of his affections and spiritual life upon another; each leaves the passionate lover, or the no less passionate hater, forlorn and desolate by the withdrawal of his object. Philosophically considered, therefore, the two passions seem essentially the same, except that one happens to be seen in a celestial radiance, and the other in a dusky and lurid glow. In the spiritual world, the old physician and the minister—mutual victims as they have been—may, unawares, have found their earthly stock of hatred and antipathy transmuted into golden love.

Leaving this discussion apart, we have a matter of business to communicate to the reader. At old Roger Chillingworth's decease (which took place within the year), and by his last will and testament, of which Governor Bellingham and the Reverend Mr. Wilson were executors, he bequeathed a very considerable amount of property, both here and in England, to little Pearl, the daughter of Hester Prynne.

So Pearl—the elf-child,—the demon offspring, as some people, up to that epoch, persisted in considering her—became the richest heiress of her day, in the New World. Not improbably, this circumstance wrought a very material change in the public estimation; and, had the mother and child remained here, little Pearl, at a marriageable period of life, might have mingled her wild blood with the lineage of the devoutest Puritan among them all. But, in no long time after the physician's death, the wearer of the scarlet letter disappeared, and Pearl along with her. For many years, though a vague report would now and then find its way across the sea,—like a shapeless piece of driftwood tost ashore, with the initials of a name upon it,—yet no tidings of them unquestionably authentic were received. The story of the scarlet letter grew into legend. Its spell, however, was still potent, and kept the scaffold awful where the poor minister had died, and likewise the cottage by the sea-shore, where Hester Prynne had dwelt. Near this latter spot, one afternoon, some children were at play, when they beheld a tall woman,

one person depend on another for their emotional and spiritual life. Each leaves the passionate lover—or the passionate hater—abandoned and depressed when his subject departs. And so, considered philosophically, the two passions seem essentially the same. One is thought of with a heavenly glow, while the other seems dark and disturbing. But they are remarkably similar. Perhaps, in the afterlife, the old doctor and the minister—each the victim of the other—found their earthly hatred transformed into golden love.

But leaving this discussion aside, there are some final details to communicate. Old Roger Chillingworth died less than a year after Mr. Dimmesdale, and he left a great deal of property, both in Boston and in England, to little Pearl, the daughter of Hester Prynne.

And so Pearl—the elf-child, the offspring of demons, as some people had continued to think of her up to that point—became the richest heiress in the New World. As one might expect, this change in her material fortunes changed the popular opinion of her. If mother and child had remained here, little Pearl could have married the most devout Puritan around. But shortly after the doctor's death, Hester disappeared, and little Pearl along with her. For many years, no news of them was heard, apart from vague rumors, which floated ashore like shapeless driftwood. The story of the scarlet letter grew into a legend. Yet its spell was still powerful. The platform where the poor minister had died and the cottage by the seashore where Hester had lived were thought of with awe. One afternoon, some children were playing near the cottage when they saw a tall woman in a gray robe approach the door. In all those years it had never once been opened, but either she unlocked it or the decaying wood and iron gave way—or else she glided through the door like a ghost. In any case, she entered.

in a gray robe, approach the cottage-door. In all those years it had never once been opened; but either she unlocked it, or the decaying wood and iron yielded to her hand, or she glided shadow-like through these impediments,—and, at all events, went in.

On the threshold she paused,—turned partly round,—for, perchance, the idea of entering, all alone, and all so changed, the home of so intense a former life, was more dreary and desolate than even she could bear. But her hesitation was only for an instant, though long enough to display a scarlet letter on her breast.

And Hester Prynne had returned, and taken up her long-forsaken shame. But where was little Pearl? If still alive, she must now have been in the flush and bloom of early womanhood. None knew— nor ever learned, with the fulness of perfect certainty—whether the elf-child had gone thus untimely to a maiden grave; or whether her wild, rich nature had been softened and subdued, and made capable of a woman's gentle happiness. But, through the remainder of Hester's life, there were indications that the recluse of the scarlet letter was the object of love and interest with some inhabitant of another land. Letters came, with armorial seals upon them, though of bearings unknown to English heraldry. In the cottage there were articles of comfort and luxury, such as Hester never cared to use, but which only wealth could have purchased, and affection have imagined for her. There were trifles, too, little ornaments, beautiful tokens of a continual remembrance, that must have been wrought by delicate fingers at the impulse of a fond heart. And, once, Hester was seen embroidering a baby-garment, with such a lavish richness of golden fancy as would have raised a public tumult, had any infant, thus apparelled, been shown to our sobre-hued community.

In fine, the gossips of that day believed,—and Mr. Surveyor Pue, who made investigations a century later, believed,—and one of his recent successors in office, moreover, faithfully believes,—that Pearl was not only alive, but married, and happy, and mindful of her mother; and that she would most joyfully have entertained that sad and lonely mother at her fireside.

But there was a more real life for Hester Prynne, here, in New England, than in that unknown region where Pearl had found a home. Here had been her sin; here, her sorrow; and here was yet to be her penitence. She had returned, therefore, and resumed,—

NO FEAR

She paused in the entryway and looked over her shoulder. Perhaps now that she was so different, the thought of entering alone the home where her life had been so intense was more dreary and lonely than she could bear. But she only hesitated for a moment, just long enough for the children to see the scarlet letter on her breast.

Hester Prynne had returned to take up her long-abandoned shame. But where was little Pearl? If she were still alive, she must have been in the prime of her young womanhood by now. No one knew, nor ever learned for sure, whether the child had died young or whether her wild, extravagant nature had mellowed into a woman's gentle happiness. But for the rest of Hester's life, there was evidence that someone in a faraway land cared for the aging woman. She received letters affixed with seals of nobility, though not the familiar English seals. Luxurious items decorated her cottage, though Hester never used them. The gifts were expensive, though thoughtful too. And there were trinkets, pretty little things that must have been made for Hester by nimble fingers moved by a loving heart. And once Hester was seen making a baby's dress with embroidery so lavish, it would have raised a public outcry if an infant in her community had worn them.

All the gossips at that time believed—and Mr. Surveyor Pue, who looked into the matter a century later, agreed, as do I—that Pearl was not only alive but happily married and mindful of her mother, such that she would gladly have had her mother live with her.

But there was more of a life for Hester Prynne here in New England than in that far-off land where Pearl lived. Hester's sin had been here, her sorrow was here, and her penance would be here. So she had returned and freely assumed—for no public official would

of her own free will, for not the sternest magistrate of that iron period would have imposed it,—resumed the symbol of which we have related so dark a tale. Never afterwards did it quit her bosom. But, in the lapse of the toilsome, thoughtful, and self-devoted years that made up Hester's life, the scarlet letter ceased to be a stigma which attracted the world's scorn and bitterness, and became a type of something to be sorrowed over, and looked upon with awe, yet with reverence too. And, as Hester Prynne had no selfish ends, nor lived in any measure for her own profit and enjoyment, people brought all their sorrows and perplexities, and besought her counsel, as one who had herself gone through a mighty trouble. Women, more especially,—in the continually recurring trials of wounded, wasted, wronged, misplaced, or erring and sinful passion,—or with the dreary burden of a heart unyielded, because unvalued and unsought,—came to Hester's cottage, demanding why they were so wretched, and what the remedy! Hester comforted and counselled them, as best she might. She assured them, too, of her firm belief, that, at some brighter period, when the world should have grown ripe for it, in Heaven's own time, a new truth would be revealed, in order to establish the whole relation between man and woman on a surer ground of mutual happiness. Earlier in life, Hester had vainly imagined that she herself might be the destined prophetess, but had long since recognized the impossibility that any mission of divine and mysterious truth should be confided to a woman stained with sin, bowed down with shame, or even burdened with a life-long sorrow. The angel and apostle of the coming revelation must be a woman, indeed, but lofty, pure, and beautiful; and wise, moreover, not through dusky grief, but the ethereal medium of joy; and showing how sacred love should make us happy, by the truest test of a life successful to such an end!

So said Hester Prynne, and glanced her sad eyes downward at the scarlet letter. And, after many, many years, a new grave was delved, near an old and sunken one, in that burial-ground beside which King's Chapel has since been built. It was near that old and sunken grave, yet with a space between, as if the dust of the two sleepers had no right to mingle. Yet one tombstone served for both. All around, there were monuments carved with armorial bearings; and on this simple slab of slate—as the curious investigator may still

have dared to impose it—the symbol at the heart of this sad story. It never left her bosom again. But, in the passage of the hard working, considerate, devoted years that made up the remainder of Hester's life, the scarlet letter ceased to be an object of regret. Instead, it was looked at with awe and reverence. Hester Prynne had no selfish desires, since she did not live in any way for her own benefit and enjoyment. And so people brought their troubles to her, this woman who had suffered so much herself. Women in particular— those either wrestling with the constant trials of their passions or bearing the burden of an unloved and therefore unloving heart— came to Hester's cottage to ask why they were so miserable and what they could do about it! Hester comforted and counseled them as best she could. And she assured them of her firm belief that, at some better time to come, Heaven would reveal a new order in which men and women acted for their mutual happiness. Earlier in her life, Hester had imagined that she might be the prophetess of such a new world. But for a long time now, she had recognized that no mission of divine and mysterious truth would be given to a woman stained with sin, bowed with shame, and burdened with a life-long sorrow. The herald of the revelation to come would certainly be a woman, but one who is pure, beautiful, and noble, whose wisdom springs from joy rather than grief. It would be a woman whose successful life could demonstrate to others how sacred love can make us happy.

Hester Prynne would say this, and glance down at the scarlet letter with her sad eyes. And, after many years, a new grave was dug near an old and sunken one in the burial yard beside which King's Chapel was later built. It was close to that old and sunken grave, but separated a space, as if the dust of the two eternal sleepers had no right to mix. Yet one tombstone was carved for the two of graves. All around were large monuments with coats of arms. On this simple slab—as the curious investigator can still observe and discern, and perplex himself with the purport—there appeared the semblance of an engraved escutcheon. It bore a device, a herald's wording of which might serve for a motto and brief description of our now concluded legend; so sombre is it, and relieved only by one ever-glowing point of light gloomier than the shadow:—

"On a field, sable, the letter A, gules."

NO FEAR

puzzle over—there appeared something that looked like a coat of arms. On it was written a motto, which can serve to conclude our story, now that it is finished:

"On a field of black, the letter *A* in scarlet."